10-33 ON
THE WEST YARD

A TRUE CRIME STORY
ABOUT POLITICS, POLICIES,
AND PRISON GANGS

The August 8, 2009 Riot at
The California Institution for Men
Chino, California

BY RICHARD A. ALVARADO

INFINITY
PUBLISHING

Copyright © 2015 by Richard A. Alvarado

ISBN 978-1-4958-0568-4
ISBN 978-1-4958-0569-1 eBook

Published May 2015

INFINITY PUBLISHING
1094 New DeHaven Street, Suite 100
West Conshohocken, PA 19428-2713
Toll-free (877) BUY BOOK
Local Phone (610) 941-9999
Fax (610) 941-9959
Info@buybooksontheweb.com
www.buybooksontheweb.com

DEDICATION

To my wife Yan Sum,
our children and grandchildren.
The road to peace is never straight and always rocky,
but it is well-traveled by those who persevere.

Despues mi dijo una arriero,
Que no hay que llegar primero,
Pero hay que saber llegar...

Jose Alfredo Jimenez
"El Rey"

TABLE OF CONTENTS

FOREWORD

Richard Alvarado's discussion in the following pages provides a unique insider's perspective on California crime, policies, gangs, and the political "stew" that guided the national "War on Crime" effort. He didn't acquire his point of view by fighting crime in the streets. He picked it up by engaging felons in prison. His career growth from group counselor and deputy probation officer with the Riverside County Probation Department, to correctional officer, counselor, captain, and administrator with the California Department of Corrections and Rehabilitation (CDCR), gave him firsthand experience with criminals. It has offered him an intimate look at unbridled violence, personal despair and the persistent gang mentality that continues to plague our communities and the prison system today.

As you read the following chapters, you'll view the day-to-day prison experience much differently from what you may have imagined. Richard outlines the national fervor that captured citizens' hearts to be tough on crime. When you peel back the many faceted layers of the criminal justice arena, you can no longer view crime as a simple equation of good versus evil. Although "good versus evil" exists, Richard persuasively shares the ideas of scholars and other criminologists to make his case about how we view crime. He smartly blends real life examples supplied by peace officers with the actions of offenders to reveal the complexity of the criminal justice system. It goes without saying, the roles played by law enforcement, district attorney, public defender, courts, victims, probation, corrections, and community stakeholders and where they intersect, is a complicated dynamic.

I, too, understood the dynamics of the criminal justice system. I served twenty-four years with the Riverside County Sheriff's Department, as a deputy, detective and the last twelve years as the Undersheriff. I witnessed, firsthand, the suffering of victims and the brutality of crime. That experience cemented my commitment to continuing the "War on Crime" when I became a legislator. I served in the California senate from 1974 to 1994 and carried many of the major anticrime and prison construction legislation. I also chaired the Senate Public Safety Committee. I was committed to ensure the penal code statutes that passed the legislature would be a deterrent to crime. Richard points out in his review of the "War on Crime" history that there was reason to be tough on criminals since California maintained a higher crime rate than the rest of the nation between 1970 and 1988. In fact, the attorney general reported in 1992 that violent crime, including homicides, were at high levels in California. My public safety mission was clear during that period. But my commitment to justice did not end with crime suppression and deterrence. I also recognized the value in balancing justice with treatment efforts.

I was among the few legislators who fought for rehabilitative programs in the prison and in the community. I carried the bill in the early 1980s that established the Prison Industries Authority (PIA). PIA was a semiautonomous agency that received no funding appropriations from the state. PIA, working with CDCR, was intended to reduce inmate idle time by providing viable work experience to assist parolees' re-integration to the community with employable skills. PIA also provided higher wages that allowed inmates a chance to save money while also paying restitution to victims. PIA had prided itself over the years for being fiscally prudent while providing inmates meaningful work skills and self-esteem that have proven to reduce recidivism rates. Richard guides the reader to the question of rehabilitation in his discussion about the AB 109 Public Safety Realignment Act. He describes how AB 109 has substantially changed the criminal justice dialogue in California, especially for local communities. It is my hope that this book will aid in the discussion to make Realignment more effective whether you are supportive of the policy or not.

After leaving the state senate, I was appointed in 1995, by Governor Pete Wilson as chair of the Youthful Offender Parole Board. Upon election of Gray Davis as Governor in 1999, I was appointed as the secretary for the Youth and Adult Correctional Agency (YACA). At that time, YACA oversaw a 5.7 billion dollar budget with 163,000 inmates, 110,000 parolees, and 51,000 employees statewide. Although, incarceration numbers continued to increase during my administration, I was committed to enhancing our therapeutic treatment and vocational programs. My efforts were, at best, piecemeal, given the tremendous budget restraints placed on all agencies during my tenure. Richard exposes the impact of the department's growth during this period of time for prisons and parole functions.

I remained as secretary until 2003 after the special election of Arnold Schwarzenegger. The burden of court-driven inmate lawsuits soon took control of the department when a federal court receiver was ultimately placed over all of the medical operations statewide in 2006. That oversight continues today unrestricted with a Corrections budget that has doubled since I left the job. More troubling to me was the realization that the enormous Corrections bureaucracy was slow to change and even slower in acknowledging its own weaknesses.

Richard gives an eye opening look at the daunting challenges local prison officials and staff faced trying to satisfy the federal court mandates while the Prison Law Office was expanding its influence in day-to-day prison business. Similarly, Richard's views about street and prison gangs are not stand-alone conversations. The real threat posed by the prison gangs is neatly found in the thread he weaves connecting the riot of August 8, 2009 at the Chino Prison to the hunger strike that occurred July of 2013.

From his perspective, the *War on Crime* shouldn't be applied like a broad brush on all the youth hanging out on urban street corners. Like most young people, they want attention and guidance, too. As Richard says, "Some need a hand, some need a swift kick in the rear, and some need to be locked up." Our youth are precisely the topic where our community leaders and elected representatives need to be totally committed. If our youth are not the focus for today, they may well be the problem for tomorrow.

It is no secret that after school programs, parks and recreation activities, not-for-profit and/or community-sponsored programs are all effective remedies for juvenile delinquency. We cannot end juvenile delinquency, but a community, county, and state government united can certainly reduce the rate of occurrence. If we don't provide some kind of constructive option, we will only see our jails and prisons continue to grow. To ignore our youth during these tough economic and unsettled social times is akin to ignoring a gaping wound in our gut that, left untreated, will only become infected.

Richard concludes with the alarming threat posed by the infection called "prison gangs." The real war on crime should be focused on the insidious nature of organized predators within the California prisons and their influence on the many confused but loyal street gang members who look up to them as role models. When those troubled youth see meaningful choices to "being a homie" in the community, they tend to be attracted to those opportunities. But when they believe they have no options, they become the prey prison gangs victimize. Until we find the political will, budget, and committed focus to provide meaningful programs and activities for all our youth, we will continue to see the "idle time" breeding ground the prison gangs earnestly stalk.

ROBERT PRESLEY
Former, California State Senator and
Secretary, California Youth and Adult Correctional Agency

ACKNOWLEDGEMENTS

Since this is my first book, it is hard not to include everyone that has taken the time to read, comment, or simply listen to my babble about the subject of crime, gangs, and law enforcement. First and foremost, I thank my immediate family who gave me their blessing and initial support when I sent them the first draft on my upbringing in Bakersfield and Los Angeles. Likewise, I cannot forget the email correspondence and lunches with my first draft reader Desiree Alaniz. Her grammar review and commentary on each succeeding chapter were timely. More importantly, her positive feedback kept me motivated during the hard stretches of research and writing.

Also, I had the benefit of many professionals I worked with who would later become Wardens and Chief Deputies who inspired and sometimes "perspired" my calling as a correctional practitioner. A few who made a profound impact on my career include the following: Jerry Stainer, Bill Duncan, Rusty Snider, Ernie Roe, Donald Hill, Jeannie Anderson, Dawn Davison, Patricia Vasquez, Lori DiCarlo, Mike Poulos, Guillermina Hall, Matt Martel, Henry Provencher, Ricco Johnston, Guillermo Garcia, Tim Busby, Cynthia Tampkins, and Brian Pahel. Other peace officers that helped me hone my perspectives included; Danny Macias, Al Quinones, George Tapia, Louie Morris, Louie Chavarria, Donna Orta, Xavier Aponte, Jerry and Amy Baker, Danny Macias, Nal Pedrosian, Mark Hargrove, Molly Hill, Steve Dye, Mark Epstein and Steve Aboytes to name a few.

Special thanks to my University of California, Riverside (UCR) mentor, Professor Alfredo Mirande who unknowing introduced me to my career path via a community outreach class at the California Rehabilitation Center. Likewise, I cannot begin to express my gratitude to my former law enforcement partners and *Wandering Dog* band musicians, Richard

De La Rosa, Thomas Ybarra, and Steve Slaton—especially Steve for his critically stinging but constructive review of the gang chapters. His expertise helped me immensely in refining my argument about the statewide hunger strike and recommendations for an effective criminal justice future.

I also thank my very dear friend Gabriel "Eddie" Gutierrez. Without his encouragement, I never would have considered a prison career. We grew together as young men and watched our children grow up, too. As we got older, hopefully we became a bit wiser for our efforts. Gabe is a great storyteller and unpublished writer. He is responsible for many of my chapter headings and quotes, including the title of the book. Also, thanks to Yvette Dominguez who created my informative website and has only scratched the surface of her superb web design talents. Similarly, I learned that you are only as good as your editor. Patricia Fry is a writer, author and professional editor whom I met in passing at the Los Angeles Times Book Fair at the University of Southern California. Patricia provided a no nonsense review of my manuscript. There are no words to adequately express my gratitude, but if I did, no doubt she'd correct them.

Lastly, my wife Yan Sum, whose thirty-four years in law enforcement was put to good use throughout the production of this book. For the last two years, she patiently read each chapter and provided appropriate revisions or commentary when I went too far off point or simply went too far. Without her support this book would not exist. It goes without saying, but I'll say it anyway, all omissions, mistakes and opinions belong to me. I am grateful to have finished a book that hopefully is a testament to the aforementioned family, friends and work companions that, at times, motivated, challenged, disagreed and ultimately channeled my desire to share a different outlook about crime.

INTRODUCTION

I am not a former gang member or prison gang dropout. Yet, in the following pages, I'll talk a lot about both. My only "claim to fame" is that I have over thirty-two years of experience in the criminal justice arena. Having worked in boys' homes, juvenile hall, adult probation, and corrections, I have had a bird's eye view of the deprivation juveniles and adult offenders face from their encounters and predicaments on the streets. I've also observed the carnivorous juvenile institution and prison experiences that epitomize their journey through the justice system. Likewise, I have experienced the challenges faced by criminal justice practitioners in maintaining order amid chaos, "fighting crime" among criminally oriented offenders, and half-heartedly seeking meaningful therapeutic solutions for rehabilitation.

To those who came before me and those who continue to work in the California criminal justice arena, it is a stretch of the imagination to say we seek to heal the emotional wounds and tortured souls of those persons under our charge. On the contrary, that was never the mission; it was all about "warehousing" bodies and if they—the offenders—were lucky, finding a modicum of healing success along the way. This admission is neither a confession nor a revelation, but it is a fact considering the intent of the California penal code was first and foremost about punishment.[1]

****

This book started out as an essay regarding the immediate circumstances leading to a full-scale riot at the California Institution for Men (CIM) on August 8, 2009. As the acting warden the week of the riot and incident commander during the riot, I had a firsthand view of the dynamics that led to the crisis. An alert officer had discovered a "kite" (inmate message to others) secreted deep within a mattress during a routine cell search.

The kite described a planned assault by Latino inmates against Black inmates. The circumstances leading to the planned assault were unique to prison politics for a number of reasons which will be delineated in the following chapters. The planned assault was so cleverly orchestrated it could not be stopped.

On August 8, 2009, a "10-33" (alarm sounding) code was broadcast throughout the Chino Prison's four facilities housing well over 5,500 inmates.[2] The 10-33 code signaled the start of a mass disturbance that all the staff had known was going to occur. The ensuing *Reception Center West (RC-West) Riot* involved over 1,100 inmates, one of the largest prison riots in the state's history.[3] Black inmates were attacked without warning by White and Latino inmates. The Blacks were outnumbered three-to-one. Trapped in 200-man locked dormitory housing units, Black inmates had to fight off multiple attackers as they struggled to pry open steel-caged windows and doors or break out dilapidated wooden barrack walls to escape from their assailants.

The initial essay was thought to be a treatise about "best practices" and strategic considerations for correctional practitioners; the heroic and successful ending of the riot, which lasted roughly eight hours without loss of life among staff and inmates. The calculated response to unrelenting racial terror and brutality resulted in serious injury to over 200 inmates with over fifty inmates requiring emergency transportation to outside hospitals. The paper was to be a testament to the exemplary actions of all the correctional officers, medical staff, fire personnel, and mutual aid responders. But that would have not told the whole story.

Despite my best intentions, an essay approach that was limited to the immediate scope of the riot and the brave men and women who prevailed would have failed to capture the "big picture." The big picture was the forces outside the prison walls which caused, complicated, and ultimately combined to "brew the stew" of rage that followed. More importantly, a short essay could not have provided any degree of thought about what the collective focus should be for our communities, political leaders, and public agencies in addressing the incarceration/rehabilitation struggle statewide. The RC-West, August 8, 2009 prison riot was not only the worst case scenario for the failed efforts of criminal justice practitioners, it was also symbolic of the failed politics and policies addressing crime in general and California, in particular. Hence, my motive for writing a book became clear.

****

I will use the August 8, 2009 prison riot at CIM as the focal point for this story. From the circumstances leading to the riot, I will introduce what I believe are the key elements: gangs, crowding, and public policy, for a discussion on systemic criminal justice issues. From my perspective, these systemic issues provided the fodder for the eventual spark that set the riot off. They are also the key issues for understanding where we, as a state, may continue to be led. However, my views about riots, crime, prison culture, and public safety, may be different from the public's perception of them. The words themselves can spark an emotional chord. The same is true when we translate those words to specifics like; overcrowding, 3 Strikes, prison gangs, and rehabilitation. We all may have different interpretations, but our understanding is usually buoyed by facts or statistics that support our views.

It is my hope that the details surrounding the August 8, 2009 riot can provide a better understanding of the words we use to describe crime issues and may also provide a meaningful gauge of how our crime prevention model has worked and where it has failed.

****

Crime has a face, both victim and perpetrator. My intent is to "put a face" on criminals, criminality, and the corrections culture that is tasked with handling it. We have found out the hard way how expensive it is to house, care for, and feed criminals. Likewise, it costs dearly to ensure criminals have adequate medical and mental health treatment. The federal courts have made that very clear in California. As a result, the criminal justice conversation has changed, but not by much. Now, our conversation about crime is framed by the "cost of criminality." California, in particular, had been mired in unprecedented incarceration levels and the corresponding cost of that effort demanded transformation—a transformation that is presently being debated by criminal justice practitioners, scholars, and politicians.

It is my belief that, until our paradigm about addressing criminality changes, our remedies will continue to be more of the current profiling, suppression, and incarceration model; a model that *targets, arrests, and detains* the "bad guys." I'm certainly not alone in this view. Much has already been documented about the "War on Crime"; the unprecedented increase in California's prison population during the past forty years;

and the cost of incarceration.[4] The question remains: Has this model succeeded in reducing crime and recidivism?

Here's the problem: you have an opinion and so do I. Trying to keep a neutral position about the criminal justice system is like a recovering alcoholic claiming to be only a social drinker. It can't happen. So I must confess that the following pages have an agenda which will seek to dispute some myths about prison/jails and offenders too. I will also try to shed some light on staff dynamics and the correctional culture that is tasked with managing these dysfunctional environments.

My arguments are simple: First, "overcrowding" and "racial tension" didn't start the August 8, 2009 riot as was portrayed by the media, crime pundits, and politicians. A Mexican Mafia "shot caller" started it. Second, politics and policies created the parole violator "frequent flyer" pool which provided the human ammunition to make the riot happen. Third, the unprecedented influence of the Mexican Mafia in California prisons and among Latino street gangs in Southern California cannot be effectively challenged simply by continuing our profiling, suppression, and incarceration strategies. If that were true, then today the Mexican Mafia would be weaker. Instead, today they have more influence and power in prison and the community having gained powerful allies.

****

Each chapter in this book is preceded by the story of a true criminal justice experience related to the topic at hand. In most cases, only first names are used; in some, public record allows for a more complete picture. The intent is to make topics such as, inmate population growth, prison violence, gangs, and prison culture real and personal to the general reader. It may be difficult to comprehend, but prisons are a microcosm of our communities, with one important distinction. All of our worst social features are prominently on display in prison. This is where the predators become prey, the overseer becomes a casualty, and the truth is often lost in frustration, anger, and despair.

It is arguable that political discourse, public perceptions, and prison gang influence—precursors of the riot—may have had their beginnings in how we, as a nation, view crime. When we see crime reported on the TV or read about some horrendous gang assault or brutalized innocent victim, we are appalled, and rightly so. It is natural to be scared of and angry at vicious criminals. It is another to think about what circumstances brought a person to commit a crime. Why should we care? They don't deserve our attention! Just "lock 'em up and throw away the key" has been the prevailing attitude. Politicians have become "tough on crime." "Law and Order" has become the standard by which we judge others in society.[5] As a result, we are committed to suppression and incarceration in this state if not the nation.[6] Moreover, we don't want these criminals back in our community.

This NIMBY (not in my backyard) psychosis has, more often than not, paralyzed the political arena. No politician wants to be seen as weak on crime. We have created a dialogue of criminal alarm that mirrors our social and political response.[7] Even our language to describe crime and criminals reflects our attitude. Terms such as; criminal gangsters, street terrorists, War on Crime, War on Drugs, and Super Predators create fear and demand a militaristic response as the solution. One-dimensional views about public safety and fears about the increase in crime have incited debate only about increased bed-funding for county jails and more law enforcement personnel. This view supports the NIMBY psychosis by repeating a familiar public safety argument; more police, more crime supression, and more incarceration.

It is far from certain as to whether we have succeeded in reducing the criminal elements in our society, unless, of course, we are measuring success by the numbers. By 2006, California had the largest prison population in the nation and third largest in the world.[8] Even with the burden of federal lawsuits and budget-busting population increases, CDCR was unwilling and/or unable to stay the course for meaningful offender intervention. Instead, change came about through prisoner lawsuits that challenged CDCR's inability to provide adequate medical and mental health care to an ever-increasing inmate population.[9] The federal courts found the need to assign a "receiver" to monitor compliance throughout the state on health care delivery. California had simply too many inmates needing health care services and consistently failed to adequately meet the federal court compliance mandates. The federal courts agreed and ultimately, "overcrowding" became the central issue of debate.

****

The aforementioned criticism should not be interpreted as the polar opposite of being tough on crime. There is no "hug-a-thug" preaching being offered. The consideration is to find a political middle ground that seeks to hold offenders accountable for their crimes while also allowing them a realistic opportunity to find a way out of the criminal mindset. The public conversation about crime has always been offered as an "either/ or" choice. Are we tough on crime or weak on crime? That is the same simplistic thinking that has guided our political decisions about crime for forty years. The crime debate should not be about being tougher; instead, it should be about getting smarter about crime intervention. But how we get to a constructive option requires a change in our collective public thinking about crime.

If we don't seize the moment and change our dialogue about crime, we are sure to see a prison population filled with more violent offenders serving more time and with fewer programs; a "perfect storm" ripe for creating unremitting prison and jail mayhem. We have already seen the antecedents in past disturbances throughout the state's prison system. The August 8, 2009 riot at the Chino prison, is symbolic of the perfect storm that developed between misguided public perceptions, narcissistic political dogma, and percolating prison gang culture. Our criminal justice system has taken an ever-increasing share of the general fund, but has provided no lasting value to taxpayers or public safety. It is arguable that things are markedly worse today as the counties have geared up for more offenders at their doors and fewer resources afforded to prisons and jails.

****

My contrarian perspective of the criminal justice arena, if it is one, is a direct outcome of who I am as a person. Accordingly, my views on these matters began long before I established a career in law enforcement. Like most folks, my moral worldview was formed in my youth. It's my belief that significant moments in our lives define who we are as a person and sets us on a path which motivates and defines our actions. Some intimate moments I call "**wow**" events in my life, I have chosen to share because I think they influenced my perspective on crime, criminals, and effective intervention strategies.

I chose to begin this book with some of my personal "wow" moments for another reason, too. Some of the experiences are similar to what many youth and young adults in the inner city have encountered, but with much different results. I had some "**whoa!**" events, too, but those were much too revealing, painful and, in many cases, regretful and embarrassing to expose for public consumption. Together, the character-building "**wow and whoa**" moments I experienced were glued together by the strong values my family instilled in me as a child. Most offenders lack this strong family aspect because they are lost to the streets at too early an age without direction. I can recall many encounters with young and old offenders alike where the abundance of excuses included the refrain, "I couldn't catch a break." I couldn't agree more; they were unlucky.

The story about "luck" and its antecedents are no doubt long and much too complicated to address here. However, there is a troubling pattern where many incarcerated offenders have become victims of their own negative views about life. Those views are reinforced by the multitude of law enforcement contacts they attract. As I view it, "luck" is the same as "success" because both require preparation and opportunity. Offenders, like all of us, control part of the "luck" equation; preparation. They can prepare to succeed or prepare to fail. Unfortunately, they don't usually act; instead, they are acted upon. You will read the term "lucky" in quotations throughout the book. I mean it to signify "success" as I believe luck and success are the same, albeit good luck (successful) or bad luck (unsuccessful).

I have no doubt that you have had similar "wow" events that have narrowed or expanded your views of the world around you. As such, I believe some of my "wow" events are illustrative of the impact politics and policy decisions had in the California criminal justice arena that led to the unprecedented increase in prison populations. The other "wow" events I share are only to partially explain why I was so "lucky."

Sharing intimate moments from my youth is important for two other reasons. First, my experience with law enforcement contacts as a young man coupled with growing up during the civil rights era was a catharsis of sorts for me. What I view today as the criminality model—profiling, suppression, and incarceration—is what I observed and was subjected to as a teenager and young adult. Ironically, it is also the paradigm I practiced as a peace officer and ultimately directed as a supervisor, manager, and administrator. Even though it is sometimes funny to recount these personal life-changing experiences, I realize there was a thin line of intolerance and inequity threaded throughout those events.

Like most baby-boomers, I grew up during a turbulent period in our nation; the Vietnam war, civil rights movement, and the assassination of cherished leaders, which led to social protests. I certainly didn't understand most of it at the time, but I kept those experiences close to my heart. You'll see examples of it in my choice of music lyrics that precede each section. Music, as the saying goes, *struck a chord* with me growing up learning to play guitar. The poetry of the oldies-but-goodies, the rhythm of the Motown sound, the energy of classic rock, and the tradition of hearing my father, a World War II veteran, alternately playing Jose Alfredo Jimenez and Frank Sinatra on the stereo, left an indelible mark on my psyche. Music became a means to drown myself out of the moment as a young man or express myself with others as I matured. So bear with me as I share a peek into the cloudy lens of my youth that influenced my perspective on people and ultimately guided my actions throughout my law enforcement career.

CHAPTER 1

And if I say to you tomorrow
Take my hand, child, come with me
It's to a castle I will take you
Where what's to be, they say will be

Led Zeppelin
"What Is and What Should Never Be"

A DIFFERENT BEAT

I was born in Oildale, California, in 1955. That's right Oildale, the smelly armpit of Bakersfield! I'm not joking; Oildale has oil rigs scattered throughout its sterile fields and cut-rate houses. The pungent smell of dirty oil always permeates the air. We actually lived in Bakersfield, but as "luck" would have it, my birthplace would be greased in oil. Hence, I can honestly be called a "greaser" from the dusty dirt fields of Oildale. Fortunately, my father moved us to East Los Angeles looking for better employment opportunities when I was nearly one year old.

My dad was a single father with two small children, and whose seven sisters took turns overseeing our development. I was fortunate to have two "mamas." Mama Lupe, my tia (aunt), gave me unconditional love throughout my life. Still today, I cherish her as my mama. My abuelita (grandmother) Mama Jesse, also cared for me and my sister during our childhood years, but would cut us no slack if we were naughty. Mama Jesse expressed her love through food. Every morning she would make tortillas de mano (handmade tortillas) and fresh salsa. The smell from the kitchen was soothing. I could hear the slaps of the masa in her hands and the thumping of the roller as she made dozens of tortillas for the day. The other slaps I recall were to the back of my head when I misbehaved!

As a little "travieso" (trouble-maker), I couldn't catch a break, with a lot of loving discipline to guide me. I used to think my tias would have to draw straws to see who would take care of me and my sister, the loser having to put up with us. I used to tease my seven tias about how a line would form when it came to spanking me for something I did. The truth of the matter is that they all sacrificed their time and energy providing a loving environment for my sister and me during our childhood. I love them all for their patience, the stories they shared, and the many nights of Chinese checkers, Scrabble, and Lotería (bingo) games we played.

One other family member who made a profound impact on my life as a youth was my nino (godfather) Ernie. As a pre-teen and teenager living in the Los Angeles area, it wasn't hard to find trouble or feel overwhelmed at times with family issues. My nino was always there for me to bend his ear with my juvenile problems. He was patient and earnestly allowed me to vent my thoughts without judgement. I could tell him what I would never tell my father. He never told me if I was right or wrong; instead, he gave advice that allowed me to find the answer myself. On hindsight, I'm sure he guided my decisions to their obvious conclusions. It didn't matter because he made me feel important. For a confused young man, self-esteem is the balance maker.

My sister and I were raised in apartments until we turned twenty and eighteen, respectively. Apartment-living is not conducive to putting down roots in any community, especially when you move frequently. During my youth, we moved from Norwalk to Estrada Courts in East Los Angeles and ultimately to Montebello during my formative years. I recall getting really sick and bed-ridden from strep throat when I was fifteen. I would lose my balance just trying to walk, so I had to stay in bed for nearly two weeks. I was bored and full of energy. But as "luck" would have it, my sister gave me her guitar to pass the time. I learned about four chords pretty quickly and realized I had met my love for life, music!

As a young man, I found it necessary to acquaint myself with new friends each time I moved. I developed the "gift of gab," probably more as a means to survive. I never joined any gangs, but ran into plenty of gangbangers from Varrio Nuevo Estrada Courts, Jardin, White Fence, Mara Villa, and Southside Montebello. I spent the last five years of my youth in Southside Montebello. Southside was right at the border of the Cities of Commerce and Norwalk. I hung out with about four guys in Southside. One was a Greek named Dino. He, who introduced me to classic rock guitar jams and his father's homemade licorice wine called Uzo. It never tasted very good, but it made our guitar playing sound better. Dino had the voice of Credence Clearwater Revival's John Fogerty, and the songs fit the four chords I had learned. We were a garage band overnight!

Dino and my other friends went to Montebello Junior and Senior High School together. Even though Southside wasn't really a barrio, it sounded good so I claimed it whenever I was asked, "de honde?" (Where are you from?). I responded, "Southside." Most of the time, I'd get a puzzled look, "Where's that?"

****

I was a child of the '60s civil rights movement. The Chicano movement and the protest against the Vietnam War were at their zenith from 1968 through 1975. I recall this young Latino from Los Angeles Community College canvassing Montebello Junior and Senior High School students at Gardino's on Garfield Avenue and Curry's Ice Cream Parlor on Whittier Boulevard. He was really passionate and got our attention by saying things like, "You don't have Chicano teachers or administrators at your school, but you have Chicano gardeners and janitors. Why is that? You need to fight for Chicano representation in your school. We want all the Chicanos to join the protest walk-out next week…" It made me think.

I recalled sitting in Spanish class with my Japanese teacher. She asked each student to say a food item in Spanish. As with most bright, forward-thinking students, I sat in the corner back row. As she made her way around the class, I quickly realized I would be the last student to speak. Having never mastered my own language, I started to panic. Everyone was picking words I knew; burrito, manzana, leche, frijoles, carne, tacos…I was quickly running out of words. Finally, when she got to me, the whole class was staring in my direction. I was drenched in a pool of perspiration. My teacher finally broke the silence, "Well, Richard, can you give us a food word?"

I responded, "Sure, chicharones!"

The whole class started laughing and I was smiling, proud that I had beat the test. My teacher wasn't so happy, she ordered me to the principal's office. I sat there for about an hour wondering why chicharones (dried pork rinds) wasn't a food since I ate them nearly every week when Mama Jesse cooked them with chile. I can only imagine that the teacher thought I was disrespecting her or worse, she hadn't had the pleasure of tasting this fine Mexican delicacy.

I did participate in the walk-out but only because practically the whole school did. We mostly stood around laughing and pointing at each other for ditching classes, never realizing the significance of the moment. We went back inside at lunchtime…we were hungry.

****

That was the first time I realized "I" was a minority. I never saw my best friend Jimmy Lopez as anything other than Jimmy. I didn't know what racism was. I hadn't cared about or even paid attention to the ethnicity of other students I went to school with. I was in the seventh grade and pretty naive about racism. In fact, I never realized that those monthly police contacts on our way to school were because of our color and appearance. Jimmy and I would be asked, "Where are you going? Where do you live? Where were you born?" It wasn't the police; it was "La Migra," the border patrol. We were a little nervous, but answered the questions innocently without knowing the reason for being stopped.

Jimmy suffered from epilepsy. I was introduced to the condition during our walk to school. He lived only three short blocks from my apartment. While we waited for the bus one day, I heard a large "thud." I turned around and Jimmy was no longer standing next to me, he was on the ground shaking furiously. I didn't know what to do, so I tried to hold him, shouting his name, "Jimmy, Jimmy, what's wrong?" His body shook so violently we were both shaking. He recovered after a few minutes and I sat him up and asked if he was okay. He didn't remember falling and his head hurt. I guess he felt good that I didn't leave him or make fun of him. We remained close friends until I graduated from high school, when we eventually lost touch.

Jimmy had a temper; he got it from his father, who petrified both of us. I got in more fights because of Jimmy's mouth than I can remember. He'd say something to some guys who were staring at us, and the fight was on. I was no fighter. Neither was Jimmy, but we stood up for each other. We never really got hurt much, except for our egos.

Jimmy's dad would allow him to pull the car out in the mornings. I'd be at his house at 6:00 a.m. and we'd joyride for about thirty minutes. One time, the police were behind us, Jimmy and I, eighth grade car-jackers, didn't know what to do. The police put their lights on and we both flew out of the car. Jimmy one way, and I the other. I didn't see Jimmy for two weeks. His father had reported the car stolen. I have no doubt that Jimmy got a serious beating at home.

****

Fortunately, Montebello Junior High and High School were the most integrated schools in the area. They were considered better schools than Garfield or Roosevelt in East Los Angeles. That was the main reason my father moved us to Montebello. Latinos accounted for about 45 percent of the school population, Armenians about 20 percent, Anglos 20 percent, and Asians 15 percent. I could consciously identify Armenians because they always seemed bigger and hairier than everyone else. One of my friends at Montebello High was Danny Agajanian, a sharp kid who would later become a dentist. I would wrestle Danny almost every week after school on his front lawn. We weren't angry at each other, just gregarious juveniles jostling to see who'd win…he won most of the time.

I witnessed knife fights at the park on Whittier Boulevard. It was scary to see, but exciting, nonetheless. All the kids would know about the semi-planned fight between some gang members from opposing barrios or some vatos (guys) just angry about a girl or disrespect issue. A simple stare beyond three seconds was enough for a fight to start. If word got out or someone reported the fight, police would charge in and take control—swinging billy clubs and banging heads on their patrol units if someone was resistive. Kids would be running in all directions to escape arrest.

It was, as if I was watching a movie. It was never real, but captivating, until it was my turn to be the star in the movie. It seems that my friend Gilbert decided he wanted to join a gang and he picked me as his opponent for a fight. He told everyone that he was going to fight me after school. I didn't understand why he wanted to fight, but I knew it was for real because everyone was talking about it. Some girl had put him up to it.

That day, after school, I met my sister at the donut shop on Whittier Boulevard. Inside, I could see Gilbert at a table looking out at me. I was scared to death, but couldn't move. Gilbert came outside and the crowd formed around us. I was the proverbial "deer in the headlights." I told Gilbert, I didn't want to fight him. It didn't matter; Gilbert raised his fists and started doing some sort of "cock-fight" dance. I raised my fists, too, and tears began to well up in my eyes. Everybody was yelling, but I couldn't hear what they were saying. I obviously didn't know the dance steps yet! Unfortunately, I did learn it in high school as I was suspended a couple of times for fighting.

I would go home after fighting at school, sure that the vice principal had called my father already. It would be quiet at the dinner table, my sister knowing and smiling as I sweated the outcome. I would spill my guts, "Dad, I got suspended for fighting."

There would be a momentary pause, then, he'd ask, without looking at me, "Who won?"

I'd respond, "It was a tie" or "Nobody, the teacher broke it up." When I did win a fight, I'd look forward to him asking the question, but he never did...just my "luck!" He never punished me for fighting, but I always felt guilty about getting in trouble at school, so I tried to avoid problems. Thankfully, my first "main event" with Gilbert on Whittier Boulevard never materialized! My sister, who was very athletic and tougher than me in our youth, stepped between us yelling at Gilbert to knock it off and saved me the embarrassment of possibly losing a fight. I guess Gilbert didn't really want to fight, either. Besides, my sister would have kicked his butt. She would save me from myself many more times in my youthful life.

****

My first job was as a janitor for a small beauty salon. I saw this sign on the door soliciting part-time work. One thing I had learned watching my family, they all valued work. Work was a testament of who you were in the community. Work enabled our family to succeed from the fields in Kern County to the city and, as I would later learn, hard work solidified a successful future. I went inside to get an application. The owner was a likeable person, not much on small talk, but very driven about his business. I guess he kind of sized me up, and then asked me if I could work after school some days. I said yes, and began working that week.

One thing about apartment living is that there are always chores to do inside the house. So cleaning toilets, floors, and walls had already been my life punishment as a youngster, or so I thought. Now, my cleaning "skills" had a payoff! After about six weeks, the owner pulled me aside and said, "Richard, you are doing a good job, but I want a more complete cleaning done on Saturdays after we're closed. Can you do that?" I answered in the affirmative, nodding my head. "Good," he said. "Here are the keys." I remember him looking at me closely, as if saying, "I trust you." I can't explain the shock and pride that overwhelmed me at that moment. He had given me the keys to the beauty salon. I was so proud that he trusted me, and couldn't wait to share the news with my family.

****

My family was active in politics. My father was one of the original members of the Mexican American Political Association in Los Angeles. He used to drag my sister and me around East L.A. to put flyers on cars during the weekend at supermarkets. We were embarrassed and always complained, but did our duty…for him. When he retired from sales, he returned to Bakersfield to open up his own business. There he remained active in politics and helped establish the Kern County Hispanic Chamber of Commerce.

I remember the 1970 Chicano moratorium protest march. My father had taken my sister and me to listen to the political speeches at the park. We were walking down Whittier Boulevard that day, not consciously aware of the significance, but enjoying the excitement and music with all the other familias headed to the park. All of a sudden, my father says, "Let's go, now!" We saw people moving quickly toward us and we turned and left the park, too. Later, we saw on the news that Los Angeles journalist, Ruben Salazar had been killed by a sheriff's deputy who fired a tear gas round into the Silver Dollar Bar. The projectile hitting him in the head and killing him instantly.

My uncles were also politically involved having served on the city councils in Visalia and Porterville, California for many years. My dad would send me to Porterville during the summer to work at my Uncle Gilbert's flower shop. I was cheap labor for him I suppose, but I think the real reason I was sent there was to keep me out of trouble in Los Angeles. In Porterville, I met this young Chicano, Michael Salcedo who drove the flower delivery truck for my uncle. Michael would talk politics all the time and I was his captive listener. While he drove, I would jump out of the van and deliver the flower arrangements and run back to hear his next tale of Chicano activism. He was a radical and I loved his passion about people and the community. He would later become a principal and administrator in education.

One time Michael convinced me to attend a protest at the local Catholic Church. The priest had demanded payment for conducting the last rites ceremony for a campesino (farm worker) who had passed away. Michael was angry that the priest would charge poor people who go to church each week and put what little money they have into the church basket.

"Why is the richest church in the world charging loyal church goers for a prayer?" he would say. So, there I was, holding a protest sign in front of the church, about four blocks from my Tia Rosa's house. I was excited being part of a protest against injustice but I was also worried. I wasn't fearful of the wrath of God; I was terrified about the wrath of Mama Jesse! If she found out, she'd punish me for sure. I couldn't bear to go on "*tortilla restriction!*" Not that she would ever do that, but she had a knack for putting the fear of God in me for questioning the church or her!

Fortunately, my Tio Gilbert, a successful businessman and community leader convinced the church to reconsider the "last rites" payment requirement. The protest was a success! But I was in real trouble with "Mama Jesse" for protesting and disturbing the church! She scolded my father and he blamed my uncle, as they both laughed about it. I recall the many political arguments my dad would have with my tios at the kitchen table until the wee hours of the morning toasting their own opinions with Crown Royal (not the cola, either). I know they tried, but, like the rest of us, they couldn't solve the world problems. At least not at one sitting!

****

I graduated high school in June of 1973. It was also the year that the military draft ended in the United States. No more mandatory military service signups. I had not thought about my future at that point. My father had volunteered to serve in the Army at age seventeen. He was a World War II veteran having served in Persia (Iran) and North Africa. My uncles Joe and Pete were both lifers in the service; one in the Army and the other in the Air Force. Both of them were "tough-as-nails" master sergeants. Both had "lost" their chevrons a few times for solving disputes without authorization (fighting). I recall hearing my Uncle Pete describe a fight he had in a bar with some guy that was a Judo Master. He said, "Man, did I pick the wrong guy to have a fight with! No matter what I tried, he'd grab my arm, hand, or pinkie finger and toss me around the room…I'd have felt better if he had just hit me!"

I remember when I was about seventeen years old, flipping one of my Uncle Joe's cigarettes around in my hand while my tios and dad played poker one night. My Uncle Joe grabbed my arm and looked me in the eye saying sternly, "If I ever catch you smoking a cigarette, I will break your arm."

I think it was his way of saying, "I love you Mijo (son), but this is bad for your health." I didn't listen. Some years later, I began smoking cigarettes. It was about ten years before I quit cold turkey. In fact, I quit smoking the day my father passed away. He died of cancer at age fifty-nine.

Sometime before I graduated high school, my Uncle Joe had told my dad, "If he's drafted, it might be better to send him to Mexico." He had served two tours of duty in Vietnam and had received medals for his service, but he refused to talk about those days and didn't want any celebratory party after he returned. I doubt I would have gone to Mexico, rebellious as most youth are to parental interference; instead, I ended up on a different path. My father had never encouraged military service; instead, he always spoke about attending college. The seed had been planted.

****

Out of school and looking for work in 1974, I found a job at Zacky Farms in El Monte. It was a large storage warehouse that moved meat and chicken throughout the region. As I recall, the back side of the warehouse housed the "chicken plucking" area, and the front side housed the receiving docks and cold storage freezer. The freezer was almost the size of a football field. I got a job as the freezer man. I had to dress up like an Eskimo—in a full body jumpsuit and hood outfit. It was summertime in Southern California, and I was sweating like a pig. I landed the job because I lied about my experience. I told the supervisor that I could drive a forklift. Instead, of asking me to demonstrate, he just said, "Good, you start tomorrow morning."

I would employ my newfound interviewing technique—*lying*—many times in the future on job interviews. I remember getting a summer job in 1980 at the Mission Inn Hotel in Riverside, California. The Mission Inn maintenance supervisor asked if I could weld. I said yes. I didn't even have a clue how to turn a blow torch on! The Mission Inn had tunnels that extended for miles underground. Large steel water tanks were located below the main floor and the management wanted to remove them. That required torches to shear off large pieces to make them convenient for removal. When I went down to start my work, one of the older Latino maintenance workers accompanied me. He looked me over; probably aware I was a first year student from the University of California, Riverside, and asked, "Puede, hacerlo?" (Can you do it?)

I smiled at him and said, "No, pero puedo aprender!" (No, but I can learn.) He proceeded to show me how to work the torch and I survived my first day.

****

It was about 7:00 a.m. I was putting on my Eskimo outfit when the Zacky Farms supervisor came by to show me around the plant. On the back dock, a large trailer truck had arrived filled with live chickens. He indicated I wouldn't be working this area in the morning, but I would help load the trucks later in the day. I observed this one guy on the top of the truck pushing the live chickens onto a conveyer-type rack that led to a large machine. Another guy was standing above us on a platform near the machine and was quickly yanking the chickens into a moving conveyer that held the chicken by the neck in a slot-lock apparatus as it went into a feather removal machine. I'm not sure when the chicken met his death, but I could see the blood on the slot locks and rack. I was happy not to have his job.

As I started my new job as the freezer man, I quickly figured out how to handle the forklift. I was by myself in the freezer warehouse, so I had time to practice. Moving frozen bull meat and other types of meat piled neatly on pallets was easy. Stacking them by hand was difficult. The meat weighed about fifty to seventy-five pounds per bag and the bags were not easy to grip with my baseball mitt-sized gloves. I was constantly cold inside and couldn't wait for a break or lunch to feel some welcome heat.

I recall leaving the freezer one day to eat my bologna sandwich on the dock. I had peeled off the freezer jumpsuit down to my waist and was ready to eat when the guy who'd been slinging chickens in the back came and sat next to me to eat his lunch—a fat torta filled with pork meat, cheese, lettuce, and chili. He was smeared in blood from head to toe. Oblivious to the blood all over him, he wolfed down that torta. The thought of fresh blood and torta was too much for me to take. I waddled like a penguin back to my cold, but clean environment.

About a month into my freezer work, I felt a sharp pain, as if a knife got stuck in my shoulder blade. It continued to hurt for about two weeks. Finally, I mentioned to the supervisor that I hurt my back. He quickly asked me when I got hurt. The question caught me off guard. I don't know why, but in the silence of our stare, I responded dryly, "yesterday."

He said, "Okay, but you'll have to wait until after work to go to the clinic."

One of my duties included assisting the loading dock in the afternoon. The trucks would roll in and we would load them as quickly as we could. A large fifteen-foot loading tray with rollers would be placed in the front of the truck bed and it extended half way into the truck. Guys on each side of the tray would grab the frozen chickens and bull meat from the pallets and push them on the rollers into the bed of the truck where two guys would toss them to the back. After seeing frozen chickens and bull meat flying all over the place, I was no longer feeling good about the meat products my family purchased at the market. This loading practice would continue until the purchase orders were completed. Supervisors always watched the loading. We all knew our day was done when the loading was finished, so we'd hustle just to leave work early. This happened every day. I would soon learn there was another benefit for our hustle.

After attending the medical clinic, I received an off-work order for two weeks, which I gave to the supervisor. He said, "Fine, but we can't pay you while you're off work."

I agreed and left for home. My pop asked me why I wasn't working and I explained what had happened. He looked at me and said, "Pendejo (dummy), they can't do that, you should be covered by workers compensation." I had no clue what he was talking about. He immediately called a friend. When he got off the phone, he told me to go to see an attorney, Manuel Lopez, the following day.

Mr. Lopez was the Los Angeles Chapter President of the Mexican American Political Association. His staff walked me through the workers compensation process and I received my pay for about six months while I attended therapy. My pain subsided about two months after therapy, but it didn't matter. Zacky Farms would not take me back because of my injury. I didn't care because my workers compensation was calculated at a forty-hour work week. The company rarely allowed employees to work a full eight-hour day (my weekly hours never reached thirty). As a result, I was making the same amount of pay on workers comp that I was when I was working! After two years, Zacky Farms settled with my attorney and I received a lump sum check for two thousand dollars. I was a rich young man with money that lasted me all of about one month!

****

Following my "medical recovery" from Zacky Farms, I landed a job at Wamsutta Knitting Mills. It was a large fabric factory on Azusa Avenue in Valinda, California, which was about five miles from home. I had applied for the $7.00-an- hour janitor job—big money for a high school graduate. Instead, I was told I didn't have the experience, but they could offer me the "sample expeditor" position for $2.50 an hour. I wasn't greedy, just needy, so I jumped on it! This wasn't the first time I had been told that "line" about lacking experience. When I was in tenth grade, I had applied for weekend work at the nearby car wash. They told me the same thing, I lacked the requisite experience. I told my dad about it and he just laughed, saying, "Pendejo, they only hire Mexicans there."

"But I'm a Mexican, too!" I said emphatically.

"Apparently, not Mexican enough for the job," he replied.

Wamsutta had hired someone else for the janitor position. I realized why when I met him; he was an older guy probably mid-forties, a family man. I figured he needed the pay more than I did. My job entailed that I send five-yard sample pieces of the different Trivera yarn cloth to different clothing and fashion merchants across the country. I had to inventory and organize the work area that sat between the manufacturing and receiving and release sections. I worked alone and ate my lunch alone. To get to my work site, I'd pass the large washer and dryer machines that each had to be the size of two large conference rooms. I'd make eye contact with many workers, nodding my head to say "Q-vo", (hi) and continue to my site. The job lasted about four month. One day, without warning, Wamsutta announced that it was closing and moving across the border.

The announcement was made late in the afternoon. They herded the employees into a large conference room. At the large rectangular table sat the Wamsutta president, management staff, and some clerical personnel. They were all white. Facing them were about forty to sixty workers, all standing in the back of the room. These workers were the backbone of the business. They ran the large knitting, dye, and drying machines that spanned across what seemed like two football fields inside the factory. They were all Latinos except the janitor, he was black.

The floor manager started to explain that the company was closing, but that we would all receive a two-week severance check the following day, and free turkeys (it was Thanksgiving week). One of the older workers translated in Spanish as the manager spoke. I could see many of the workers; mostly older women, begin to weep. It hurt me to see these women in pain. They all looked like my tias, especially my Mama Lupe who, like them, worked in a factory, too.

One of the clerical employees sitting at the table asked the president what he would be doing. His response, "I'll probably open up a taco stand." The people at the table laughed. That was it; I went off. I was insulted by the statement. Maybe, if he had said burger stand I would have been fine, but tacos…it hit a nerve! I was standing on the side facing both the table and the other factory workers. I shouted out, "You can open your fucking taco stand, but there are people here who have families; what are they supposed to do?" I quickly surveyed the crowd who stood quiet, but gave me no support.

The floor manager quickly stepped up and said, "That is why you're all getting the severance check."

I continued, "That's not right, you gave the workers no notice and they have families to support. I'm young. I can find a job, but they have worked here a lot of years and for what; a small check and a turkey? Go open your damn taco stand, I don't want your turkey, I could care less!" I looked at the crowd of workers and not one moved or said a word. It was a protest of one.

I was disgusted that they wouldn't say or do anything. I'm not even sure what I wanted them to do, but I was pissed that they accepted the bullshit coming from the management. I stormed out of the room. The meeting had ended on that note and I couldn't get out of the building quick enough. When I got home, I told my dad about what had happened.

I was mad that the workers just accepted the abuse. He studied my face for a minute and then said, "They couldn't do anything, but they'll find work...don't forget to get your check and *my* turkey tomorrow."

I did not look forward to entering the large warehouse factory again. I was angry at the workers and feeling humiliated that I had to go get my check and turkey from the office staff. As I had every morning for four months, I walked into the knitting building area where there were twenty large freezer-size sewing machines being operated. As I entered the rotunda, all of the workers faced toward me and began applauding. I looked around wondering what was going on and suddenly realized they were applauding for me. I was caught off guard. An older worker came up to me and said, "I told everyone what you said yesterday, tienes ganas hijo (you have passion, kid, thanks) gracias."

I nodded with embarrassment and looked at the smiling faces. I put my head down and kept walking; I was truly ashamed for having doubted them. No one had translated what the president had said or my response until after I had left. I had done nothing but speak my mind, but I learned a lesson about valuing the worth of others.

****

Since I had no job and nothing to do, my sister suggested I go to college. She said the smartest and prettiest girls were there. She always had my best interest in mind! College was also something my father had talked to us about regularly. He didn't know how to help us realize our dreams, but he made sure we knew what was important. I enrolled at Mt. San Antonio and, about two years later, transferred to the University of California, Riverside. My close friends during my college days were guys that came from different Barrios—Benny from Valinda Flats; Richard from Puente; Javier and Julio from Puente Trece; Andres from Blythe, which he referred to as "La Cuna de Aztlan"; and Eddie from Varrio Trece.

Andres always pronounced Blythe "Blee-tay" and I would tease him, "Blee-tay? What's that a rash?" Andres never did laugh, but just looked at me like I didn't get it. He was correct. Andres is an attorney now, but his true love was the guitar and horses. Benny retired as the clerk of the court in Los Angeles, California. Richard is a drafting engineer in Riverside County. Javier is an executive administrator for charter schools in San Bernardino, California. Julio is a professor in Colorado. Eddie was a Marine who later retired as a correctional officer and became known by his fellow officers as "Gabe" (Gabriel was his first name). We all were young men looking for adventure; but mostly, we were just looking for steady jobs and the attention of women.

Benny, Richard, and Eddie had "firme ranflas" (nice rides). Everyone referred to Richard and me as "Los Dos" ("The Two" Richards). Because we were always together in his '64 Impala low rider, people mistook us for brothers. We were both tall, dark, and handsome. Okay, maybe we shared only two of the three characteristics! We'd cruise Whittier Boulevard in East L. A. playing tape decks of Led Zeppelin, Jimmy Hendrix, Santana, Credence Clearwater, and the Rolling Stones while everyone else played oldies. We were different and preferred it that way. I drove a '74 Buick Wildcat; it was fast, with dull paint and dented all over like the dimples on a golf ball! But I didn't care because it ran!

****

That Wildcat was also the cause of my arrest for assaulting a peace officer. It was 1978. Richard and I had met some girls at a party and they invited us to another party the following weekend. They gave us a flyer from a girls club in Norwalk. We thought, let's go! We decided not to take Richard's '64 Impala or Benny's '68 Impala, or Eddie's '69 Monte Carlo, "the Green Burrito." We always made fun of the nasty green color. If we ever tried to deny our Mexican heritage, the Monte Carlo wouldn't allow it! We decided to take the Wildcat. We knew we were going into some strange barrio, and we didn't want to attract any unnecessary attention. We never worried about trouble because we weren't looking for any. But we knew there was always some danger. We were right. That night, we danced and partied with the girls until about midnight. Then we heard some commotion outside.

We moved to the back patio and realized it was coming from the street, so we hopped on the brick wall to get a better look. From our vantage point, we could see about a dozen dudes yelling out their barrio name, "Jardin, y que putos" (The Gardens and what of it, fuckers). We weren't concerned because it was all talk, but some other guys at the party were. They had driven their "firme ranflas" (good-looking cars) to the party.

Low rider cars were a "high maintenance" endeavor for young men. It cost money to fix them and to make them look good. They cost nearly as much to drive. Anyone owning a "ranfla" had two things going for them, a job and some basic mechanic skills. Those guys had brought their beautiful rides to a bad part of town. By the time they exited the house, the damage was done: tires slashed, windows busted, fenders and hoods dented. We were standing on the wall, holding our beers and chucking over their losses, content in knowing that my ugly Buick Wildcat, sitting smack in the middle of the battlefield, was ignored by everyone.

The sheriff's deputies finally arrived and ordered everyone to leave immediately. As I started to walk across the street from the house, I was accosted by a deputy who demanded that I leave the area. He grabbed my arm and yelled, "Leave now!"

I was about five feet from my car. Angry, I pulled my arm away and yelled back, "I am leaving; my car is right there."

At that moment, I was taken down by three deputies and cuffed in the street. They put me in a patrol unit with two other guys who had been at the party. The one in the middle was drunk and screaming profanities all the way to the Norwalk Substation. "Putos (fuckers) take these cuffs off and see what happens, pinche putos. You ain't about shit mother fuckers." He was spitting on the window grill as he cursed. This continued throughout the whole ride.

I whispered to him, "Shut up man, these guys don't know who's saying what, shut up!"

"Fuck'em," he replied. "These mother fuckers ain't about nothing."

When we arrived at the substation, we were herded like cattle into the receiving area, still in cuffs, and ordered to face the wall with our noses glued to it. About eight of us, all Latinos, did as directed. The "cursing boy" was right next to me. He was quiet now as we waited to be searched. A deputy walked up and poked his head between the two of us and whispered to cursing boy, "So what were you saying about my mother?" Cursing boy was quiet with his nose pressed on the wall. The officer asked again sarcastically, "Come on now, you were a tough guy in the car, what about my mom?"

Cursing Boy couldn't hold back any longer, turning his head he yelled, "Fuck you, puto!"

The deputy, in one quick move, grabbed cursing boy's head by the hair and slammed it back against the wall. I could feel the splatter of blood hit the side of my face. Cursing boy was silent but still standing.

"Say it again, tough guy!" the deputy hollered. Cursing Boy didn't say a word, and the whole place got really quiet. The deputy with full bravado, said, "That's what I thought; another little bitch!" He then pulled Cursing Boy from the wall and slammed him again, this time harder. Cursing Boy fell to the ground nearly unconscious. I was frozen in place, scared shitless that I was up next for a beating.

****

I had a habit of leaving my driver's license in the car. I kept it with my registration for quick access. I was used to being pulled over by police late at night, since I cleaned burger joints from two to five on Friday and Saturday mornings. (That's right, those damn cleaning skills I honed in apartment living were paying off tons of dimes and nickels!) A Latino out on the streets at that time of night got lots of attention. I was pulled over every weekend and sometimes twice in one night. They'd look in the backseat of the Buick Wildcat asking suspiciously, "So if you do janitor work, where are your cleaning supplies?" I'd jump out and open the very spacious trunk that had all my gear; bucket, mop, broom, cleansers, rags. I had it all! This happened so often I just kept my paperwork; driver's license, registration, and insurance, bundled together in the glove compartment to save time. However, because of my arrest at the party, I had no chance to get my license from the car. As a result, the substation sergeant informed me that I would get one call but I was on my way to Los Angeles County Jail for further processing because I had no ID.

I arrived at the county jail in Los Angeles about 2:30 a.m. I was strip-searched, power sprayed with lice powder, and herded again like cattle with another forty guys to a large holding cell. I sat on a long wooden bench when another Chicano sat next to me. He looked at me and asked, "What are you here for?"

"They said I assaulted an officer," I responded.

He smiled, "Orale." (Alright!)

I tried to appear disinterested. I'll admit I was scared. This was my first time in jail, but I wasn't going to show it. In fact, I was more concerned that my father not find out. He had told me in the past that if I ever got arrested not to bother calling him. How did he know I'd get myself into this predicament?

About two hours or so passed and I finally heard my name called. I was being bailed out. These two black guys approached me as I walked toward the grill gate. The older one, in his forties, asked, "Hey man, you leaving?"

I answered, "Yeah, I guess."

He responded, "Let me have your shoes."

I was startled by the question and felt insulted wondering why this guy wanted my shoes. I blurted out, "My shoes? Fuck you, I ain't giving you shit!"

He just looked at me as I stared at him neither of us saying a word. The holding cell fell quiet. Not wanting to press my "luck" I left the module without incident…until I got outside.

****

Eddie had driven the *Green Burrito* from La Puente to pick me up. The ranfla was a dark-lime green color with pinstripe designs all around it. It had the clean lines of the Monte Carlo and no dents. The color was an eye-catcher. This was not the appropriate vehicle to drive into Los Angeles. But I didn't care. I was just happy to see him, Benny, and Richard. They teased me about doing "time," asking if I still preferred girls, etc, etc. Didn't matter. I was happy my father didn't know I had been arrested and I was out safely…or so I thought.

About a block from the jail, we saw this car approaching us from the opposite direction. It was a black low-rider with two guys inside. It was about five on a Sunday morning, so there was no one around. To make things worse, neither Eddie nor the rest of us knew how to get to the freeway. The low-rider passed slowly then sped up and whipped a U-turn coming along side us at the signal light with the windows down.

We looked over and could see the occupants were mad-dogging us. Benny chuckled, saying, "There's only two of them, do they know who their fucking with?" Richard and I laughed. Eddie didn't, he had been out of the Marines less than a year.

He looked over at the black low-rider saying, "Something's not right, they must have a gun or something in the car. Let's get out of here."

Benny and Eddie were "one hit" wonders. When they got into a fight they were fearless. When they connected a punch with their opponent that was it; lights out, game over. Richard and I were the opposite; we'd do the "rooster dance", jumping around and flailing away, looking like unskilled ballerinas hoping to land any kind of solid punch. None of us however, ever ran away from a fight, until then.

Eddie gunned it at the green light and the black low-rider sped along with us, until they passed us speeding along the road. We thought they were done, but they weren't. From a distance, we watched as the vehicle made a screeching U-turn and came back. The passenger now was sticking half-way out of the car with something in his hand. For a moment, we thought it was a gun. Luckily, it wasn't. It was a pipe. He threw it and it missed us but hit the hood of the Green Burrito. Eddie was pissed. He made a U-turn and headed after them; luckily we couldn't catch up and eventually lost sight of them on the streets. My dance with crime had ended before it started.

****

I appeared in court about four months later. My witnesses were Benny and Eddie for the charge of assaulting an officer and resisting arrest. I was assigned a deputy public defender. He was a Jewish fellow who was short on words. As I tried to argue that I wanted a jury trial, he said, "Look, you don't want a trial and the court won't entertain it anyway. Just answer my questions directly when I call you up to the stand." I sat next to him and watched as he stared at his legal notepad. He scribbled away as the deputy district attorney had the arresting officer describe my actions leading to the arrest.

My attorney never looked up; never made eye contact with the witnesses or the judge. I wondered if this guy was paying any attention. So I looked at his legal pad and I realized he was writing in shorthand every word that was being spoken. Occasionally, he'd bark, "Objection, your honor, leading the witness," or "Not relevant, your honor," and he'd continue to write. When it was his turn, my attorney put each of us, Benny, Eddie, and I on the stand. For each one of us, he asked the same question, "What is your occupation?"

The reply was the same, "I'm a student at Mt. San Antonio College." I realized later, he was only trying to establish that we were not what we appeared to be.

At that time, I wasn't sure what we appeared to be, either! When he cross-examined the deputy, he cleverly guided the deputy through his original testimony, stopping him to correct what he had already testified to. Of course, it was in his notes! The deputy was changing his testimony without realizing what was happening. The deputy couldn't articulate if I was coming or going that night and in what direction. The judge dismissed the case. At the time, I was not happy because I wanted to be found "not guilty," but I was glad the case was dropped. I was really impressed with the attorney's skill. However, I was not impressed with the justice system—a thought that would echo in my mind many more times during my career.

****

Attending the University of California, Riverside (UCR) was instrumental in my introduction and eventual career in the criminal justice arena. I had occasion in the winter of 1979, to complete an internship at the Riverside County Juvenile Hall. The summer before, I had worked at a boys home in the Woodcrest area of Riverside. All the juvenile placements were from Los Angeles County, mostly Crip gangsters—a tough group of misunderstood and angry kids. But I was familiar with the "breed" having grown up in L.A. Comparing these group home kids to the delinquents placed at the juvenile hall was like comparing salsa to catsup; it was hot vs. bland. The juvenile hall youths were neither very sophisticated nor street savvy. As an intern, I was watching the group counselors and thinking, "I could do just as good of a job, if not better, at managing these punks."

About the same time, my college mentor, Professor Alfredo Mirande had organized a group of students to conduct "Chicano Issues" classes at the California Rehabilitation Center in Norco. It was around 1980-81 when we would meet for an evening each month to discuss topics like; machismo images, conflict management, mujeres (women) in the workforce, etc. The students were primarily graduate students, all women except me and one other guy. It was always funny to see these inmates strut their male egos, talking about where their woman belonged and how it was the man's role to care for the family, then to hear the educated women remind them that what they do is more important than what they say. Sometimes, the women would have to cut through all the double-talk and ask the critical question to a stubborn convict, "Then why are you here?"

I applied and started working at the Riverside Juvenile Hall in 1979 while I continued my studies at UCR. Going to school during the day and working full time in the afternoons became my modus operandi for the next four years until I completed my bachelor's degree. I also had just begun my own family so a career was my primary objective.

****

Eddie was a Marine Corp veteran and became one of my closest friends. He comes first in my mind when I think about my career. He told me on many occasions, when I worked for the Riverside County Probation Department, that I should join corrections. He had already been at the Chino Prison about four years. By then, he was using his first name, "Gabriel." Everyone at work just called him "Gabe." The department was already changing him, but neither of us recognized it, yet. It would change us both as the years passed, as it does with all peace officers. He said, "Look, you'll move up quickly to lieutenant or captain. You can do this." I honestly didn't see myself working with adults in prison, but he made a good point, I would make more money. Because of him, I left my seemingly safe and secure employment as a deputy probation officer assigned to Adult Investigations in Riverside County and entered what was then called the California Department of Corrections (CDC). The year was 1985.

I recall the initial CDC employment interview panel asking me, "Why would you want to leave your secure job in probation to work in a prison?"

I responded, using my now finely honed "lying" interview technique, stating, "I want to gain experience in different areas of law enforcement, so I can be a better peace officer."

The panel wasn't buying it. One administrator quipped, "You have a college degree and you are already a peace officer. Tell us the truth, why do you want to be a correctional officer?"

I looked right at him and told the truth, "So I can make more money."

He replied, "Good, that's what we thought and that's all we needed to hear!"

The CDC was in the process of massive growth at that time having had twelve original prisons built between 1852 and 1984. Since 1984, the California Department of Corrections and Rehabilitation (CDCR) has built twenty-one new prisons. When I began my career in 1985, the statewide corrections budget of California went from roughly 950 million dollars to over nine billion dollars and thirty-three prisons in 2011, the year I retired. Along the way, the CDC would also add *Rehabilitation* to its name. I guess I got what I wanted, more money. But personal triumphs aside, the massive corrections growth and disingenuous name change would be cause for considerable consternation in my mind.

Got a baby's brain and an old man's heart,
Took eighteen years to get this far,
Don't always know what I'm talking about,
Feels like I'm living in the middle of doubt,

Alice Cooper
"18"

ROMEO

On March 23, 2000, nineteen-year-old Pete G. aka "Romeo," escaped from the California Rehabilitation Center (CRC) at Norco. He had been assigned to the forestry work crew that left prison grounds daily to complete community service projects in the area. Only low custody level, non-violent, non-sex or non-serious offenders were allowed to work the forestry crews. The inmate work crew had been clearing brush from the river bottom in the Norco area when the escape occurred. Romeo walked away from the bus during the crew's lunch break.

The prison was notified and our escape pursuit plan was immediately initiated by the watch commander. All units were locked down and all available staff was sent to pre-determined areas in the community to search for the escapee. It was estimated that Romeo had a two-hour advantage. CRC staff had taken pride in the fact that previous escape attempts had been thwarted by CDCR correctional staff, who captured the escapees before the aid of local law enforcement was necessary. We were determined to do it again.

As the captain assigned to Facility III, I was responsible for oversight of the forestry crews. Approximately fifty inmates were assigned to the program and they had their own dorm. My first instinct was to determine what Romeo's motive was for escaping. Romeo had less than three months to serve at the time. He had been serving an eighteen-month sentence for possession of drugs for sale. The unit lieutenant and I made a beeline for Romeo's room and locker to identify all information relative to family and friends. Normally, we would delegate the task, but all available staff had been reassigned to the search teams that were combing the community. The warden had already established the Emergency Operations Center where we first met to outline possible locations to search. I was perplexed, wondering, did he receive a

"Dear John" letter from a girlfriend? Was it a death of a loved one? Or was there a threat to his life on the yard?

Sometime immediately after the escape, Romeo had entered a home in Norco. Early reports indicated that he broke in, commandeered a vehicle, and kidnapped a minor sixteen-year-old girl using a gun he had found in the home. An all-points bulletin of the suspect went out statewide. There was now an urgency to determine his next move.

Records and letters revealed that he was from McFarland, a small town just north of Bakersfield, California. Close friends were noted in his central file, and phone records reflected previous contacts he made during his stay at CRC. Romeo had many girlfriends; hence the nickname "Romeo." The dorm officer and counselor were interviewed regarding any unusual activity related to Romeo. We recognized that Romeo was looking at a potential thirty-five years in additional time if he was found guilty of all the apparent crimes he was committing!

The dorm officer advised us that some weeks prior, Romeo had come to his office and reported that he had not stolen "Gangster's" cigarettes. The officer looked at him puzzled and stated, "That's okay, you're not supposed to have them anyway." (Departmental policy prohibited smoking by inmates.) The officer indicated that Romeo would come back from the work crew each day, shower, eat dinner, and begin doing "bunk time" (never leaving his room). The officer reported his observations to the unit counselor. He agreed that Romeo's behavior had changed, but when questioned, Romeo declined to provide any information, saying he was fine, just tired. No further action was taken.

Work crew inmates, interviewed after the escape, disclosed that Romeo was in trouble with Surenos for snitching to the dorm officer about stolen cigarettes. 18th Street gang members and one identified as "Gangster" were suspected of pressuring Romeo. The pieces of this escape puzzle were becoming apparent, but not clear enough for me. I was determined to somehow glean any useful intelligence of his whereabouts from contacts listed in his central file and letters. The day was getting late and no new leads had developed.

However, the Investigative Services Lieutenant, Xavier Aponte reported unusual circumstances regarding the crime scene at the home of the kidnapped girl. Sheriff's detectives reported that there was no forced entry into the home. Although, a bathroom window was opened, it didn't appear to have been used as an entry point since items on the window and below it were intact. Likewise, the parents had reported that their gun was in a bedroom drawer *below some sweaters, and the drawer didn't appear to have been disturbed when the gun was removed...almost as if someone familiar with the home simply retrieved it without making a mess. I was becoming more suspicious about the circumstances of the alleged crimes and Romeo's role.*

With the help of the watch lieutenant, I decided to make a call to one of Romeo's girlfriends. I pretended to be a convict and claimed that I was trying to get Romeo some help out of state. To make the call seem realistic, I used the inmate pay telephone in the facility and dialed collect. The inmate phones automatically announce to the listener every three to five minutes that the call is coming from a state prison facility. It was late in the evening after chow, so all the inmates were on their bunks for count time. The lieutenant and dorm officer kept an eye on the inmates in the unit on their bunks while I pretended to be an inmate using my best gangster accent!

"Orale' Carmen, you don't know me...soy Gangster de 18ᵗʰ Street... Romeo's homie. Look I can't talk too long, but I need to get at him about some feria (money) he needs and a place to stay, mi entiendes (understand)? The placa (police) is looking for him and I told him I'd take care it...Can you get at him? Donde esta? (Where is he)...I need a number to call him, now!"

The girlfriend took the bait and seemed genuinely concerned for Romeo's well-being. We chatted, small talk, and after some time, she felt secure enough to admit that he had called once. She would not or could not offer any additional information only that he was all right. She didn't believe he was in McFarland because he would have just gone to her house. This information was relayed to the teams who were staked out at various locations in the city of McFarland.

Early morning, March 25, 2000, the victim's vehicle was spotted in Bakersfield. The victim was the driver and was taken to the sheriff's department for questioning. The girl stated that she was taken by Romeo to McFarland and he left from there. She was unharmed. The sheriff detective shared with Lieutenant Aponte that she did not act in a manner consistent with being a kidnap victim. She was neither scared nor concerned about having been with Romeo. In fact, that was the name she used in speaking about him. She would not offer or admit to having helped Romeo. When questioned about the gun, she said she thought he might sell it to get money. No further information was provided.

At approximately 11:40 p.m., escapee Pete "Romeo" G. was captured by CDCR special services agents as he sat on a Greyhound bus in Los Angeles.

His destination was Arizona. Earlier in the day, Lieutenant Aponte had convinced family members that Romeo would be safer if he surrendered to CDCR. He reminded them that Romeo's commitment offense for drugs was not a violent offense and we believed he was probably afraid of getting hurt in prison which is why he escaped. He led the family to believe that local law enforcement would not be so forgiving. Eventually, they relented and revealed that he had called and was headed to Arizona by bus from Los Angeles.

At the Greyhound Depot in Los Angeles, the CDCR special services agent, a no nonsense warrior, calmly approached Romeo in the back of the bus, looked him square in the eye, with gun in hand, and asked, "Do you want to go peacefully?"

Romeo quietly nodded yes. He was returned for placement in administrative segregation at CIM pending disciplinary action. Lieutenant Aponte and the ISU sergeant were the first staff from CRC to interview Romeo. Upon their return to CRC, they came directly to my office. They were seasoned correctional personnel who had seen their share of convict stories and incidents. These were some tough-minded and closed-hearted men who rarely provided any empathy for criminals, yet, I could see from their faces they were troubled by Romeo's dilemma.

Romeo told them he had met a "Veterano" named "Gangster" from 18th Street while he was in LA County jail awaiting placement at CRC. Gangster, was in his early thirties, seemed sincere and took care of him providing cigarettes and sharing food during their stay. Gangster told him to look out for some of his homies (CRC had a large contingent of 18th Street inmates at the time) when Romeo arrived to CRC and he would be okay. Romeo believed Gangster and did as he was told. Romeo said everything was going well until Gangster arrived a few months later to CRC. By then, Romeo was assigned on the work crew detail.

Gangster had begun to pressure Romeo for a favor; would he bring packages (drugs) in for the homies. Romeo refused, stating that he was close to release and didn't want to get in any trouble. Gangster continued to "sweat" Romeo and insisted that he meet on the yard with the homies to discuss the issue. Gangster did not have access to the work crew dormitory so he had to lean on the other Surenos for information. Romeo refused to go to the yard. About this time, Gangster told his 18th Street homies that Romeo had stolen his cigarettes. Other Surenos became aware that Romeo had informed the dorm officer about his cigarette troubles. Now, Romeo was not only a thief but a rat. The only thing worse than being a prison thief or a rat was being a child molester. Romeo had committed two out of the three taboos. This time, a message was sent to Romeo by Surenos on the work crew that he must attend a "mandatory meeting" on the yard. Romeo had no alternative, but to attend.

Romero told the investigators that he was scared for his life and didn't know what to do, so the next morning he decided to run. He informed them that he had no idea what city he was in or where to go, so he approached a house that looked empty, hoping he could find money or something to trade for a ride. Instead, he found the young girl, three years his junior. He knocked on the door to see if anyone was home. The young girl opened the door and looked at him. He told her he had escaped and needed help or a ride to McFarland. She agreed to help him.

When he told her he needed something to sell, she got the gun and gave it to him. When questioned about the gun, he admitted selling it in McFarland for the bus and food money. He revealed that he stayed at the park in McFarland and watched the surveillance cars until he could get to a friend's house. Lieutenant Aponte, upon hearing Romeo's story, knew that his ignorance about prison "inmate codes" and his fear of being assaulted could result in his receiving many more years in prison. He and the sergeant surmised that Romeo would have only received a beating on the yard at best and maybe be forced to pay rent (canteen or money) until he paroled, but he would not have been killed for his actions.

I saw Romeo the following day to conduct his "CDC114D Hearing" regarding placement in administrative segregation. I knew he was looking at many years in prison if the district attorney filed all the charges: escape, burglary, kidnapping, grand theft auto, and a sentence enhancement for the gun. Given the statement from the young girl and the circumstances found at the home, there was some credence for believing his story. He asked me what was going to happen, as the tears welled up in his eyes.

I told him, "I'm not an attorney, but if I were you, I'd fight the case and request a public defender."

He then asked, "How much time am I looking at?"

I responded, "Probably a lot, young man; you should get an attorney."

Weeks later, I was informed he plead out to over eighteen years for kidnapping, escape, and felony weapon possession.

The "WAR ON CRIME"

Romeo's experience is not unlike many others who come to prison only to see their incarceration time increased because of poor decisions. Inmates get into fights, buy and traffic drugs, assault other inmates, refuse to work or go to school, and sexually abuse others. These offenses can result in Rule Violation Reports submitted by staff that can extend inmate release dates, if found guilty. Some felony offenses are referred to the court, like Romeo's case was, and result in years added to their sentence. These scenarios are real and happen every day in prison; a direct consequence of the environment in which they live. We may question Romeos' decisions and those of others like him, who are led further into the prison subculture abyss. However, the more revealing question is; what were the circumstances that led to his incarceration in the first place?

Romeo was a "first termer" in prison. A "fish," meaning new to prison, like a fish-out-of-water. He was completing an eighteen-month sentence for sales of a controlled substance. He was not a trafficker of large quantities—kilos or pounds—of drugs. His crime was for selling some "dime" (single use) bags of dope to off-set the cost of *his* dope. He was a drug addict. There is no doubt he had multiple arrests for possession and/or under the influence of a controlled substance. He probably got a pass from local law enforcement many times as well, and was released without detention. In a small town like McFarland, he was not hard to find. His conduct made him an easy target for police. Regardless, of how many "passes" he may have been given by law enforcement, he quickly used them up. Unfortunately, his case example can be multiplied by thousands of others just like him. Romeo was not simply a casualty of his own poor decisions; he was also representative of a much larger national "War on Drugs" policy mindset.

Most scholars are in agreement that the increase in incarceration began in earnest during the 1970s. The facts support it.[10] The number of offenders in state and federal prison per 100,000 population averaged around 115 per 100,000 from 1930 to 1963—a fairly stagnant period of incarceration nationally. From 1963 to 1972, the nation began to turn away from imprisonment as the ratio went from 114 per 100,000 in 1963 to a low of 96 per 100,000 in 1972. However, by 1989, the ratio was 276 to every 100,000 residents.

What accounted for the increased incarceration rate? Some sociologists have characterized the '60s social movements as "…a shock to the [social] system…"[11] The civil rights movement and civic unrest over the war in Vietnam all created a heightened anxiety and sense of insecurity that generated growing concerns about stability and crime. Other scholars saw the popularity of harsh sentencing coupled with politicians serving up tough crime agendas as primary causes for the increase in incarceration. Regardless of the cause, an increase in crime laws became the norm during the late '60s and early '70s, and this changed the prison landscape nationwide.

It's believed that the start of the "War on Drugs" (the term first coined by President Nixon in 1971) began with the Comprehensive Drug Abuse Prevention and Control Act of 1970. The law categorized controlled substances based on their medicinal use and potential for addiction. The Act codified rules regarding the manufacture and identification of drugs with potential for abuse. In 1973, the Drug Enforcement Administration (DEA) was created and tasked with combating drug smuggling. These policies, independent of each other, had all been influenced by the national dialogue about safe communities and fear of crime. Drug abuse and gang warfare had become the principle targets.

The DEA effort overlapped state and local drug interdiction efforts which, over time, became the same view of "organized street gang drug traffickers." Very little evidence supports the notion that street gangs are "organized" and are committed to trafficking drugs, but that view slowly became the norm.[12] At the same time, media and politicians alike began to frame enhanced crime legislation as "law and order" or "public safety" bills. They gathered a lot of public support and those who would argue against them were ridiculed or labeled as "soft on crime." Politicians who may have disagreed had very little choice but to support the bills.

The numbers don't lie. Between 1987 and 2007, the national prison population had nearly doubled.[13] During that period, the prison population in our nation increased from 585,084 to 1,596,127. That marked an unprecedented expansion of over one million more offenders in just twenty years (see Figure 1). As a nation, we may have won the battles for safe streets, but clearly we were losing the war on crime and drugs at the expense of non-violent offenders like Romeo.

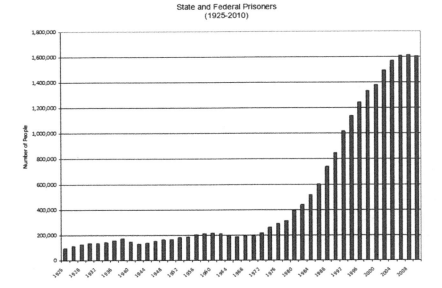

State and Federal Prisoners
(1925-2010)

(Figure 1. Sentencing Project, 2013)

How did the nation become hardened in its public perception of offenders, drug abuse, and gang violence? Those of us who believe in an "eye for an eye" or "reap what you sow" mindset find it easy to put all the responsibility on "Johnny" the criminal and his wayward ways. Conservative pundits had no qualms about the need for being tough on crime. But what about those who claim to believe rehabilitation to be the better alternative—those so-called "bleeding heart" liberals who view the world through a utopian lens. Tom Hayden, activist and former public official offers an interesting view on the liberal mindset regarding crime and gangs. He maintains that liberal progressive minded people try to distance themselves from the "gang problem" which they find "indefensible and morally discomforting."[14] Yet, not enough to act on what many consider to be an unsolvable issue. Hence, it is easier to ignore gang violence and drug abuse and focus on other pressing social issues.

The unprecedented incarceration numbers in our nation certainly makes the case that our public discourse about crime, violence, and gangs is centered on a law-and-order agenda. This view was neither a partisan effort nor a neo-conservative attitude; it was the prevailing attitude among all of us and, as Hayden describes, included liberal and progressive-minded citizens, as well. If Romeo and other street gang members like him are vilified, and fear and panic caused by celebrated horrific crimes is the norm, then the public dialogue will continue to be centered on expanding police and prison budgets, which has been the trend since the 1970s to the present time.

Only recently has the discussion changed about prison alternatives in California. But the motivator was not an enlightened view of the world; it was massive budget hits caused by the 2008 economic debacle. We simply could not afford to house so many offenders any more. California's response was AB 109, the Public Safety Realignment Act. AB 109 redirected responsibility for low level offenders back to the counties in California. More will be said about AB 109 in the last chapter.

Is AB 109 a change in our crime dialogue or only a change in budget and housing alternatives? What is driving our criminal justice agenda in the United States? Is it a humanistic philosophical notion of a "better man?" Is it a scholarly treatise about best intervention practices or adherence to social norms of deterrence and retribution? Perhaps it's more emotional—a common denominator that transcends all levels—fear.

It is arguable that we don't see crime like we view the rest of our human environment. For example, usable clean water is becoming scarcer as our earth's resources are challenged by the unending increase in the world's population. So citizenry have no problem looking at all the options available to protect and enhance our water sources. We recycle gray water, restrict usage in commercial and residential communities, we siphon salt water from the sea and convert it to public use in desalination plants. We test water daily, weekly, monthly to ensure it is clean. We legislate, regulate, and never hesitate to question, prod, and demand the purest form of a primary life-giving element. We fear the worst, if we fail to constantly manage water, so we are willing to do anything.

Yet we don't make the same expansive effort when it comes to crime. Crime is a wicked problem, like war and poverty that has always plagued mankind.[15] Regardless of the cause or nature of crime, we've consciously and unconsciously decided that only one cure or methodology works best; arrest, convict, and incarcerate. Figure 1, amply reflects our national criminal justice outcome. What has been the motivator for such a single-minded option, is also our collective emotional reaction to crime—fear.

We can do the innuendo,
We can dance and sing,
When it's said and done,
We haven't told you a thing,
We all know crap is king,

Don Henley
"Dirty Laundry"

15 MINUTES OF FAME

The artist, Andy Warhol, during the late 1960s, is credited with coining the phase, "15 minutes of fame." The adage is meant to describe the influence and spread of media exposure and the likelihood that we all will get some of that attention. Especially today with the Internet and the multitude of media outlets like YouTube, Facebook, Twitter… it seems inconceivable that personal attention can be totally avoided. Likewise, with modern "smart" phones having video and web streaming at your fingertips, everyday occurrences that were once private or unseen can now become public fodder. At some point, we are all potential "fame" victims whether we want to be or not. I can attest to that point. I finally got my "15 minutes" and then some, on November 17, 2010. It's not all that it's cracked up to be when the political agenda is at your expense.

On the afternoon of Tuesday, November 16, 2010, I was advised by the RC-West Facility Lieutenant S. Moore of possible safety concerns regarding inmate/parolee Lawrence J. Brown. Television and radio news reports identified him as a sex offender with an imminent parole date and news reports were being telecast throughout the day. Lieutenant Moore had wisely removed Brown from the RC-West dormitory setting and placed him in a single cell at Reception Center Central. Other inmates watching the news would surely know who inmate Brown was and would assault him immediately if he remained in general population. By evening, Chino Prison had a significant media presence at the front gate that continued the following day on November 17, 2010, the scheduled release date for Brown.

Brown's commitment offense was for five counts of PC 288(B) forcible lewd and lascivious acts with a minor below the age of fourteen years, with enhancements for force and violence and use of a firearm. He received a total term of forty-nine years in 1985 and had paroled on April 27, 2010. He had remained free only nine days before arriving at CIM on May 6, 2010, pending a revocation hearing for violating conditions of his parole. He had received a five-month parole violation on June 1, 2010 by the Board of Parole Hearings (BPH) for failure to comply with GPS conditions and changing residence without informing his parole agent.

All paroling inmates must be released before midnight, the day of their scheduled parole date, but rarely, if ever, do they leave so late at night. Normally, we release them in the morning or noon and sometimes in the afternoon. In those cases where parole agents indicate pick up, we may keep them longer for evening pick-up. Case records staff, who prepared the release documents for Brown, had already received a request by the Division of Adult Parole Operations (DAPO) staff to not release him at 8:00 a.m. to a female friend who was waiting for Brown that morning. We agreed because DAPO had been in contact with the Orange County District Attorney's Office on arranging surveillance teams to follow and arrest him for any violation of parole conditions.

This was the parole plan as I understood it. This was not new territory for the prison administration or DAPO on sensitive cases posing a legitimate threat to the community; it was "CDC 101!" It had been my experience that, when a high-profile or high-risk inmate was paroling, they would be closely monitored and violated the moment they failed to comply with their conditions of parole. The rationale behind the overbearing surveillance was based on the very real demonstrated threat posed to the public by these predators. If the inmate had served his time and was legally entitled to parole, the only avenue to maintain strict oversight was through parole supervision and subsequent violation for conditions of parole. The higher the threat posed to the public, the more stringent the conditions and supervision. This case was no different.

As "Murphy's Law" would dictate, I was acting warden and I was fully aware of the media interest in Brown's release. During the course of the day, I was in contact with Sacramento CDCR Headquarters delineating the details of the Board of Prison hearing and Department of Mental Health decisions. Both of which required by law that we release Brown on parole November 17, 2010. Technically, I had until 11:59 p.m. to execute the release. Sounds simple right? Wrong!

Unbeknownst to me, the Orange County District Attorney (DA) Tony Rackauckas had been hyping Inmate/Parolee Brown's case to the media as a public safety threat. The DA used the terms "ticking time bomb" and "free to roam the streets" with the Orange County Register Newspaper in describing the threat posed by Brown. I couldn't agree more with the DA's assessment. This pedophile should not be released given the nature of his sickening crimes. He had kidnapped and sexually assaulted two girls aged eight and seven, forcing oral copulation, rape, and sodomy during the commission of the crimes. However, I wasn't paid to impose my personal opinion on offenders, but to meet the public service mission. In this case, Brown had completed his sentence and was entitled to be released by law. I had no option but to comply with the law.

Truth be told, the DA had a legitimate beef with the Department of Mental Health (DMH) for not designating Brown as a Sexual Violent Predator (SVP). As an SVP, he could be transferred to a DMH facility for treatment to remain until doctors decide he is not a threat to the community. Under the law, inmate/parolee Brown didn't meet the legal criteria. The DA's office was trying to get DMH to re-review the case based on new information and also aggressively trying to get a court order to hold him. Unfortunately, this information was not relayed to me by the DA's staff until after the predator was paroled. Funny how hindsight is always 20/20!

I had kept the warden (who was attending the statewide warden's conference in Sacramento) advised on what Classification Services Unit and DAPO had advised our Case Records staff throughout the day. At no time was any directive given by any CDCR department head to extend the release to the last minutes before midnight. In fact, all the phone calls and correspondence between me and Sacramento was regarding how the release would take place. This was done to accommodate the surveillance teams from both the DA's office and DAPO.

My Case Records team at CIM predicted that Brown would violate his conditions of parole within a block from the prison. He could not be alone with a woman, which was one of over 100 parole conditions placed on him. However, we were aware that a woman was intending to pick him up. To avoid the media crush at the front gate, it was agreed that he would leave from the east entrance to avoid media attention. I and the CIM Records team surmised that, after paroling with the woman alone, he'd leave through one gate, be stopped by DAPO and quickly return through the other gate!

At approximately 4:30 p.m., the decision to release Brown was made after I had consulted with the warden in Sacramento and he had conferred with the regional administrator on the matter. DAPO's team was in place as well as the DA and Tustin Police Department teams. Brown would drive off grounds in the car of his woman friend and, upon hitting the street, would be pulled over and arrested for violating terms of parole...or so I thought! Instead, the teams followed in traffic until the predator arrived in Orange County, City of Tustin before being pulled over by the Tustin Police and Parole Surveillance team. The media portrayed the arrest in a positive light for the DA and Tustin Police Department; they had "saved the public" from this human menace.

Here's what disturbed me; there was no public furor from the DA's office when this child predator originally paroled in April of 2010. Only after he returned in May of 2010, did he suddenly become a "blip on the DA's radar." This is significant because the basis for my public "tar-and-feather" moment was orchestrated on the mistaken belief that CDCR had "placed a hold on inmate Brown until 11:59 p.m." which I had somehow "overruled." This was the story the Orange County Register provided to the public based on what the DA, Tony Rackauckas and his staff reported. Joining the tarring were Tustin Police Chief Scott Jordan and State Senator Lou Correa, who both criticized my alleged "overruling" and "dropping the ball...made a bad decision by releasing him."

If any of the aforementioned parties had bothered to ask me, I would have told them that no such "hold" was ever placed nor was any directive given to "stand down" on his release until <u>after</u> the predator was released. In fact, I had received a call from the warden to rescind the release, but Brown had paroled about five minutes before I received the call. Just my "luck," I guess. I wasn't concerned because I was confident that Predator Brown would not remain in the community for long. I was right, but I was now in the cross-hairs of the DA.

Why the DA would specifically announce my name to the media is a mystery. I have no doubt he truly was making a concerted effort to keep the predator in custody. Given his frustration with the release, he could have contacted the agency secretary to voice his displeasure. He could have also called the warden. Instead, he used me as a scapegoat for the media and a lightning rod for his political agenda.

The decision to release Predator Brown wasn't based on what the Orange County DA wanted. Predator Brown's release was based on what CDCR had to do in compliance with the law and in accordance with DAPO. DAPO would have jurisdiction on this parolee and had routinely advised on holds or instructions for delaying releases in the past. That call never happened. Had all parties been on the same communication corridor, perhaps another outcome would have occurred. Instead, my alleged "overruling decision to hold" went viral but the surveillance plan initiated by DAPO and the DA's office did not.

Despite the fact that Brown was returned to CIM within a couple of hours, the news stations were broadcasting my name and my decision to release a sex offender contrary to an alleged "hold." While on my way home about 7:30 p.m., I received a call from CIM Public Information Officer Mark Hargrove. He was chuckling a bit when he said, "Check out the 'John and Ken' show on the radio; they're talking about you."

"What about?" I responded.

Mark retorted, "You got to hear them!"

I immediately switched on the AM station. John Kobylt and Ken Chiampou are the popular hosts of the KFI 640AM "John & Ken" radio show. They are what I refer to as "yellow journalists." The term is derived from the early nineteenth century public battles between newspapers owned by William Randolph Hearst and Joseph Pulitzer. Critics argued that both newspapers sensationalized stories to drive up circulation. Today, the term refers to newspapers or so-called news personalities that present little or no legitimate well-researched news and, instead, use eye-catching headlines to get attention. John and Ken have been accused of exaggerating news events, scandal-mongering, and sensationalism. However, my use of the term "yellow" has more to do with them being cowards. They, like DA Tony Rackauckas, never contacted me to check the facts. It appeared that releasing a known predator made for a good, eye-catching headline—"ammunition" to fire at me, regardless of the truth!

As I listened, John and Ken described the DA's version of my alleged bureaucratic failure. Then came the "hit" in a slow, dramatic monotone, "Who is this Rich-ard Al-va-ra-do…what an Ass! Why would he ignore a superior's order and let a sex offender free" Again, they slowly repeated my name and the vulgarity.

I started to laugh as I'm driving in my car, yelling at my radio out loud, "This is my 15 minutes of fame?" It made no sense to me to get angry at them, but it was humorous to hear the distorted version of what had happened.

I suspected they were baiting me, hoping I would call in to defend myself. But considering the source, I wouldn't bite. I had no respect or time for the ignorant rants of publicity opportunists, nor would I support any journalism that treats news in an unprofessional or unethical fashion. Unfortunately, CDCR Headquarters in Sacramento did bite. The following day, I was directed to submit a memorandum outlining the circumstances leading to the release of the sexual predator. CDCR Directorate was reacting to the unqualified rants from the DA and local politicians. Not long thereafter, I was made aware that an "inquiry" was being conducted by the Office of Inspector General (OIG) regarding the release.

When I got the call months later from the OIG attorney, he used the term "inquiry." I challenged his euphemism since any so-called inquiry of a career executive appointment really amounts to an investigation. I asked him if he had reviewed my memorandum that I authored for Headquarters. He indicated that he had not been made privy to it. I forwarded my copy to him and encouraged him to interview Lieutenant Hargrove, who had been at my side during all the "speaker phone" telephone calls with Headquarters, parole personnel, and the DA deputy district attorney to corroborate the facts. I also advised him to read the email correspondence between the director and DAPO and CIM, who were all on board regarding the release circumstances. Wisely, I had retained all email correspondence for just this reason. A few weeks later, the attorney gave me a "courtesy" call to advise that the matter had been closed. I quickly asked, "Will I be receiving anything in writing?"

He responded, "No."

I guess that is the difference between an "inquiry" and "investigation." I obviously prefer the former!

As a footnote; the warden half-heartedly tried to support me with the local politicians and the DA in Orange County. He scheduled a meeting with them to voice his displeasure with the DA identifying me publicly. The meeting eventually occurred many months later with a slew of attorneys and political representatives in attendance. The DA did not attend, but one of his representatives did. I wasn't asked to, nor did I want to, attend the circus. As I suspected, no admission or apology was forthcoming from the DA. Apparently, my 15 minutes of fame was all used up!

BELLY OF THE BEAST

The public furor over the release of inmate/parolee Brown is a good example of the type of fear mongering that develops about offenders. Don't misunderstand the point. This sex offender was a real threat to public safety. That's why the media likes to talk about these offenders, because it gets our attention. Sex offenders, like murderers, dictate the hard-edged response by law enforcement, courts, and corrections. They are also the "TV profile" of how most citizens see criminals. The media frenzy on predators like the Manson family, or Richard Ramirez, the Night Stalker, or parolee Richard Allen Davis, is firmly etched in our minds.

In fact, Davis' heinous crime (brutally assaulting and murdering the young girl, Polly Klass) was used by media commentators and politicians to argue for the passage of Proposition 184 (Three Strikes Law) in California. The media barrage over the crime made passage of Proposition 184 a foregone conclusion.[16] Likewise, the reoccurring media visits during parole hearings of the Manson family murderers, reminds us all to be mindful of the evil twisted psyche of drug-crazed killers. Thus, it is easy to see why we, as a nation, support and encourage "tough on crime" policies and laws. We are inundated with the worst crimes occurring every day in the news.

But these celebrated cases are not representative of the vast majority of offenders doing time in prison. There is a consequence to our pursuit of justice, when it is overwhelmingly based on our feelings. Emotions should never be the basis for creating criminal laws. Yet, fear, outrage, and danger have been the *political Kool-Aid* that we've been drinking. Our collective thirst for safety has driven our criminal justice policies for the past forty years. We fear being victimized by predators, and we are outraged by violent street gangs and their wanton disregard for the law and lack of respect for our communities. We desire a safe haven for our babies and young children that only law and order can deliver. We arguably may have achieved a "safe haven" or at least a safer one in our nation with the largest prison population in the world, but at what cost?

The state of California had seen the largest increase in prison and parole population since the early 1980s which resulted in the largest incarceration rate in the nation (CDCR Expert Panel 2007). What caused the increase in incarceration was a combination of two primary contributors. The first contributor was the Determinate Sentencing Law (DSL) implemented in 1976, which changed the legal basis for incarceration of all new offenders.[17] Instead of an indeterminate sentence (five to ten years, five to life, etc.) where the Board of Parole Hearings determined if prisoners were ready to reinter society, offenders now had a defined prison sentence. The DSL enacted determinate sentences based on a range of time (low, medium, high) with enhancements or mitigating criteria for adjusting sentencing. Thus, inmates entering prison generally knew how much time they would serve which was not the case under Indeterminate Sentencing.[18]

Californians have seen its prisons swell to gargantuan proportions since the 1980s. The "belly of the beast" swelling to well over 170,000 inmates by 2007.[19] In California, the politics of public safety had led to draconian laws. Carole D'Elia, Deputy Executive Director for the Little Hoover Commission describes the sentencing whirlwind that occurred in California following the Determinate Sentencing Act (DSA) in 1977:

> "As soon as the ink was dried on the DSA, lawmakers began enacting layer upon layer of new sentencing laws…today more than 1,000 felony sentencing laws are on California's books…supplemented by more than 100 felony sentencing enhancements. The incremental changes have been dubbed "drive by" sentencing laws-often enacted as knee-jerk responses to horrific, high-profile, and frequently isolated crimes…"

(Federal Sentencing Reporter (2010). Vol. 22, No. 3.)

The intent of the DSL law was to provide a measure of uniformity in sentencing and punishment that was proportional to the crime. Unfortunately, DSL literally morphed into a *punishment-on-steroids* bonanza for suppression and incarceration proponents. The result was an unprecedented spike in parole violators being returned to prison in California. The tough-on-crime proponents in the legislature, media, and law enforcement supported draconian laws that not only enhanced determinate sentences but also made parole revocation hearings little more than rubber stamps of "guilty" as roughly 85 percent of all parolees were returned for technical violations, spending an average of approximately four months in prison. This phenomenon created an incredible burden on correctional resources. Criminologist, Joan Petersillia, the renowned scholar put it best:

> "...two thirds of all released parolees in California are back in prison within three years, a proportion twice the national average...parolees account for the bulk of the California prison admissions. In 2008, nearly 70,000 parolees returned to California prisons for parole violations...This catch-and-release system is costly...and is at the root of the state's overcrowding situation."[20]

The second contributor was the Three Strikes Law, enacted by the voters by passage of Proposition 184 in 1994. The law provided stiffer sentencing for repeat offenders who met certain criteria. Those who committed a "Third Strike" felony would serve a minimum twenty-five to life sentence. In 2008, CDCR admitted approximately 1,000 murderers serving indeterminate life sentences. Our nation's prison population is the highest in the world, but the principle cause of this offender growth, isn't crime, it's policy driven:

> "...lawmakers are learning that current prison growth is not driven primarily by a parallel increase in crime, or a corresponding surge in the population at large. Rather, it flows principally from a wave of policy choices that are sending more lawbreakers to prison and, through popular "three-strike" measures and other sentencing enhancements, keeping them there longer..." (Pew Center, One in One Hundred, 2008)

Former California State Senator and human rights activist Tom Hayden describes the intent of the Three Strikes Law as a means to lock up "repeat violent offenders." Instead, it became a means to lock up "the dangerous classes." Hayden revealed less than 1 percent of the Three Strike commitments "...involved murder and only one-fifth other violent offenses, while two-thirds were property, drugs, and alcohol offenses."[21]

There has been much debate on the effectiveness of this "tough on crime" approach, but for our discussion we are limiting it to the outcome; increased offenders in prison and county jails. Both DSL and the Three Strikes Law has accounted for the unprecedented incarceration numbers in California. In fact, the prison population grew exponentially during the 1980s, from twelve prisons housing approximately 55,000 offenders in 1978, to thirty-three prisons housing over 170,000 by 2007. During this period, California enacted over eighty laws that lengthened sentences for offenders (Little Hoover Commission, 2007). The population trend since 2000 for the California Department of Corrections and Rehabilitation (CDCR) reflect the continued impact of the laws:

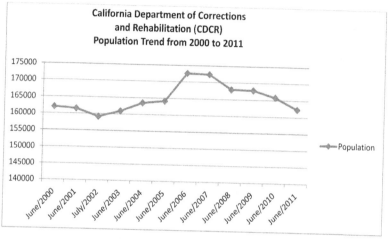

(Figure 2. Alvarado, 2012)

Although the state had passed legislation and CDCR had implemented policy changes intended to assist the reduction in population, the prison population numbers (Fig. 2) reflect little change from 2000 to 2011.[22] Unfortunately, our public acceptance of what is presented as factual—the threat posed by crime, drugs, and gangs—is presented as an assumption with only one solution model: the profiling, suppression, and incarceration paradigm.

THE SPIN DOCTORS

To illustrate, the Orange County District Attorney's (DA) Office spun the threat posed by inmate/parolee Brown with great aplomb before the media. To be fair, the Orange County DA's office was correct in identifying the threat posed by inmate/parolee Brown. But did DA Rackauckas need to use the "bully pulpit" to somehow influence CDCR or DMH to change or reinterpret the law? He was presumably seeking court relief to hold Brown in prison. Instead, Rackauckas acted to manipulate media outlets to send a message. His message served to reinforce the power of persuasive politics about criminals; the idea that the community is not safe with inmate/parolee Brown loose on the streets. He was correct that Brown posed a significant threat to society. Unfortunately, the message about Brown also painted a broad brush message about all parolees.

The public media "spin" regarding this sex offender is readily applied to all offenders, as if they all pose an equal risk to the community. To be sure, inmate/parolee Brown is a dangerous pedophile. But not all sex offenders pose the same risk as he did. Take for example, the nineteen-year-old who has sexual relations with his girlfriend, a seventeen-year-old minor. If convicted, he would also be required to register as a sex offender. Adolescent behavior is clearly different from a pedophile who commits a sexually perverse act with child minors. The bigger questions are: Do all offenders pose the same demonstrated risk as inmate/parolee Brown? Do all street gang members sell drugs like Romeo? Prior to his escape, was Romeo a serious threat to public safety? The short answer is, No! The longer answer is, highly unlikely.

Expand the question to include all of the inmates that now meet California's AB 109, Public Safety Realignment Act criteria. Clearly Romeo would have been eligible had he not made the poor choice to escape. Is the community at risk from the 30,000 offenders released under AB 109 Realignment? If so, what is the actual risk? Is it imminently genuine or is the risk simply perceived to be real? If it is real, then we would be seeing roughly 30,000 *additional* detainees in the county jails at any given time but that isn't happening.[23] Offenders released under AB 109 represent less than 15 percent of that increase. But, if we perceive all AB 109 offenders as a continued threat, then what is driving our perceptions? Alternatively, if we view all criminals as a danger to civil society, then why is there disparate treatment of other criminals having arguably more victims?

FEAR MONGERING

Take, for example, the corporate raiders, ponzi schemes, and "banksters"[24] who sold shaky derivatives and the like, which led to or, at the very least, were the precursors of the 2008 Wall Street debacle. Was there a consequence to the public trust and significant financial losses stemming from those corporate crimes? How do we articulate trillions of dollars in loss to the public trust and national economy? Our collective view is not as emotional when it comes to those crimes as it is for robbery, rape, and murder. The latter we can see with our eyes and feel with our hearts and bodies; the former is done in the silence of a board room or corner office with a computer.

We can't easily discern the immediate impact of the finance industry debauchery, but we can easily understand street crimes. There is an emotional reaction to what we see and feel on the streets and on TV. Likewise, most Americans agree with the adage, "Do the crime; do the time." The point being made here is that not all criminals are doing "the time" and some doing time don't really need to be.

There cannot be an "either/or" proposition to the discussion on crime. Instead, let's challenge our deeply rooted beliefs with regard to the causes and responses to crime in general. There needs to be a place for predators like Brown as well as white collar criminals; just as there needs to be alternative solutions to a large portion of offenders that do not pose significant risk to the public. Scholar John Hagan has argued about reframing our perspective on crime and criminals so that we can "…redistribute the risks and punishments of *street and suite* crimes in America."[25] But that dialogue can't begin until we truly understand what has been driving our beliefs about crime.

Hagan argues that "fear" is the common denominator for how we view crime and ultimately how we address crime. He says, "The lesson is that fear trumps hope in the American crime equation, and in particular, it does so through its designations of crime and punishment."[26]

The history of our so-called war on crime directly led to our aversion to allowing criminals back into our neighborhoods. This NIMBY (not in my backyard) phobia reveals our apprehensions and fears. This is the "spin" Orange County D.A. Rackauckas was exercising effectively. Playing to the public emotion is great theater and makes for good twenty-second news briefs, but it has done little to remedy the overall crime and recidivism challenges we've faced for the past forty years.

So where does the blame lie? Maybe, it's a lack of courage among our elected leaders who won't challenge the prevailing wisdom on crime. Or maybe it's the rest of us who can't seem to shake our hesitation about seeing crime as a multitude of shades instead of the more simplistic "black-and-white" comparison. But crime in our communities is not that straightforward. It requires more considerations than the current model, which demands only the profiling, suppression, and incarceration remedy.

Oh, I was born six-gun in my hand,
Behind a gun I'll make my final stand,
That's why they call me,
Bad company, I can't deny...

Bad Company
"Bad Company"

LEOS & LIONS

Why is it you can always spot a cop in a crowd? Is it the way they look? Or perhaps the way they carry themselves? Could it be the manner in which they speak? Or is it all of the above? Why do cops maintain an emotional distance between themselves and the people they encounter? Especially with strangers, a peace officer will allow only minimal expressive outbursts save maybe a laugh or two. They are generally polite and observant. They may offer some sarcastic humor, but they're always in control of themselves while they simultaneously listen to the conversation and survey the crowd around them.

More often than not, they stand or sit with their backs to the wall, which allows them to see everything going on in front of them before it happens. This is the Law Enforcement Officer (LEO) in "restraint mode." The only time they let go, relax, and reveal any aspect of emotional feelings is with their immediate family, friends, and partners. Although, some find it hard to relax at any time.

However, when a LEO is in "engaged mode," their training, knowledge, and experience kicks in. He or she adopts a "take charge" attitude that is meant to protect the officer by focusing on controlling or containing a potential crime scene upon arrival to the location. The location could be a house, street, jail holding cell, courtroom, or prison cafeteria. This is the persona that citizens see every day from police officers, sheriff's deputies, parole and probation personnel, jail and prison peace officers. There is a reason for this behavior. You can't roll up to an incident and passively hope to determine who the perpetrator, victim, and witnesses are without exerting some definitive voice of authority. Every LEO, regardless of the agency he or she works for, is taught at the academy and nurtured by their partners to exhibit a "command presence" on the job.

Former Senator Robert "Bob" Presley, who was a LEO with the Riverside County Sheriff's Department for twenty-four years, shared his view about the "command presence" demeanor of a cop:

> *"...You know, when I was a homicide detective, I used to teach criminal justice classes and I'd walk them thru a day of a deputy describing the "power" they had over citizens. Just putting on the uniform and driving a patrol unit was a sign of power. People are more conscious of their behavior when a cop is around. They obey the cop—unless they are the bad guy—because citizens are more inclined to obey the law when they see a patrol unit. Pulling someone over; giving simple instructions, like directing traffic or frisking them is power only a cop can exercise. But that power can also escalate; like issuing a citation. The "power" officers have increases too when you take a person's freedom away by detaining or arresting them or ultimately having their life in your hands, if deadly force is required...all this starts with a cop's attitude about who is in control. They are, because they're supposed to be, they are trained to be!"*

Senator Presley's description of a LEO's "power" poignantly explains why LEOs behave the way they do. This was the mindset of officers who worked a beat during the '50s and '60s and remains the same today. Although, much has changed in terms of tactics, technology, and weaponry since Detective Presley worked a beat, little has changed in describing the LEO state of mind today.

****

In November of 2013, I interviewed a former LEO, we'll call him Jerry, who worked for a large law enforcement agency in Southern California. Jerry had worked for twelve years before he was forced to medically retire from injuries sustained on the job. However, he continues to work today as a use of force trainer and armory officer for the same agency. Jerry describes the on-the-job training he received from a "seasoned" officer on the force after he graduated from the Academy at twenty-one years of age.

> *"I was shocked at his appearance...No undershirt, chest hairs sticking out with a gold chain around his neck. This*

guy, Barry, was about fifty to fifty-five years old, about twenty-five years in the department. No slob, his uniform was clean, you know, but he had that 70s look, smiling and easy going. Not like what I had been trained to be...you know...have your shit squared away, be bad-ass, we go into every scene and own it! I remember as a kid running from the cops because they were tough. Barry didn't have a billy club, no bullet-proof vest on or cuffs. We were taught to be ready to rock and roll...but Barry taught me to not make a scene because our job (evictions, till-taps, restraining orders, etc) was always going to upset someone so accept it... [Barry would say] you got to learn to use your words, verbal judo and stuff to get the job done...we don't have time to arrest them, just push them out of the way...No reports, besides, the field sergeant didn't have time to respond to our concerns."

Jerry's first field assignment, his second day on the job, was service of a restraining order. The person in question was home, but took off when he peeked outside the window and saw the deputies. Jerry and Barry knocked again and an older man answered the door. Barry knew him and admonished him about the son they were trying to find. The homeowner refused to help. Barry ordered the man to remain on the porch. The restraining order had revealed some history of violence and guns, so Jerry entered the house with his veteran partner Barry; both had guns drawn. They couldn't locate the subject, but when Jerry exited the house he saw the homeowner loading a shotgun and noticed a gun and holster strapped to his chest. Jerry, his gun already drawn, aimed at the man and ordered him to put the shotgun down. The man ignored his orders.

Barry, having heard Jerry's order, also begins to yell commands as he exits the house with his gun at the ready. The man was calm, but agitated about them being at the house. Jerry is within four yards of the man. Barry orders the man to take the gun from his holster with his left hand. The man goes for the gun with his right and Jerry, his arms fully extended, squeezing the trigger and seeing the hammer going back, is thinking, Oh shit, I'm going to be the first one from the academy to fire my weapon and kill some guy.

Barry, glancing over at Jerry, immediately rushes in Jerry's line of fire and grabs the guns from the homeowner. Barry is going at it verbally with the man, telling him, "What the hell's wrong with you? You want to get shot over this stupid shit?" Barry directs Jerry to the car and they leave. Jerry is puzzled about why Barry let this guy off the hook. Barry explains...the man was a former captain and Barry had worked for him.

No reports were filed and Jerry ran six miles that evening to burn off his adrenalin...he had just become hooked to his new career!

****

After a few years, Jerry found himself on patrol in a rural area of the county. He had earned himself a reputation as the "Runner" a result of him having outrun a fleeing suspect on foot. Jerry ran alongside the suspect and was calmly extolling him as they jogged to give up or get shot...with OC spray. As they both ran down the street, the suspect refused to stop, so Jerry, still jogging alongside him, sprayed his face which quickly persuaded the suspect to comply. Henceforth, on any foot chase, the field sergeant would routinely unleash Jerry who would run off in foot pursuit, always getting his man! Jerry's last foot pursuit would be no different. In 2006, he was on routine patrol about 11:00 p.m. in a rural city of Southern California's desert community. Jerry observed an old beat up Eclipse approaching him. It looked like a "tweaker mobile." No headlights were on, so Jerry "lights up" the vehicle and it pulled over on a dark street about five feet from the curb. Jerry reported the stop via radio to the dispatcher; identifying the car, license plate, and two occupants.

Jerry had plenty of experience with suspects fleeing the scene after being pulled over, so he exited his patrol car, but continues to stand by the door watching the movement inside the other car. He observed a male driver with a girl in the passenger seat. Jerry had no backup in this area of town since his partner had made an arrest and was at the jail forty miles away. Jerry, like many other deputies, had gone out alone for traffic stop cruises in order to stay busy. He and other deputies did it all the time. His sergeant could be anywhere in the county for all he knew. This looked to be another routine "cuff and stuff" if drugs were found. However, in police work, "routine" can turn "obscene" in the blink of an eye!

Jerry didn't even take two steps toward the Eclipse when he saw the tires squealing and the car heading northbound on the road. He immediately jumped back into his patrol vehicle and pursued, alerting the dispatch as he chased the vehicle on some deserted residential streets. Suddenly, the car made a right turn and stops in the middle of a dead end street. As Jerry makes the turn, he observes the vehicle driver side door swing open. Jerry put his unit *in park as the driver quickly runs between two houses. Jerry's got a rabbit! He sprints after him without any hesitation; leaving the suspect car and female occupant behind. Jerry didn't have to chase this guy and, when queried, he agreed but stated, "That's all balls! But that's what we do in our department."*

****

This is the Law Enforcement Officer (LEO) mindset in a nutshell—a combination of training, experience, and bravado; that acknowledges policies and procedures while simultaneously ignoring them when challenged. I recall a young correctional officer named "Mark" who worked at the California Rehabilitation Center (CRC) for me when I was a captain in 1998. His demeanor and adventurous spirit reminded me of Jerry.

Mark stood maybe, five feet-four in his boots, but stood tall as a giant among his peers in determination and grit. Many times, I would receive reports stating that he had chased down inmates in the living units who were headed for the toilet to dump and flush their contraband. A fight would ensue for the dope in the presence of nearby inmates. This was the "old guard" experience that officers practiced for years and still do today.

Unfortunately, we had a new "use of force" policy that was being implemented and I was obliged to enforce it as captain. The days of "fighting convicts for the dope" was no longer acceptable as the primary reason to engage a fight. Instead, we were expected to use force to gain compliance with a lawful order and effect custody. I encouraged the custody staff to include that specific language in every use of force incident report to avoid any confusion regarding an officer's intent. Truth be told, it was a matter of pride for officers to get the dope—a felony offense in prison. I recall when I was an officer, Lieutenant F. Rubio, who would challenge the facility units at the CRC prison to compete for the most felony busts during the week. On Saturday, he would treat the winning unit to free beer at the American Legion. Motivation came in all forms, and we were motivated!

Mark understood the policy, but couldn't help himself. One day he chased an inmate, who was suspected of having dope, in the CRC Unit 3 corridor (with inmate traffic all around him). He tackled the inmate and immediately grabbed the inmate's hand preventing him from swallowing the dope. As they wrestled on the floor, the inmate was able to get the balloon into his mouth, whereupon Mark made a quick sweeping motion with his fingers to dislodge it. When I heard what had transpired, I directed him to report to my office.

49

"Mark!" I yelled, "hold up your hands and spread your fingers."

He calmly complied, as I said, "Good, you still have ten fingers! Don't you EVER put your fingers in some convicts mouth again…you know exactly where that dope is eventually going to come out, right?"

He nodded smiling, as I finished. "Good! So potty-watch the bastard and save yourself from losing a finger next time!"

****

I doubt my barking ever influenced Mark's approach at work and the same can be said about Jerry. Jerry had been influenced by his peers and encouraged by his supervisors to make pursuit on any "failure to stop." For deputies in this particular agency, like most others, it was a matter of pride that suspects don't evade arrest. And if they did, then a visit to the hospital was expected. Jerry, had heard it directly from patrol sergeants, that anyone disrespecting a deputy, "would get a ride to the hospital." Jerry, as experience had taught him, was only following the "LEO code."

Jerry chased the suspect that September 2006 night. The suspect had jumped a six-foot chain-link fence with a lock on it. Jerry, in hot pursuit, approached the fence. Being the smart deputy that he was, he saw it was a horse shoe lock which he quickly kicked to spin the gate free. He followed the suspect into a dark backyard and, as he gained ground, swung his large mag light to give the suspect a "distractionary" blow.

Jerry missed his target—the shoulder. Instead, he hit the suspect across the top of his head. He said later, "I wasn't mad yet, I'd just missed my target. But that was okay; it stopped his attempt to jump over the back fence into an empty field."

The suspect then ran back toward a clothes line trying to avoid further hits. The backyard was all gravel rock with no lighting or even moon light and Jerry quickly realized this would be his fighting arena. He and the suspect began fighting as Jerry yells orders to "get down."

The suspect is yelling back, "Fuck you…I'm not going back to the joint."

Jerry pulled his radio with one hand as he's fighting with the other and the suspect knocks it out of his hand, and it shatters on the ground. As they continued to tussle, Jerry pulled out his OC spray and gave him a solid spray-ing to his face. The seconds, quickly turned to minutes as the fight continued both falling to the ground and getting up, sliding again with Jerry swinging at whatever he can hit.

Jerry quipped, "I'm not big or muscular, it might take me ten (shots) for one, but I was throwing haymakers from way back here behind my shoulder. There were no jabs."

Jerry could feel the suspect grabbing at his belt as Jerry was swinging blind; punches, boot stomps, knee kicks whatever it would take to distract and disable the suspect. Finally, Jerry was able to pull his ASP (expandable baton) and starts swinging in the dark. "Every time I swing my baton, I start hearing metal...I'm hearing metal on some of my shots. Well I didn't know we were tied up in this clothes line pole...he was wrapped around it...I'd hear this crunch, crunch, ping, crunch, crunch, ping, ting, as I was swinging the ASP. So finally, I get one good punch with my right hand and get a really sharp pain. Simultaneously, I feel something tugging on my leg as the lights go on in the backyard.

"The homeowner looks out his back porch door and sees a deputy and this guy wrapped around the clothes line pole. I look down and I see the owner's ten-pound Shiatsu—a 'shit dog'—chewing on my leg! The whole backyard looked like a rummage sale; battery here, top end over there, my OC spray here, my flash light is in fifteen pieces and all I've got is my ASP. I was lucky because my holster only has a thumb break and my gun was still there. Just leather with a strap..."

Jerry asked the suspect, "Are you done?"

The suspect, still hugging the pole, responded, "I'm not going back to the joint. You're not taking me."

Jerry tried to take one last good swing to let the suspect know that he was serious when he realizes, "I've got no balls in my swing. There's nothing there. I kind of limp it with him and I know I'm in trouble now."

But the suspect didn't swing back at Jerry, instead he jumped up and ran to the back fence. Jerry, without hesitating, put the ASP in his left hand and chased after him.

As Jerry reached the fence, the suspect has already flipped over, but he got his fingers caught in the top of the chain-link fence stability wire. As the suspect is dangling with his back against the chain-link fence, he tried to pull away, but can't get his fingers free. Jerry quickly starts to strike at his fingers. "I just start crushing his fingers [thinking], you may get away from me, fool, but I'm breaking every one of your fingers. I know I'm getting him because he's screaming and every time I hit a finger it turns into a bloody mess." The suspect finally pulled his fingers out of the wire and flees. Jerry, physically spent, is thinking, "I'm done...I got nothing...I don't know how long I've been fighting and I don't hear anybody (unit back up) yet."

Jerry started to focus, "Okay, slow down, you got the car, hopefully the female is still there, and we can ID him from her. I'm thinking, I got to let someone know I'm okay. So I put the battery back in my radio and its going nuts, sirens, multiple responder location calls. My call sign was 14-Paul 30... are you code 4? [He hears]. I get on my radio, okay, I'm code 4, I've got one white male I've been fighting with, start me medical, I'm hurt, um...but he's in a white t-shirt, grey shorts, orange face, northbound...I was trying to be funny with the orange face [OC spray]...it's in the radio call history."

I asked Jerry, if anyone caught the joke and he responded, "Oh, yeah, my partners told me later they were thinking 'Fucking Jerry he's hurt and he's still throwing one-liners out!'"

Jerry continues, "I know I lumped the dude up because, as I'm picking my stuff off the ground, there's blood everywhere. I know I got him from the head hit—the accidental midnight special to the head." Jerry walked out to where the vehicle was parked and saw that the female passenger was gone. He found nothing in the vehicle to identify the suspect.

When code responders arrived, Jerry wanted to remain in the hunt. He first tried to grab his holstered gun with his shooting hand; the gun fell to the ground. He then tried to use the sergeant's beanbag shotgun. That, too, fell to the ground. Jerry could only watch as his partners quickly found the suspect, who was curled up in a fetal position in an old wood shed about a quarter-mile away. One shotgun blast of a beanbag was enough to effectively convince him to give up.

The suspect had sustained a gaping head wound requiring seventeen staples to close his skull, eight broken fingers, and a cracked sternum where the beanbag struck his chest. Curiously, he pled to battery on a peace officer and parole violations without fighting the case. It didn't make sense, why would he voluntarily take a second strike? Turns out he was trying to avoid any connection to another crime he committed. But, as "luck" would have it, a DNA swab, required on every prison commitment, came back as a "hit" in an unsolved armed robbery that had occurred a week prior to this event in the *same county. The parolee ended up receiving a third strike commitment and is presently serving a life term in Pelican Bay State Prison.*

Only five minutes had transpired from when Jerry went in foot pursuit to when he radioed dispatch that he was code 4. It would be the longest five minutes of Jerry's career. Unfortunately, Jerry had torn all the tendons across the top of his wrist on the right hand. This injury would be the third and last time he had injured the same hand. It was five minutes that turned out to be a career "deal breaker" for this LEO. But Jerry's decisive foot-pursuit had, no doubt, resulted in the capture of a violent criminal. This offender would no longer be committing crimes in the community. When asked, on reflection, if he'd do anything different in that same situation, Jerry responded, "No, not at all…I'd done it plenty of times before…to avoid injury? Never, I'd jump out of my car every damn time!"

****

Jerry's law enforcement perspective is based on his personal drive to accomplish his public safety mission and the LEO mindset that has been trained and nurtured over years of working the streets. A recent thank-you letter [for inviting him to speak to students] in Southern California from the police chief of a small community lends itself admirably in describing the LEO call to duty and the impact the public safety mission has on their view of humanity:

> "…Our society can only thrive when we all live by the rules. Of course, I include all law enforcement officers in that requirement, as well. In fact, we are held to an even higher standard, and we should be. We must follow the Constitution of the United States, the California Constitution, and all other laws enacted by the legislature or generated through case decisions. Citizens are also required to live according to the law.

> The statistical truth is, most citizens only interact with a police officer once or twice in their lifetimes. For many, it may be a traffic stop during which a citation or a stern lecture is issued for a violation such as speeding. For others, their only contact may be when they report the theft of their car or a burglary at their home. None of these scenarios is pleasant and, therefore, police officers are often associated with a negative experience.

A very small segment of society may have much more frequent and negative contact with law enforcement officers and the criminal justice system. That contact is almost always driven by the choices that portion of society makes. Of course, I am referring to that small portion of the population who choose to live outside the law. That small segment of the population can be very violent and dangerous for the rest of humanity, including the police officers who are duty-bound to stand against them. That very real danger is why officers must always be vigilant. Vigilance is often mistaken for anger, condescension, or aloofness. In some cases, it might be one or all of those. However, most often, it is hyper-vigilance and an inordinate amount of exposure to man's inhumanity to man..."

****

Not all LEOs are built the same, it's human nature. Most are able to absorb the training and fulfill the role of a LEO. Some find it hard to maintain a "command presence" revealing, perhaps, too much empathy for the situation and/or not enough authority. Some LEOs take a "command presence" demeanor naturally, as an extension of their own character traits. And there remain a few zealots of the peace officer community that epitomize the "command presence" demeanor. They readily "show no quarter"; meaning showing no mercy, retreat, or refuge. These LEO types are "lions" in the midst of sheep! As you read the stories that start each chapter, you may discern a few of these lions.

Lions are usually the ones that "take the lead." They give the term "hyper-vigilance" new meaning. They are "the point of the arrow" that everyone else follows. Whether the intentions are good or bad, other officers follow their lead. They have proven themselves in crisis situations, hostile encounters, and deadly altercations. The lion, a carnivore, readily seeks conflict because they feed off of it. Every department needs lions who willingly put themselves in harm's way.

It is the nature of the "beast" to show courage and bravery, an instinctive response to crisis that draws the best or worst from others around them. But there is a consequence for having lions in the midst? Because, without great "trainers" (supervision), some lions can easily forget the mission of law enforcement and become a threat to those around them and worse, pose a liability to public service.

My friend Gabe was a lion. He would never refer to himself that way or suggest it to others, but his character had been born from strong family values, weaned in a community riddled with strife, honed to a razor's edge in the Marine Corp, and seasoned on the tiers and yards of Chino Prison. It was never his intention nor did he consciously reflect on being the "point of the arrow" in prison. When I asked him about my characterization of LEOs and lions, he readily agreed and, as always, had a quick story to share:

> "I remember this sergeant who knew me and had just been assigned to the Reception Center (RC)-Central facility at the Chino prison. She pulled me aside and said, 'You know Gabe, you don't always have to be the first one to go in when something happens…that's why you always get in trouble [under investigation]. Let someone else do it.' I looked at her, pondering the statement, and quietly stated, 'Sergeant, I would, if there was someone else willing to do it.' She just looked at me and said no more."

This is a curious thing about law enforcement. There's always someone to take the lion's role when a leadership void occurs. In Gabe's case, everyone was satisfied with his leadership (or perhaps didn't want to challenge it), so no one felt the need to "step up."

From my experience, the LEO/Lion phenomenon is a direct result of the culture that peace officers encounter on the job. The LEO culture is derived from the environment, social interactions, training, and the unique experience of the team working that locale. There's an unavoidable transference of behavior that comes with the job: the unique language, training, mannerisms, and frame of mind. The trappings that come with being a peace officer—seeing the most negative aspects of humanity daily—leads to an officer being leery of everyone except those they work with directly.

Within law enforcement, there's a real "circle of trust," much like that humorously referred to in the movie, Meet the Parents. The larger circle of trust is the law enforcement community, the middle circle is the agency you work for and the inner circle would be the unit, squad, or particular watch to which you are assigned. LEOs develop a special camaraderie with those they have fought side-by-side with. Similar to military combat veterans who *fought side by side in battle, there's a kinship that is derived from knowing that those persons have "your back" when something kicks off while on duty.*

Robert Presley, when he was a Riverside County Sheriff's Homicide Detective, used to encourage deputies to maintain and cultivate outside friendships to avoid the pitfalls of only seeing the world from a LEO's perspective. "When you are dealing with 'bad people' everyday, then you tend to develop a negative view of people in general." He credits long-term friendships outside law enforcement circles, as having enabled him to maintain a positive and reflective frame of mind about society.

THE NEW CENTURIONS

There is an implied resistance to criticism when public perception, law, and policy become one. Hence, the trail of negative bias regarding criminals, repeat offenders, and parole/probation violators begins with law enforcement contact, parole/probation supervision, and legal or administrative actions that end in repeated incarceration. The training and experience that Detective Presley, Deputy Jerry, or Correctional Officer Mark received, underscores the bravado attitude and "command presence" that characterizes most LEOs in California, if not, the nation.

It is arguable that the LEO "I'm in charge" mindset, established at the turn of the century with prohibition and the east coast "mob" wars, became galvanized during the 1970s, 80s and 90s, when "cleaning up" our communities became synonymous with purging society of criminal elements. For the "War on Crime" supporters and the eager "New Centurion" warriors keeping peace in the streets, the concept of profiling, suppressing, and incarcerating "bad guys" was a fitting aspiration.

Centurions were Roman soldiers who enforced the strict codes and traditions during the Roman Empire. Author and former L.A. Police Department Crash Officer and gang expert, William Dunn, speaks about the historical background of the Roman centurions who were "skilled in the art of mediation" with powers of arrest.[27] The term "new centurions" refers to the modern cop on the beat who must be skilled in both mediation and information-gathering, but also geared for the suppression of crime. Getting "undesirables" off the street appealed to everyday folks who wanted safer neighborhoods. Politicians, public officials, district attorneys, and law enforcement leaders were quickly learning what the public clamored for when it came to crime. *Where* these forces merged and cemented the "profiling, suppression, incarceration" paradigm can be traced to the concept called, "broken windows."

Academia notions of what causes crime have centered on two sometimes competing ideas: environmental vs. sociological stimulus. Environmental stimuli are characterized as specific ecological attributes of the community; poor lighting, trash, graffiti, building decay, etc. Sociological stimuli refer to issues like, income, education, values, and beliefs [culture]. In 1982, George L Kelling and James Q. Wilson argued, in what is now considered a seminal piece in the *Atlantic Journal*, that environmental stimuli is just as influential, if not more so, in determining rates of crime, as social stimuli. Kelling and Wilson argued that something as simple as a broken window could lead to more crime:

> "...at the community level, disorder and crime are usually inextricably linked, in a kind of developmental sequence. Social psychologists and police officers tend to agree that if a window in a building is broken and is left unrepaired, all the rest of the windows will soon be broken. This is as true in nice neighborhoods as in rundown ones...one unrepaired broken window is a signal that no one cares, and so breaking more windows costs nothing...Untended property becomes fair game for people out for fun or plunder and even for people who ordinarily would not dream of doing such things and who probably consider themselves law-abiding... Such an area is vulnerable to criminal invasion."[28]

The idea that crime could be contagious if the environment was left untended, was a convincing theory, and it spread like a virus. It made heartfelt sense to most folks—the thought that, before you can help someone (rehabilitation), you must first have order and accountability. All the talk about poverty, educational opportunities, discrimination, and other social niceties could be brushed aside. The so called "root causes" of crime: poverty, poor education, inequality, was not as important as neighborhood stability and safety. The suggestion that "disorder" in the form of such things as; broken windows, graffiti, pan handling, and other nuisance violations was the precursors of serious crime, seemed logical to the public. In fact, it was readily embraced by key leaders in

New York; one of whom was William Bratton. Bratton would make a profound reputation and career in law enforcement implementing the broken windows theory.

William Bratton was an admirer of researcher George Kelling and made his mark with the broken windows theory, or as it was sometimes referred to "Quality of Life" or "Order-Maintenance" policing, when he tested it as the head of the New York Transit Authority.[29] Early in 1990, he was hired to reduce crime in the subway system which was at an all-time high. Chief Bratton decided that focusing on subway fare-beaters was the best strategy. Malcolm Gladwell, in his book, *Tipping Point,* explains Bratton's strategy in the subways:

> "...he believed that, like graffiti, fare-beating could be a signal, a small expression of disorder that invited much more serious crimes...police had been wary of pursuing fare-beaters because the arrest, the trip to the station house, the filing out of forms...took an entire day—all for a crime that usually merited no more than a slap on the wrist..." (Pages 144-145)

Bratton was creative in his quest to make his focus on fare-beating work. First, he had his police officers in plainclothes at the worst station turnstiles, arresting and cuffing fare-beaters one-by-one and leaving them standing at the platform for all to see. The result was that subsequent would-be fare-beaters either left the station or paid the fare. He then retrofitted a city bus with all the necessary phones, fax machines, and fingerprinting needs necessary to book offenders at the subway stations. As "luck" would have it, nearly "one out of seven arrestees had an outstanding warrant for a previous crime."[30]

Bratton was successful in cleaning up drunkenness and improper behavior, as well as increasing arrests for misdemeanors fivefold between 1990 and 1994. Serious and misdemeanor crimes that were once considered rampant in the subways suddenly saw a significant drop as a result of Bratton's "broken windows" fare-beaters spotlight. His success would soon lead to his appointment as the head of the New York City Police Department. The Mayor, Rudolph Giuliani and Chief Bratton were confirmed *broken windows theory* devotees. Chief Bratton was encouraged to go after quality-of-life crimes: public drunkenness, public urination, graffiti, and the "squeegee men"—the persons that demanded money for washing car windows at busy intersections. Gladwell and others have asserted that these types of crime are referred to as "tipping points" or one aspect of the criminal pendulum that leads to other crimes.[31]

The new centurions, our LEOs, boots-on-the-ground, eagerly embraced the concept, although not consciously. Agencies established policies that set aside civil liberties or conveniently ignored some aspects of due process in the quest for keeping neighborhoods safe.[32] Cops were encouraged to stop, frisk, and arrest anyone who was violating quality-of-life offenses. In New York, Chief Bratton focused on the subway graffiti and squeegee men, and when he moved to Los Angeles he focused for some time on gang members and taggers.[33] The idea that graffiti, gang members, and serious crime were somehow related was easy for street cops, deputies, parole agents, and probation officers to consider. The communities they patrolled easily depicted the rat-infested, trash-strewn, and crime-ridden quality-of-life challenges spoken of in the broken windows theory. Regardless, if the connection points were blurred, it didn't matter because "potentially" dangerous criminals were being taken off the street.

In 1994, Bratton had also introduced computer statistics "Compstat" to pinpoint crime hotspots in the city. A data-driven management model, Compstat enabled the police to redirect attention (rapid deployment of patrols and resources) to areas in the city with the most criminal activity. By pinpointing crime hotspots, the New Your Police Department could immediately make an impact. As Compstat evolved over the years, specialization in law enforcement strategies followed the broken windows concept. Law enforcement agencies across the nation saw an increase in foot patrols, community service cops, gang interdiction teams, parolee apprehension teams, cyber-crime teams, etc, all based, in part, on preventing or solving crime before it happens.[34]

For LEOs, the broken windows theory was nirvana. The belief that focusing on minor offenses could prevent more dangerous crimes became the mantra in most law enforcement agencies. It made sense that if you stop and search: would-be gang members, known criminals, vagrants, panhandlers, you are probably going to get one of two results. First, a possible arrest for contraband or warrant hit, and second, an avoidance of crime in your area because of the contact. The public was supportive, too, since crime numbers fell in both New York and Los Angeles. Imagine encouraging, by policy, a broad brush approach to policing, where "suspicious behavior" includes anyone who looks like, dresses like, or acts like a thug. This was the proverbial "win-win"; one for the beat cop and one for agency leaders—LEOs catching bad guys and city leaders enjoying the political fruits of fighting crime. By 1995, this law enforcement approach had become the norm.

I was slippin' into darkness…
Take my mind beyond the dreams
Where I talk to my brother
Who never said their name…

WAR
Slipping Into Darkness

LEO SCHOOLED

*My LEO experience and training never had the drama, excitement, or danger-
ous experiences that Jerry, Mark, and other LEOs, had. On the contrary, my
LEO development was much more modest. I started my LEO career with the
Riverside County Probation Department. I had my share of scuffles when
responding to aid others, but never did I feel any sense of real danger. That's
probably because of the great "trainers" I encountered at the juvenile hall who
showed me the ropes by example.*

*"Juan" was a group counselor who I befriended at the juvenile hall. We
were about the same age and ran very active units. The kids always appreciated our shifts because we'd have our units compete in some kind of activity
together. They'd forget where they were for few hours and we'd have very few
problems managing them. The kids were simply too busy having fun to cause
trouble for us. Juan was athletic—a ladies' man with the body of an Aztec
warrior. In LEO terms, Juan was a lion! I was trim and fit, too, but sorely
came a distant third in any comparison with him. (Juan would take first and
second place.) But that only made me work harder to keep up with him. He
was someone I wanted to emulate because he was good at the job.*

*One evening, we had organized a war ball game between our units in
the gym. We had about 100 kids ranging from ages ten to eighteen slinging six
dodge balls at each other. It was fast-paced fun. Juan and I would play alongside our unit wards, daring the other team to hit us. In fact, anyone getting
a head shot on us would be rewarded with late night privileges. Of course, I
held my dodge ball and would bounce balls off it to protect my head until I
could get a shot on some unsuspecting kid. Juan would sling "stinger" shots at
the kids and a few of the older boy would be head hunters trying their best to
get us, but none ever did. We were pretty agile and one day, we unknowingly
proved it to the amazement of the kids and ourselves.*

We were both working the "Ricardo M" program in the gym. This was a pilot juvenile hall placement program where minors served their time at the hall instead of another location. Most of the kids were serving less than six months. One day, a code alarm sounded from Unit II where seventeen and eighteen-year-old boys were housed. Two other counselors were in the gym when the alarm sounded, so Juan and I took off running in response. He was ahead of me by a foot.

As we entered the adjacent unit, we noticed that all of the boys were seated on the dayroom bench as the assigned group counselor waved us through, yelling, "Go, go, I got the door." Juan ran toward the bunkroom corridor, but the ping pong table, which was made of a solid wood frame, blocked the entrance. It was blocking the entryway lengthwise, so the only way past it was to slide your body on either side. Making matters worse, the entrance was steel framed with a steel sliding door that was secured at night.

Without hesitation, Juan ran right up to the ping pong table and hurdled over it. Like an Olympic sprinter, dropping his head and upper body to avoid the top of the steel frame door. He leaped pushing his front foot off the far end of the table. I was directly behind him and, seeing him make this incredible feat, I had no choice but to follow him, making the same jump. As we reached the Unit II door and entered, we saw the group counselor for the dorm waving us off. This guy was a monster. He stood about six feet five inches and he was built like a tank. He smiled, saying, "It's all good. No one's gonna act the fool in my house." It was a false alarm.

We laughed, nodding in agreement, and exited heading back the same way we came. As we both were now cautiously sliding past the length of the ping pong table, I had no doubt we were thinking the same thing: how the hell was I able to jump across this table?

The boys, all sitting quietly in the dayroom, waiting for permission to resume activities, had observed us make the jump and, as we reappeared, they gave us a round of applause, yelling, "Aw man, that was cool."

"Do it again, do it again!"

We just smiled and headed back to the gym. Right before we entered the gym, I looked at Juan and said, "Shit, when I saw you hurdle the table I had no fucking choice but to jump, too, because I knew all those kids were watching."

Juan replied, "Hell, I didn't know what to do! I knew you were right behind me and figured you were gonna jump the table. So I didn't have a choice but to try or get run over." We both started laughing realizing how lucky we had been.

We both agreed that if we tried that jump again we would never make it without getting hurt. That event sealed our reputations at the hall amongst the staff and wards. We were rarely challenged by juveniles again. Juan would soon transfer to the California Youth Authority—prison for delinquent youths, where he was injured while responding to a fight; his back broken while trying to help another counselor who had been assaulted. He was medically retired soon after.

****

"Donna" my "main squeeze," was a senior group counselor I befriended at the juvenile hall. Donna ran a unit with the delivery of a drill sergeant, but the heart of a saint. She was always fair and cognizant of the personal drama young wards were experiencing. She was a surrogate "mom" to some and "big sister" to others. She also had a sharp sarcastic wit that caught most kids and her adult peers off guard. You didn't want to "trash talk" this woman because you would lose the verbal jousting and lose quickly. She definitely had the gift-of-gab!

The only thing more attractive than a pretty woman is a pretty woman with intellect. That was Donna. I affectionately called Donna my "main squeeze" because, she was a leader and had no need for anyone to help run a unit. Hence, my desire to want to work with her. More often than not, male counselors appreciated her assistance to help maintain control of a unit.

She could handle herself in a fight quite well and the kids knew it! One evening, two hefty juveniles got into a fight at the gym. I was at the far end of the gym when the boys started swinging. I could see Donna about three feet away barking orders for them to stop. I quickly moved toward them, as I yelled for all the wards in the gym to freeze movement and get down. But before I got even ten feet, she'd already jumped between the boys, grabbing them by the shirt collars, and tossing them to the ground yelling, "What the hell did I tell you? You want to fight here you better start with me?"

They didn't move, just hung their heads probably embarrassed that a woman had just tossed them up!

****

"Richard" was another group counselor who I called a friend. We worked together on many a shift and never had any problems...but we did spend time running to "response calls" to other housing units. Richard and I would drink and play dominoes at his house after work to kick off the adrenaline after a busy night. I recall, the first time I went to his place in Riverside. As we approached his front door, he motioned with his finger on his lips for silence. I thought he was kidding around, but he wasn't.

His roommate Gary, another senior group counselor, was a Vietnam veteran who suffered sleeping memories from being "in country." Richard would quietly open the front door of the house and calmly say, "Gary, I'm home...Gary, its Richard, I'm home."

From the dark recesses of the house, a voice would say, "Okay, come in."

Richard later told me that Gary would squat and sleep in a dark corner of the living room with his gun by his side...a sleeping habit he hadn't yet kicked. Gary was about ten years older than we were, and carried a "no bull shit" demeanor all the time. In fact, during all the years I knew him at the juvenile hall, I never saw him consume anything but coffee, unfiltered Camel cigarettes, and, when off duty, Jack Daniels whiskey. But he wasn't the only Vet that I would get to know and learn from at the hall.

My first unit assignment was with Tino, another Vietnam veteran. Tino had been a reconnaissance ranger in Nam. He stood about five feet two at best, but his demeanor towered above mine and that of anyone else in the room with him. I was five feet eleven and weighed 195 pounds and Richard, a former lineman in college football, was about six feet two and weighed 290 pounds (probably more, but I'm being nice). Tino, without even trying to, could make you feel like an adolescent in his presence. We knew who was in charge and it was him.

Tino had seen, attracted, fought, and delivered death during his tours of duty in Nam, and you could see it in his eyes. Tino and Gary, like my Tio Joe, who had done two tours in Nam, had no problems. They had "lost" their problems in wartime, because problems were useless burdens to carry when you're in survival mode. Survival mode doesn't feel courage or fear. It feels nothing but the will to live, by any means necessary. Most servicemen in time of war find a way to deal with it, and let it go, a few never do.

My first juvenile hall use of force event occurred when I was working with Tino. I had only been on the job one week. Tino had a habit of telling all new "fish" counselors to remain in the office and hand out medications. He would do everything else. I, of course, listened and followed his directive. However, medications were always passed out at the beginning of the shift and, after about fifteen minutes of fidgeting around, I started to get frustrated and angry about the order he gave. The unit office had glass panels all around it, so I could see Tino making the rounds between the TV room, living area, and dorm area. I kept asking myself, "Why was I not allowed out there, too?" Finally, out of frustration, I walked out and toured the unit, walking and talking with the kids, too. Tino said nothing about it.

At the end of the shift, Richard and some other counselors asked me if I was in the office all shift. I said, "No, I got bored and wandered around to see what was going on. Why?"

Richard laughed and said, "That's good. Tino tells all the new counselors the same thing just to see what they will do...some of them don't move...and they don't last very long on the job. You passed the test, little brother."

I thought to myself, "That SOB. I had been feeling guilty about leaving the damn office!"

A couple of weeks later, we had a fire drill in the unit early in the morning. Unit II, where Tino and I were assigned, housed the older wards—sixteen to eighteen years of age. The unit also had a lock-up corridor that led to the intake office. Tino directed me to unlock the doors to get the kids ready to exit the unit. As I walked down the hallway unlocking doors, I would motion for the kids to dress and form a line in the corridor for the fire drill. The drills were monitored on the yard by supervisors for timeliness. They would watch as each dorm unit exited to the yard and count wards to see if the unit staff had accounted for everyone. Orderly and speedy compliance was necessary. We had about sixty testosterone-filled boys in our unit at the time.

As I was reaching the end of the hallway, I opened the last door and announced, "Let's go son, get your clothes and shoes on for the fire drill." He was sitting on the metal bunk with his head down when he mumbled, "I don't care; I just want to die."

I was taken aback by the comment; I had never heard someone talk like that before. I responded louder, "What did you say? Let's go we have a drill!"

The young boy repeated in a mousey monotone, "I don't care; I just want to die?"

Within seconds of our exchange, Tino, who had been standing about sixty yards away in the living area, had already gotten to the door and slid past me. How he managed to have heard the kid's mumblings from afar amazed me. I looked down the hall and the forty-plus wards were lined up at the door and looking in my direction like scared chickens in the henhouse. They'd apparently seen Tino in "assault mode" before. This would be my first time. Tino, who was now inches from the boy, calmly stated, "What's the problem?"

The boy repeated his suicidal statement, "I just want to die."

Tino responded, "Oh, you want to die? Well to die, YOU HAVE TO FEEL PAIN!" he screamed. In an instant, Tino snatched the kid up from the bunk to the floor and was straddling the boy choking him by the neck with both hands, screaming, "DO YOU WANT TO DIE? DO YOU WANT TO DIE? THEN YOU'RE GONNA HAVE TO FEEL PAIN!"

I was startled; not sure if I should try to save this kid from Tino (as if I could win that fight) and also save myself from unemployment. (Yeah, I had priorities—three young children to feed.) But I couldn't move in that instance. I looked down the hallway like a deer looking at the lights of an on-coming train. The kids, all bundled up in line, must have read my face because they were frozen, too, like sheep hearing the snarling wolf. I had no idea what I was going to do in the next moment. Fortunately, I didn't have to do anything. The kid decided he wanted to live more than die as he gurgled, trying to cry out, "I wanna liv…wanna liveee!"

Tino shouted back, "THAT'S WHAT I THOUGHT; GET YOUR ASS IN LINE NOW!" Tino let go of his death grip and the boy jumped up and ran out the door grabbing his gear. He never had a suicidal thought again… at least not in Tino's unit. More importantly, our group was the first out for the fire drill.

****

My second episode with force occurred with Gary. I was working the Juvenile Hall Intake Office, about my second year on the job. By then I had earned a solid reputation as a fair but firm group counselor. The kids called me "Mr. A." I reminded them that the "A" meant, "Where I will be if you don't follow the rules." Gary was working Unit II which connected down the hallway from the Intake Office. We shared responsibility for the ten hallway cells.

A young man of about sixteen was brought in by Riverside PD. He had stolen some candy and soda from a grocery store and refused to cooperate with the officers. The boy had no identification on him and he wouldn't speak a word to them—name, address, nothing. He'd just look them in the eye, bold and defiant. They were pissed off with his cockiness. I took custody of him, returning the officer his cuffs, and advised him that "Silent Boy" would be held pending contact with the parents for juvenile court.

"No problem," I thought to myself. I had dealt with strong-willed youths before and prevailed. I'd get this punk's attention!

The kid and I were sitting at the intake desk when I asked him his name. He just looked at me without saying anything. I tried a few more times and got no response as he stared at me with a blank look. He was stoic, so I got up and said, "Well, I don't have time for games right now, get up and take it down the hall." I pointed as I made the statement. The kid got up and walked into the hallway and I walked next to him. Gary approached us from the opposite direction. I guess he could tell by my demeanor that I was in "alert" mode. I motioned with my hand in front of an empty cell and told Silent Boy to take his shoes off at the door. He stopped by the door, but wouldn't move to take his shoes off. I repeated my instructions, but he ignored the order. He just looked me in the eye.

I had already contemplated my next move, which was to grab his arm and shoulder and take him to the ground. But I was too slow; Gary used a leg sweep that was so fast I didn't even see it. That was Gary's and Tino's modus operandi. They don't contemplate anything, they just act affirmatively! The kid hit the ground in short order. I instinctively followed him to the ground grabbing his legs and twisting them as Gary spun him face down. We hogtied him like a calf ready for branding and carried him to the "rubber room" a small rubber-padded cell in the intake office used for unmanageable wards. Usually the rubber room was used for kids suffering mental health episodes (banging their heads, hands, or feet into walls, etc) or violent, screaming kids that disrupted the other cells.

As we approached the cell, I swung it open with my left hand, and we heaved the poor kid into the rubber room. I figured after ten minutes or so he would be more receptive to my instructions. What I didn't figure was the noise I heard. As soon as he bounced off the padded mat, a whining whistle sound *emanated from the room. Gary heard it, too, and we both had the same curious look. I entered the cell and looked at the light fixture but it wasn't coming from there, it was coming from the floor. As I followed the sound I saw it—a little grey earplug-size object. "Oh, shit Gary, it's a hearing aid!" I shouted. I retrieved it and, sure enough, it had a little wheel that turned the sound up or down. I turned it down.*

Neither of us said a word, as we took off the chains and cuffs, and lifted the boy up. I sat him down at the desk and quickly grabbed a paper and pencil. "Can you read?" I wrote as he attentively nodded, "Yes." I continued writing, "Is your hearing aid working?" He shook his head, "No."

He motioned for the pencil. I hesitated and looked at him squarely as I handed him the weapon. Quickly, he wrote, "Hear aid no work. I read some lip."

Sure you do, I thought as I wrote, "Family phone number?" He nodded, in the affirmative. Fortunately, the kid didn't suffer any injuries from the episode and never reported it to anyone. For that matter, neither did Gary or I. I felt deeply embarrassed for not realizing the kid couldn't hear a word I had been saying. It was obvious, the kid was deaf, and I was dumb!

"BROKE BACK" THEORY

There are always two sides, if not more, to any concept that has a profound impact on society. It is ironic that in 1975, scholar James Q. Wilson, who, with Kelling, had coined the *broken windows theory*, speculated that "the gains from merely incapacitating convicted criminals might be very large." He was correct, if the "gains" he spoke of referred to the burgeoning prison population nationwide. However, by 1994, his own view on incarceration had waned when he argued, "Very large increases in the prison population can produce only modest reductions in crime rates."[35] By then, it was too late. The broken windows theory had gained nationwide acceptance as an effective policing strategy.

For LEOs, incarceration numbers didn't matter since their mission was to "fight crime." Besides, the bustling prison populations were proof of their successful efforts; the "bad guys" were locked up and off the streets! But there was a bigger alarm that was not being readily sounded in law enforcement that the broken windows theory had propelled. While it was true, the disorderly were getting "screwed" for nuisance crimes (tagging, panhandling, fare-beating, gang banging, public intoxication, etc), the laws and codes LEOs were enforcing were primarily suffered by minorities. Social activist Tom Haden reported from 1980 to 1989 "felony arrests nearly doubled in New York City, mainly in response to crack cocaine; however, the implementation of "broken windows" shifted the emphasis from felony arrests, which leveled off after 1994, to misdemeanor arrests, which mushroomed by 53 percent between 1993 and 1998." The arrests targeted African American and Latino youth, the "unimportant collateral damage" from the crime fighting strategy.[36]

The concept of establishing order by clearing the streets of "disorder" made indiscriminate and regular contact with *profiled* hoodlums the norm. The hoodlums profiled were mostly young minorities living in the poorest sectors of the city. Most were considered to be associated with gangs simply by their dress and location. A crime need not have been committed to justify the stopping and frisking of these suspected hoodlums.

In New York, Chicago, and Los Angeles, the pattern was repeated. What transpired in practice was a focus on "minority disorder" in the communities. In an NPR Interview on October 17, 2002, scholar Bernard E. Harcourt explains the impact of broken windows on minorities:

> "...in the big cities...African-Americans represent about 13 percent of the population. But folks arrested for vagrancy are 46.3 percent African-American. Folks arrested for disorderly conduct are 37 percent African-American. Folks arrested on suspicion are 58.7 percent African-American."

During the same time in California, the felony property damage threshold dropped from $2,000.00 to $400.00 for graffiti offenses. As a direct result, juvenile prosecution jumped "...from 160 in 1999 to 546 through the first nine months of 2002."[37] California was a "three strikes" state which meant that any third felony conviction could result in a life term in prison. Of the individuals sentenced to second and third strikes in California (numbering 50,000 by 1999) nearly 65 percent were for property and drug offenses. Three Strikes was intended to put away repeat violent offenders, instead it became "an instrument to put away countless individuals from the 'dangerous classes' of life."[38]

Today, California's prison population demography reflects the outcome of the broken windows theory in practice. The total combined CDCR population (both in-prison and parolee) reached 287,444 by December 31, 2010; the largest prison population in the nation. The in-prison population was 39.8 percent Latino; 28.9 percent Black; 25.2 percent White; and 6.1 percent other (Asian, Middle East, and Islanders). In comparison, the overall California population numbers reflect that Whites were under represented (39.4 percent) and Blacks over represented (6.6 percent) in prison. Professor Harcourt described the idea behind the broken windows theory as having:

> "...two categories of people around: the law abiders and the disorderly...we feel like we can identify in some natural way...some kind of intuitive sense...But of course, that's not true...It is a category that we just create, that's created through policies...through the policy of cracking down on the squeegee men..."

The pattern of profiling quality-of-life offenders shouldn't be construed as a formal racial profiling initiative, consciously endorsed by LEOs or their agencies. On the contrary, the broken windows theory, as it applied to what some scholars referred to as "order-maintenance" policing strategies, pushed LEOs to focus on crime predictors, both natural (biological) and nurtured (environmental). Poorly educated, impoverished, unstable homes, neighborhood and community malaise all feed into the vicious cycle of disorder. And as broken windows proponents argued, these predictors lead to criminality. Regrettably, in large urban areas like Chicago, New York, and Los Angeles, Blacks and Latinos overwhelmingly represented that criminogenic profile because they overrepresented the people exhibiting those crime predictors.

The irony to the broken windows theory was that its originators, Kelling and Wilson, hoped to reduce crime by reducing disorder. If it's a crime to steal or not pay the turnstile or seek attention defacing a public building, wall, or train, then regardless of your status, rich or poor, black or white, young or old, educated or not, arrest and punishment awaits. The truth of the matter was, more often than not, the only persons behaving "disorderly" were the young, poor, uneducated minorities in the inner cities. Our California jails and prisons provide ample proof of that outcome. Despite the broken window theory's best efforts, disorder continues to plague those same poor, young, uneducated, minority communities.

For LEOs, it is already engrained that quality-of-life offenders are, in fact, a species of the criminal class. Scholar Joseph S. Fulda, in his defense of broken windows theory extorts:

> "Would trying mightily to apprehend criminals also net terrorists?...terrorists commit bank fraud, grand theft, weapons violations, immigration violations...and a wide variety of other offenses before an act of terror is consummated...Efforts that are therefore directed at criminals will also catch terrorists...just as efforts to catch quality-of-life offenders catch some criminals who are also quality-of-life offenders. [39]

Fulda's circular argument is simple: cast a wide enough net and you're bound to catch the big prize. The rest of the nuisance "fish" may not have been guilty of something, but it didn't matter because the outcome was the real objective.

Over the years that the broken windows theory has been carried out nationally, it is clearly the "game changer" in police practice. Despite the mountainous evidence that reflects its focus on poor communities of color and unending allegations of unwarranted and unethical police tactics against citizenry, the broken windows theory remains the best law enforcement strategy. Despite unintended outcomes, the broken windows theory moved law enforcement from merely *reacting* to crimes to becoming *proactive* about crime.

During the period when Bratton successfully applied the broken windows theory in New York, crime was already on the decline nationally in other cities not practicing the theory. Some scholars point to the decline in crack cocaine use, others to economic improvement during the same period as the cause for decline. That debate continues today.

It didn't matter what caused the national decline in crime, because the public discourse was effectively tied to the broken windows theory. The "War on Crime" had conveniently found a palatable theory touted by politicians, scholars, and law enforcement, and one that the public could understand.

I see the bad moon arising,
I see trouble on the way,
I see earthquakes and lightening,
I see bad times today...

**Credence Clearwater Revival
"Bad Moon Rising"**

THE "NO PEE" POLICY

My first CDCR encounter with the LEO mindset came early on as a "fish" officer at CRC. CDCR didn't have any field training officer posts, but seasoned officers were always around to observe and learn from. I had met Officer Terrazas when I was first assigned to a facility dorm. He was, for all practical purposes, my "training officer." I called him "T." Very quickly, I realized that "T" was a younger version of senior group counselor "Tino." Not just in height and weight, but attitude, as well. A carbon copy! My very first "training" observation occurred as he visited my dorm one morning.

It was about 8:00 a.m. and the inmates normally would be up and dressed for work and school. Those that weren't assigned to day activities would sleep in late. "T" was the unit's search and escort officer and one of his duties required him to locate inmates who had not reported to work or school. On this day, "T" was looking for a particular inmate. He walked into my office, stating, "I need to find this dude" as he gave me the inmates name and CDC number.

I looked on the dorm roster board and responded, "Yeah, he lives here, but he's probably at work right now."

"T" sarcastically quips, "You think so? Let's go check his bunk!"

As we start touring the dorm, I'm just hoping the damn inmate is out of my unit, because I know "T" will just ride my ass about it if he is still here. Just my luck! "T" stops in front of a bunk.

"T" barks out, "Johnson, get up and get to work!" There is no response. "T" starts to bump the bunk mattress with his fist to wake him up.

Inmate Johnson peeks from his blanket and states, "Leave me the fuck alone, I'm sick."

"T" bumps the mattress again with his fist and responds dryly, "Get up and go to the medical clinic or to work, now!"

Inmate Johnson, getting angry states, "Fuck you Terrazas, don't hit my bunk again mother fucker or I'll kick your ass." He attempts to pull the sheet over his eyes.

"T" quickly grabs the sheet and blanket and yanks them to the floor shouting, "Fuck you and YOUR MOTHER! Get up and kick my ass right now!"

I'm standing there expressionless thinking to myself, "Oh, shit, it's on now," as I survey the room and notice that all the remaining forty-plus convicts have stopped and are now watching what has just transpired.

Inmate Johnson is now wide awake and slides off the bunk with "T" standing less than two feet from him between the bunks. Inmate Johnson quickly picks up his sheet and blanket and grabs his clothes to dress stating, "You're fucking crazy Terrazas, you're not right, man."

"T" responds, "That's what I thought mother fucker." "T" still not moving and looking directly at the inmate, states, "You better be at work when I come back."

The inmate says nothing, as he cautiously slides past us to the restroom.

I asked "T" later, "Hey, were you trying to set that knucklehead off or what?"

"T" casually replied, "Not really, usually nine out of ten 'pee.' Besides, you can't let them talk shit and get away with it. Otherwise, you won't get nothing done."

The concept of "peeing on yourself" in prison meant, you chickened out, you got scared and didn't fight back which is what Inmate Johnson did. This applied to staff too. I was absorbing the LEO code…and didn't even know it!

****

I was working as a correctional counselor at the CCI, Tehachapi Prison IVB Security Housing Unit (SHU) when I was called out by the facility lieutenant to talk to an inmate who was refusing to move. IVB SHU had a unique team approach—everybody's important and everyone's involved— which was readily encouraged by Program Administrator, "Rusty." Rusty was a red-headed (literally) All-American basketball player from Indiana and a seasoned veteran of many years in prison. I could never beat him in our *"one-on-one" lunch basketball drills in the prison gym. He played like an All-American basketball player and I played like a hacker.*

Rusty had a pleasant demeanor with a critical eye when it came to prison business. He was also astute in keeping high energy staff around him and he welcomed opinions from all ranks on keeping the facility running smoothly. Rusty empowered his teams in the SHU unit. For example, as a unit correctional counselor, I had responsibility for all cell bed moves. Only in emergencies, could a lieutenant make bed-moves. It made sense since the counselors saw more details in the Central file of an inmate than the Lieutenants. But this was a unique practice since most prisons bed moves are maintained by uniformed custody staff. I was keenly aware of the impact and rationale behind this unique function in a SHU environment.

Rusty liked the facility lieutenant (Kevin) and so did I. Kevin was an even-tempered, amiable workplace friend. During this period of time, the SHU units statewide were getting full, and single-cell living was no longer possible. I knew, when Kevin called me that day, what was needed. Get this inmate to move voluntarily or else Kevin would make it happen the hard way.

As I approached the cell, I recognized the inmate as a newly arrived Crip. The day prior, I had asked him about moving in with another Crip temporarily until he could find someone more compatible. The other Crip was okay with the temporary move. Unfortunately, this inmate refused. As I approached the cell, I started thinking about what approach to take since I didn't know much about him. The other cells' windows were mashed with convict faces observing the afternoon entertainment.

On both sides of the cell, the extraction team was waiting. Kevin was armed with a 37mm projectile launcher that fired wood block baton rounds. It looked like a miniature bazooka and sounded horrific when fired in the tier block echo chamber. Kevin stood calmly by the side of the door and smiled as I glanced at him straight faced and focused my attention back to the cell door window I was approaching.

As I looked into the window, I saw that the Crip was lying quietly on his bunk. He saw me looking, as I nodded an acknowledgement. He started the conversation, "I know what you want and I ain't doing it."

I responded, "I don't know why not, I give you my word that as soon as you find someone you can live with, we can make that move."

He sat up. "Bull shit, I don't fuckin' believe you."

Without pausing, I stated, "Look, I have no reason to BS you, that's why I'm here right now. We are crowded and need to make space. The other guy is cool with you moving in and understands this is all temporary. It's got to happen."

"No way," he replied.

There was a momentary silence as we looked at each other, I, knowing what was coming next and he, having played his last "pawn" move. "Okay," I said, "but understand this, when I walk away from this cell there is a "No Pee" policy here."

"A what?" he asked quizzically.

I responded, "A No Pee policy, which means when I walk away, if we don't have an agreement, then you can't change your mind when they come in to get you."

"Fuck that shit, bring it on!" he shouted.

I shook my head in disappointment and, as I walked away, I made eye contact with Kevin who nodded in the affirmative.

Kevin signaled the control officer to crack the door. As the door slowly opened, Kevin stuck the nozzle of the wood baton launcher into the cell yelling, "Get down, get down" as he fired into the cell. The inmate had already barricaded himself behind a mattress for protection as the extraction team entered. The Crip was forcibly removed from the cell without serious injury except maybe to his pride. This scenario is routinely scripted and played out at most prisons by inmates presenting a "tough guy" stance and officers ensuring consequences for inmates failing to follow directives. It might not make sense to public perceptions of right and wrong, but it is part and parcel to the culture in a prison setting.

Later, I spoke with the inmate who was living in his new cell with another Crip homie. He apologized for doubting my word after receiving reassurance from others on the tier. One of the Crip shot callers, a member of the defunct Consolidated Crip Organization, told me the next day that they had "got at him about the program" in IVB SHU. "We told him, if Alvarado says he'll move you, he will." I thanked him for the assist. Too bad it was a day late on that communication!

****

I wish I could claim the "No Pee" policy speech, but it belonged to Gabe. I recalled one of our many "consultations" regarding the department's disciplinary policies, when he shared with me the "orientation" speech he'd give to inmates just arriving to his unit. He'd remind all the inmates that he had a "No Pee" policy, and there was always a "fish" inmate asking what that meant. Seasoned convicts would laugh or smirk at the comment, but understood the message: You can't back off, or change your mind or be a coward; meaning you can't pee on yourself, because you will face the consequences regardless of your change of heart. Of course, there was always one or two who would challenge the No Pee policy. And Gabe, a man of his word, would oblige. He was the lion amongst the sheep!

This take-no-bullshit approach to behavior modification scenarios has been played out in every city, county, and state correctional facility since they first were established. Some officer behavior is, at times, more brutal, callous, and life-threatening, while other times more subtle, but mentally taxing just the same. All have the same intention, control and power. To the general public, this can be a very cruel and inhumane behavior and attitude for public servants to exhibit.

I'm not making excuses for unbridled violence by professionals tasked with protecting the public, staff, and offenders, nor am I condoning those occasions when officers exceed the limits of their duty and punish offenders with unnecessary or excessive use of force. Those instances are the exception to the rule. Hard as it is to believe, it's true. The problem for law enforcement is that public opinion thinks otherwise. And I have no doubt this book will only serve to reinforce the perception of rampant excessive or unnecessary use of force if taken out of context.

The stories shared in these pages can illicit debate and opinion about what could or should have been done differently without resorting to violence. But what works in a "normal" social setting such as, work, school, or the mall cannot be applied in a prison setting. Nothing is really "normal" in a prison setting because things we take for granted in the street are magnified behind steel and concrete walls. An inmate cutting in line, extended eye contact, an insignificant gesture or simple misstatement can be cause for trouble between inmates. The same applies to inmate and staff relations. Minor infractions and seemingly trivial offenses can escalate quickly into violence. This is one of those psycho-sociological mysteries for scholars to figure out.

What I have learned from experience is that civility simply won't work in prison because the human dynamic is entirely different. For one thing, the characters locked up have already proven to be anti-social and untrustworthy law breakers, whereas, LEOs are trained to enforce the law and are culturally inundated with the expectation to take charge. As a consequence, between offenders and LEOs, there is always an underlying tension and hostility. But this debate detracts from the primary point of the discussion I'm sharing, which can only be described as a "cop-think" mentality that permeates every law enforcement agency today. LEOs are expected to be professional, and that includes the expectation to affirmatively act when a suspect or offender is not compliant.

Maintaining control of a situation and containing it from getting worse, demands absolute adherence to an officer's directives. This is peace officer 101—controlling the scene of a potential or active incident. When those directives are challenged—even ever so slightly—it can result in a definitive armed or physical response by LEOs. Likewise, when those disruptive events occur (whether it is a boisterous citizen refusing to stay calm or an inmate that refuses to exit his cell or keep his hands on the wall during a search) LEOs will not hesitate to act. The awareness that some type of action will occur for failing to oblige the directives of a peace officer makes sense with most citizens. Except when they see it on television, then it is examined at nauseam. But for career offenders, it becomes a constant game of stretching boundaries or simply testing officer resolve.

BARBARIAN BARRAGE

The focus in this chapter concerns LEO behavior and how policies like broken windows influenced the new centurions' collective mindset and actions. Before the broken windows theory, the *national policing strategy* was as Peter Moskos, Professor of Law and Criminal Justice referred to as "little more than picking up the pieces of broken windows." Cops on the beat responded to crime, they didn't prevent crime. The broken windows theory changed that dynamic as Moskos argues:

> "In truth, Broken Windows rests primarily on little more than...urban concepts of eyes on the streets...to keep the 'barbarians' from winning...while one must never assume that correlation equals causation...the

concept at least got the police back in the crime-prevention game. That was a seismic shift, nothing short of a law-enforcement scientific revolution."[40]

The LEO way of thinking continues unabated both in the community and behind the jail and prison walls, where sometimes disorder can appear to be the order of the day. For the "new centurions" working in jails, prisons, and parole units, the LEO mindset is no different and perhaps more engrained throughout the state of California since they are the keepers of the so-called "barbarians."

Jail deputies and prison correctional officers have been trained to "walk their beat" managing the daily programs and activities (yard, school, work, clinics, living units, meals, etc) and ferreting out suspects who may be involved in nefarious business such as, drug trafficking, larceny, and gang activity. But, more often than not, officers are kept busy "sweating the small stuff," like; a hostile attitude, verbal taunts, expletives, and failing to follow minor rules (extra laundry, out-of-bounds, failure to appear, etc). Rules and regulations enforcement is a critical tool of correctional science. It can be verbal, informal or formal, but, without consistent enforcement, havoc can strike quickly. When issues or conflicts arise that may result in officers using force to gain compliance, the offender can face administrative hearings or possible felony prosecution. More time in jail or prison is the result of that formalized process. It is a daily part of the LEO routine.

Correctional officers in the '70s and '80s carried a flashlight, handcuffs, whistle, and pen (some had radios, but not all) while on duty. These officers wore "Class A or B" uniforms that looked like officer "suits." These were his/her official equipment, unless they were assigned an armed post requiring both a revolver and mini-14 rifle. By mid-1990, officers were better equipped: radio, stab-proof vest, cuffs, whistle, OC canister, ASP (baton). The majority of the officers now wear jumpsuits similar to those worn in the military. Jumpsuits provide more comfort and body movement and make carrying equipment easier. Like equipment and uniforms, officer training has also improved over the years which today highlights emergency response capabilities and use of force options.

These new centurions now look and act like "Robo-Cops." They are physically prepared and departmentally trained for conflict engagement, and that is the expectation when working their beat. The departmental standard expectation is to be, "firm, fair and consistent" with the offender population. However, the practice of interacting with offenders may have had a different outcome.

The change in officer equipment and dress was a practical matter for "celled environments" like; Level III, IV, Administrative Segregation Units, and Security Housing Unit facilities where the infrastructure and daily routine was highly structured and made interaction between inmates and officers impractical. These higher level of custody environments demanded a *command presence* profile from LEOs based on the inmate population and higher security risk level. But for Level I and II inmates, interaction was unavoidable since those inmates were not behind cell doors, but in dormitory-living with the officers on patrol. Unfortunately, a Robo-Cop "look" and demeanor doesn't invite much interaction. Accordingly, over time, effective communication between inmate and staff would suffer the consequences of enhanced officer safety.[41] Officers were not actively engaging prisoners, but more often than not, over time, only reacting to prisoner behavior.

These same new centurions have been recruited to the Division of Adult Parole Operations (DAPO) of CDCR and continue the street LEO tradition of keeping order of the "disorderly."[42] Correctional officers also brought the new centurion attitude, training, and experience derived from prison to the streets. The problem is that "disorder" is a relative term for all peace officers to judge. A common *quality-of-life* offense, like pan handling or graffiti, may result in arrest in some cases, but for parolees, any violation of the law is a *violation of parole conditions* that could result in the return to prison.

Parole agents naturally followed the LEO rules-of-engagement with assurance that parolee behavior be held to a higher conduct since they were already deemed "barbarians" owing to their prison history. Violations were increasingly brought to the Board of Prison Hearings (formerly called Board of Prison Terms) as basis for re-incarceration. By 2008, felons in California were returning to prison at twice the national average for violations, averaging three to six months stints. The new centurions working in parole division were indeed keeping local communities safe.

The parole division also mirrored local law enforcement broken windows theory strategies statewide. High Risk Offender programs,

Parolee-at-Large (absconders), Gang Task Force, and Sex Offender programs became specialized units.[43] These functions had at one time been the responsibility of the individual parole agent. But just as local law enforcement agencies use Compstat data to allocate staff and resources at high crime areas, DAPO eventually created specialized units to attack the barbarian disorder. However, it is arguable as to whether specialized law enforcement tactics have provided any real public value to community safety.

Take, for example, the massive expansion of electronic monitoring that has taken place in nearly every county of California. Journalist Page St. John calls it the "massive expansion of the virtual jail" using GPS technology to track "criminals on the street rather than incarcerate them."[44] Electronic monitoring has been a challenge for CDCR since its inception. Unfortunately, this is a national problem not limited to California's parole and probation departments. The issue surrounds the GPS "alerts" that are triggered by dead zones, low batteries, broken ankle bracelets, and parolee/probationer tampering. For example, California's parole system sent out nearly 40,000 alerts *each month* to parole agents in 2013.

In Los Angeles County, the probation department has the system activate an alert whenever a device passes a school or park. The *Los Angeles Times* reported that there are approximately 4,800 prohibited places for sex offenders in the county—one every square mile—resulting in a "total of 7,500 messages generated by some 300 probationers each month." Probation officers also receive email alerts in their email in-boxes, generating 20,000 messages each month. Following up with those alerts is both untenable and costly. Matthew DeMichele, former researcher for the American Probation and Parole Association, commenting on GPS technology, stated "In some ways, GPS vendors are selling law enforcement agencies, politicians, the public a false bag of goods."[45]

The California Parole Apprehension Team (CPAT) provides another example of the CDCR broken windows theory "mirroring" local law enforcement practices. Parolee-At-Large (PAL) teams were created statewide specifically to target the apprehension of parolees who had absconded from parole supervision. It is estimated that California had approximately 17,688 parolees at large during that time. In January 2010, those duties were incorporated into the current CPAT teams. In early 2014, California's PAL population was approximately 12.5 percent

(13,387) of the total parolee population. The 2014 "high control" PAL population is 4,245.[46]

While the CPAT effort seeks to provide measurable results in public safety, it ignores other potential avenues to remedy the onset or continuation of criminal activity. This is the broken windows theory "disorder" as it is applied by all law enforcement; Gang Task Forces, GPS programs, sex offender programs, and similar specialized units. It attacks a crime problem, but serves no other public value purpose. In other words, there is no socio-political solution or remedy, only continued *maintenance* of the crime problem.

BONDAGE VS. BANDAGE

Mario Paparozzi, Ph.D., law and justice professor has suggested a new paradigm twist for the broken windows theory. He argues that public safety and social justice paradigms should not be treated as separate ideological concepts that are mutually exclusive. He questions the personal and professional ideologues who "dig in their collective heels" defending their own perspective:

> "For some, broken windows is viewed as part of a conservative agenda, while 'what works' is considered the liberal version. However, when polarized views such as criticisms related to the gender and race of the proponents are set aside, it becomes apparent that the two models are neither liberal [nor] conservative. Rather, they are forced into narrowly construed ideological categories by critics whose personal views derive mainly from visions of what should be rather than what is, and who have anemic foundations in 'street experience.'"[47]

Instead, Paparozzi maintains that the idea of addressing crime "disorder" with the social justice "what works strategies" should be reconciled. For law enforcement, the broken windows theory seeks to reduce criminal activity. For community corrections, the "what works" theory refers to "…reducing the individual offender recidivism." Ironically, both models seek a reduction of crime as the foundation for their stated outcomes yet, as a nation, we have only endorsed one avenue of redemption, the law enforcement model.

Put another way, fixing broken windows shouldn't begin and end with the "potential" for crime disorders as espoused by scholars enamored with Wilson's and Kelling's crime philosophy. On the contrary, the broken windows theory needs to embrace the whole spectrum of criminality from the "potential" crime to potential rehabilitation. That means equal and passionate attention to the practice of repairing social ills. Public agencies, as well as non-profit and religious organizations, that provide social programs geared to help offenders successfully integrate back into society, are the community corrections component of "what works." Paparozzi argues that the public's view on justice is generally limited to suppression and incarceration. Further, in practice, the courts, police, probation, and parole responses to offender accountability is little more than punishment-based strategies.

What is needed is a synergistic approach that blends the new centurion mindset with the community corrections professional. Paparozzi maintains that including the broken windows concept to the community corrections component "presents an opportunity for what works principles to become compelling rather than optional."[48] This inclusive rather than exclusive modeling of the broken windows theory may be the new paradigm that AB 109, Public Safety Realignment needs to transform the *tough-on-crime* model the new centurions have been proliferating for the past thirty years. Borrowing a line from Connie Rice, the civil rights litigator who cautioned Chief Bratton upon his arrival to Los Angeles in 2002, "…get a new playbook…our emergency isn't broken windows; it's broken communities. And broken children."[49]

CHAPTER 2

Mama, take this badge off of me
I can't use it anymore.
It's gettin' dark, too dark to see
I feel I'm knockin' on heaven's door

Bob Dylan
"Knockin on Heaven's Door"

CHINO PRISON BEDLAM

The California Institution for Men, commonly known as "Chino Prison" has a storied history. It is the third oldest prison housing male inmates in the state after San Quentin and Folsom prisons. Chino has established itself as a primary Reception Center and largest minimum support facility in the state. It was also the largest prison in the southern region. All prisons have their own unique history and Chino was no different. It began as the "Prison with no Walls," it housed some of the most notorious prison gangsters in Palm Hall, and became the busiest of Reception Centers in the state for many years. The culture of Chino Prison was unique to its experiences. I experienced a few of Chino Prison's major incidents my last years in the department, which became the backdrop for the August 8, 2009 Reception Center (RC)-West Riot.

Homicide of an Officer:

In December of 2004, I arrived at the California Institution for Men, the Chino Prison, as the new Associate Warden (AW) for Health Care Services. My primary duties required that I oversee access to care at all the facilities and monitor follow-up for compliance with court mandates under the Plata, Coleman, Armstrong, Valdivia, and Perez litigation. As such, I was involved in most management meetings that could impact inmate movement (population, lockdowns, classification, etc). On January 10, 2005, during a morning meeting with the warden and a number of facility AWs and captains, the warden's phone rang. She put the call on speaker phone and we all heard the same news. The RC-Central captain, his voice urgent, but clear, reported that Officer Gonzalez had been stabbed by an inmate. "He doesn't look good. The ambulance is en route. The inmate is on the tier with two other inmates, possible hostages".

We immediately responded to RC-Central, which was located about 250 yards west of the administration building. Two large cooper grill doors separated the front lobby easement from the secure interior facility like the shiny teeth of a hungry shark. The officer manning the control room hurriedly passed the warden and the rest of us through the gate, as we flashed our identifications. As I entered the main corridor, I could see on my immediate right, a trail of blood that extended from Sycamore Hall down the long hallway to the medical clinic where I was standing. The warden and others went immediately inside the medical clinic. I followed the trail of blood down the corridor past R & R, where I observed a highly agitated officer yelling and stomping back and forth in the corridor stating, "I told those mother fuckers to do something…I told them someone could get killed…I told them…" He wasn't speaking to anyone in particular only looking down at the floor, angry, with his hands balled up into fists.

Ignoring him, I continued down the corridor where I saw officers lined up in two rows, assembled in riot gear in front of Sycamore Hall. I noticed that one of them had a blank stare as if he were on medication—numb to the circumstances. I had seen that look before. I quietly asked him, "You work this unit?" He nodded, yes. I put my hand on his shoulder and told him to "stay focused until this is over." His eyes welled with tears; he nodded in agreement as he tried to fight them back. He wasn't scared; he was in shock at what he had seen. I quietly told the sergeant, who was standing nearby, to make sure the officer was not part of any extraction team.

It was controlled bedlam. Inmates in Madrone Hall, on one side of the corridor facing Sycamore Hall, were yelling. You could hear inmates in both units yelling obscenities at staff. Multiple staff paced back and forth, others awaited orders on how and when to extract the assailant. Inside Sycamore Unit, two captains, both seasoned Special Emergency Response Team members, had been observing the situation and trying to negotiate the suspects to end the siege. One captain had already lobbed an impact grenade in the direction of the main suspect without effect. The suspect had discarded the weapon used to stab the officer and the other two inmates on the tier had already agreed to cuff up. They had not been involved in the assault. Lieutenant M. Acuna directed the staff in front of the tier grill gate. The suspects agreed to be handcuffed. All the inmates surrendered and the standoff had ended within the hour.

Thirty minutes after Officer Gonzalez had been sent by ambulance to the hospital, we were notified of the bad news. Officer Manual Gonzalez had expired from a stab wound that tore directly into his heart.

I had seen inmates that had been stabbed, murdered, and shot from gunners in the towers and I had seen officers that had been assaulted. I was indifferent to those episodes. Perhaps it was because I was engaged in assisting matters in those events and over time had become a little hardened to trauma. Now, as a new AW at CIM I felt like a bystander watching a horrific scene that I could do nothing about. This was the first time I had seen so much blood on the tier and, knowing it was from an officer, it is an image I will never forget.

The records department sits in front of the RC-Central lobby area, the same area that Officer Gonzalez was rushed out from by ambulance personnel. Many records department staff knew Gonzalez. They appreciated his pleasant demeanor and casual conversation when delivering paperwork to the office. The staff was horrified about what they had seen and heard and didn't know yet that he had expired. I entered the records area asking the manager if I could have a minute to talk with the staff. She gathered about forty women in the main records area. I began, "As you have all seen and heard, Officer Gonzalez was assaulted this morning and we just received word that he passed away at the hospital."

Some staff members began to cry, others looked shell-shocked, seeking to understand the moment. I continued, "I feel for his family and friends at this time. But even after receiving this terrible news, we need to keep our

85

focus. We are trying to secure the suspect for immediate transfer. It's our job to make sure any outstanding documents that are not in the suspect's central file, are found and immediately placed there." I looked at the manager and she nodded. "The unit lieutenant will be asking for it, if he hasn't already. This is a sad reminder of where we work and why all of our jobs are important. We should never take for granted the routine nature of our work because, at any given time, it could be one of us. Please keep Officer Gonzalez and his family in your prayers."

As I spoke, the executive staff team for the warden had regrouped in the RC-Central Associate Warden's Office which was directly next to the records office. The warden inquired where the suspect was being detained. The captain for RC-Central stated, "The Palm Hall holding cell."

"Who's with him?" the warden asked.

The captain didn't know, but believed a sergeant and lieutenant escorted him there. I made eye contact with the warden and stated, "I'll go," and immediately left the meeting. She didn't say it, but everyone knew what she was getting at...keep this animal safe from staff until we can get him out of here!

When I arrived at the Palm Hall holding cell, I observed a camera in the hallway pointed directly at the cell holding the suspect. Two lieutenants, one of them assigned to Investigative Services, had remained with him. I was relieved because, if any harm came to the suspect, it would only serve to muddy the case against him for murder. We didn't want any roadblocks to his case.

The inmate, identified as Jon Christopher Blaylock, was already serving a seventy-five year sentence for the attempted murder of a police officer. Blaylock was a well-known Crip who was both despised and feared by other black inmates. He had already assaulted another inmate during his reception center processing. Blaylock sat quietly, but stared directly at me as I glanced his way. He sat motionless in waist chains. The lieutenants motioned for me to follow them and we quickly entered the adjacent office. Excited, one of them stated, "We got him on tape...we never said a word, just set up the camera and he started mouthing off about stabbing Officer Gonzalez."

I responded in a soft voice, "You got that on tape? That's good." Make sure you document it and be ready for the DA's office to speak to you about the circumstances here." I then informed them that Officer Gonzalez didn't make it, that he had passed away at the hospital. The room got quiet.

I exited the room and approached the cell. Inmate Blaylock rose from his seat and asked, "Who are you?"

I sternly replied, "I'm Associate Warden Alvarado." I sensed he knew that I had the utmost contempt for him at that moment. I was trying to stay calm and collected, but my disgust was overwhelming what little professionalism I had left to muster for this animal. I clenched my jaw and kept my eyes fixed on him as I spoke. (To be honest, I kept my composure only because the video recorder was running.) I continued, "I'm here to inform you that you will be transferred within the hour to Corcoran, Lancaster, or Tehachapi…"

He interrupted, "Yeah, it's about fucking time! I have to stab a mother fucker to get it done…this shit wouldn't have happened if you mother fuckers had transferred me!"

I responded, more forcefully, but without raising my voice, "I could care less about what you have to say or what you think. Just know you're leaving this institution very soon."

As I walked out of the area, the lieutenants joined me. I whispered, "Tell me you got that on tape."

"We sure did, boss. Hopefully, that will be enough for the DA to give this guy the death penalty."

"I hope so," I responded, and I quickly left to advise the warden.

Inmate Blaylock's case has been repeatedly delayed pending court determination regarding legalities of doctor/client confidentiality privilege and of his mental competency to be tried in court. As of this writing, his pre-trial for murder was scheduled March 21, 2014 in Fontana Superior Court…he has yet to be tried for the crime of murder ten years later!

2005 RC-East Riot:

Not much media attention surrounded what was perhaps one of CDCR's most critical tactical response episodes in recent history. In September of 2005, RC-East had an inmate disturbance in Butte Hall, requiring the Crisis Response Team (CRT) to enter the housing unit "hot" (armed with lethal weapons). Butte Hall was a two-story unit with 200 reception center inmates living in a celled housing environment. Additionally, thirty-six inmates were bunked in the TV living areas of both floors because of overcrowding.

The inmates had rioted in the lower Butte dayroom which was open to foot traffic through the main living area in front of the officers' station. As the disturbance grew out of control, inmates began throwing chairs and tables at the officers' station office window, ultimately breaking it. The officers' station control panel operated all the doors on both sides of the unit housing fifty inmates each. As the inmates began to breech the windows to seize control of the officers' station, the officers quickly retreated via a ladder leading to the second floor officers' station and closed the hatch. Once there, the officers realized that the inmates could take the whole unit, if they scaled the ladder, too. The officers quickly scrambled up to the roof hatch, but could not open the roof top door; it was locked from the outside.

The 2005 RC-East Riot was notable for a number of reasons. This was the first time in nearly twenty years since guns had been brought into the facility to quell a major disturbance. Second, the department was under a microscope for a number of systemic failures. As a result, the governor had created the Inspector General's (IG) Office to investigate and report on CDCR and gave the IG carte blanche access to prisons. During this disturbance, the IG representative came into the Emergency Operations Center and took notes while Acting Warden Mike Poulos made the hard decision to assault the building.

****

Ironically, Mike Poulos was being vetted for the warden position at the time, so every move he made was being closely monitored. If anyone could handle the pressure, it was this man. My frustration was that he didn't deserve the enormous scrutiny, nor should any warden during times of emergency. It was akin to having FEMA inspectors arrive just as response teams are busy trying to save lives and assess needs in a natural disaster. Only in California, where CDCR had probably earned the worst ranking among agencies, would legislators and the governor's office accept such an intrusion in the middle of a crisis.

The department had a unique warden vetting process. It was like getting free work at no cost. If the candidate didn't meet muster, there was no risk; simply replace the candidate. Administrators have no union privileges, so it was understood by any candidate that the playing field was not theirs to control. Some candidates did not meet muster. However, that was not the case with Warden Poulos. His experience through the ranks, including a tour of duty with another prison's CRT, made him the best trained leader to be incident commander at that moment.

****

Outside the RC-East housing unit, the CRT awaited the green light to enter the building. They had already developed a tactical plan for entry and containment. Their advanced tactical training and past crisis intervention experience made them the best option in any assault scenario. During that period, it was discovered that a Medical Technical Assistant (MTA) remained trapped inside an office. He had called for assistance on the office telephone and remained on the line with staff. He reported that the inmates were trying to break down the steel door that separated them from him and the medications he was carrying for the unit. Time was running out.

No one could find a key to the maintenance door leading to the roof. A quick-thinking yard sergeant directed staff to make a human ladder and they scaled the two-story building and forced open the access door on the roof freeing the officers inside. That sergeant's quick thinking and his team's actions also prevented the inmates inside Butte Hall from gaining the field of vision over staff below. During the roof extraction, the warden received the call: The inmates were breaching the door where the MTA was located. The MTA was pleading for help as the steel door was already bent partway giving the inmates a view of the medications and access to a possible hostage.

Staff monitoring the phone call could hear the banging of metal on metal in the background. A decision had to be made. Warden Poulos didn't hesitate. He gave the green light and the CRT entered the unit and took control within minutes. The shock and awe of the flash grenades and CRT formidable tactical actions quickly dissuaded the inmates from continuing the melee. The inmate takeover of the housing unit ended within minutes.

Vetting a Warden:

Many months later, I was interviewed by Inspector General, Matthew Cates regarding the candidacy of Mike Poulos for warden. The IG's office was interviewing management and line-staff regarding their thoughts about Mike's character. I was one of the last to be interviewed. I really disliked the vetting process. Maybe, it was the invasion of privacy; inspecting your financial status, asking neighbors to comment about you, querying employees at random about decisions made. It gave the appearance of an objective selection process, but was fraught with subjective opinion and innuendo.

From my perspective, the IG would be hard pressed to find a nexus between what my neighbors or staff thought of me and the duties of the warden. If the intent was to determine character traits, it could hardly matter at that point in a correctional career. Vetting character traits should have occurred when candidates sought positions for captain, associate warden, and chief deputy warden, where the field leadership of prison business is developed. Besides, the IG's office had little to no experience regarding the nuances of the prison culture, prison employee group interactions, or the operational intricacies of correctional facilities. Yet, the IG staff was tasked with gleaning key elements of a candidate's worthiness to be warden.

I walked into the executive staff meeting room for the interview. Mr. Cates shut the door behind me and, after a few pleasantries, the interview began. Mr. Cates, a former attorney general office staff lawyer, opened the discussion stating, "This is a confidential interview, Richard." Next to him another attorney sat quietly taking notes.

I quickly responded, "No it isn't, Mr. Cates. Nothing's confidential."

He smiled, looked at me, and said, "I guess you're right." He continued, "We just want to know if you think Mike Poulos is warden material and why."

I looked at him and without hesitation, said, "He is absolutely warden material. He not only has created a positive atmosphere with the management team and line-staff, who are still recovering from the homicide of Officer Gonzalez, he resolved the riot at RC-East without loss of life. He did that while being under the microscope of your staff—an unprecedented act. He doesn't pretend to have all the answers, but readily seeks his management teams' advice on the best course to take. He also doesn't second guess his decisions; he takes responsibility for the prison, good and bad, which to me is a mark of a leader."

Mr. Cates, looked me over, contemplating his next question. "You've known him for how long?"

I responded, "I first worked for him at CRC in Norco; he was the AW for my unit when I was a captain."

Mr. Cates paused and asked, "Is there anything that you don't like about him?"

I answered quickly. "Absolutely, he is a tight wad who's always going through my trash can hunting for plastic bottles or soda cans to recycle!"

Cates and the other attorney laughed. Warden Poulos was confirmed by the senate not long after the vetting process was completed. Mathew Cate would also become the secretary of the department in a few short years.

2006 Riot at RC-West:

A year and half after the homicide of Officer Gonzalez, I was at home with my wife enjoying the company of some close friends when I got the call from the Administrator of the Day (AOD), Molly H. She advised that a riot was in progress at RC-West, Cleveland and Sequoia Halls, housing 400 inmates. She was en route to the prison. At that time, AODs were required to do four-hour tours of the prison at a time of their choosing, one day on the weekend. They were not required to report to work each day Saturday or Sunday, but were to be on-call 24/7. I lived in Los Angeles a thirty-minute drive without traffic.

It was Sunday, December 23, 2006. I reported to work within twenty minutes time, obeying all speed laws, of course. As I walked on to the yard, I observed a row of four officers facing Cleveland Hall's North Yard side entrance with Black inmates lying prone on the ground in front of them. The unit door appeared to have been forced open and bent off the hinges. On the west side, I could see a number of officers by the entrance door. I could hear noise coming from inside the dorms. In the middle of the yard I saw AOD Molly, wearing a very colorful baseball jersey. She had left a softball game when she got the call.

As I approached her, I stated, "Nice jacket, it will be easy to spot by the media helicopters. What do we have?"

AOD Molly responded, "I knew you'd say something, but I didn't have time to go home and get dressed." She advised that a fight broke out in Cleveland between Black and Hispanic inmates. The inmates had barricaded the dorms using the steel bunks, and some Blacks had forced the north side door ajar where they escaped and surrendered to officers. Inmates in Sequoia heard the commotion and, once they realized what was happening, they (Black and Hispanic) attacked each other, too. The last two dorms, Laguna and Borrego, followed suit. Eight hundred inmates had taken control of the units on the east side of the facility.

As she spoke, I realized that we didn't have very many staff on the scene. I asked, "Where are the lieutenant and sergeants?

91

AOD Molly looked at me and stated, "Richard, this is it. That's why the lieutenant is assisting the assault team by the door. The officers you see are it; the rest are covering the medical triage area with the injured inmates that got out."

"What about the other dorms?"

She looked at me, and deadpanned, "I don't know. If they go, too, we're screwed." We both chuckled a bit. AOD Molly was a recently promoted captain from Lancaster. A very level-headed, experienced correctional employee who had worked all levels and had gained notoriety for her leadership skills and prison security awareness. I was associate warden for the RC-East and West Facilities at that time. The East and West Facilities were about one mile apart. Neither of us had any concern for our immediate safety, as we were focused on identifying control and containment options. We both knew time was not on our side. Inside my head, I was already calculating plans B and C and I have no doubt AOD Hill had already done the same.

****

It may be that with experience comes a "calmness in crisis" attitude that law enforcement officers (LEOs) exhibit when trouble starts. Maybe, for some, an unconcerned attitude is a way to shield themselves from appearing weak or unsure, but I think it has more to do with having survived a multitude of incidents and learning a few things along the way. Peace officers are trained to maintain a "command/control" demeanor. We see this daily with police and deputies on patrol. On the street, it is readily apparent that LEOs entering an unknown environment (store, car, house, street scene, etc) always behave in a manner that is vigilant. When they engage citizens and suspects on the street, they project a demeanor that is neither excited nor relaxed, but always observant and authoritative.

The same demeanor applies to a correctional officer entering an office, unit, prison yard, and work or school area full of angry, suspicious, or guarded inmates. It goes without saying (but I'll say it anyway) that a command presence among LEOs is a mandate on the job. In fact, more so in a prison setting where all the "citizens" are convicted felons.

****

As AOD Molly and I stood on the RC-West yard, I received a call from an associate in Sacramento. An associate is a professional acquaintance, but not necessarily a friend, so the assistance given is rarely the same as given to a friend. He was a member of the Office of Correctional Safety. He was calling from the Emergency Operations Center (EOC) in headquarters. He needed information for the EOC. He started, "Hey Alvarado, are you at Chino?"

I responded, "Yeah, but we're up to our earlobes in alligators right now, I'm on the RC-West yard."

Excited, he said, "You are? We need to know what's going on!"

I responded, curtly, "Look, we don't even have control/containment. We need more staff and I can't tell you anything beyond that. Injuries to staff and inmates remain fluid with no accountability for either at this point. Tell your people to wait for our EOC to advise you. I gotta go."

AOD Molly got a call on her cell phone, she needed to report to CIM's EOC. About five minutes later, I was called out, too, by the warden.

Fortunately, the 2006 RC-West riot ended without expanding to other units. It was a "spontaneous combustion" event caused by some disrespect issue between races which could not be resolved in time before it blew up. Disrespect issues can arise from the simplest of things. For example, the housing units at RC-West had notoriously bad restrooms with showers, sinks, and toilets always needing repair. More often than not, inmates would claim a sink, toilet, or shower for "their people." If the wrong race was on the commode, it was on! This may be where the adage, "Shit Happens" came from…Okay, maybe not!

****

One notable exception to the rule occurred that day. In one of the housing units, a seasoned officer, who was respected by all the inmates, put the inmates on their bunks when the riot alarms sounded. He calmly reassured the inmates as he toured the 200-man dormitory unit, that it wasn't their fight or issue. He reminded them that most were "short-to-the-house" (pending immediate release dates). Because of his efforts, the inmates decided not to "play."

Following the riot, we began to replace all the old "spring loaded" bunk beds and bolted the bunk frames to the cement floor. This would prove to be a critical security preventive measure that probably saved lives when the August 8, 2009 riot occurred. The inmates could no longer barricade the doors with bunks or use the springs from the bunks as weapons, as they had in 2006. More importantly, at CIM, Warden Poulos readily encouraged "reality-based training." Reality-based training included, but was not limited to, simulated weapon usage, hostage/victim extraction exercises, classroom or *office scenarios, and skirmish line assault training at the range and on facility yards using inert gas grenades and amplified sounds to simulate riots.*

Warden Poulos supported a constant training cycle throughout the prison facility that afforded staff more than just familiarity with non-lethal and lethal weaponry, but also provided a comfort zone for "what ifs" in their immediate work locations. The training allowed staff to practice with their collective game faces on. It also sent a strong message to inmates who could overhear the staff cadence calls during training exercises in the facilities. The training would pay for itself in life-saving dividends three years later when RC-West exploded in violence. Together, the 2005 RC-East Riot and 2006 RC-West Riot experiences and the reality-based training regime honed the proverbial "correctional awareness" sword of the many men and women who would ultimately prevail in the 2009 riot.

California Institution for Men

On August 8, 2009, the California Department of Corrections and Rehabilitation suffered one of the largest prison riots in departmental history. At approximately 8:30 p.m., the riot erupted at the California Institution for Men (CIM), Reception Center West (RCW) facility, as a result of Hispanic and White inmates attacking Black inmates.

The riot began in one building and, less than a minute after the first housing unit alarm sounded, alarms went off in all seven inmate-occupied housing units. Approximately 1,175 inmates were involved, of which 249 received injuries requiring immediate medical treatment. Another fifty-five inmates required transport to area hospitals for treatment of more life-threatening injuries. It took approximately seven long hours for staff to quell the disturbance with no fatalities incurred by staff or inmates. The heroic efforts of staff to quell the riot most assuredly began those few days prior to the event. But the antecedents that developed and became the catalyst for the riot probably began many years before.

Dedicated on June 21, 1941, the California Institution for Men (CIM) (commonly referred to as Chino Prison) was the first major minimum security institution built and operated in the United States. It was the State of California's third male correctional institution[50] and was constructed to relieve the overcrowded conditions of San Quentin State Prison (1852) and Folsom State Prison (1881). CIM was unique in the field of penology because it was known as the "prison without walls." The only "security" fence around the facility units was a five-strand livestock fence, intended mainly to keep the dairy cows from wandering through the living areas.[51]

Kenyon Scudder, a remarkable and innovative superintendent of his time, sought to develop a rehabilitative environment where behavior change could be achieved through non-punitive measures.[52] Scudder believed that "rehabilitation must come from within the individual and not through coercion" so he sought and trained staff who would guide and allow personal growth to occur with each prisoner sent to CIM. Scudder even demonstrated how to scale the barbed wire fence for incoming inmates, so that they would know there was a choice and it was theirs to make:

> "...if you stay on the inside of the fence you can enjoy limited freedom. When you drop down on the other side you are a fugitive felon and we will bring you back no matter how long it takes. Many more years will be added to your sentence and you can never come back to Chino."[53]

Scudder's belief that inmates wouldn't choose to escape if treated with dignity and programs, proved to be correct. Very few inmates tried to escape. Since that time, CIM has increased security measures to meet the challenges of a vastly different inmate population. While no longer known as "the prison without walls," CIM's Minimum Support Facility (MSF) housed the largest level I inmate population within the California prison system. At the time of the riot in 2009, the MSF had approximately 2,700 minimum custody level beds at the facility.

The MSF provided a number of educational and vocational programs over the years, most notably the Prison Industry Authority Diary Program and the Chino Divers Program. However, since the 2008 economic upheaval and severe budget cutbacks, all prisons have seen a substantial cut in program opportunities. As a result, since October of 2011, and the implementation of AB 109, Public Safety Realignment[54], the MSF population has been significantly reduced to below 2,100 beds.

CIM Expansion

In addition to the MSF, CIM expanded its operation to include three reception centers (RC): RC-Central (1951), RC-West (1961), and RC-East (which was acquired from the California Youth Authority in 1970). The prison and outlying state property extends 2,700 acres between Central and Euclid Avenue and is adjacent to the former Heman G. Stark, Youth Correctional Facility (See Figure 3).

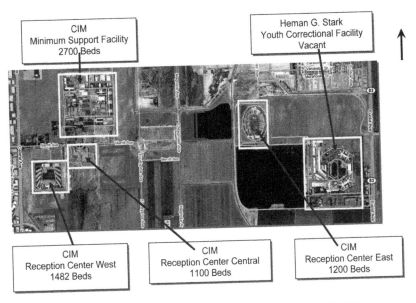

Figure 3. Source: CDCR, After Action Report January 25, 2010.

Reception Center West

The RC-West facility was originally designed to be a California Department of Forestry (CDF) Fire Training Camp. All eight 198-bed housing units are constructed of wood (Figure 4). Since that time, RC-West's mission had changed to become one of three (3) Reception Center (RC) Facilities at CIM. RC-West had a total housing capacity of 1,482. On the day of the riot, 198 beds in Laguna Hall were closed due to renovation with a facility inmate population of 1,292. RC-West provided housing for reception center inmates awaiting parole revocation processing. [55]

CALIFORNIA INSTITUTION FOR MEN RECEPTION CENTER WEST (RC-West) FACILITY MAP

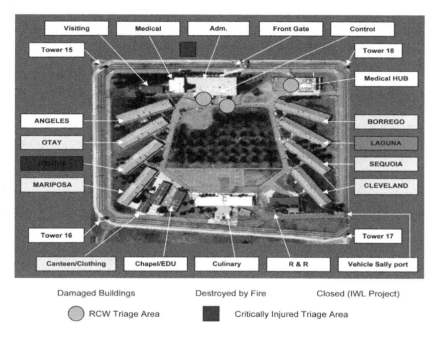

Figure 4. Source: CDCR; After Action Report, January 25, 2010.

"Frequent Flyers"

The CIM received intake from several Southern California counties including, Orange, Riverside, San Bernardino, and Los Angeles Counties. During the year of 2009, CIM received approximately 400 parolees back into custody on a weekly basis and, on some occasions as high as 600 parole violators per week. Those inmates were reviewed by staff for proper housing, custody level, medical/mental health needs and tracked for Board of Prison Hearing review and/or program placement. California was unique, not only for the high number of recycled offenders, but for placing a three-year parole term for every prisoner released back to the public.[56]

The term "frequent flyers" was first coined by staff at CIM in reference to the large, continual turnover in the Parole Violator (PV) population for the RCs and level I and II facilities. This unique PV population trend was not limited to CIM. Throughout all statewide RCs and level I & II facilities in California, it remained a challenge to maintain stability and provide meaningful program needs with the constant migratory nature of the PV population.[57]

The ebb and flow of PVs returning to prison was coordinated with the number of parolee releases, which made bed management a daily priority. Bed space for these "RC" cases was managed between the three reception centers; RC-Central, RC-East, and RC-West. This population changeover was monitored statewide by administrative personnel in Population Management Division at CDCR headquarters. They, in turn, were in communication with county jail personnel on their bed needs arising from arrests, court convictions, and out-to-court felon cases housed in the local counties. It was a daily statewide exercise for prison and county jail staffers to maintain bed availability.

The sheer number of PVs returned to prison to serve revocation periods or new terms became a significant management quagmire not easily addressed nor readily acknowledged departmentally. From early 1990 through 2005, the California prison population had increased by 73 percent. California prisons held approximately 55,000 people in 1985; nearly doubling to 96,794 in 1990 and housing 167,698 in 2005. The population eventually reached 173,614 in August of 2007 before a gradual decline was observed.[58] The parolee population showed a similar trend.

In 1990, the parolee population in California communities was approximately 65,144; however, by 2000 the parolee numbers swelled to 118,000 and peaked at 127,722 in August of 2007. The majority of the admissions in California prisons consisted of felons returned to prison from parole status, either for a new crime or a violation of parole conditions. In 1990, 41 percent of admissions were new commitments. By 2004, they only accounted for 33 percent of admissions. Parolees were returning at a rate of nearly 70 percent.[59]

RC-West Culture

At CIM, RC-West the PV population would roll over (change) by nearly 50 percent each month. This migratory population of PVs made safety among the inmates untenable since they always had to watch who was coming or going that may be a potential enemy on the street. The RC-West inmates were primarily low-level custody inmates cleared to be housed in a dorm setting.[60] Seasoned convicts would try to remind younger inmates about the rules-of-engagement and more often than not, were challenged. The pecking order usually seen in stable prison units was not entirely welcomed or solidified in the RCs, since many inmates serving thirty days or less had no reason to be tied to anything or anyone. Likewise, the inmates had no interest in keeping their surroundings clean or bed space orderly as they knew that they would not be in prison or the facility for any extended length of time. However, this unique subculture phenomenon didn't apply when it came to race relations.

Race consciousness is reinforced daily in prison and was no different for RC-West. First, by gangs: for street gang members the pecking order remained tied to the prison gangs and each gang is tied to race or regional allegiances. Secondly, race identity is reinforced institutionally: Inmates are placed in bed or cell assignment according to race. Staff document inmates based on racial designations and classification committees acknowledge race concerns relative to gang affiliations and ethnic balancing in facilities. Inmates themselves segregate for yard time and chow lines, so as not to be seen with another race. Phone lines, TV schedules, and some yard programs are given designated race periods for equitable access between all groups.

For staff assigned to RC-West, the constant PV changeover did not allow for establishing a rapport or routine with all inmates. The inmates were simply not there long enough. Enforcing simple rules about keeping the units and dorms clean became a constant challenge. Most PVs were doing "straight time" and were not eligible for "good time credits" which meant any rule violations like disobeying orders, out-of-bounds, or similar infractions, would not result in more time to serve. As a result, custody staff had no formal "hammer" to enforce rule compliance with most PVs. Likewise, staff was hard pressed to move recalcitrant inmates from their units or the facility since bed space at the other CIM RCs was limited, at best. Informal measures of control became the routine.[61]

Making matters worse, the RC-West dorms all had deteriorating restroom facilities that were not equipped to handle 200 inmates on a twenty-four-hour basis. The conditions of inoperable sinks, showers, and toilets, constant fungus and mildew, and crumbling ceilings were well documented by CIM, CDCR and court overseers. The subject of the deplorable living conditions was a constant issue for all the inmates and it was the most pressing issue facing RC-West staff and CIM administration.

It was a routine occurrence during public tours of the RC-West facility that inmates of all races would ask two questions of visitors: "Are you from Sacramento?" And, "Have you seen the restroom?" Inmates perceived anyone from Sacramento as having authority over the warden and/or some influence with politicians. Ironically, however frustrated inmates may have been about the poor conditions of the restrooms, it was not a factor which led to the riot. Yet, the very nature of the "frequent flyer" population housed at RCW would prove to be a primary factor in the resulting riot that occurred on August 8, 2009.

The August 8, 2009 at the RC-West facility was a planned attack orchestrated by only a few inmate shot callers on the yard. But it didn't behave as a planned attack. Inmates used weapons of opportunity (broken shards of sinks, metal window sill frames, broom and mop handles, etc). Had more inmates been made aware of the planned assault in advance, inmate-manufactured weapons (with handles and sharpened to a point) would have been found in abundance. Likewise, if the planned assault was shared with more inmates, it is highly likely, snitches would have warned staff. Unique to this riot was the fact that it was intended to be a surprise attack against black inmates and that aspect of the riot was cleverly achieved.

Race relations in prison are based primarily on power and who has it. Latino and White inmates constituted approximately 70 percent of the RC-West inmate population. The ethnic race that has the numbers and leadership usually controls the yard for drugs and contraband. Regardless of any other deterrent like a pending release date or the possibility of catching more time in prison, inmates cannot ignore racial conflicts. The PVs at RC-West and East facilities were no exception. They gained nothing by involving themselves in the eventual riot of August 8, 2009. But they had no realistic options. When inmate "shot callers" attack another race (which will be explained in greater detail in the next chapter) the Latino and White PVs were obligated to attack the Blacks without really knowing why.

Had this been a general population (GP) environment, instead of a reception center, maybe a riot could have been avoided. GP facilities have the luxury of more programs and earning time off their sentence for working or going to school. GP inmates live in a more stable environment since they are doing their time at that location, unlike RC inmates who are in transient mode, open to constant movement. Accordingly, GP inmates generally try to avoid prison politics as much as possible. But as the saying goes, "The proof is in the pudding."

Prison "Pudding"

The "pudding" in this case is the Minimum Support Facility (MSF) at CIM. It housed approximately 2,600 inmates at the time of the riot in a very large dormitory environment. The MSF did not riot. There are a number of reasons to explore: First, it occurred in a GP programming yard. Second, and perhaps most important, Blacks constituted about 51 percent of the population. If White and Latino inmates had decided to assault inmates on the MSF yard, it would have been a fair fight. The third reason the MSF didn't join the riot was because nearly all the inmates on the GP had known release dates. Since, the population at the minimum yard rolled over about 30 percent every sixty to ninety days, it was reasonable to assume that a sizable portion of the inmates would be leaving within three to eight months of their arrival. Combining these three points gave some pause to management and line-staff that the MSF would not blow up. But why take any chances?

On August 14, 2009, five days after the largest prison riot in recent California history occurred, executive leadership at the state level, in concert with CIM executive staff, came up with a preemptive strike plan called "Operation E-Brake." Teams from around the state, comprised of Crisis Response Team, Investigative Services Unit, Special Services Unit, Parole Apprehension Teams, and CIM facility staff, made a surprise visit to the MSF at "0-dark-thirty" and other targeted housing units throughout the prison. The MSF was the primary objective and the goal was to send a message and round up any gang leadership targeted or discovered. Roughly 200 specially trained officers in drug interdiction and gang identification came to CIM and targeted suspects for searching, documenting, and validation of gang status. But the massive operation had a more striking affect.

It was made clear by the management team that the night-time raid on the MSF would be conducted in a calm and respectful manner. The E-Brake teams would quickly enter a housing unit, and, within seconds, assemble a tactical advantage while sergeants barked orders to, "Lie face down on your bunk, now!" The inmates were asleep at the time, and when startled awake saw the tactical teams among the bunk areas with weapons drawn and quickly complied. The show of force had an immediate *shock and awe* affect; the inmates didn't want any trouble. Once they realized what was going on, they simply obeyed directives, understanding that at least some troublemakers would be carted off without others being blamed. A number of prison gang members were identified as a result.[62] The MSF never participated in any disturbance, which was a relief to all staff.

CHAPTER 3

We are all just prisoners here, of our own device,
And in the master's chambers,
They gathered for the feast,
The stab it with their steely knives,
But they just can't kill the beast...

Eagles
"Hotel California"

THE "BIG ONE"

Riot Parlance

The largest prison riot in modern times for CDCR started for me on August 6, 2013, but I didn't know it then. None of us working at CIM did, but we knew the potential was there for a disastrous event. It was about 10:30 a.m. when the operations captain came into my office with the Investigative Services Unit (ISU) Lieutenant and Sergeant, the Institutional Gang Investigator (IGI), and Gang Investigative Officers. Just my "luck" I was acting warden during the week, covering for the warden who was attending a CDCR conference in Sacramento. I looked up from my "paper chase" and could see the seriousness of the occasion on their faces. Captain Acuna started the dialogue, "Boss, we got a kite that indicates a riot may jump off soon, the lieutenant will give you the details."

The lieutenant was a seasoned correctional peace officer. He knew the games inmates played and he knew the games the staff played, too. He was the lead investigator for employee misconduct matters for the prison. I trusted his prison judgment but, when it came to his personal agendas, I had to keep both eyes wide open. This isn't a criticism of him, but more of an observation of what happens to most "A" type (take charge, ambitious, proactive, multi-tasking workaholic) personalities, especially, peace officers in positions of authority. They have control issues; myself included!

The lieutenant reported that an officer, during a routine cell search, found a kite in the cell of suspected EME associates. The officer contacted the gang squad who determined that the contents indicated that a race riot would kick off soon. The IGI lieutenant and his gang officers were able to discern which inmates were identified in the kite; all EME sympathizers. The kite was written by an inmate that had just left RC-East, Butte Hall and was housed in RC-Central at the time of the discovery. Another kite anonymously sent through institutional mail the day before, now corroborated the August 6th kite's information, specifying RC-East as the starting point for the riot on Friday.

The ISU squad had put "feelers" out to known informants and the ISU lieutenant and sergeant spoke with facility supervisors on all the yards. No staff reported any racial tension or noticed any unusual behavior changes in the inmate population. Generally, if a kite was regarded as legitimate, there were always tell-tale signs in the units or rumor/leaks coming in to corroborate the information. We had received nothing of the sort.

During the IGI lieutenant's briefing, I was handed the kite. As I read it, I was immediately taken aback. I looked up at the IGI lieutenant and asked, "Have you verified the information?"

He responded, "No."

I immediately called the RC-East facility sergeant and inquired as to which inmate housing units would be using the main yard on third watch (afternoon) Friday. I had the phone on speaker so all could hear. The sergeant responded, "Butte."

I thanked him, hung up the phone, and looked at the group saying, "It's been verified. Captain, lockdown the prison, now!"

I have seen many kites in my years, but I had never seen one that provided so much information; where the riot would start, why it would happen, and how to proceed. In fact, this kite even directed a tactical strategy for the EME sympathizers to follow for escalating the planned assault throughout the prison.

The kite was supposed to be cleverly coded by the EME, but was easily interpreted by the gang squad. The concern was how to intercede effectively before tomorrow—the targeted riot date. More importantly, how do we confirm the threat on all the yards without creating undue racial tension? Within the hour, I met with the executive staff team for the prison and spelled out the situation. None had heard of any issues in the unit, but they all agreed that a modified program was necessary.

Modified programs meant that the inmates would be restricted to the dorms or cells. Critical inmate workers, like clerks, cooks, maintenance, would remain on the job sites, but no yard would be permitted for the duration of the threat. Movement within the dorms was okay. All movement outside the units would be effected by escort. This protocol allowed for the redirection of select staff to assist with searches and enabled the units to quickly isolate and contain potential suspects in the event of any disturbance. It was a simple "CDC 101" security decision. Headquarters (HQ) was not in agreement. Why wasn't I surprised?

****

My boss in HQ was a retired annuitant (RA), acting as the regional administrator for reception centers. RAs were a blessing and, at times, a curse for CDCR. They provided valuable experience for vacant posts in critical areas while not costing the state the burden of any additional benefit package (medical, dental, and leave credit or retirement earnings). From the public view, or at least the one projected by the media, they were often characterized as some sort of "blood suckers" milking the state twice; a paycheck for working as an RA and a retirement check from CALPERS the state retirement agency. Among staff, we referred to RAs as "retired irritants" mostly in jest. But, on this occasion, the name fit.

I emailed the acting regional administrator explaining the circumstances and identifying my decision to "...modify program, including cancellation of visiting, pending further investigation (interviews and searches)..." I had already called his cell phone, but he was notorious for not answering and always late returning calls. I knew the bold print change in program and cancelling of visiting font used in the email would get his attention and it did. He called me and wanted to know why I was cancelling visiting. I

105

reiterated the contents of the email and explained the urgency in minimizing inmate movement.

He disagreed. He advised that he would have to discuss the matter with the director and get back with me. He didn't get it...I wasn't asking his permission, I was advising him of the situation and the actions I was going to take. I knew now I had another problem to overcome. It was clear to me that the issue wasn't whether a riot would occur, but when it would occur. Maybe, he viewed me as not having the requisite experience or maybe he didn't have the confidence to make a decision. It didn't matter because time was working against us.

Visiting for CIM at the MSF yard and all the other facilities involved the use of at least six to eight officers. I needed to redirect them to other areas of the prison where additional staff were needed for coverage. Visiting personnel processed approximately 200-300 visitors on weekends. Imagine visitors with inmates of all races enjoying time together in the visiting compounds at all the facilities and a race riot kicks off. We would have no staff to assist in processing the visitors out or extracting the inmates back into the facilities. All available custody responders would be needed for the riot. Why would I need to explain in minute detail the consequences of such a scenario to a seasoned veteran regional administrator? The "what ifs" were enormous: rioting in the Visitors Room, potential hostages, untold injuries... Imagine the liability. This is part of the disconnect that can happen between the field and HQ. No one is at fault, because it has more to do with what drives decision-making in CDCR.

Potential controversy is always a fear for anyone working in Sacramento. To be put under the spotlight and get grilled by the perception of things rather than the reality of the circumstances is the burden CDCR leaders share in Sacramento. That's why having a "fall guy" is a great option. From my experience, there always seemed to be plenty of them in the department. I remember a seasoned warden advising me, when I was working at Tehachapi, not to be in a hurry to promote to warden. When I asked why, he said, "It's simple math. The longer you're in the position, the more likely you'll hit a landmine...you won't even see it coming." His words were prophetic, as I had observed it happen to wardens and HQ's Directorate personnel many times throughout my career.

To be fair, the CDCR Directorate team in Sacramento was driven by bigger considerations; some of which conflicted at times with managing *prisons effectively. For example, the inmates have a sizable stakeholder voice in Sacramento. It is most readily seen when issues arise surrounding access to or restrictions on visiting privileges, mail, religious groups, and food. These are sensitive issues for adult offenders having little or no options in programming. In fact, these are constitutionally protected areas. CDCR had had a history of subjective application on criteria and protocols for the aforementioned. CDCR, in its quest for uniformity, had effectively addressed most of those inconsistencies, but trouble always rears its ugly head when "A" type leaders in the field decide to interpret policy their own way to meet their needs.*

That is why HQ and prison managers track citizen complaints, disciplinary, program participation, inmate appeals, and other key operational areas. Given the situation and my decision to shut down visiting, I suspect the regional administrator didn't want to make the call on his own. Canceling inmate visiting was one of those sensitive inmate privileges potentially fraught with negative citizenry blowback, but not under the present circumstances. CIM had credible intelligence that the EME planned an attack on Black inmates. Safety of staff and inmates was always priority number one in prisons and this situation met that threshold.

****

I contacted the warden about the visiting issue. We didn't have to discuss the relevance of the kite because we both recognized the urgency. He agreed with my decision and spoke directly with the regional and director who concurred with him. The mini-crisis in leadership was averted. It was a good thing, because I had already given the order to cancel visiting at the prison and inmates were already notifying family members not to come on the weekend. My "A" type personality notwithstanding, it had been my practice, learned from other seasoned field generals (wardens), that "it is sometimes better to ask forgiveness than to ask permission!"

The Riot Begins

As described in the August 6, kite, the planned EME riot started at RC-East in the Butte and Alpine Dayrooms at 2:18 p.m. on August 7, 2013. All four dayrooms, housing approximately thirty-six inmates each, erupted in fighting between Hispanic and Black inmates. The housing sergeants and unit officers gave orders to stop fighting. All the inmates ignored the orders and continued to riot. Staff used pepper spray in the form of MK-9, MK-46,

Instantaneous Blast Grenades and T-16s. In addition, 40mm and 37mm launchers were utilized, firing numerous XM 1006 direct impact (rubber) rounds. The aforementioned less-than-lethal use of force quickly stopped the assault with inmates finally lying in a prone position on the dayroom floors.

At 9:40 p.m., the same day, the EME-orchestrated riot continued, but this time at the RC-Central facility, Madrone Hall Dayroom. Nine Hispanic and nine Black inmates were identified by housing unit staff as participants in the racial disturbance. Curiously, the White inmates remained on their bunks. Orders by staff to "get down!" were ignored by the combatants and one officer deployed a continuous burst of OC pepper spray from his MK-46 with negative results. One of the ISU gang officers was on duty that evening and launched an OC Blast Dispersion Grenade approximately three feet above the inmates' heads and they immediately complied with staff directives to lie prone on the ground. RC-Central staff had smartly separated Blacks in the Sycamore Dayroom earlier in the day to avoid another riot situation. After medical review, all the inmates involved in the riot were re-housed in the dayrooms with Hispanic and White inmates in one and Blacks in the other.

The warden had returned to CIM on Friday, August 7th and was apprised of the situation. No changes were made to the additional response teams assigned at the MSF and RC-West facilities. However, some adjustments were made to the regular code response teams based on what was surmised from the August 6th kite. In the kite, the EME associate was telling the inmates how the assault would take place: "…Okay, when they [inmates] come out to yard. So the East [facility] would go off first and everybody else [in the facility] will follow suit. I'm sure that we will know when this is taking place. Every yard and dayrooms are to follow suit…"

Inmates know when an incident occurs because they can hear the code alert on officers' radio transmissions. They also know that some pre-selected staff will leave the unit in response to another facility's radio call for assistance. That would signal the time for inmates to initiate their own attack on Black inmates, when staff response in their housing unit would be weakest. The EME game plan almost worked.

However, the supervisory staff at RC-West had already been directed to not send a response team, thereby ensuring adequate staff remained at RC-West in the event of any disturbance. This was a wise decision given the fact that RC-West was a dormitory setting housing nearly 1,200 inmates at the time. Since the RC-West inmates didn't see any staff leaving the facility, *they were not sure any assault had been initiated at RC-East or RCC. We had bought ourselves a twenty-four-hour reprieve.*

The Incident Command Team

I got the call from the administrative officer of the day (AOD) about 8:30 p.m., on August 8, 2009 that a disturbance had erupted on the RC-West yard. Captain Acuna was the AOD and he also lived within minutes of the prison. I knew I could count on him to give me a good assessment. I was almost relieved that the drama was unfolding so we could get the business done once and for all. But it was only a fleeting thought, as I hurriedly got into my car for the drive to Chino. What I didn't know was the magnitude of what was about to unfold in rather short order and with much ferocity.

Captain Acuna had received a call from the Security Administration Building (SAB), watch commander's office. The lieutenant was yelling on the phone that the riot had just kicked off at Mariposa and what followed didn't make any sense. Captain Acuna told him to calm down and start again. The lieutenant had just recently been promoted and had been left at SAB to run the institution while Watch Commander, Lieutenant Quiroz had gone to the administration building to establish the Emergency Operations Center. As they spoke, the Joshua unit went off, the lieutenant telling the captain, "We lost one." Repeated radio transmissions kept coming to the SAB, the lieutenant finally reporting to Captain Acuna, "We lost them all," (referring to all the dorms).

I was about half way to work when Captain Acuna contacted me on my state cell phone advising about Joshua. He contacted me two more times before he stated, "We've lost the facility and a fire has started at one of the buildings." I couldn't get there fast enough.

After the captain called, I received a call from Chief Physician and Surgeon, Muhammad Farooq. He was a competent and capable medical practitioner who was relatively new to the department, but was committed to making CIM's health care services better, a gargantuan task, to say the least! He began the conversation, "Richard, I got a call from the nursing station. Do you need me to come in?"

I responded, "Yeah, Mu, we need everyone. It's the whole facility; you'll need to set up a triage area—the works."

Without hesitation, Mu responded, "Okay, I'm on my way in."

****

Dr. Farooq was formerly a medical educator and also worked as a doctor for Kaiser Hospital. He had a calm style of leadership that was very much needed in the complex and agitated world he inherited at CIM. CIM was one of the original twelve prisons whose infrastructure was sorely antiquated and not suitable for the resources (computer, telephone, water, and privacy rooms) needed to meet the mandates imposed by the federal court. Making matters worse, Medical Technical Assistants (MTAs), a "nurse with a Badge" positions had been eliminated throughout the state because, as the court appointed receiver for health care delivery proclaimed, "Nurses cannot serve two masters (custody and medical)."

I agreed with the concept, but wholeheartedly disagreed with the implementation plan. MTAs were the backbone of the health care delivery system at all prisons. They were the principal means by which inmates received medical care. By removing and replacing them with less paid nurses, many of whom were unfamiliar with prison policies, this created a roadblock to the very thing the receiver wanted accomplished—improved health care delivery.

Fortunately, Dr. Farooq was adept at creating an environment where multiple stakeholders (doctors, nurses, psychologists, psychiatrists, pharmacists, and medical clerical staff) could voice concerns and provide solutions. More importantly, he readily saw custody staff as a resource and not as a deterrent to getting the job done. His leadership and the strong work ethic of the doctors and nursing team would be given its biggest challenge on this night. As time would prove, they met the challenge successfully.

****

Captain Acuna arrived at the Emergency Operations Center (EOC) as Lieutenant Quiroz was initiating the Incident Command System protocols. As they spoke, more management team members arrived and took positions: Operations, Logistics, Planning, and Finance. CIM executive staff had had its share of disturbances requiring large-scale EOC activation. So EOC protocols were almost second nature to the crisis. Whether a major riot, homicide, power outage, or a deadly commuter plane crash—CIM had them all during my tenure there—the EOC staff had plenty of on-the-job experience. Fortunately, the boots-on-the-ground on this night were no different. They were also primed and ready.

It had been my experience that "Johnny" (euphemism for inmates and convicts) was less a concern for me in the housing units when I worked. What

110

did concern me as an officer was "who" I was working with, because you are only as good as your partner when something bad happens. In prison, it is likely that something bad can happen at any moment. As an officer and as a correctional counselor, I didn't shy from reminding my peers that "we don't get paid good money for what we do each day, but we for damn sure can earn our pay for the year in one day!" Most of my peers understood the message, "shit happens" and we get paid to deal with it! This bottom line credo struck a chord with me and the many staff I worked with during my CDC travels from Norco, Tehachapi, Headquarters, and Chino. It continues to strike a chord with me today when I read about or see any LEO in harm's way.

As I was heading into the city of Chino, I got a call from my wife regarding my stepdaughter, Amy, a San Bernardino County Deputy Sheriff. Little did I know that this call would be useful later that evening. Amy was on patrol that evening in the Chino area and had gotten a radio call to respond to the Chino Prison and provide perimeter support. Amy informed my wife that a fire could be seen from Central Avenue. My wife, a retired parole district administrator and former officer and sergeant, who had worked at the Chino Prison, calmly knew the crisis unfolding was significant. As she relayed the information, I thanked her and advised I'd call when time permitted, stating, "Don't expect me home tonight."

"Okay, be careful," she responded.

My mind raced thinking about what options lay before us for quickly quelling the disturbance. I had a sudden fear about how many staff and inmates might be seriously injured or dead. I shook the thought away, as I approached the entrance to the prison on Central Avenue. I could see that Chino PD had already barricaded the street. As my car slowly approached the officer waving traffic away, I "badged" him for entry to the prison grounds. To my right, I observed the Chino PD Mobile Command Post and Chino Valley Fire District triage area set up outside the main entrance in support of the fracas inside the prison grounds. They were stationed in the visitor parking area, a stone's throw away from the incident.

****

I reported to the EOC at about 9:30 p.m. I looked around. The room buzzed with staff; some on the phone, others posting logistical maps, and some posting scribe notes on the wall. I saw Acting Warden, A. Fakhoury and Regional Administrator, Mike Poulos talking with Steve Miller, Special Agent for the Inspector General's (IG) Office. I whispered to the acting warden that

I was going to take over the Incident Command and that he should exit with the Regional and IG to his office. He looked at me and nodded in agreement.

This was not, by any stretch of the imagination, a heroic overture on my part. The heroics were occurring at the facility. It also was not a moment of clear-headed thinking, as we had more capable and intelligent leaders already there working the EOC. My decision to take control was a selfish one. I realized at the moment I walked into the EOC that there were only two people who would be held accountable for the outcome; both the acting warden and me. As "career executive appointments" we had no real employment right to our positions and could be removed without notice. I quickly surmised that, if anything was going to happen, then it would happen on my terms.

I took command of the EOC and relieved the watch commander, who was serving as the interim incident commander. There are prescribed command and organizational functions and duties that are spelled out by the Incident Command System (ICS) framework outlined in the National Incident Management System (NIMS), a consistent nationwide template that all law enforcement, emergency responders and fire agencies have been directed to use. Using familiar phrases and protocols in large disaster events makes it easier for competing agencies to blend and flow with nuances of different city, county, or local departments.

Communication and "Murphy's Law" (if anything can go wrong, it will) are always a concern in any emergency and the ICS seeks to reduce those missteps as much as humanly possible. But as I have learned over the years, poor communication and unknowns are a part of any crisis event. The CIM riot would prove to be no different!

As the incident commander, I asked the section chiefs to address the following: Verify staff accountability and injuries; especially if anyone remained in Joshua Hall. In addition, we needed the estimated time of arrival for additional responding staff to help quell the riot.

It was the shortest section briefing I had ever been part of since these individuals had already been doing just what I asked before my arrival to the EOC. To a person, this was not their first rodeo (riot or EOC experience). All had plenty of riding time on this horse! The EOC personnel all had a history of crisis management and all had experience with the ICS protocols. Together, we had been involved in two prior full scale riots (one 220 man gym riot and one 800 man riot at RC-West), not to mention a fatal plane crash on grounds. In fact, they had all been "boots on the ground" at some time in their careers. They knew what the facility staff personnel were facing and used the ICS framework to get the necessary help and resources needed without missing a beat. They were experienced correctional leaders: Operations Chief, Captain T. Diaz; Logistics Chief, Captain M. Hill; Planning and Intelligence Chief, Captain D. King, and Finance Chief, H. Provencher, CDW.

Nearly 200 years of correctional service was in the EOC. I was merely directing traffic, knowing full well these adept men and women already knew what direction to go and how to get there. They were all working within their own "silo" teams reaching for the same result: control/containment of the riot. Unfortunately, any organization acting from a "silo syndrome" unknowingly has each department or function interacting primarily within that "silo" rather than with other groups across the organization or, in this case, the EOC. Which in lay terms means, we weren't necessarily communicating in unison. This may not have been an ICS postcard of perfection—working in silos—but it was absolutely what CIM did best when responding to crisis. Besides, I had confidence in a successful outcome, knowing full well the caliber of the men and women working at CIM and in the hot zone, RC-West.

Boots on the Ground

The Crisis Response Team (CRT) leader, CCI Ross. G., arrived at the EOC for direction. I was happy to see his steely-eyed face because that meant his team was at the ready to enter the facility. I motioned him over to an aerial map and told him the objective. "Commander, I need you to clear a path from the Sally Port around the southwest tower by the canteen and laundry rooms to Joshua. I need a clear path of travel for the fire trucks. I don't know if staff or inmates remain in the building. I don't know what you're gonna find, so expect the worst. Any questions?"

He had none; he nodded in agreement. His job was to figure out a way to make it happen. Tactically, the CRT for the southern region was second to none. They had a history of competent and capable members and leaders before Ross; T.J. Padilla, F. Fulk, B. Pahel, L. Neff, and C. Caldwell. Together that CRT group had collectively set the tone for excellence that subsequent teams sought to maintain. The CRT was a compilation of highly trained correctional peace officers from the local prisons; CRC, CIW, and CIM. On this night, the measure of their excellence would be tested and won!

As it happened, the CRT element on the yard first had to address the inmates locked up in the culinary. Working on the assumption that the kitchen was a hostage retrieval situation, the team quickly entered and pulled the officer from the kitchen safely, leaving the inmates locked up for the time being. During the same period, it was reported that about 150 inmates had barricaded themselves between Mariposa and the canteen/laundry room area. Complicating matters, the EOC was informed that lighting was poor in the southwest corner making an assault to clear the area far more dangerous for the staff.

Upon hearing the news, efforts to contact the Chino PD mobile command post was interrupted. Good ole "Murphy's Law" again! Our law enforcement liaison, Sergeant S. Cleland's radio battery had died. Unbeknownst to me at the time, she had wisely used her personal cell phone to maintain contact with operations and logistics chiefs. I didn't wait for what I thought was a life-threatening situation, I called my stepdaughter, a Deputy Sheriff who posted on the outside perimeter fence line on her cell phone. "Amy, I need you to get a hold of the mobile command post or your immediate supervisor. I need more light on the southwest corner by the tower."

She responded, "Okay, can I give him your number?"

"Yes, please, I need it now!" I replied. Moments passed before I got the call. I informed the sergeant about what was happening and what I needed. Not only was the Chino PD helicopter used, the sheriff's vehicles on Central Avenue trained their lights against the southwest corner, as well. CRT with assistance from unit officers on the skirmish lines used their "shock and awe" tactics to retake the corner. CRT had succeeded in clearing a path of travel for the fire crews.

****

Nothing is ever completed so neatly without some drama. First, the CRT had been hampered by facility commanders who were being overwhelmed by the sheer number of inmates being placed on the main yard. They were overcome by victims and combatants flooding out of the dorms, who were both giving up and/or being victimized. This was a legitimate concern, but not consistent with the level of threat posed by an uncontrolled fire on the yard.

We had an officer providing lethal force coverage from the tower on the yard, plus all combatants detained were in flex restraints and lying prone. It was easier to stack the yard than ignore the fire and rioting in the "no-man's land" zones. When I first became aware of the concern regarding the number of inmates being detained on the main yard, the answer to me was pretty simple. SERT Commander Guerrero asked, "Are we supposed to follow the orders of the facility commanders?"

I told him, "You and everyone else here are under my direction right now. You have them call me if they have a question and you get the job done as I've outlined."

His only reply was, "Thank you, sir."

The urgency for getting the fire trucks into the facility was foremost on my mind. All the dorms were of wood construction, like dry match sticks waiting to be lit. We had some assurance that no inmates or staff remained in the burning building, but we could not validate that until the fire was extinguished. However, the more urgent concern was that the adjacent wooden dorms still had inmates inside actively trying to ignite more fires or fighting.

CRT Commander Guerrero again entered the EOC sometime after midnight. He reported that the Chino Valley Fire District would not allow their fire fighters to enter the facility without an armed escort. I didn't want to believe what I was hearing—another delay—but it made sense. In the community, a riotous encounter must first be controlled by local law enforcement before the fire department can do their job and they would do it, only under police protection.

The CDCR policy does not allow lethal weapons inside the secure perimeter, period. It's a good policy that is in place to prevent the possibility of inmates getting their hands on weapons. I looked at the CRT commander and asked, "Does the team have side arms immediately available?"

"Yes," he responded.

I motioned at the aerial map and replied, "Only side arms and only to remain with the fire trucks for protection."

I got a "Yes sir!" as he quickly was off to get it done.

It so happened that Regional Administrator Mike Poulos had entered the EOC during the exchange. Mike was a former Crisis Response Team (CRT) member of many years. I caught his eye, as the CRT commander hurried off, he nodded in the affirmative. If I was going to second-guess any decision this was it. Unbeknownst to me, the RC-West facility electrified fence was turned off by request of the fire department. Escape was never a consideration in my *mind. Fortunately, the EOC chiefs had already armed the facility towers to provide extra gun coverage. Another routine protocol and for me a "lucky" turn of events!*

****

Everything after my exchange with the CRT commander remains a blur to me today. Calls made and received, section chief status reports; I honestly don't remember any details. Once the Joshua fire had been controlled and the units started falling to staff control, my thoughts switched to the Minimum Support Facility (MSF) which had twice the number of inmates and acreage four times the size of the RC-West facility. The MSF had only one fence line and the distance between the armed towers made escape opportunities more tenable. Simply put, we didn't have the resources to prevent any escape attempts if the MSF yard, housing over 2,600 inmates, rioted.

Fortunately, the EOC section chiefs had already prepared contingencies for such an event. A response team with newly arriving officers was assigned to "float" throughout the MSF with select CIM staff that were familiar with the logistics. Also staff coverage, boarding, transfer of inmates, medical and mental health follow up, and feeding for both staff and inmates at RC-West was already being handled by the chiefs. Truth be told, they had the harder job in the EOC and they deserve much credit for keeping CIM on task. It is important to note that most of the third watch staff that had battled throughout the night had been ordered over that shift and would reach twenty-four hours on-the-job by morning. Relief of those officers became a priority.

****

The RC-West facility was managed by Associate Warden L. Moser and Captain T. Diaz (who was working the EOC), both with over fifty years combined correctional service. The facility had Lieutenant A. Lazarus (who was acting in a limited-term capacity) as the on-site response commander and RC-Central Lieutenant E. Hernandez assisting him. Sergeants Alva, Barbon, Duarte and Lara were also on the yard that evening. All had extensive experience dealing with hostile inmate situations.

The culinary officer assigned to the facility dining room had fifteen inmates working at the time of the riot. The culinary workers were a mixture of Black, Latino, and White inmates. As the alarms sounded in all the living units, the culinary officer directed the workers to remain calm. The Hispanic inmates approached him about fear of being confronted by Sureno inmates if they didn't participate. The Officer was in harm's way but realizing the threat to his work crew he took it upon himself to shut off the lights inside the dining area so the inmate workers could not be viewed from outside. He also smartly remained in radio contact with the EOC.

Meanwhile, a seasoned female officer working the Sequoia Dorm saw the inmates begin to riot in her dorm. Any orders by her for inmates to "get down or stop" were futile. She immediately retreated back into her office and locked the door. She could hear the radio calls as the riot expanded to all the units. The inmates, seeing her in the office began to pound and kick the door to gain access. She alertly kicked out the small air conditioning unit in the office window and climbed from a chair out the window. Before escaping harm's way, she grabbed two MK-47 OC weaponry that were in the office.

As she exited the office window, she discovered that she could not exit the fire safety area between the units because the gates were locked with plant operation key locks. She then traversed amid the screams and noise in the dorms on both sides of her to the back of the unit where she freed herself into the "no-man's zone" next to Receiving and Release. She was scared by the magnitude of the incident, but who wouldn't be? To her credit, she quickly regrouped with other officers joining a skirmish line to re-establish control in the immediate area. By 10:00 p.m., nearly 100 reinforcements from local prisons and parole units began to pour into the facility. Surprisingly, in prison, 1,100-plus inmates versus 143 officers is considered a "fair fight." Its par for the course in all state prisons: We are always outnumbered, but better trained, equipped and committed.

****

Retired lieutenant Edward "Eddie" Hernandez was interviewed on December 17, 2014 regarding his on-site observations of the riot. His candid view of the drama and hands on preemptive actions was reflective of the courage and tenacity of the CIM officers and supervisors the night of the riot:

Q: *Eddie please describe your work experience with CDCR.*

A: *I had 27 years with CDCR. I worked 8 years at CRC as an officer and limited term Sergeant before promoting to a permanent sergeant position at CIM in January of 1995. I worked all posts and facilities at CIM including, SAB, Palm Hall and RC-West. I promoted to lieutenant in July of 2000. I had been a lieutenant for nine years before the riot occurred at RC-West. I retired in January of 2014.*

Q: When did you first hear about the circumstances of the riot?

A: I was working as the disciplinary officer at CIM at the time I first was informed. The captain called us in and told us about the kite that was found in Palm and the details regarding how the riot was to occur at a certain time at RC-East, Butte Hall and then spread to all the other prison facilities once staff went to assist. Basically we were told to keep our eyes and ears open and that the prison would go on modified program while the matter was investigated.

Q: The day before the RC-West riot, were you working when the East dayrooms rioted?

A: Yes, I was working an overtime as the Health Care Lieutenant when the Alpine and Butte dayrooms rioted. I responded to the radio call and saw inmates' laid out prone on the floor in Butte and Alpine lowers. The dayroom uppers (second floor) didn't go off. Pepper spray had been used to quell the fighting.

Q: Did you hear anything from staff about the cause of the fighting?

A: They just said the inmates (White and Latino inmates against Blacks) started fighting in the dayroom. I realized it was started based on what the kite had indicated—that the riot would start in Butte and go to each unit after that.

Q: So when did RC-Central dayrooms riot?

A: It was later that night, Madrone Dayroom. I responded and observed staff bringing inmates that had been pepper sprayed out of the dayroom.

Q: That evening did you have any discussion with the lieutenants and sergeants about what you were seeing now?

A: Yes. At that point, one of the sergeants made the comment that when East went off, RC-Central dayrooms were supposed to as well, but it didn't until later that night. Staff also commented that some inmates on the West yard were seen getting off their bunks and dressing but extra staff had been sent there. I made a suggestion to the supervisors that everyone was going to be cell fed, except the dayrooms which were still integrated. The races needed to be separated to avoid any problems. They agreed and the Black inmates were removed from the dayrooms and housed together in one. That was on Friday night. It kept the dayrooms from rioting at Central.

Q: *Where were you on Saturday and what role, if any, did you take before and during the riot that ensued that night?*

A: *I did a double overtime on Saturday 2nd Watch and Third Watch. I sat down with the Central sergeants Saturday morning. We talked about what happened the night before at East and Central and decided that we should create another response team for the Minimum yard since that was going to be the big problem if it goes off. What we talked about was having a team of five officers respond to Minimum. If something were to happen at West, we'd take additional S&E's and send them to West yard if there were incidents occurring simultaneously.*

Q: *Were you hearing anything from staff or inmates about tension or issues with the inmate population during the days prior to the riot?*

A: *No, there was no tension. Inmates were talking amongst each other during chow release, yelling and screaming across the tier like they normally do. We (staff) weren't hearing anything from inmates or seeing any unusual behavior.*

Q: *So where were you when the 10-33 radio call went out that RC-West needed assistance?*

A: *All day long we were waiting for something to happen. I was at East, Central and visited the West yard to see if there was any problems. I was doing paperwork at the Health Care office in Residence 2. It was a little after 8pm when I hear a radio call from West saying once the last dorm, Mariposa, was secured designated staff were to report to the front of the yard pedestrian gate to begin a search of the dorms. At that point I thought to myself, "crap I think this place is about to kick off."*

Q: *What made you think that?*

A: *I don't know it was just a gut feeling. In fact, I was on the phone with a sergeant from Central when I heard the radio call and I told him, "Hey, get everyone ready, I think it's going to happen." As soon as I said it, Control announced on the radio that a personal alarm sounded at Mariposa. At that point I left for the West yard. It took me three minutes to get to the front gate at West. On the way over, I heard calls by multiple officers on the radio of fights in the dorms.*

Q: *So it was a domino effect on all the dorms after Mariposa?*

A: *Yes, I'm still hearing chatter on the radio as I enter the facility and as I reach the yard behind the fence line…all I see is chaos. The inmates were pouring out of the housing units onto the mini-yard. Numerous inmates were armed with pipes, utilizing the pipes as weapons to swing toward other inmates. I heard the sound of glass breaking. All the dorm alarm lights were activated except for Laguna which had been closed for renovation and Angeles which housed the minimum support workers. I remember running up to Lt. Lazarus, who was the facility lieutenant and asking him what was happening and if all staff were accounted for yet. He said all the dorms went off and no accountability had been made.*

Q: *What did you do then?*

A: *At that time, I told him to call control and get everyone (staff) out the dorms and on the main yard for accountability. I radioed minimum control and told them I needed all available staff on the West yard. I heard the Watch Commander, Lt. Quiroz announce on the radio that he was initiating the Emergency Operations Center (EOC). I radioed him to contact CRC and CIW for immediate assistance too. I knew from experience we couldn't handle it without more assistance.*

Q: *Were you essentially advising and helping the West Lieutenant?*

A: *Yes, he was overwhelmed at that point, just trying to get all his staff accounted for.*

Q: *How many riots have you been involved in during your career as an officer, sergeant and lieutenant?*

A: *Maybe fifteen to twenty.*

Q: *How did the RC-West riot compare to those other riots?*

A: *It was the worst I've ever seen. I just seen all the inmates fighting or breaking things inside the dorms. The Black inmates were trying to break out of the dorms to get away. They were way outnumbered. The way the inmates looked, the wounds that were inflicted. The destruction of the dorms.*

Q: *How long do you think you and Lt. Lazarus had to stand off 1100 inmates before outside mutual aid responders from other prisons arrived?*

A: *I would say about an hour maybe an hour and a half. It seems longer when you're there. I mean at one point, we knew we were overwhelmed. But we also knew we'd have to break off (leave the skirmish lines) to* get some of the victims. If not they would have died. I remember seeing inmates carrying other inmates for medical help.

Q: Who was leading the skirmish lines?

A: I believe it was Sergeants Alva, Barbon, Matute, Duarte and Lara. I saw one Hispanic inmate just swinging what looked like a pipe at any black inmate. He was just beating the hell out of the inmate on the ground. I recall looking up at the tower and screaming at the Control officer, "Why aren't you doing anything." And he tells me "What do you want me to do?" I said "shoot something!" At the time, I thought we still had scat rounds (tear gas) in the towers so if he had had some gas, it would have calmed things down. Inmates were trying to breach the main yard gates by kicking and beating the doors. As soon as we started to move forward (skirmish lines) I remember that I did hear a shot over my head that got the inmates down. I remember hearing Officer O'Neil, one of the code responders, on the radio advising staff to "be careful, we got shots fired on the West yard." But the first shot effectively got the inmates down.

Q: So what happened with the skirmish lines when the inmates did breach the main yard gates?

A: The inmates were scattered all over the mini-yards. I believe at one point the inmates did kick out the main-yard door from Cleveland. All this stuff was happening on all the dorm mini-yards. The skirmish line officers stood their ground on the main yard, yelling for the inmates to get down. The majority were Blacks who were trying to escape. They were yelling, "You're supposed to help but you're letting us get killed." I responded, "We are trying to help, comply with the officers." Officers continued to tell them to get down on the ground. They refused, so staff fired OC and baton rounds to gain compliance.

Q: What was happening with Mariposa during this period?

A: I remember Mariposa, they didn't really have a mini-yard but they broke out of the dorms and broke into the clothing room and canteen offices next to their dorm. They started tearing down shelves to block staff from entering or clearing the area.

Q: Were you in contact with the EOC during the riot?

A: I was on my personal cell phone with Lt. Ross Guerrero.

Q: He was the Crisis Response Team (CRT) leader, what about the EOC's Operations Chief?

A: No, I think Laz (Lt. Lazarus) was maintaining contact with the EOC. We did get Sheriff's helicopter provide light coverage for about 15 minutes but the noise interfered with staff communication on the ground. I got word that an officer remained in the culinary so I told Laz I would take a team and retrieve him. He told me to hold off because the CRT was entering the yard. At which point, I went to the rear sally port and met up with Lt. Caldwell who was leading the CRT. He told me he needed a key to the culinary which I got from a skirmish line officer in front of Cleveland. My team assisted the CRT in extracting the culinary officer safely from the kitchen and the remaining fifteen inmate workers were locked back inside. Lt. Caldwell indicated that we were going to clear each area around the perimeter and place the inmates on the main yard. He requested my team's assistance on clearing the barricaded inmates in the laundry/canteen southwest corner. I took some Central response team members and assisted the CRT.

Q: What happened?

A: As we engaged the inmates staff were met with rocks and batteries. CRT utilized flash bang grenades to quell the assault and we proceeded to clear the laundry and canteen areas following CRT's tactical entry.

Q: What were you seeing and feeling at this point?

A: Mass destruction and evilness. I was amazed and overwhelmed...but the blood...I started seeing blood all over the place. At this point, Joshua which had been smoldering for about 45 minutes was now on fire.

Q: As the Incident Commander, I never received confirmation regarding the status of staff or inmate accountability in Joshua. Was this a concern discussed between you and Lt. Lazarus at any time when the fire started?

A: Yes, when I first got on the yard, I told Laz we needed all the staff up front (on the main yard) to account for them and establish a skirmish line. I didn't know till later on about the officer in the culinary.

Q: Were you aware that officers initially responding to Mariposa had gone back inside to retrieve an officer that was trapped inside and another officer in Cleveland or Otay had to kick out an air conditioner to escape from the staff office as inmates were trying to breach the office door?

A: No, I didn't know about the Mariposa officer but I did know about the officer that I think was working in the dorm next to Cleveland. She told me she had to kick the air conditioner out the window and got to the back side of the dorm before she made it to the main yard. When I talked to her she was shaking and had a cut on her forehead from the dorm window. I told her to go to medical to get it checked out she said, "No, I'm going to stay here." I told her just to go and get it checked anyway.

Q: What else did you see?

A: We cleared the canteen, laundry, and began clearing the dorms. Lancaster staff arrived after 2 and a half hours. For me it felt like time was standing still. At the time, were thinking, Ok, were dealing with Mariposa but what if the other side breaches the main yard. We don't have anyone watching our backs, possibly take us hostage. You're tired and looking for staff to help and take over. It's hard to explain, it just seems like it took forever for assistance to get there.

Q: What do you think got the staff through it? For example, why was that female officer willing to stay there after narrowly escaping from the dorm and being injured?

A: At that point, you just want to take care of one another. You know, you don't want to leave anyone behind and don't want to give up...at least, that was what I was thinking to myself. I know that afterwards a lot of people were scared. I noticed, after four hours into the riot, staff were coming in from off-duty...that is just dedication and drive. That is comradery...you know, I want to be there for my brothers and sisters.

Q: When or did it ever come to your mind that you finally had the advantage?

A: Well it never came to my mind that we had the advantage. But I felt we had it under control once we cleared the first three housing units. But we didn't have the advantage because we still had about 800 inmates running around the other dorms and mini-yards. Once we had those individuals in flex-cuffs and on the ground on the main yard we had some control. That was about 2:00AM. That was when the first bus arrived to move inmates off the yard. At one point we had to stop bringing inmates on the yard because we had nowhere to put them.

Q: Anything you think people need to know about these kind of major events?

A: Just watch your back. The one thing we had going for us was training about a year or two prior we had started hands-on training...reality *based training on a monthly basis at each facility and on the range. At first I kind of thought it was a waste of time. But as I watched it, I realized that it was helping staff understand a tactical response to situations. Before staff would just all run into an incident without any tactical plan. I think the training kept staff from getting seriously injured. I know without this training if we had a riot like this five or six years prior, some staff would have been seriously injured, held hostage or killed. If you train for it, it's probably going to happen...you don't ask, "Why are we doing this."*

Q: *What made the training effective?*

A: *Basically, if you train for it (scenarios)...hands on training...reality based training...if you made a mistake they'd stop you and show you what you're doing wrong in a skirmish line advance, extraction and/ or recovery situation. You'd talk about it and they'd always film it to show the class later. Sometimes they'd film the training take place on the facilities too.*

Q: *Who was responsible for creating this training environment for staff?*

A: *I give kudos to the In-Service Training (IST) team. Lt. Neff at the time, Lt. Caldwell was a housing lieutenant but also an IST training instructor. The administration...when IST went to Warden Poulos, along with yourself you both approved and supported the training. I give kudos to RC-Central staff who took the reality based training seriously because that facility had the most incidents at CIM...a lot of those staff responded to West that night.. Officers O'Neil, Bonfil, Sgt. Lopez. Also Lt. Lazarus at the West yard and the CRT. I give kudos to the EOC for letting us do what we needed to do on the yard and getting us help. They didn't tie our hands like they had in the past. Sometimes you have to think outside the box and do things differently. Sometimes it works sometimes it doesn't. We got it done that night and no one was injured or killed.*

Q: *Any final thoughts about the riot that night?*

A: *I was frustrated knowing that one of the response teams was cut from 8 to four earlier in the day. I don't know why that was done. Also, I do remember a lot of the inmates (Latinos) that were detained on the main yard had their property rolled up which we didn't allow them to bring. Also, most of them had jackets and shoes on which tells me they knew this was going to happen. I wasn't on the yard during chow so I can't say when all this (pre-planning) happened. But it could have been* something we missed. Staff need to be more attentive...they (inmates) were "booted and suited" but it probably wouldn't have made a difference in this situation.

Q: Eddie, I speculated and no one has refuted it...that the Sureno shot caller that happened to live in Mariposa got the word out before Saturday's evening chow that the Blacks would be assaulted. That may have been what you were observing that night. How did you feel after the riot?

A: I had been up twenty-three hours by the time I left the prison. I had done a sixteen the day before. Yeah, I was burnt out...but it was adrenalin that kept me up, I wasn't tired. I was still in control but as soon as I went home and jumped in the shower and laid down...that's when it hit me...when I noticed my arms and hands were shaking. But I remembered my son, he had only been in the department two years. I thought about my son, who was there that night.

Q: Your son was at West that night?

A: Yes, he was on the skirmish line...he was part of the secondary response team. He came from Central and also was on a sixteen hour shift that turned to twenty-three hours too. I called him at home and asked, "Are you ok son?" He said, "I was scared as fuck dad." I told him, "So was I." Maybe, I didn't react during the riot because my mind was focused on protecting staff and getting our job done. Someone had to take control. I told Laz, Ok, this is yours but stay with me. But at some point he had to go his own way. Which he did. When CRT came in I figured Laz must have it so I assisted them. When talking with the staff afterwards they all were saying, "That was the worst we had ever seen." Knowing later on it was one of the worst in CDC history. At the time, we didn't know it. We were just trying to get things under control and send staff home safely.

****

Weeks later, during a debriefing with local law enforcement personnel from the various mutual aid agencies, the question of our tactical assault plan was brought up. How was staff able to deal with the sheer number of inmates rioting? Three points were shared. First, we had previously bolted down all the bunks after the RC-West 2006 riot so that inmates could no longer move them to blockade the doors from staff gaining entrance. Secondly, all the dorms had been individually fenced off as a fire safety measure required by the Fire Marshall. The fencing was a bone of contention among some staff since it effectively locked staff up within each dorm slowing their egress during emergencies. However, during the riot, the fencing prevented the inmates from charging the yard indiscriminately and seriously slowed their movements between the dorms. Thirdly, the officer skirmish lines fluctuated according to the need for extracting victims and combatants, deployment of less lethal force options, and support for the Crisis Response Team element. It was a constantly moving line of committed LEOs amid chaos taking one bite of the rebellious elephant at a time.

As Lt. Hernandez aptly stated, tactics in the facility (field of engagement) should never be made by the EOC. This is the function of field commanders. They have to be able to change course and take action given the situation. Akin to fighters in Mixed Martial Arts, you might get good advice and training, but when the fight starts, you're on your own and have to fight according to the opponent's weakness or strengths. The EOC staff realized that some of the best trained staff and supervisors were assigned the yard that night. It was just a matter of letting them get tactical advantage and supporting their needs. Later in the year, officers, sergeants, lieutenants, nurses, doctors and plant operations staff that played a significant role on-site at the RC-West facility riot, received medals of valor and commendation for their courageous efforts.

****

In the meantime, the EOC was now tasked with quickly identifying and housing 1,100 inmates from the RC-West—an enormous task for the recovery phase of the EOC. The RC-West facility dorms were in complete shambles and unlivable after the riot. Inmates remained scattered in large and small holding cells and cement yard enclosures throughout the prison facility's three reception centers. Staff was also gearing up for the possibility of a bigger fight with as many as 2,700 inmates on the MSF yard. The EOC would remain active for well over one week.

Events Preceding the RC-West Riot

On **Thursday, May 21, 2009**, at approximately 1110 hours, a racial riot occurred at the RC-Central facility, main yard. The active participants consisted of 43 Hispanics and 3 White inmates who were attacked by 21 Black inmates. According to inmate witnesses and staff reports, the attack was unexpected and appeared to be an organized assault. Only minor injuries resulted from the skirmish.[63]

An investigation later determined that the Black inmates attacked the Southern Hispanic inmates due to a verbal confrontation between members of the "Black P-Stones" (BPS), a Piru street gang set and members of "Eighteen Street", a well-established southern Hispanic street gang. The Los Angeles County Sheriff's Department confirmed the racial street war between BPS and 18th has been ongoing for several years and had caused problems in the community and county jails.[64]

On **August 5, 2009**, an anonymous inmate note ("kite") was sent via institutional mail to the Appeals Coordinator's Office. The kite revealed that *"...a big riot is going to jump off. Us Homies on the Blacks Friday, all day rooms are to jump off on the East Yard and the Yard as well if we get the yard..."* Investigative Services Unit (ISU) staff could not confirm the validity of the kite via interviews with inmates and staff observations on the yard did not suggest any racial tension to confirm the kite's message. However, the anonymous kite would later prove to be accurate.

On **August 6, 2009**, during a routine cell search at Reception Center Central (RCC), staff discovered another unsigned inmate kite in the cell of an inmate, who was later validated as an associate of the Mexican Mafia (EME) Prison Gang. The kite stated, in part:

> *"P & Mesa*[65]*...alright homies I would like to share the latest mail that came through the east yard mesa, it was from the Pilli* (EME Leader or recognized shot caller) *himself.*[66] *I've seen it with my own eyes. It was regarding on the incident* (referring to the May 21, 2009 riot at RC-Central) *that happened here in central with the tintos* (pejorative term for Blacks).

> *Last week a homie came out of Birch* (RC-Central) *that's were the Pilli's are and the homie had two amapils* (Aztec/ Mayan term for prison notes) *giving us instructions on how to go about this. He put the vatos* (slang for dudes) *on the verde* (approval for assault "green" light), *he gave us two days to pick, he also told us that it was our duties to let all yards know so we started writing and started sending the* [word] *out. So they should be in rout* [en route]. *I know that this is a very serious matter. I would never. I*

127

would never misjudge you. I know that is hard to make a call especially without any paper confirm.

But I feel that is my job to let you know since I was a team player myself in the East Yard (RC-East). *Okay, when they come out to yard. So the East would go off first and everybody else will follow suit. I'm sure that we will know when this is taking place. Every yard and dayrooms are to follow suit. The Pilli said no questions ask.*

My avise to you maybe you should let a firme camarada (referring to an EME associate) *somebody that you trust so that nothing starts leaking. The only one's that know about this is the meseros* ("table members"- a reference to RC-East "shot callers" for the EME) *in the East. We were and are keeping this in the down low. We will let the homies know a day before or maybe that same day, but regardless the house will rock.*

I left the East Monday morning and everything that I'm telling still stands to my knowledge that's why I'm saying that we should play it by ear and have some solid as homies on stand by. Well homies this is just my advise at the same time that how the East is doing it & also that's how them amapils where written. I'm hoping that this amapil is well received & all understand. So for know I will exit just like enter with my upmost respect and love to you & those with you..."

The kite described, in detail, the plan to assault Black inmates throughout the California Institution for Men (CIM) facilities numbering approximately 5,600 inmates at the time. The inmate kite was considered by staff to be highly unusual given the amount of information it contained. The kite described where, when, why, and how the assault would take place. The prison was "locked down" and appropriate security measures were initiated to identify potential suspects and prevent any disturbance. Inevitably, all the preemptive measures failed to stop the plan.[67]

Staff confirmed that Butte Low at RCE was scheduled for yard the following day. Coupled with the previously discovered inmate kite, the management team elected to place the institution on "Modified Program" (confinement to cell and/or dormitory, no yard privileges or visiting) pending further investigation. In addition, notification to Division of Adult Institution administrative staff in Sacramento was completed. Interviews and searches of the entire prison were initiated.

On **August 7, 2009**, at 1418 hours, a riot erupted in **Alpine and Butte Hall** dayrooms between Black and Hispanic general population inmates at **RC-East**. Facility staff was deployed and quickly quelled the rioting inmates. The information identified in the August 5th and 6th kites that indicated the disturbance would start at RCE, had been proven to be true. Since inmates at RC-East were prohibited from using the main yard, the disturbance in the dayrooms were isolated and easier to stop.

On the same day, at 2140 hours, a riot erupted in the **Madrone Hall dayroom** at **RC-Central** between Black and Hispanic General Population Inmates. Staff was able to quickly quell the disturbance. Before the other dorms in RC-Central had an opportunity to clash, the watch commander removed the Black inmates from the dayrooms at RCC.[68]

The CIM management team assigned additional officers to the RC-West and MSF facility to provide extra security. Facility searches and interviews continued throughout the day to determine the volatility of the inmate population. During a search of the RC-West **Mariposa Housing Unit** on August 7, 2009, two inmate manufactured weapons made of flat metal stock were found in the trashcans.

Management, supervisors, and line staff were primarily concerned about the MSF and RC-West facility since the bulk of the prison population (about 3,700 inmates) were housed in dormitory settings. Despite the best efforts of all concerned, the RC-West riot had already been pre-determined by EME sympathizing Surenos and White Skinhead inmates. The circumstances amounted to an "observe, identify, and respond" situation for correctional staff.

Additional patrol teams had been assigned to the RC-West and MSF facility after the initial riots at RC-East and RC-Central had occurred.[69] A total of forty-three correctional officers and supervisors were on duty at RC-West during the third watch evening shift. The RC-West and MSF facility had undergone unit-by-unit searches and interviews had been conducted during the day, but no additional contraband and/or information was revealed to suggest tension on the yards existed. This was a troubling fact that management couldn't get its head around until after the riot, realizing the tactics used by the EME in this riot had even kept the inmate population in the dark.

An ethnic breakdown of the housing units at RC-West reflected that they were ethnically balance and integrated commensurate to the overall makeup of the facility. Hispanics made up 40 percent of the RCW population, Whites 29 percent, and Blacks 27 percent with the remaining 4 percent other ethnic races (Asian, Native American and Middle Eastern descent). Regardless, Black inmates were outnumbered nearly seven to three in all the housing units.

Riot Chronology

On **Friday, August 8, 2009**, the evening meal at RCW was "control released" (one dorm at a time) to keep the flow of inmate movement to a minimum. At approximately, 2030 hours (8:30 p.m.), the last dorm fed was returning to **Mariposa Hall**. Upon the last inmate entering the dorm, the expectation by staff was that all inmates would retire to their bunks and disrobe (remove pants, shirts, and shoes) to await continued searches. The Hispanic and White inmates, who made up nearly 70 percent of the RCW population, had a different plan:

One of the officers assigned to Mariposa Hall observed multiple inmates begin to fight at approximately 2030 hours. She sounded her personal alarm and yelled for the inmates to "get down." Responding staff formed a skirmish line outside the door and observed multiple inmates fighting throughout the dorm. They used chemical agents in an attempt to quell the fighting, but to no avail. Responders observed the other officer in the dorm office, and tactically entered the unit and extracted the officer to safety.[70]

Within thirty seconds of the first alarm in the Mariposa housing unit, alarms sounded in all seven occupied housing units. (One housing unit, Laguna, was unoccupied due to a fire sprinkler retrofit.) The riot quickly escalated. The attacking Hispanic and White inmates utilized weapons of opportunity such as broom handles, metal window frames, plumbing pipe fixtures, and shards of broken glass to attack the black inmates. Hispanic and White inmates used fire extinguishers, pipes, and other items to breach the secured areas within the affected housing units, the laundry, and the canteen. The Hispanic and White inmates secured doors with tied sheets or knocked off the door handles to prevent the Black inmates from leaving. Although, Black inmates tried to protect themselves, they were clearly outmanned and received the brunt of the injuries.

At this time, Code II and Code III responders were requested by RC-West Control.[71] Soon thereafter, the initial responders began forming skirmish lines in front of the units to contain the inmates to the housing units and the Fire Refuge Areas (FRA), also known as "mini-yards" that are located around each unit. Black inmates were initially trapped in the locked units and had to force open steel windows and kick out the walls of the units to escape. Staff began retrieval of injured Black inmates as the Blacks escaped from the housing units amid unrelenting assaults by Hispanic and White inmates.

Requests for assistance were made by the watch commander in accordance with established procedures to fire, police, and ambulance mutual aid responders. The time-line for actions to control, contain, and secure the RCW facility was as follows:

2040 to 2050 hours: As inmates exited the buildings and the number of inmates grew on the main yard, some inmates began climbing on rooftops and throwing items at responding staff from behind the unit fences. In response, the skirmish lines fell back from the roadways in front of the housing units to form one continuous line in front of RCW Control. This enabled staff to monitor the situation, and maintain security of the administration area while awaiting further assistance.

2040 to 2055 hours: The Emergency Operations Center (EOC) is activated by the watch commander who assumes the incident commander (IC) position.[72] Mutual Aid responders begin to arrive: Ontario Police Department (OPD), Chino Police Department (CPD), San Bernardino Sheriff's Department (SBSD), and the Chino Valley Independent Fire Department (CVIFD). The Medical Triage and the CPD Mobile Command Center is established in the CIM Visiting Parking Lot.[73] The IC activates the Crisis Response Team (CRT) and requests any available staff from local prison watch Commanders.[74] Sheriff's Deputies and OPD patrol vehicles set an outside perimeter to the CIM prison.

During this period of the riot, the Incident Commander (IC) learned that one correctional officer and nineteen inmates remained in the culinary in a secured area. The IC maintained radio contact with the officer who advised him that he was not in imminent danger as the inmates in the culinary were compliant.

The EOC is notified that inmates have set fire to the Joshua housing unit. Due to the violence, fire crews cannot enter the facility until sufficient control and containment can be achieved in the area.

2110 to 2150 hours: The associate director arrives to the institution and contacts headquarters staff to declare a State of Emergency at CIM. Additional managers arrive and begin to coordinate EOC functions.[75] The EOC initiates Staff Accountability procedures. The chief deputy warden assumes the duties of the IC.[76]

The IC directs the CRT commander to establish a tactical plan to clear a path of travel from the RCW Sally Port to the west side inside perimeter to allow for the safe entry of fire personnel and apparatus. The CRT mission was three-fold: retrieve the trapped officer in the culinary; clear a path and provide security for the fire personnel and equipment; and clear the remaining housing units.

Approximately eighty officers arrive from various locations to the RC-West facility. They are logged in and assigned to various locations on the yard, triage, and holding areas as the riot continues unabated. Officers continue "cover-contact" retrieval of injured Black inmates from the FRAs.

At 2130 hours, all facilities institutional counts clear except RC-West.[77]

Media Staging Area:

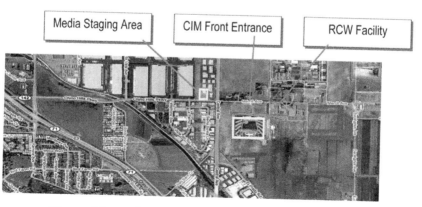

The public information officer assembles media off Central Avenue in a business park across the street from the prison. The media are able to view RCW from the location. National, state, and International television and radio news stations are also present.

Newspapers:	Radio Stations:	Television Stations:
Associated Press	National Public Radio	KCBS Channel 2, Los Angeles
Chino Champion	KPFK Radio, Los Angeles	KNBC Channel 4, Los Angeles
Inland Valley Daily Bulletin		KTLA, Channel 5, Los Angeles
La Opinion		KABC, Channel 7, Los Angeles
Los Angeles Times		FOX, Channel 11, Los Angeles
New York Times		Univision KNBX Channel 34
Orange County Register		CNN (Casper News)
Press Enterprise		German TV
San Bernardino Sun		
Independent (United Kingdom)		

Other:
Canada Council

2150 to 2300 hours: All the RC-West Towers are posted with officers.[78] Upon arrival of the Crisis Response Team (CRT), they tactically entered the culinary area and safely removed the officer without incident.[79]

At 2250 hours: The RCW Library and Chapel areas are cleared by CRT.

The EOC is informed that approximately 300 inmates have barricaded themselves in the clothing room and canteen area which is located in the southwest corner of RCW. Inmates are throwing objects at staff and taunting them to respond.

EOC is advised that there is poor lighting at the RCW southwest corner. IC contacts sheriff's personnel to assist with lighting for the corner. SBSD Helicopter and Patrol Vehicles shine lights on the RCW southwest corner.

At 2257 hours: The clothing room and canteen area is cleared by skirmish Line elements and CRT.

At 2325 hours: The EOC grants approval for the de-energizing of the west side lethal electrified fence upon request of the CVIFD.

2300 to 2358 hours: The DOC is activated at 2300 hours. The Mariposa Housing Unit staff office is reported to be on fire. At 2351 hours, the CRT secures Mariposa.

The CRTs from R.J. Donovan State Prison and California State Prison, Lancaster, arrive and are activated by the EOC.

The DOC and EOC coordinate the activation of a secure adult unit at neighboring Heman G. Stark

Facility. The EOC directs movement of 200 mattresses, 1000 "fish kits" and 500 bedrolls sent to Stark.[80]

0005-0200 hours: CVIFD enters RCW yard to extinguish the fire in the Joshua Dormitory.

Fifty-four inmates are transported to outside hospitals. Surrendering Black inmates are placed in the medical hub holding cells. White and Hispanic inmates are placed in flex-cuffs and staged on the yard in front of the culinary.

0040 hours: Maintenance staff cut off gas in Joshua Dormitory. The Otay and Mariposa housing units are cleared by CRT. CSP-LAC CRT arrives on grounds to assist tactical plan. The first transportation bus arrives at RCW at 0130 hours.

CIM chief medical officer requests additional medical support staff from sister institutions (CRC and CIW).

0200 to 0500 hours: All Southern California prisons are placed on lockdown status by the DOC. Inmate visiting is cancelled statewide.

A statewide conference call with all administrative officers of the day is made to discuss staffing, housing, and transportation needs. The incident commander, warden, and associate director share critical information with DOC, BIR, and HQ.

Joshua Dorm fire is extinguished by CVIFD.

Inmates begin to be moved to RCC and the RCC yard for temporary housing.

EOC completes a tactical assault plan for Laguna, Sequoia, and Cleveland Dorms.

Borrego and Laguna are cleared by CRT.

EOC completes a contingency plan for the CIM-MSF. Intelligence received that they may be next to riot.

0500 to 0938 hours: Angeles, Sequoia, and Cleveland are cleared by CRT.

Cal Fire serves 500 staff breakfasts at 0725 hours.

0756 hours: EOC reports that all dormitories have been secured. Remaining inmate combatants are controlled on the yard or placed in Medical Hub Tanks. All inmates awaiting transfer to housing at RC-Central, RC-East, HGS, other prisons or the RC-Central yard.

CIM medical team demobilizes the RC-West Triage areas.

0830 hours: The CVIFD, SBSD, and OPD demobilize the Visitor Center Parking areas.

0938 hours: On August 10, 2009, the CPD demobilizes the Mobil Command Post.

Recovery Phase

On **Sunday, August 9, 2009**, the Emergency Operations Center, headed by CDW C. Tampkins, began the Recovery Phase at the conclusion of the inmate containment and securing of the RCW dormitories. The assessment for alternate housing locations at other institutions was an immediate priority. As soon as bed vacancies were identified, inmates were transported to those locations. Alternative institutions identified to relocate and re-house inmates included the California Rehabilitation Center (CRC), the Correctional Training Facility (CTF), Calipatria State Prison (CSP), and the Heman G. Stark YCF.

Inmates continued to be transferred throughout the following Monday and Tuesday, August 10th and 11th, 2009. On Tuesday, August 11th, all inmates temporarily confined in outside areas were appropriately housed, leaving only ninety-two inmates remaining inside CIM RC Central Holding Tanks. On Wednesday, August 12, 2009, all inmates displaced due to the RC-West riot had been transferred to permanent housing.[81] No staff or inmate lives were lost throughout the ordeal.[82]

Primary recovery issues also included: name verification of each inmate previously housed at RCW; appropriate medical and mental health follow up of the nearly 1,100 inmates involved in the riot; Investigation, Evidence Collection and Disciplinary Reports for submission of cases to the district attorney's office; coordinated security review and evidence collection at the MSF facility; RCW housing infrastructure damage assessments; and, lastly, coordination of continued reception center processing (Intake) that was cancelled for a brief period. All of the aforementioned was a tremendous chore and was completed with a remarkable amount of teamwork and individual sweat.[83]

On **Monday, August 17, 2009**, all inmates had been accounted for in accordance with DOC requirements.[84] Both the EOC and DOC were demobilized at 1800 hours.

CHAPTER 4

Save the strong lose the weak,
Never turning the other cheek,
Trust nobody don't be no fool,
Whatever happened to the golden rule,
We got stranded....caught in the crossfire

**Stevie Ray Vaughn & Double Trouble
"Crossfire"**

"Sweating the Small Stuff"

*A*s a peace officer, you never forget the first time you are involved in a fight. You also learn from those incidents, what not to do, what to do better, and, most certainly, what to report. I recall my friend Gabe sharing a story about an incident he was involved in. The sergeant, arriving at the scene, asked him, "What the hell happened here?"

Gabe deadpanned. "Do you want the truth or do you want to read my report?"

The sergeant paused, as he looked at Gabe, mumbling, "I'll wait for your report."

Maybe it's just human nature, wanting to be right or simply just getting it right. I was learning the job like most LEOs, only as experience and training can teach best.

I was working the morning chow line at the Unit 1 "Hotel" at CRC in 1985. The "Hotel" was a section of the original Lake Norconian Club Hotel in Norco, California, that opened for the rich and famous in 1929. The section of the hotel used as a prison was an eight-story building that sat adjacent to a hill and attached at its apex to the main hotel which served as the administration office on top of the hill. Many staff members and inmates believed that the Eagles song "Hotel California" was derived from CRC's "Hotel," but that was just local folklore with no validity to it. Although, it sure did fit the song! The "Hotel" had twelve dorms each housing 100 inmates with one officer for each dorm. I was assigned as the security and escort officer for Unit 1, with duties that included assisting the morning coverage of chow.

Inmates would be released by dorm, forming a long line in the stairwell up to the kitchen mess hall. At the entrance to the chow hall, they would show their picture identification cards (IDs) as I checked off their names. The intent was to discourage "2nds," meaning no sneaking back in line for another plate. You always knew when inmates would be encouraged to get 2nds—when the food was good. Hamburgers, sloppy Joes, and meatloaf in the evening were big feasts. In the morning, it was all about the cinnamon rolls, hash browns, and sausage links. I don't recall the menu the morning of my fight, but it must have been good because the line traversed down the hallway and stairwell past two floors!

Just my "luck" I noticed a six foot two, buffed-out, 230 pound Crip approaching the chow hall entrance. I have no doubt he saw me, as he should have every other day, checking inmate IDs before they entered. Upon reaching me in line, he ignored my request for the ID and walked on by. I called him back, but he ignored me. I wasn't worried about him because there was only one way in and one way out; he'd have to face me again. I stopped the traffic with my hand and looked into the culinary to make sure I would recognize him when he exited. What concerned me was that the next twenty or so inmates had seen what had just transpired. Would they, too, try to ignore me? I guess no one wanted to find out because, when I re-started the line, it was back to business checking ID's, until he came out, about ten minutes later.

I had been watching for him. When I saw him coming, I stopped the chow line again and took a position blocking the door path. I put my hand up and ordered him to give me his ID. He responded, "Fuck you; get out of my way," and kept walking directly toward me.

I took a step back, still blocking his path and again ordered him to stop and give up the ID.

He replied, "What the fuck are you going to do?"

So much for trying to de-escalate the situation. I threw the clipboard to the ground and moved forward as he took a swing and missed. It was too late. He couldn't get a clean shot at my head because I ducked and simultaneously bear-hugged him to the wall.

As we wrestled and rolled along the corridor wall, the fight fans in attendance (inmates in line) began to yell, "Kick his ass...fuck that mother fucker...kill him." I assumed they weren't rooting for me. I had a fairly good reputation with the convict population as a fair but firm officer. I gave the inmates respect, but I did enforce the rules. However, respect can only get you so far in prison; everything else is about power and coercion.

I could not get any advantage on this guy, he was too strong. I knew if I pulled my body away, he'd be able to swing his hammer fist down my throat. I wasn't going to let it happen! I recall my CDC "Peace Officer's Survival Creed" issued to all cadets at the academy in 1985. At the time, I thought it was a joke, but it wasn't. It was the final lesson:

> The will to live, to survive the attack, must be uppermost in every officer's mind. Fight back against the odds. Turn the tables. Get off the ground. Seize the initiative. Take the advantage. Kick. Punch. Scratch. Bite. Don't give up!
>
> You don't bleed. You don't hurt. You're going to make it. You're not just fighting for God and country; you're fighting for yourself. I. Me. To see your kids again!
>
> If your attacker knocks your teeth out, swallow them and keep punching. Don't let them waste you in some dirty, stinking tier...

Of course, this fight wasn't nearly life-threatening yet, but not wanting to lose the fight was foremost on my mind! It might seem trivial that a fight could happen over 2nds, but that wasn't the issue.

****

Food was thrown away every day because the cooks were required to make enough food to feed every inmate whether they chose to eat or not. Some leftovers would be eaten by staff and the culinary inmate workers, the rest would be dumped in the trash bins. Tray upon tray of eggs, hash browns, burgers, "SOS" (gravy and biscuits that Navy personnel refer to as Shit On a Shingle) and dinner leftovers were dumped in the garbage bins. The dumping of good food occurs every day at every prison. I have no doubt there may be better options for using perfectly good food and some prisons may have solved that problem...but that's another story.

So why fight over 2nds? The real issue was that the inmate failed to follow my directive. Good officers have to "sweat the small stuff" to keep the bigger problems from overtaking us. Enforcing simple rules sends a message about obeying the law—something convicted felons need constant reminders of in prison. The less we enforce the rules, the more inmates are likely to ignore them. This isn't an opinion, it's an observed fact!

You can traverse a facility unit-by-unit and see the difference in cleanliness, orderliness, and demeanor of the inmate population. The difference is a direct reflection of the unit officer and a reflection of the unit supervisors and management team, as well. But the cardinal rule for all inmates is they must obey a direct order. There can be no flexibility with it. It is basic "CDC 101" for the rules-of-engagement among staff and inmates. Inmates must comply with the directives of staff.

If I had let the Crip get away with ignoring my orders, there was sure to be 100 more inmates doing the same to me in rather short order. This is no exaggeration, the Hotel housed 1,200 inmates at that time. Word gets out about officers who don't enforce the rules! In my mind, it wasn't going to happen on my shift. Inmates know which staff will not be likely to monitor the rules and which will aggressively enforce the rules. I like to think I was somewhere in the middle of that pendulum.

The officer who worked Dorm 106 adjacent to the kitchen had observed the whole situation. She stood there frozen as the inmate and I did the prison "two-step" dance. There is always someone who has no business being in uniform, they despise the job, they can't enforce the rules and they are of no use to anyone when trouble arrives. And just my "luck" I was in trouble and she was my only backup.

My partner, Officer Galvan, worked Dorm 107 in the Hotel, one floor up from the culinary chow hall. He was a beefy officer monitoring traffic in the hallway by the stairwell when he heard the fight fan commotion coming from downstairs. To his credit (and my health) he came flying down the stairwell to my rescue. When he got there, we were able to turn the inmate on the wall and cuff him. The inmate resisted the escort, refusing to walk, as we bounced him off the floor and walls in the stairwell all the way to the sergeant's office.

As I held the inmate against the wall in the sergeant's office, one hand on the cuffs and the other hand gripping the hair on his head, the lieutenant walked in and bellowed, "What's going on?"

I responded, dryly, "This guy beat me up, Lieutenant."

The inmate started squirming and yelling, "I never hit him."

The lieutenant directed me to sit him down on the bench and told the inmate to "shut the fuck up or it's gonna get worse."

I smiled at the inmate telling him, "Now I get to beat you up, with my pen!" The inmate, now seething, insisted to the lieutenant that he had done nothing and that I attacked him. Fight over, at least for me.

When an inmate is charged with assaulting an officer, he is placed in Administrative Segregation (Ad-Seg) pending the disciplinary hearing process. For CRC, our Ad-Seg was located at the Chino Prison, in Palm Hall. As "luck" would have it, Gabe worked Palm Hall. We spoke the next evening and I told him about the incident. He related that a Crip had arrived from CRC and had been mouthing off and was being belligerent with staff at Receiving & Release (R&R) when he arrived. The inmate refused to comply with staff in the R&R tank, then in the main hallway enroute to "Palm." Gabe joked, "This guy had a big mouth, but he was "counseled" by staff twice before he ever got to Palm. He was quiet as a mouse when I got him in the unit!"

The Crip got the message the hard way and was no longer a management problem for staff. When he returned to CRC months later, he made a point to find me and apologize. It didn't go well for him as he approached me in the unit hallway and stated, "Officer Alvarado, I wanted to find you and apologize like a man about that incident."

I responded matter-of-factly, "You're not a man. Men don't break the law and men don't go to prison. You're an inmate. Remember that next time we meet. Now keep moving."

He just looked at me dumbfounded by my disregard for his apology and walked away. I think he was shocked by my response. Frankly, I didn't represent the badge well that day, it was unprofessional and not how I normally engaged inmates. I always regretted what came out of my mouth. At the time, I was still angry at him. Knowing if he had gotten the better of me, it would have been pretty ugly. And he had the nerve to approach me and apologize? Shame on him for thinking I was a man of character and shame on me for lacking it at the very moment when it should have mattered most. Humanity is the rare coin that once dropped in prison, is ever rarely found again.

****

Gabe probably had more violent inmate encounters during his tenure than most other officers. Some were on the record, and some were off the record. Some were investigated, but most were found wanting.

One thing Gabe could never be accused of is shying away from conflict. On the contrary, conflict followed him like a dark cloud. He was a leader among his peers, always a shining light of self-assurance and cooperation, but that dark cloud would always find him. I'd seen him in action before he joined the department. He would never start a fight—always trying to be a peacemaker, but, if the other guy wouldn't back off, he'd absolutely finish it. He shared a story, among a litany of them, about a convict that didn't "get the program" when Gabe worked RC-Central.

It was during the evening after chow and it was time for "lock-up." Inmates were returning to their cells for the night. Gabe was on the third tier checking and locking cells when he saw a Black convict talking at a cell at the end of the tier. "Let's go! Lock it up!" Gabe shouted across the tier.

The convict looked over at him, ignoring the directive and continued talking.

Gabe played off the non-response as he worked his way over to the convict. When he got closer to him, Gabe said, "Did you hear what I said? Lock it up now!"

The convict kept talking to the inmate in the cell ignoring Gabe's orders.

Gabe's tolerance was done and he walked directly to the convict saying, "Hey I'm talking to you; lock it up NOW!"

The inmate stopped talking and turned toward Gabe saying, "Don't be coming up on me!"

Here you had it; two Alpha males in prison. The convict didn't want to back down with inmates looking out from their cells, and Gabe would not back down knowing he'd already ordered this convict twice to lock up without effect.

Gabe was in the prime of his athletic life at the time of this altercation. He was bench pressing 300-plus sets and hitting the body bag and me off the ground when we'd work out. He was the bull-on-the-tier, but so was the convict. Both were thinking the same thing: get an advantage and strike first. They charged simultaneously with neither able to get a hit in or a grappling edge. The tier railing had two bars that ran horizontally with a large gap in the middle. A gap that was big enough to fall through. Both fighters, off balance, fell against the third tier railing. They both grabbed and pulled the other but neither could get control or advantage. It was serious muscling and gasping for air between the two of them. The convict tried, but was not strong enough to heave Gabe over or through the railing, and Gabe, with all his strength, was not able to put the convict on the floor. Neither realized the power of the other until that moment.

Gabe knew he was in serious trouble, but didn't consider yelling out for assistance. It never entered his mind. His instinct was to get this convict under control. Below him, the other officers working the unit floor sat at a table talking, not hearing or knowing about his dilemma.

Both Gabe and the convict knew either one or both could fall between the railing gap. They made eye contact and almost instinctively moved together in a silhouetted gorilla-grip dance to the wall. Having eluded the danger of falling off the tier, Gabe and the convict finally released each other. Both had expended all their energy, each knowing they survived. But the convict knew he had met his match and who was still in charge.

"Move down stairs NOW!" Gabe roared. The convict wanted no more and quickly walked down to the lower tier. As he followed the convict down the steps, Gabe could see the officers now looking in their direction. None had heard the scuffle, but all of them could see that Gabe was breathing heavy, and that his uniform shirt was in disarray and torn. Gabe locked the convict up without words being spoken.

"What the fuck happened?" the officers queried.

Gabe described what had occurred and then pointedly asked, "Where were you guys?" Gabe had a piercing look when he wanted the truth and this was one of those times.

The group fell silent. They knew they had fucked up. He was the leader in Madrone Hall and they had failed to watch his back. Words were never spoken again about it, but they didn't forget the lesson...you stay alert until the last inmate is in his cell.

Funny how prison culture works. Gabe never wrote the convict up. When Gabe returned to work in the unit the next day, he noticed that all the Black inmates acknowledged him with respect, obeying his directives without so much as a shrug. The inmates knew he could have done more, but had given the convict "a pass." In prison, power is everything and that power can be expressed in a variety of ways. But on the tier, it really is about who's in charge. For Madrone Hall, it was Gabe and everyone knew it.

Prison Violence

Prison violence, like Gabe's encounter on the tier or the large-scale disturbance that occurred on August 8, 2009, is not a new phenomenon within correctional institutions. There is an underlying assumption that violence is symptomatic of prison life for incarcerated felons. The characteristics attributed to prisoners are; poorly educated, drug users, and violence-prone, all the while being subjugated by correctional overseers is the common public perception. Based on these assumed traits, it is easy to surmise that brutality, then, becomes a self-fulfilling prophecy. History supports this notion.

The past few years alone have been witness to horrible major prison riots worldwide: January 4, 2012, thirty-one prisoners died in a riot in Mexico's northeastern state of Tamaulipas; February 14, 2012, 359 prisoners died in the Comayagua Prison of Honduras; February 19, 2012, forty-four prisoners died inside the Apodoca Prison in Nuevo Leon, Mexico; March 29, 2012, eighteen prisoners died in the Tegucigalpa Prison in Honduras; August 21, 2012, twenty-five prisoners at the Caracas Prison in Venezuela; and on November 10, 2012, twenty-seven prisoners died at the Colombo Prison in Sri Lanka. The heavy-handed or derelict manner of prison administration, degree of governmental support, and varied socio-cultural differences in these countries may speak volumes about the causes of the riots. But the horrific outcomes are the same for all these countries: violence begets violence.

The United States has had its own history of prison violence over the years and fortunately not as bleak as other countries: The 1959 Montana State Prison riot where three inmates led a thirty-six-hour prison takeover until the state National Guard stepped in to quell the disturbance; the 1971 Attica Correctional Facility Riot in New York, which was sparked by the death of a Black inmate and dire living conditions (inmates occupied the yard for five days until the governor ordered an attack that left ten hostages and twenty-nine inmates dead; the 1973 Oklahoma State Penitentiary riot that left three inmates dead; the 1980 New Mexico State Penitentiary riot that was mired in gruesome inmate-on-inmate violence leaving thirty-three inmates dead and twelve guards held hostage; the 1981 State Prison of Southern Michigan riot where *rebellious guards* took over the facility because of unruly inmates, a lenient warden and severe budget cuts; the 1987 US Federal Penitentiary, Atlanta, and Federal Detention Center, Louisiana riots that found Cuban "Mariel boat" refugees take 120 hostages at the two prisons which resulted in the temporary stop of deportations; and the 1993 Southern Ohio Correctional Facility riot that occurred over a ten day period on Easter, by Muslims angered over TB shots. In that riot, nine inmates and one guard were killed with forty million dollars in damages.[85]

California Riots

California, likewise, has not been exempt from riotous behavior in its prisons. As was previously discussed, on September 22, 2005, 200 inmates rioted at the CIM RC-East facility. Eight inmates were sent to local hospitals. The riot lasted approximately six to eight hours. One year later, on December 31, 2006, 800 inmates rioted at the Chino, RC-West facility, after two inmates (Black and White) began fighting and the melee quickly spread to neighboring dorms. Fighting was controlled within two to four hours. Fifty-one inmates were injured and twenty-seven inmates were sent to area hospitals, with three inmates air lifted to trauma centers.[86]

On May 20, 2011, 150 inmates on the recreation yard of the California State Prison, Sacramento (known commonly as *New Folsom*) began fighting. Six inmates were hospitalized with stab wounds. Fighting stopped after five minutes when officers fired warning shots and used pepper spray to quell the disturbance. On September 19, 2012, sixty inmates on the general population yard at New Folsom began fighting. Staff used less-than-lethal methods to restore order. Thirteen inmates were injured, one from a "blast dispersion round" the others from stab wounds.[87] More recently, on October 9, 2012, 100 Black and Latino inmates fought on the exercise yard at the Ironwood State Prison in Blythe. The fighting spread to two day rooms in other housing units. Three inmates were injured. Many more disturbances have occurred since that time throughout the state.

Major or Minor Incident

There are many examples of disturbances and violent behavior in California prisons that need to be clearly delineated for describing the difference between "riotous" or "large-scale incidents" as distinct from minor incidents and/or fights. To be clear, all fights are *violent behavior* that share common features of "riots" such as a loss of control, containment, and order. Likewise, the causes of incidents and/or fights may also be the same as those you find in a riot: poor living conditions, sudden change in administrative rules, individual or group unrest, etc. However, for this discussion, "riots" or "large-scale disturbances" will have some unique features that distinguish them from the other conflicts.

First and foremost, a riot (also called a "large-scale" or "major" disturbance) involves an extended period of unrest, generally, well beyond an hour or two. Second, riots involve a large number of inmates which result in numerous acute or deadly injuries sustained by inmates and/or staff. Third, they involve more than one or two groups. Whereas, incidents and/or fights may share one or two of the aforementioned features, riots share all those attributes.

For example, two inmates argue and become involved in a fight (or an assault) and attract other inmates to participate. This incident is normally controlled and contained within minutes after staff are alerted and respond to quell the matter. Some injuries may have resulted from the skirmish; likewise, the ruckus may have triggered many inmates to join. However, this example does not meet the definition of a riot in the context of our general discussion. A riot is not easily contained, as was the case in this example. A riot involves more than just the immediate participants (the example partially meets the criteria). Lastly, a riot can result in multiple serious injuries or death to staff and/or inmates. In the example, it is possible some injuries may have occurred; however, *span-of-time* and *number of participants* are the key dividers between claiming an event to be viewed as a riot.

There are exceptions, like the New Folsom riot in May of 2011 or the 2012 Ironwood State Prison disturbance. Staff were able to contain and control the matter within a relatively short period of time. This is probably more a testament to good custodial policing than an exception to the riot definition proposed for this discussion.

The question is; what "elements" makes a violent event a riot? If "three or more participants" fighting becomes the basis for calling an incident a riot, then CDCR is having riots on a daily basis. That might make a good argument for adding resources to reduce "riotous" events, but it lacks merit. In fact, it implies that existing staff are not capable of managing housing units without incident and/or management is failing to properly supervise and train staff in security protocols. More importantly, that simplistic definition minimizes the seriousness and impact of larger forces that influence large-scale incidents. Correctional Officers can't stop riots from occurring just like police officers can't stop crime from happening on the street. But both can minimize the likelihood if they follow proper protocols. Touring, observing, communication and documentation, to name a few.

Delineating the components of a "riot" from everyday incidents provides a clearer context for identifying factors that can contribute to and/or reduce the likelihood of prison violence. This is important for the discussion relative to the August 8, 2009 RC-West Riot because, by understanding the "drivers" of that riot, we can point criminal justice practitioners toward more definitive solutions. However, regardless of how we define riots, disturbances, or a fight, in California the rise in overall prison violence remains high.

California Dreaming

The public perception that prisons breed violence seems irrefutable. The facts support this belief: From 1989 to 1998, the Department of Corrections and Rehabilitation saw the average daily rate of Inmate Incidents rise from 4.3 in 1991 to a high of 6.7 in 1998. Recent data reflects a jump from 7.1 in 1999 to high of 9.2 in 2006. The increase in incidents corresponded with the years when CDCR saw the prison population steadily increasing to its highest number of well over 170,000.[88] Despite this history of violence, *the number of prison riots has steadily decreased o*ver the years in the United States.

Prison riots in the United States, in particular, California, remain an enigma because their declining numbers appear contrary to the customary prison violence assumptions seen worldwide. Bert Useem, esteemed Purdue sociologist who has studied prison riots for three decades, maintains that as prison populations have increased dramatically nationwide, America's correctional facilities have become noticeably less violent:

> "...The statistics bear this out: In 1972, the year after 29 prisoners and 10 guards were killed at Attica, there were more than 90 prison riots nationwide, yet by the mid-2000s, Useem writes, "prison riots had become rare." And non-riot-related violence has waned too. Between 1995 and 2008, inmate violence in New York City jails dropped 95 percent..." (*Mother Jones*, Nov/Dec. 2009)

Although, for California, the violence trend continued to remain high among individual prisoners, the rate of large scale disturbances (riots) was notably reduced. To be fair, not all scholars agree that prison violence has been reduced since no reliable data exists that accurately measures non-lethal violence across the states, nationally (Vera Institute, 2006). However, California does track inmate incidents which reflect an increase in inmate violent behavior, but no corresponding increase in the rate of riots.

You would think the reduction in California prison riots over the past ten years would be a "feather in the cap" for CDCR. It hasn't been, because the perception by all the stakeholders has been focused on violence in general as a problem. Of course, there may be a political agenda that supports the violence equation, too. Where there's a problem, there's potential for more funding and resources. However, by not delineating the difference between riots and fights, CDCR has failed to give proper credence to improved training, better equipped staff, and more effective security policies and procedures over the years. CDCR may be getting failing grades in health care delivery and unrealized rehabilitative programs, but it has consistently received very good marks when it comes to the security and safety of staff and inmates.

Causes of the RC-West Riot

Most researchers point to two primary theories in describing the causes for riots. The first is the "powder keg" theory that assumes poor prison living conditions (overcrowding, inadequate food, administration/guard brutality, etc) as the basis for "blowing up." The second popular theory is the "group conflict" where the prisoners have political conflict based on race or group dynamics among the prison subculture (Larsen, 1988). Another theory called the "state-centered theory of revolution" argues that prison riots arise from the combination of five conditions: cuts in budget that reduce amenities for inmates and increase the ratio of prisoner to staff; those cuts undermine staff morale, increase staff turnover and confrontations with inmates; inmate perceptions of conditions of confinement and/or treatment by staff are worsened; inmate ideologies foster alienation and outrage among the population; and actions by administration is viewed as arbitrary, capricious and unjust (Goldstone and Useem, 2002).

The August 8, 2009 riot at RC-West does not meet the criteria described for either the "powder keg" or "state-centered theory of revolution" regarding riots. Although, poor living conditions and nearly non-existent programming was evident at RCW, those conditions had been prevalent for well over four years (although it could be argued that the 2006 riot met the "group conflict" theory). More importantly, the "frequent flyers" status of the parole violators doing less than a month or two, made it easier for them to put up with the inconveniences. From the inmate perspective, RC-West wasn't going to be "home" so who cares about the amenities since they knew they'd be leaving *sooner-than-later*. Likewise, the issue of "overcrowding" was not easily applied to RC-West. RC-West had dayrooms that were used for T.V. and gaming tables.

Unlike at RC-East and RC-Central facilities that housed inmates in day rooms—*ugly beds*—that normally were used for T.V. and gaming excluding other inmates from access.[89]

The media and politicians used terms like "racial tension" and "overcrowding" to describe the causes of the August 8, 2009, RC-West riot. Yet, the Office of Inspector General (OIG), Special Report on the riot did not view those as principal causes:

> "...In addition to the history of significant riots at RC West, CDCR also received information from outside agencies warning against housing reception center inmates in an open dormitory setting. In a November 2007 report filed after touring one of RC West's dormitories, the former director of the Texas Department of Corrections, Wayne Scott, declared, "*The housing unit was a serious disturbance waiting to happen. If the prisoners wanted to take over the dorm, they could do so in a second and no one would know.*" In November 2008, the Office of the Inspector General (OIG) also warned that "placing inmates with histories of disruptive or assaultive behavior in an open setting where they can roam freely and where fights among inmates can quickly escalate and spread, creates a more dangerous environment for inmates and staff members."...Days before the riot, staff learned of a particular inmate group's intention to cause an institution-wide riot..." (OIG, Page 4-5).

The OIG report pointed the finger directly at the Reception Center status of the inmates (parole violators) and reception center dormitory housing practice at CIM as principle factors causing the riot. More importantly, the IG also identified the Mexican Mafia, although not by name, as instigating the riot.

Inmates at RC-West didn't complain about overcrowding but did voice concerns regarding the lack of activities on the yard. The dormitories had 198 bunks each, which originally was designed for 100 bunks each to house fire camp inmates. Double-bunking began in the 1980s when the statewide population began to increase. The RC-West had suffered two riots since that time, the last one in 2006. It is true that cuts in budget, poor staff morale, and increased confrontations between staff and inmates did occur at a more pronounced level over the years at RC-West. Moreover, it is likely those issues contributed to the rise in inmate incidents, too. But those issues were not solely limited to RC-West; they were relevant statewide in California, which begs the question: Why was CIM-RC-West more prone to riot?

The PV Crucifixion

Another theory for the cause of riots seeks to look beyond facility, operation, and administration issues and examine the "individual-level perspective" (Graeve, et al, 2007). The characteristics of the individual inmate (values, beliefs, and behaviors) are viewed to determine the potential for violence:

> "...criminologists have furnished impressive empirical support for the importation model of inmate behavior. Offenders with more extensive arrest and incarceration histories, prior involvement with gangs or security-threat groups, serious substance abuse problems, or previous use of violence were among the inmates most difficult to manage..." (Prison Rioters, Page 410).

Although, inconclusive, this theory found the following "in-prison" infractions for criminal violations as predictors of prison riots: weapon possession, theft, threatening staff, and drug possession. Also noteworthy were two social risk factors; low work skills and poor vocational history. Other variables such as: security level; celled or dorm settings; program availability; and access to yard visits and phones have significant influence on either individual or group behaviors.[90]

RC-West was housed with parole violator "frequent flyers," most of whom had returned to prison numerous times for violating conditions of parole. Most of the PVs fit the characteristics Graeve used to describe "... difficult to manage..." inmates. Even though RC-West PVs were determined by CDCR policy to be "low level" offenders, they generally met Graeve's characteristic profile of extensive arrest histories, drug abuse, and previous violent behavior. They also had limited work or vocational skills experience.

Other considerations also may have contributed to the PV culture that prevailed at RC-West. Lin, Grattet, and Petersilia have described ethnicity and gender as having a greater likelihood for incarceration of PVs. Their research revealed that minorities (Hispanic and Black) and men are more likely to be re-incarcerated. More importantly, they found that "community political punitiveness" also affects the likelihood that sex offenders and serious offenders will be violated on parole. These scholars argue, in part, that the CDCR Board of Parole Hearings labeled:

> ...*the pivotal categories of registered sex offender and serious or violent offender, which mark highly stigmatized types of parolees. When these parolees violate their conditions of supervision, they are far more likely than others to be re-imprisoned, even when holding constant other relevant factors... Failing to imprison them for new criminal behavior leaves parole board members highly vulnerable to criticism if any of these parolees subsequently should commit heinous crimes. So exercising caution with stigmatized parolees, at least in part, could be functioning as a prophylactic against potential public or political scrutiny...parolees in pivotal categories are mandatorily referred to the board for any violation behavior. Our findings show that when they come before the board, they have significantly higher chances of prison return. Thus, the board's propensity to return these parolees to prison is an extension of the increased scrutiny that they receive throughout the parole process. To a certain extent, mandatory referral leads to near-mandatory return for these parolees...*

(Predictors of Back Door Parole Decisions, 2010. Page 23-25)

The aforementioned research paints a disturbing picture of how CIM came to house "frequent flyers" at RC-West in 2009. The RC-West PVs comprised a large portion of the "stigmatized parolees" Lin, Grattet, and Petersilia describe. Parolees with a history of violence were subject to the mandatory referral to the Parole Board endemic to the parole process. These scholars suggest, and the data supports their contention, that parolees having an offender status for sex and/or violent or serious offenses are "stigmatized" or branded as undesirable. This stigmatization is both formal (mandatory referral on violations) and informal (public perception).[91]

Graeve's contention that the characteristics of inmates are the best indicators of violence cannot be easily dismissed. CDCR uses these same indicators (arrest history, gang ties, drug usage, etc) as well as others to determine appropriate levels of custody needs for inmate placement. Likewise, the argument Lin, Grattet, and Petersilia present is also persuasive regarding the "systemic" parole process which minimizes characteristics of the inmate and, instead, relies on crime status (sex, serious, and/or violent offender) designations.

The PV stigmatized offenders represented the bulk of the RC-West inmate population. When you combine violence-prone attributes with the Sureno street gang mindset which comprised nearly 40 percent of the population at RC-West, it is not hard to imagine that the Latino inmates could be predisposed to assaulting Black inmates, especially, when given the "green light" by the Mexican Mafia.

Latino inmates were marked, like the stigmata marks on the hands and feet of Jesus Christ from the crucifixion. But they were far from being saintly. They were Sureno street gang members marked with tattoos of "Sur" or "13" depicting their allegiance to the EME. It was the combination of the Sureno street gang mentality, the prison culture of race consciousness, and the Board of Parole Hearing stigmatization of PVs that made the inmate population at RC-West easy prey for manipulation by the EME. The former director of the Texas Department of Corrections, Wayne Scott and the OIG's apparent riot predictions were only half right. The RC-West housing units were not "…*a serious disturbance waiting to happen.*" On the contrary, it was the street gangs and EME that were waiting to happen. They easily orchestrated the parole violator attack on Black inmates.

CHAPTER 5

Nights in white satin, never reaching the end,
Letters I've written, never meaning to send,
Beauty I'd always missed, with these eyes before,
Just what the truth is, I can't say anymore,

The Moody Blues
"Nights in White Satin"

God's Will?

*I had been assigned to the 4B Security Housing Unit (SHU), at the
California Correctional Institution in Tehachapi for about three years
beginning in 1987. 4B SHU held major prison gang leadership; including,
but not limited to, the Mexican Mafia (EME), Aryan Brotherhood, Black
Guerrilla Family, Texas Syndicate, and Nuestra Familia. Over time, I had
earned the nickname "Dick Tracy" from the prison gang members housed in
Housing Unit (HU) 5. The name probably arose, in part, from the khaki
colored trench coat I routinely wore over my suit in the winter months and
my dark rimmed glasses.*

*Having worked in a level II prison and juvenile hall, I had no problem
engaging inmates on the yard or tiers. It was a natural tendency for me
to want to know the clientele. I recall my first tour on the SHU tier, as I
approached a window of two Aryan Brotherhood gang members, "Shorty"
Schreckengost and Billy Parrot. They looked as different as the characters in
the movie "Twins." Shorty was a small, slim-statured man and Parrot, a*

hulking, strapping Viking warrior. But Shorty was the "shot caller" in this unit and I was already aware of that important fact.

As I reached the window of the cell, Billy charged the door screaming, "WHAT THE FUCK ARE YOU LOOKING AT MOTHER FUCKER? YOU WANT SOMETHING, ASSHOLE?" He was giving me looks to kill as he pounded his fists on the steel door.

Keeping my composure, which was easy, considering I had a three-inch steel door protecting me, I calmly said, with just a hint of sarcasm, "Just touring the tier. Are you okay? Do you need help?" As I said it, I looked at Shorty, who was staring at me.

Parrot bellowed, "I don't need a fucking thing from you," as he turned his back on me.

Shorty smiled and answered, "We're good Alvarado." Shorty and I had never met, but he knew who I was. The SHU, I would soon learn, is where much is never said, but communication is king!

****

From 1987 through 1990, during my tour-of-duty in the SHU, I had documented and submitted evidence to the Criminal Activities Coordinator (CAC), our in-house prison gang investigator, to validate associates and members of nearly every prison gang's activities for the previous years. It was a team effort, thanks, in large part, to the officers involvement in developing snitches, intercepting inmate messages (kites), and/or discovering hidden contraband that revealed names, Akas, and information about the intended business of the gangs. They would provide me the information, and I would document it for future reference.

My memorandums routinely started, "On this date, Officer 'So & So' discovered gang drawings or kites outlining gang activities…" The officers appreciated that I was giving them credit for their work, and rightly so. This became a regular occurrence after a few months on the job. The staff was literally "dialed in" on most every aspect of prison gang politics or activities. Sometimes we were ahead in the game, sometimes not. The inmates knew we were watching them, but never as much as they were watching us.

For example, we were able to discern that the sudden collection of empty potato chip bags found in cells were being used to fashion plastic handles for slashing weapons. Our inmate tier tender (a drop-out of the Consolidated Crip Organization and known weapon-maker) provided a video-taped example of how to make a shank using potato chip bags. The inmate would wear a wet sock over his hand, light a chip bag to melt it and immediately roll the hot melting bag on the wet sock. Continuing the process until the potato chip bags (probably thirty or more) formed a larger cone handle shape. The inmate would then fasten a broken razor blade on the end with string removed from clothing and continue to melt potato chip bags to secure the blade to the handle. The weapon could be hidden in the rectum and not easily discoverable by metal detectors. This discovery, albeit, a critical find, was miniscule to the number of other things we didn't find. It was a constant chess match played with living pawns!

Sometime in 1988, and unbeknownst to staff, the same tier tender who helped demonstrate the potato chip weapons had passed a shank from an EME member from one cell to another cell in Unit 5. The shank had been cut out of the cell wall shelf. Staff was sure that paper clips or staples may have been used to cut the shelf steel. The cell where the shank was cut belonged to "Tablas" Castellanos. Little did I know, Tablas would be an important player for the EME twenty-two years later. (See the Hunger Strike Chapter.)

Gabriel "Sleepy" Huerta, from the EME, Tablas's former cellie, was the recipient of the shank. Sleepy's new cell partner was Nick "Niko" Velasquez, also an EME member, whose reputation as a brutal carnal (brother) was well documented. For about six months prior, our SHU population was growing and, although, Niko had been single-celled for years because of his criminal history (he was serving two life terms w/o possibility of parole) and his violent prison behavior (suspected of numerous assaults and murder), I was forced to advise him, along with some other previously single-celled inmates, to find a compatible cellie. Niko agreed and signed the cell move request form to have his EME brother "Sleepy" join him. Niko had made a grave mistake.

Unbeknownst to me, Niko had created a division between EME factions when he negotiated a truce between the Black Guerilla Family and EME while at San Quentin. It did not sit well with the more aggressive faction of EME housed at Folsom, led by Ernesto "Kilroy" Roybal and Reymundo "Bevito" Alvarez. Kilroy and Bevito were now housed at Tehachapi, in my unit with Niko. Complicating matters, on or about the time Niko had been transferred to CCI SHU, he had become a Christian. Niko was no longer involved in conducting EME business on the yard. The EME, concerned that Niko may drop out or worse "confess his sins" about the EME, devised a plan to eliminate him. Sleepy used the bone-crusher (steel cut long enough to reach bone) to stab Niko approximately thirty-four times.

There is a certain irony, albeit pathetic, to prison politics among gang members. They sometimes choose to forget or ignore the obvious transgressions of some or stated rules-of-engagement in order to meet their personal agendas. Take, for example, the tier tender, a dropout from the Consolidated Crip Organization. The EME used a Black gang member and dropout to move the bone-crusher between EME members because EME member, Bevito, allegedly disliked Niko for not supporting his call to assault Blacks while at Folsom. Yet, within a year, Bevito would also drop out of the EME. The indefinable relations and judgment process of these prison gang shot callers was both disturbing and confusing. This was the nebulous world of the deadly "gangster politics" played in prison; everything goes except when it doesn't, but only if it serves your personal interests.

The control officer heard the familiar sound of "man down" on the tier. He looked out from his observation post and saw inmates pointing from their cell windows in the direction of Niko's cell. The unit floor officer looked in the cell and observed Sleepy calmly sitting on the cement slab facing the toilet by the door. Across from him laid Niko in a pool of his own blood. He had been dead for some time. Next to Sleepy was his property neatly stacked and folded. Investigative staff surmised that once Sleepy had finished with Niko, he went about breaking up and flushing the weapon and packed his property. Sleepy then announced "man down," so he could be moved.

When Sleepy was removed from the cell, he was immediately placed in the holding cell located in the living area of the unit pending removal and interview with the investigative services personnel. He looked at the sergeant and asked, "Sarge, when do you think I can get my property back?"

His unemotional and matter-of-fact demeanor infuriated the sergeant, who responded, "Who gives a shit?"

Sleepy just smirked.

During a search of the cell, the staff discovered a letter that was written by Niko to his sister, but had not been sent out. It read, in part, "Counselor Alvarado has told me that I have to have a cellie. I know the lord is doing this for a reason and I know Jesus has set me free and this may be part of God's plan to have me share his word with my brothers. To set them free, as well."

I suspected that Niko knew he was in trouble, but his faith allowed him to accept God's will...unfortunately the EME had other plans.

The Prison Gang Equation

The politics among prison gangs inside and outside of prison have been the subject of two notable EME dropouts, "Mando" Mendoza and "Boxer" Enriquez.[92] They both discussed Niko's fallout and others like him, as a consequence of prison gang business. The EME "blood in, blood out" rule had left little room for interpretation. If the carnales (EME members) believed that someone was a potential risk, a "green light" would be quickly ordered. The risk was viewed as something as mundane as a show of weakness or failure to follow orders to something intolerable, like snitching. The problem was that whoever called the order was usually someone with stature among the carnales at a particular time and place. This was a very imprecise and, at times, cloudy pecking order that could create confusion among the ranks.

The August 8, 2009 riot was one such event. "Mondo," the EME shot caller at CIM was recognized as the leader among Surenos[93] housed in Palm Hall. But some Surenos had been questioning his status at the same time.[94] Although, at the time of the riot, there was no specific proof to support Mondo's slide from grace, it can be surmised that he had some inkling of his declining status. It is arguable that the order to assault Blacks was a convenient motive with a hidden agenda. Mondo knew that Surenos would not tolerate having been blindsided by the Blacks in the earlier May riot that occurred at RC-Central. Racial tension has always been an undercurrent of prison life.

The issue of racial tension caused by long-standing disputes between Black and Hispanic street gang members cannot be dismissed lightly. In California, Blacks represented nearly 30 percent of the incarcerated population statewide and Hispanics represented roughly 40 percent for the year 2009.[95] Not all Blacks belong to the two primary street gangs or sets (Crips and Bloods); however, those street gangs draw considerable influence among the black inmate population based on their sheer numbers. Crips and Bloods are bitter rivals in and out of prison, but in a racial disturbance with White or Hispanic inmates, they become dubious but committed fighting comrades.

Surenos wield much more influence in California prisons given their sheer numbers.[96] Although, they compete with Whites and Blacks for control of illicit drug trading within the prisons, they are quick to align with Whites against Blacks in almost every instance. However, as a matter of convenience, racial disputes are usually placed on the back-burner during prison incarceration so as not to interrupt on-going illicit crime (drug trafficking, gang communication, larceny, etc). Sureno street gang members become intermediaries to the *"mesa"* (literally meaning "table"). The mesa are shot callers within the prisons, facility units, and even cell blocks (tiers). They are usually members or recognized associates of the Mexican Mafia (EME) prison gang. Suffice to say, there is a pecking order and Surenos are at the bottom. The same pecking order generally applies to other prison gangs, as well.

California has several recognized prison gangs: Aryan Brotherhood, Black Guerilla Family, Nuestra Familia, Nazi Low Riders, Texas Syndicate, the Mexican Mafia, and two other recognized Hispanic groups Nortenos and Surenos. Other groups have also emerged during the past five to ten years that have created conflict in jails and prisons. One of them, Mara Salvatrucha (MS) is a street gang from Los Angeles, formed from first generation Salvadorians. They eventually included other Central American immigrants as well (Nicaragua, Guatemala, Panama, Honduras, and Belize). The MS had presented a growing problem for the EME since their numbers were increasing and they had no fear of reprisals in the areas they controlled. After much bloodshed, they too joined the ranks of other street gangs loyal to the EME. They started using the "MS13" logo to signify their allegiance.[97]

Much has been written about prison gangs, their creation and influence. For this discussion, only the Mexican Mafia or "EME" is of significance, since the August 8, 2009 Riot appears to have been initiated by a recognized shot caller of that gang. The approval to assault a member of another race is weighed heavily by the various gangs and must have some corresponding benefit for approval or "green light" to be granted. The racial riot that occurred on May 21, 2009 at the RC-Central facility, was ignited by what staff determined was the "final straw" of disrespect between an 18th Street gang member and BPS Blood (Piru) gang members. Inmates reported to staff that, during chow or shower release, an argument ensued that caused the tension. The shot caller for the P-Stone Bloods gave the green light for the assault and the BPS surprised the Hispanics that day. (Not all inmates on the yard were from the 18th Street gang.) Ironically, as a result of being victims of the surprise assault, the Hispanic inmates on the yard were now "disrespected," and retaliation was to be expected.

During this time period in May of 2009, validated EME member "Mondo" had been housed in RCC in the Birch Housing Unit.[98] It is suspected that the May 21, 2009, Black assault on the Hispanics, may have provided him an excuse to exercise his influence among the Sureno population. During an interview with Investigative Services Unit (ISU) staff on August 6, 2009 (two days before the riot), "Mondo" related the following when asked if he had given the green light for all Surenos to assault the Blacks:

> *"...do you think if that was the case I would tell you, what do you expect me to say...?"* (The ISU Investigator advised him that if a riot occurs he would be charged and held back from paroling on his scheduled release date Monday, August 10, 2009.) *"...I came out to talk to you as a courtesy, but if you keep me here and play games, then we can play games and go that route. At the end, you will have to explain it to administration. I don't have to explain it to nobody...all bullshit aside, if it's going to happen, I know it's your job to stop it, but sometimes you can't. If you think it's okay for a black man to beat up on a Mexican, then you got another thing coming."*

The investigator had not provided any information regarding the alleged cause of the planned assault; instead, "Mondo" revealed the basis for the assault (Blacks assaulting Mexicans), and was subsequently charged for conspiracy to incite a riot after the disturbance occurred two days later.

It was revealed to ISU staff that Mondo had asked RC-Central facility personnel why he wasn't being housed in the Palm Hall Unit (referred to as "Palmas" by Hispanic inmates) which was recognized for housing notorious prison gang shot callers. They would not provide a bed move or reason for his remaining housed in the Birch Housing Unit of RC-Central. It was surmised by staff that Mondo was insulted for not being housed in "Palmas" which had some notoriety among inmates.[99]

Adding insult to injury, just prior to the August 8, 2009 riot, another validated EME member was brought from Pelican Bay State Prison out-to-court and was moved directly to Palm Hall. This was taken as an affront to Mondo, and staff speculated that he intended to send a message to administration about his reputed power among the Hispanic inmates. This motive seemed consistent with what staff deemed to be Mondo's egotistic leadership style. He had been disrespected as a self-proclaimed EME shot caller and now would use his influence to show off his power. The August 8, 2009 Riot was his cryptic claim to fame. However, this adolescent "show of power" would only be a precursor of a more calculated action by the EME and other prison gangs in 2011.

Oh mother tell your children,
Not to do what I have done,
Spend your lives in sin and misery,
In the House of the Rising Sun...

The Animals
"House of the Rising Sun"

"OUT OF GAS"

Manuel "Manos" Sosa was a member of "La Mesa," meaning "the table," the recognized leadership board of the Nuestra Familia (NF) prison gang, in 1987, at the California Correctional Institution (CCI) in Tehachapi. He was serving an Indeterminate Security Housing Unit (SHU) term based on his prison gang status. Manos had earned his membership in the NF when he murdered another inmate on orders from the NF while serving an eighteen-month drug possession term at CIM and thereafter became a lifer. His brother Robert "Babo" Sosa was also housed at CCI. Babo was one of the original members of the Nuestra Familia and "supreme commander" in the mid-1960s. But, by 1987, Babo was inactive, having lost major influence after a power struggle with Robert "Black Bob" Vasquez. Babo was, for all practical purposes, shunned by the NF, but still too dangerous to walk the mainline (general population) and remained feared among the gang.

I was required, as a correctional counselor, to complete the Board of Prison Terms, Lifer Hearing Reports for both Sosa brothers. Part of the report required an in-depth interview regarding their views on the commitment offense and discussion on plans for demonstrating readiness to re-enter society. In the SHU, inmates serving an Indeterminate SHU Term had no program other than twenty-three hours in a cell and maybe two day a week yard-access and weekly shower time. Babo politely refused to be interviewed. When I asked him on the tier to reconsider, he just smiled and said, "It makes no difference, I'm not going anywhere. Write what you want. I don't care."

Manos was the more agreeable brother. This was his second Lifer hearing. Manos was a statue of a man, handsomely chiseled with an Aztec Warrior frame. He was articulate and well-groomed. When Manos was on the yard with other NF members, it was clear who was in charge. He had a natural charisma and sharp wit that overwhelmed most convicts. Not an easy trick to do in prison. He didn't have to use fear to influence others, but every-one knew what he was capable of. Staff observing him on the yard, clearly viewed him as the most influential of the NF mobsters. He got his nickname "Manos" (meaning "hands"), as the story goes, because of his fighting skills. When Manos got busy, "he put hands on you" is what was said on the yard. Although, I was not privy to all the NF politics prior to Manos's and Babo's arrival, there was general agreement among staff that Manos "had the keys" (control) of the NF at 4B SHU.

During our interview for the Board Report, Manos readily admitted his guilt in his commitment offense for the homicide of another inmate while housed at Chino Prison. He said he knew the consequences, if caught. At the time, he was serving about eighteen months for a drug offense. When asked why he participated in the homicide, the response had a familiar ring, "You do what you have to do in prison." Manos asked what the board wanted to see before they would give him a release date. I responded that it would probably take some time before they ever considered him, as the Board of Prison Terms would say, "...demonstrably ready to re-enter society."

I told him, "Look Mr. Sosa, until you leave the SHU, you cannot estab-lish a program; an educational or vocational curriculum of any real merit. Besides, the board needs to see you in general population (GP) engaged non-violently with other inmates and staff. You can have contact visits in GP; attend programs for drug and alcohol and religion." He listened, but said nothing.

I recall the fact that he asked about what the board looked for, but didn't put it together until months after his board appearance and subsequent denial for a parole date. Around summer of 1989, an officer poked his head in my office and stated, "Alvarado, Sosa wants to talk with you, he is scheduled for the law library today at 10:00 a.m. He asked, if you could see him then." I nodded yes. Something was different. My mind quickly raced back to our interview. I wasn't sure, but knew something wasn't right with how Sosa contacted me. Maybe he was ready to talk about his business.

****

Staff would often hear the names inmates gave to describe the staff. One officer on the Investigations Squad had a penchant for entering a cell and always finding something. Inmates called him "Cucuy" (the bogey man). Cucuy was a friend of mine, Louie C., a strapping former Marine with spider web tattoos on his elbows and buff arms revealing his days growing

165

up in the barrio of Salinas, California. He was a no-nonsense officer; polite, but firm with everyone: staff, the public, and inmates when he was working. Off duty, Cucuy was much more relaxed and engaging. At work he was all business. When it came to the prison gangs, he was equal opportunity-driven. He had no favorites and they all knew it. He went after all of them with a passion, often finding weapons and coded messages. You name it, Cucuy could find it. You could literally hear toilets flushing as he entered a unit. The inmates quickly discarded weapons or kites (notes), paraphernalia, and other contraband, as another inmate shouted, "Hay viene Cucuy!" (Here comes the bogey man!)

I could trace my "Dick Tracy" nickname partly to the detective work done that validated many of the inmate sympathizers as associates or members of the various prison gangs as well as my glasses and coat that unintentionally mimicked the look of the comic book character. In actuality, the credit really went to the officers in the unit that readily reported information that I would simply document for placement in the inmates' central files. During Classification Committee, the inmate would be surprised about the amount of information uncovered that connected him to a gang. I didn't embrace my prison nickname, especially since unit staff would tease me, asking if they could just call me "dick." I'd respond, "Sure you can, as long you don't mind me calling you one, too!" It may have stuck with inmates; thankfully, it didn't with the officers in the housing units…at least not to my face!

My Dick Tracy persona didn't work with most convict leaders. I recall trying to get Ernesto "Kilroy" Roybal to "roll over." Kilroy was one of the recognized leaders of the EME when they first became entrenched. The unit staff had been presenting me with many requests from EME members to switch yards. The inmates would claim that the yard schedule was preferable for their law library and visitor timetable. I knew better. It was a ruse to move to the same yard as "Kilroy" in order to assault him. I informed him that he was "in the hat" (meaning on the hit list), and should consider walking away from all the drama. He just laughed and told me, "I'm not worried about anything or anybody. If someone wants to bring it, bring it, I'm good where I'm at."

****

At this stage in his criminal career, Kilroy looked like a senior citizen, with receding white hair and no large muscles on his body. But he was lean and still mean! Fifteen years earlier at CIM, Gabe had an encounter with *a younger Kilroy when he was housed at Palm Hall. Gabe, just fresh out of the Marine Corp, was escorting Billy Parrot, an Aryan Brotherhood (AB) member, and Kilroy from Palm Hall down the long RC-Central corridor to an appointment. The AB and EME had a good working relationship in prison—both enemies of Blacks and NF, and both wanting to control prison drug business. Parrot and Kilroy watched a line of inmates coming from the opposite direction and Kilroy recognized one of the inmates in line. Kilroy made eye contact with Parrot.*

As was protocol, the officer escorting the line of about twenty GP inmates stopped and had the inmates face the wall to allow the Palm Hall escort to proceed. Gabe was a half-step behind his two handcuffed escorts, watching the other inmates as they stopped in line facing away from his traffic. Everything appeared to be orderly but, appearances are always deceiving in a prison.

As Gabe's escort got closer, Kilroy suddenly darted toward the line with Parrott instinctively taking off with him. Both were handcuffed behind their backs, but that didn't stop them from charging the line. Kilroy found his victim like a mountain lion scatters a herd of deer, knocking down his prey and kicking him in the head and body as Parrot joined the assault. Gabe reacted to the charge one step behind and, having played high school football, he instinctively charged Kilroy going for the tackle. Gabe hit him solid in the back, chest first, only to bounce off him. Recalling the event, Gabe said, "Man, he didn't even know I hit him…it felt like I had hit a granite wall. That guy was solid!" After, the cavalry (officer backup) arrived, Kilroy and Parrot stopped the assault, barely breathing heavy and calm as kittens. Gabe told Kilroy later, "Did you know that I tried to tackle you, but I just bounced off your body?" Kilroy said he didn't know it and apologized if Gabe was hurt. At that moment, the only thing hurting Gabe was his ego!

****

Fifteen years later, Kilroy's attitude remained stronger than his body. He knew what I was after and he didn't care. This was his world and he had less than a year to serve to parole. For convicts, a year or so to serve was just another "cup of coffee and a wake-up call." His cellie, however, did roll over while out to court at CIM! Reymundo "Bevito" Alvarez ran out of gas and was debriefed by one of the most celebrated prison gang investigators in the state, Lieutenant "Leo" Years later, I had the privilege of working with Leo at CRC. We were both facility captains. Obviously, not an opportune moment to be a gangster at CRC. Tehachapi may have had the "Cucuy" but CIM and CRC was visited by the "Chupacabra"[100] of crime fighting!

Leo was as tenacious as "Cucuy," but had two distinct advantages. He had a higher rank and he was at CIM. The rank gave him more access, clout, and opportunity; he could direct staff and inmates more fluidly than an officer. More importantly, working at CIM gave him a cornucopia of convicts and information to trove. Since nearly 60 percent of all convicted felons throughout the state originated from Southern California, CIM's Reception Center was ripe for street and prison gang intelligence-gathering given the sheer number of gang members arriving daily. Likewise, the prison gang shot callers arriving for court cases were routinely housed at the CIM Palm Hall "Palmas." Leo didn't limit himself to just the prison business of gangs, he was adept at connecting the street business with the nefarious activities of the EME, AB, and high-powered Crips and Bloods. His prison gang knowledge base was so vast, law enforcement personnel around the state for many years relied on him as the CDCR gang expert to contact for information about prison activities.

****

"Joker" Mendoza of the NF was another convict I couldn't convince to call it quits. Joker was rightly named because of his penchant for always joking around with people. He was no joke having committed murder to get into prison and also committing murder in prison on behalf of the NF. He was one of the NF members who were suspected in the death of Rudy "Cheyenne" Cardenas, an original EME member and leader. In the movie, "American Me" one of the only parts of Cheyenne's murder the producers got right was that it did occur at the Chino Prison. The EME didn't kill Cheyenne, the NF did and Joker was believed to be one of the assailants.

I recall, after working the 4B SHU Facility, H.U. 5 for about six months, I had scheduled Joker for Institutional Classification Committee (ICC). Inmates were seen by ICC routinely every six months and annually for program review. The chief deputy warden, associate warden, facility program administrator (captain) would be present with me, the counselor, and my boss, the supervising counselor, was also present. I was at the bottom of the pecking order. Joker, in restraints, was escorted into the little housing unit office, crammed with the committee members and me sitting around a small table.

As I started to introduce the committee, and asked him to identify himself, he interrupted, looking at me. "Who are you? I've never seen you on the tier."

I responded, knowing he was purposely lying to the committee, "You don't remember talking to me on the tier last week or in this office a month ago?"

He looked at me with a real serious glance, and said, "You know what, Alvarado, you don't fool me, you're just another Mexican in a JC Penney suit, that's all you are!"

The committee broke out laughing; they all knew he was joking at my expense. I smiled, telling Joker, "Okay, now, you've done it. I'm going to have to write you up for lying to the committee and disrespecting my clothes!" Nothing came of the exchange and Joker knew I was just returning the verbal jabs. I ran into him two years later on the GP yard, he had run out of gas, too! No Joke!

****

About six months prior to Manos's request to see me, I had gotten the leader of the Texas Syndicate (TS), "Pajarito" to drop out. Pajarito, like most of the TS members, was a tough and stoic convict. Truth be told, the TS members worshiped him like a god. The stories of the TS always being outnumbered on the yards and refusing to take sides with either the NF or EME were almost legend. While at Folsom and San Quentin, the TS bravely went to the yard outnumbered and held their own so much so that the other groups left them alone. Those TS members that did take sides with the NF or EME were "no good" in Pajarito's eyes and no longer welcomed back to the TS.

I recall in 1988, receiving word that the EME was planning to assault the TS members. My housing unit had only four of them, including Pajarito. They would be outnumbered three to one if they went to exercise. When he was brought to committee, I informed him about our concerns for his safety and he calmly stated, "I want to go to yard; I have no problem with it."

Every TS member that followed him to committee said the same thing. The committee wisely created a separate yard for the TS. What changed for Pajarito was his inability to have contact visits. His family could only visit him through glass and speak on a phone. He had spent nearly ten years in lock up and was tired of it. It disturbed him to no end; he wanted conjugal visits with his family and wife. He was ready to give up the TS. He almost whispered the first words, "Alvarado, I'm out of gas..." When he "rolled over" (dropped out of the TS), within one week, all of the last remaining TS

members did, too. It was an emotional event to "roll over" for gang member.
In fact, two of the TS members cried like babies when they were interviewe.
about the gang debriefing process. It was like losing a valued family membe.
or a lost love. Except the "loved one" in this case, was a cunning, narcissisti.
murderous prison gang.

****

I walked into the rotunda adjacent to Unit 5 where Manos was sittin.
The rotunda was a converted chow hall dining room with steel holding ce.
routinely called "cages" by staff. I walked past Manos, saying nothing an.
looking straight ahead, continuing to the program administrator's office.
wanted him to think I was in no rush to see him and that his request to s.
me was insignificant. After about ten minutes sipping coffee, I walked ba.
to the holding cell. "Mr. Sosa, did you need to speak with me?"

"Yeah, Mr. Alvarado. Listen I'm done."

I stood there silent looking at him, and then asked, "Done with what?"

Manos responded, "I'm out of gas. I want out."

I sternly looked at him and stated, "Are you sure? Do you understand t.
process and consequences?"

Inside my mind, I was ecstatic. This was the highest ranking Nuest.
Familia Mesa leader at 4B SHU who had the history of the NF and curre.
prison and street intelligence. But I wanted to appear disinterested. I did.
want to make him feel vulnerable or worse, suspect he was being played. As.
convict, he thought like one. It was his only world view and I was essential.
his only trusted means to get out of SHU.

Manos replied, "Si mon, I'm sure. I want a program and bone ya.
(conjugal) visits."

Again, keeping the moment uneventful, I stated, "Look, I think you ne.
to think this over. If you're serious, you need to write your whole life sto.
everything you know, in detail."

I knew Manos's cellie was out to court and was expected back in t.
coming week. I reminded him of that, and said, "I'll have the officer gi.
you some paper, if you decide to go through with it, then get at me. You ok.
with that?"

He nodded his head in the affirmative, saying nothing more. About a week later, I received about twenty pages front and back of his detailed story. Manos had truly run out of gas. He was later debriefed by the criminal gang coordinator for the prison and released not long after to the mainline as an NF dropout.

Some EME dropouts in general population remained suspicious of him; other NF dropouts looked up to him. About a month after his release, I inquired with the IVB general population sergeant about Manos's transition. He responded, "That guy may be serious about walking away, but he's still running things."

I asked him, "What makes you think so?"

He replied, "Just the way he carries himself on the yard, always followed by three or four dudes watching his back. Besides, he never goes to canteen for a draw, but his cell is stacked with food and stuff given to him. You know how they do it."

However Manos was perceived, it was clear that he remained a leader on the yard. It was his character.

The Street Gang Connection

Pajarito's, Bevito's, Joker's, and Manos's defection from the Texas Syndicate, EME and Nuestra Familia prison gangs have been duplicated many times over by other validated prison gang members. That's good news. Unfortunately, just as many hardcore street gang members are readily available to take their place in the pecking order. However, stories of prison gang members "running out of gas" have been a spark of hope to some street gang members who are questioning their own lives.

Most hardcore gang members live a circular journey. They're going nowhere fast, but taking a lifetime to get there. They fail to recognize the truth about the gang lifestyle. It doesn't benefit them; it costs them precious time, despair, and sometimes their lives. They victimize strangers, friends, and family by their conduct. All the while, they are unknowingly victimizing themselves. Understanding how California became a hotbed for gangs is important, if we want to develop strategies for combating their growing influence.

Researchers have found youth gangs prevalent in the United States since the growth of urban centers and the migration of minorities to this country. During the mid-1860s to 1920s, there were many Irish, Italian, Polish, Chinese, and Jewish minorities living in impoverished neighborhoods of Chicago, Detroit, New York, and other parts of the Northeast. These areas quickly became prominent breeding grounds for youth gangs. In New York, gang members were the same age as most members of current street gangs; averaging about sixteen to twenty-four years of age. The most notable being: the Five Pointers, the Monk Eastman, the Gophers, the Hudson Dusters, and the Chinese Tongs.[101]

During the 1940s immigration and job opportunities spurred the introduction of Latinos to the Northeast region. By the 1960s, sixty percent of the New York street gangs were Puerto Rican or Black. By 2008, the Northeast region had "approximately 640 gangs with more than 17,250 members..."[102] Today; the most significant street gangs on the east coast are the Crips, Latin Kings, MS-13, Neta, and United Blood Nation. Also today, Latino gangs outnumber Black gangs in the Northeast region of the United States.

The development of gangs in the Southwest had unique origins as described by some scholars.[103] Mexican settlers in the Southwest date back to the sixteenth century. However, following the Mexican-American war, the Mexican government ceded a large portion of its northern territory to the United States, under the Treaty of Hidalgo. Mexican citizens living in Texas, Arizona, Nevada, Utah, and California became naturalized citizens. Mexicans, living in the United States, had been physically and socially separated from Mexican society after the annexation. Although, they were in their "new" homeland, the United States, they were treated as second-class citizens. Newly formed local government and economic bases viewed them as outsiders or foreigners. As a result, the isolation contributed to marginalizing the Mexican community based on language, as well as cultural and socio-economic differences.

Early signs of gang orientation were the *Palomilla* (flock of doves), a group of young male horse riders who wandered the early migration trails. This isolation further engrained the prejudices in the Anglo-American communities as immigration continued unabated following the Mexican Revolution (1910-1920). Railroad and agriculture labor needs saw nearly two million more Mexican immigrants enter into the United States during a twenty year period. The older established Mexican neighborhoods or barrios became even more isolated by cultural, racial, and socio-economic barriers.

The poorest of the marginalized immigrants, Cholos-a derivative of the Spanish *solo*, meaning "alone," could not assimilate into their new society. They were young male youth neither Anglo nor Mexican by culture. But being a Cholo allowed them to proudly assert their unique Latino identity while simultaneously denying "being enbacheado (Anglicized)."[104] These street youth shaped their own Cholo subculture. (Howell and Moore, May 2010, Page 10).

The Zoot Suit Charade

It wasn't until the early 1940s that Mexican-American youth called "Pachuco's," the "hip" version of Cholos in Los Angeles were "discovered" by the media. The *Sleepy Lagoon Case* brought young Mexican-American youth to national attention. A young gang member had been found unconscious on a rural road in the outskirts of Los Angeles. He later succumbed to his injuries. Twenty-two members of the 38th Street Gang, many of whom embraced the zoot suit style of dress, were charged with his murder.

The case was dubbed the "Sleepy Lagoon Murder." The prosecution rested much of its case on the boys' "distinctive appearance" and "love of jazz fashion was evidence of their social deviancy." The judge in the case, Charles W. Fricke of the Los Angeles Superior Court, made little secret of his bias against Mexicans, and the prosecution was allowed repeatedly to stereotype the defendants racially. The defense charged throughout the case that the defendants were being denied haircuts and change of clothing; soon they began to resemble the prosecution's stereotype of sordid Mexican hoodlums. Seventeen received sentences ranging from life in prison to a year in county jail. The Mexican community united behind what was perceived as a racially motivated trial and, with the aid of community activists, all charges against the defendants were dropped two years later on appeal. During and after the trial, the *Los Angeles Times* and Hearst newspapers exploited the trial "with sensationalist journalism emphasizing alleged Mexicano criminal activity."[105]

Many Pachucos wore distinctive clothing called a zoot suit, a colorful and brash style of clothing that was the social rage for urban youth.

The "outfit" consisted of a flat-crowned, broad-brimmed hat, lengthy draped coat, and high-waisted baggy-legged trousers with tight fitted pegged cuffs. The hair was long and combed into a ducktail. They wore long, elaborate watch chains to complete the look. The zoot suit style was made popular in the movies of the time and was worn by White, Black, Mexican, and Filipino youth, especially those that followed the jitterbug dance craze.

www.cinevegas.com

Interestingly, the zoot suiters were characterized by the media in Los Angeles as marauding Mexican thugs or gangs. But only a small percentage were from local barrios and even those Pachucos had no structure. On the contrary, "they were just boys who hung around street corners and formed shifting, informal allegiances..."[106]

The Southern California street gangs had some similarities, but also distinctive differences from the East Coast gangs. First, they were tighter-knit than other street gangs, partly, owing to a "Colonia" history. Young Mexican males, raised in the barrio communities, gave rise to street gangs loyal to their neighborhoods. This historical social context created an allegiance to the neighborhood that was somewhat equal to family, albeit because many family and extended family members lived in the same neighborhoods.

Likewise, the ancestral history extended more than one generation and was being infused with a constant surplus of new, but familiar, immigrants (primarily Mexicans) each year. This cultural infusion kept the language and customs of Mexicans intact. It also served to keep them isolated, and without the larger Anglo political arena support for education, jobs, and social services. The Sleepy Lagoon Case galvanized the Mexican community in a common cause against discrimination and racism—particularly, the Pachuco mindset of being "outsiders":

> "The 38th Street gang members' cause continued in
> prison. They maintained their dignity and demonstrated
> a type of gang pride and resolve never seen before. These
> behaviors also elevated the incarcerated 38th Street gang
> members to folk hero status in the Mexican commu-
> nity. The [other] street gang members especially held
> them in high esteem." (Howell and Moore, Page 11)

To be clear, the Mexican community didn't endorse Cholos, Pachucos or the zoot suit craze. Tradition and familial customs frowned on the youth who acted so brazen in attitude and dress. However, in Los Angeles, the zoot suit style became symbolic of racial tension and prejudice between military personnel and the Latino community that soon led to the infamous Zoot Suit Riots.[107] Scholar, Alfredo Mirande describes the Pachuco mindset:

Pachuquismo was a response not only to prejudice and discrimination, but to intergenerational conflict. Chicano youth were considered American by Mexicans, especially their parents and grandparents, and Mexican by Americans. One of the most tragic aspects of the 1943 riots is that most victims were not aliens or foreigners but second-and third-generation American citizens who, though not totally assimilated or accepted, had adopted the American style of dress. The zoot suit, after all, was not a traditional Mexican costume; it was American...Chicanos were rejecting their Mexicanness. Yet, at the same time the Pachuco also symbolized the rejection experienced by Mexican-American adolescents at the hands of American society. (Gringo Justice, Page 186-187).

kcet.org   www.research.pomona.edu

The rise of Pachuco or Cholo street gangs in California would grow during the 50s and 60s. Likewise, South and North migration of Blacks to Los Angeles fueled the growth of Black street gangs. Much of the growth stemmed from the continued isolation and marginalized ghetto and barrio experience and partly from the normal youthful zeal to be different from the older generation.

Young Blacks fell into two camps, Crips or Bloods, and began to emulate the territory-marking practices that had been developed by the early Latino gangs. Crips controlled housing projects in Watts during the '50s; in particular, Jordan Downs, Nickerson Gardens, and Imperial

Courts. Bloods became strong in South Central Los Angeles cities, such as, Compton, Pacoima, Pasadena, and Pomona.

Today, the Los Angeles Police Department describes Los Angeles County as the "gang capital" of the nation. With "…more than 450 active gangs in the City of Los Angeles. Many of these gangs have been in existence for over fifty years. These gangs have a combined membership of over 45,000 individuals."[108] But a new more powerful negative influence was on the horizon in the '50s that continues to infect Southern California street gangs in one form or another today.

The EME Infusion

There remains an embryonic connection between the Mexican and street gangs in Southern California. The Mexican Mafia had its beginning during the 1950s at Deuel Vocational Institution (DVI), a prison located in Tracy, California. DVI was referred to as "Gladiator School," since the most incorrigible of the minors doing time in youth authority would be transferred here for a presumably more secure celled environment. Youthful offenders who were former street gang leaders now doing time at DVI decided to form a group which ultimately began to prey on other inmates. Most, if not all, of the members came from street gangs in Southern California. They called themselves the Mexican Mafia and later, "La EME" (the letter "M" in Spanish). Former street gang and EME member Ramon "Mundo" Mendoza describes the new prison gang's ideals

> *"Huero Buff" Flores introduced an idea that would unite the street gangs once and for all. Huero Flores proposed a prison super gang, one in which the leaders of the street gangs represented inside could join hands as allies and "carnales"—brothers—a more appealing alternative to perpetuating their bloody gang warfare into the prison system…a purely democratic system in which everyone was equal and no single member could give orders to another. Their common goal would be to organize the barrios, at least to the point that they would not tangle while incarcerated, control the heroin trafficking within the institution, and, upon release to the free world, organize a deadly cartel for the purpose of continuing in the narcotics business*

and other lucrative criminal activities. (*"The Altar Boy,"* Page 16.)

By 1959, the EME, with less than thirty original members, very quickly established themselves as merciless and cunning in their willingness to assault anyone who might pose a risk to their power. The EME readily used violence to instill fear among general population inmates. In fact, because of their ruthlessness with other inmates, a group of inmates (mostly from Northern California) decided to organize their own prison gang calling themselves *La Nuestra Familia*. They, too, had their origins among street gangs residing in northern California.

The 1960s and '70s saw blood shed rise to its highest levels at Soledad, DVI, San Quentin, Chino, and Folsom State Prison as the EME and Nuestra Familia sought to gain control of drug and extortion activities on all the mainline prisons. Other prison gangs (Aryan Brotherhood, Black Guerilla Family, and Texas Syndicate) joined in to protect their own interests, as well as protect themselves from becoming preyed upon. By the 1980s, the EME had created a cultural morass of respect through intimidation, fear, and hatred, that extended well beyond the walls of the California prisons and into the low-income communities from which the EME members had originated.

Neighborly Protection

The EME's connection to street gangs seemed a natural extension of why young men joined street gangs in the first place. The loyalty and kinship of young, defiant youth, whose natural bonds from growing up together, sharing similar experiences—good and bad—and identifying with their neighborhoods, are important traits attributed to street gang membership. The sense of family and love, which may have been lacking in the home, was replaced by the dysfunctional companionship gang membership offers many adolescents. The gang becomes part of their individual identity and is both "protector and protected." "Mundo" Mendoza, describes the street gang mentality:

> *The street gang is a common force that draws love-hungry brown-skinned kids into the protective umbrella that hides them from what they perceive to be an insensitive*

society—the same society that thumbed its nose at them in school, during job interviews, at shopping malls, on the bus, and wherever Chicanos and Gavachos [Whites] crossed paths. On the other hand, it encouraged a complete disregard for authority, especially for those who choose crime as a way of expressing their defiant and rebellious attitudes. It is a way of receiving the recognition and acceptance they desperately crave and an avenue in which the guys could demonstrate their macho [manliness]. The gang offered complete independence. ("The Altar Boy," Page 79)

For the same reasons, the creation of the EME by leaders of various street gang members doing time had fashioned a safe haven in prison. For other inmates not aligned to their agenda, it was a living hell. This EME protective shield was the same nurturing aspect of why young men found safety in numbers in the ghettos and barrios of Southern California and eventually the prison system.

In Los Angeles, Varrio Nuevo Estrada Courts, White Fence, The Avenues, 18th Street, La Rana, Varrio Trece, Maravilla, Hazard, Artesa 13, Florencia 13, Wilmas, Monte Flores, Puente Trece, SanFer, and other less celebrated street gangs became the *raw meat* from which the EME gained its muscle. To be sure, the older street gangs had established a local hierarchy based primarily on age. Mendoza explained:

Every gang in Los Angeles contains separate "cliquas," or cliques, within the gang…This subdividing takes place as members of a common age bracket within a neighborhood claimed by a street gang decide to emulate their older idols. Customarily, these youngsters obtain the blessings from the older fellow gang members—the "Veterano"—before selecting a name for their newly formed clique. ("The Altar Boy," Page 72)

For aspiring gangsters in Southern California, the "Gang-*Ladder of Success*" starts as a street gang member, then a stint in youth authority camps and jail, followed by a prison term and finally to the firm grip of the EME. This was a dysfunctional aspiration to be sure and only limited to those "vato locos" (crazy guys) particularly suited for violence and destruction. Most street gang members did not recognize or have any interest in climbing the crime ladder. Unfortunately, some were swept away by the supposedly romantic notion that "la vida loca" (the crazy life) was somehow the only way to live.

Within the prison, the EME had established its own hierarchy. The EME "Carnales" (phonetically "meat," meaning brothers) sat at the top of the prison gang pyramid. Associates or "Camaradas" were loyal followers who were hoping to be members. Associates were usually hardcore street gang members. They did much of the work connected with directives made by EME *Carnales*.

The use of EME associates became the norm after CDCR began to lock up EME members in management control units—administrative segregation (Ad-Seg). By the 1980s, they were being placed in the newly created Security Housing Units (SHU). The SHU environments assured limited contact among EME members and other general population inmates. The associates, by default, became "shot callers" in the general population. They giving the orders, "hits" (assaults), eyes and ears for drug trafficking, etc on the mainline on behalf of the EME. Below them in the hierarchy were the "Surenos," the rest of the Southern California Hispanic population doing time in prison.

Surenos

The term "Surenos" originated in the California prison system and refers to Southern California street gang members. The 1970s prison war between the Nuestra Familia (NF) and EME forged recognition of street gang members' loyalty based on a geographic regional identity of a "North vs. South" street gang mentality.[109]

It became the norm for newly arriving Latino offenders in prison to recognize and acknowledge the regional identification tag. Latino street gang members had to pick a side; they had no choice. This is an important consideration; the "Sureno" or "Norteno" (northern street gang member) label readily used in prison became a connecting thread that regionalized street gang mentality. What was once only used in prison to denote allegiance, became a much broader street gang label honoring or acknowledging the EME or NF. The super gangs had become part of "the norm" in street gang nomenclature. Proof of which is the 13th and 14th letter of the alphabet (M & N) used in southern and northern

California by taggers, in tattoos, and part of the street gang name to signify allegiance to the prison gangs.

CDCR used various means to identify these alleged NF and EME sympathizers and, arguably, may have used a broad brush in that effort. Inmate cell partners, tattoos, letters, yard assignments, pictures, drawings, social associations (who they hung around with), and self-admission were some of the primary means by which correctional staff identified them. But this did not occur without some institutional encouragement. Housing assignments, yard assignments, Ad-Seg or SHU, required identification of inmates' allegiance as a Norteno, Sureno or "non-affiliated" status. For our discussion, we will focus on the Sureno tag, although the same outcome applies to Nortenos.

The identification of an inmate's gang status was a critical prison function to both safeguard the inmate in question and to protect others. Some inmates would admit being "Sureno" while others would not and some merely indicated that "it doesn't matter, put me where you want." This left supervisory and counseling staff to determine the best cell and yard placement based on the other factors mentioned above. One assumption made was previous gang ties in the community. If they were recognized Southern California street gang members, they were considered, by default, Surenos. The status of the inmate then would be formally noted by a classification committee in the inmates' Central File.[110]

The fluid nature of prison politics among the various inmate groups and within the EME itself led to a constant need for oversight of associates and sympathizing Surenos. But not all Surenos were loyal or even interested in supporting the EME cause. Unfortunately, they had to remain silent and cautiously avoid being "caught up in the drama."[111] When tension rose between inmates of another race, all the inmates would be obliged to "backup" their own people.

Prison race-profiling *by inmates among inmates* was mandatory to ensure some measure of protection. Thus, the races (Black, Brown, White, and Asian) generally sat separately, walked among their own race, ate and exercised separately, too. If an assault or fight were to ensue, the inmates would already be amongst their own for protection. At the same time, over the years it was expected that inmates only congregate with their own race. To do otherwise, would create tension and inmates not adhering to the practice would have to answer to *his* people.

If an issue developed between inmates of different color, the shot callers for that race would decide the best resolution for their own people. Paying the debt or paying with a beating or worse, was usually the outcome to avoid a larger racial conflict. However, it didn't matter whether an inmate had an imminent release date, or family visit, or court appearance, if a racially motivated incident occurred, all inmates were expected to participate or face negative consequences.

This wasn't a hard and fast rule. Some inmates were not necessarily affected based on their status as protective custody or **Special Needs Yard (SNY)** designation. These inmates could not walk in the general population because of their criminal record and/or prison status (rapist, informant, transgender, prison gang dropout, or child molester), others because they were in separate housing (clerks, culinary workers, off reservation work assignments, maintenance crews, etc). The latter group of inmates were usually integrated and lived in better housing so "politicking" was not high on their agenda. More importantly, their isolated living arrangement reduced the constant pressure for favors by other inmates.[112]

Prison Business

The evidence supporting the EME's role in the August 8, 2009 riot is overwhelming. The discovered kites clearly spelled out the reason and intended victims. The kites were written by an EME associate, were found in an EME associate's cell, and were meant for EME associates to be followed. The EME shot caller "Mondo" had put the word out that Black inmates would be assaulted. This would occur, coincidently, before he was scheduled to parole on August 10, 2009. It was never determined if that was his intent, but it is highly likely he wanted to be around to admire his work and bask in some sickening genocidal glory. For Surenos, their participation was strictly "prison business."

RC-West Parole Violators (PVs) were the most susceptible to EME influence. Since they were being processed back into the prison system, they knew the rules-of-engagement. But, since they had just recently arrived, they were also not privy to the details of the local prison politics. They wouldn't have a reason to question the facility shot callers, who also didn't know any details that arrived from RC-Central. In fact, one of the unique aspects of the assault order was that only key EME sympathizers or associates (maybe one or two inmates) would be aware of planned attacks on each yard. When they initiated the assault on Blacks, all the Surenos would automatically follow suit without really knowing the reason or caring to know, because it was strictly *prison business*.

The assaults that occurred Friday, August 7, 2009 in the dayrooms at the RC-East and RC-Central facilities by PVs followed the same pattern of only EME sympathizers having knowledge of the plan, except that White inmates declined to join the fracas. Interestingly, but for the discovery of the kites, the incidents would have been considered by staff to be spontaneous events since no discovery of inmate manufactured weapons were found and no telltale tension could be detected beforehand. This is what makes the riot unique among all others. For all practical purposes, the RC-West Riot was a spontaneous event (since nearly all of the inmates involved were unaware of the circumstances) despite it being planned out and executed by EME associates.

The MSF Menagerie

To illustrate the dynamic of a *reception center* Parole Violator (PV) mindset, consider why the Minimum Support Facility (MSF) did not participate in the riot. Certainly, the Surenos on the MSF yard, most of whom were parole violators, recognize and sympathize with the Mexican Mafia. So what factors influenced their non-participation? First and foremost, the MSF yard had more Black inmates in August of 2009—51 percent, in fact, a fair fight to be sure!

Surenos, as a group, don't fear Black inmates, but they were clearly outnumbered, representing only about 36 percent of the MSF population. They would not have been excited about the possibility of playing the role of General Custer in a "last stand" charge to support EME business. Likewise, it is doubtful that the Whites would participate without knowing why, and more importantly, knowing, "What's in it for us?"

Secondly, the PVs doing time on the MSF had parole dates and programs. Any participation in a riot would result in more time to serve, although, the same penalty applies to PVs on the RC-West yard. The key difference is that reception centers do not have any programs available. Program availability ensures that inmates can earn "day for day" credit on their sentence—a very important distinction.[113] The penalty for rioting on the MSF extends beyond just losing time for disciplinary action. It also means you lose your job or education/vocational program that affects your release date. Inmates know they can get some time back for disciplinary actions, but will lose time permanently for loss of jobs or programs. Probably the most important reason that the MSF was not part of the riot was due to its primary "mission" for the EME.

The MSF was the "grocery store" of sorts for the EME housed at RC-Central. Generally, information and drugs would be shuttled routinely by inmates at the MSF to "Palmas" (Palm Hall). Surenos, wanting to make an impression with the EME, would find a way to be locked up in administrative segregation to supply the "big homies" (EME members). To be sure, this wasn't the only way drugs and information found its way into Palm Hall at RC-Central. But it was the primary way and has been since Palm Hall first gained notoriety in the '70s. This rationale for the MSF not participating in the August 8, 2009 Riot is, of course, only speculation, but it is highly probable given the nature of how inmate prison business was conducted at CIM.

Weighing the circumstances of Mondo's order to assault Blacks wouldn't have made sense to inmates on the MSF yard. The disrespect issue of being attacked by Blacks on the RC-Central yard in May of 2009 was RC-Central's business, not the MSF. Also, there were EME associates in Palm Hall who were quietly questioning "Mondo's" status. These same EME associates probably had "homies" on the MSF yard conducting their business activities. They would not want any interference with their nefarious activity regardless of Mondo's proclamation.

Separately, the aforementioned factors may not hold weight to support a rationale as to why the MSF didn't participate in the riot. However, taken together, they are compelling reasons why the MSF didn't riot, and thankfully so. The MSF was the largest dormitory facility in terms of acreage and also was the largest populated MSF in the state of California, housing 2,700 inmates at the time of the riot. A riot on the MSF would have been a gargantuan challenge, if circumstances had been different. The MSF didn't have an electrified fence like RC-West nor did it have a double-fence like most prison facilities. The haunting specter of inmates rushing a single fence line and knocking it down in an area not easily covered by the armed towers, loomed large in the minds of custody personnel.

Proactively, CDCR didn't take any chances. Operation *E-Brake*, comprised of select teams of gang investigators, special services unit agents, parole personnel, and special emergency response teams converged on the MSF one week after the RC-West Riot and targeted known EME sympathizers and suspected associates for identification, documentation, and removal. As a result, any potential riot supporters were effectively neutralized.

CHAPTER 6
PRISON CULTURE

When logic and proportion
Have fallen sloppy dead
And the White Knight is talking backwards
And the Red Queen's "off with her head!"
Remember what the door mouse said;
FEED YOUR HEAD, FEED YOUR HEAD!

"White Rabbit"
Jefferson Airplane

"Who's in Charge?"

*I*n February 2005, I was an associate warden (AW) at CIM and assigned
to oversee administration of Health Care Services at the prison. Okay...
not really; those duties belonged to the chief medical officer (CMO), a distin-
guished career Naval doctor, who had served his country proud and had
retired to continue work in correctional health care over the past ten years.
My job entailed the custody portion related to health care—to make sure that
"Johnny" (inmates) had "access to care" by ensuring he was made available for
health care appointments and that the prison was meeting the federal court
health care delivery mandates. CIM was failing in its health care mission,
but the same could be said of most prisons at that time.

This was a troubling period for CDCR, since all of the key federal court litigation cases (Plata, Coleman, Armstrong, Clark, and Valdivia) were becoming too overwhelming for wardens statewide to handle. CDCR was on the verge of being held in contempt of federal court decrees with the governor as the primary defendant. CDCR was under a microscope by the governor's office, the Ninth Circuit Court monitors, prison law office attorneys (who were gaining real power by the minute), and the state legislature. They were concerned with the skyrocketing cost of corrections, and health care delivery, in particular. I recall advising my peers, who were frustrated at the "push-pull drama" coming from CDCR Headquarters with no real solutions. I said, "It's really very simple, we managers are all like the musicians on the Titanic; we need to continue playing a soothing message until the ship sinks or help arrives!"

CDCR's solution was to create an administrative post (AW) specific to health care. This person would be responsible for ensuring that custody staff complete daily tasks associated with getting inmate medical services. The key problem, as I saw it, was that health care delivery always took a backseat to custody matters. That had been the "past practice" based on security protocols and/or incident response emergencies. Safety and security always trumped medical. That mindset was about to change, but, ever so slowly and only with the assistance of a federal court "boot" to CDCR's rear quarters! By October of 2005, the Ninth Circuit Judge would appoint a Receiver to rule over all of the state's health care staff in the prisons.

****

I had been working the previous year as a facility captain, assigned out of Headquarters Health Care Division. Myself and the other "Plata" captains (so named after what headquarters staff dubbed "the mother of all lawsuits," the federal court Plata health care litigation) were tasked with completing custody audits of prisons based on specific "access to care" protocols. It was apparent from our statewide journeys as Quality Management Assessment Teams (QMAT) that prisons statewide had not been very successful at meeting the court mandates. We were tasked with documenting if "Johnny" was receiving his doctor-ordered medications in a timely fashion. Were inmates receiving basic clinic appointments or follow-up interventions? If not, what was the cause of "no show" appointments? Was documentation on Medical Activity Reports consistent? Was appropriate follow-up care received?

And that was just the medical issues. Mental health and dental arenas had their own demons to expunge!

During my QMAT tours, I had been asked to review and recommend employee actions regarding clinical personnel who had been under investigation for various issues. My previous background, as an employee relations officer at the California Correctional Institution at Tehachapi, had found a useful purpose in the Health Care Division in Sacramento. I suspect CMOs statewide had heard I was the one challenging their proposed misconduct decisions on staff or questioning their own misfeasance regarding employee actions.

Health care was a very tight and closed culture to outsiders, especially in a prison setting. Undoubtedly, in a prison setting, where everything is magnified, the dysfunctional relationship between custody and health care personnel was the primary reason CDCR could not find meaningful solutions to the delivery of care. Custody didn't think it was their job and health care personnel didn't believe they needed to explain their actions. This mindset in the field reached from the nurses and officers to the CMO and the warden's office in most prisons. Each entity blamed the other, politely in some cases and angrily in other cases, for the many health care failures.

Making matters worse, the various employee group cultures on the health care side were constantly working separately or, in some cases, against each other, as a bizarre montage of "professionals in denial." Doctors, nurses, psychologists, pharmacists, psychiatrists, Medical Technical Assistants (MTAs), and medical clerical staff, all had a hand in the delivery of care and all had their own view on what worked. They also had strong opinions about the people they worked for. Every prison had the same health care cultural rainbow working within the social context of the greater prison culture.

Confused? Don't be. From my perspective, all these health care employees were behaving just the way other groups do based on friends, associates, bosses, and organization demands. But when you have educated professionals who have a socio-economic distance to others (based on pay range) around them, a distinct caste system develops based partly on economics and partly on status. In the health care arena, everyone knows who is in charge and who is at the bottom rung.

But in CDCR, the clinics, pharmacies, and hospitals were all within the secure perimeter of a prison. You cannot go anywhere without approved access from an officer, sergeant, lieutenant, or captain. Custody blanketed all aspects of the health care delivery system in prison. The synergy created by these two clashing dysfunctional cultures was simultaneously unique and disastrous. For example, if a prison culture at a facility was more "strict and unforgiving" of inmates, health care staff tended to be the same. If the prison was more therapeutic-driven, so, too, were the staff. But if the health care leadership had any animosity against the custody or vice versa, there would be constant bickering and blame. Just like any other organization or company group, CDCR's prison culture was a reflection of its peers and environment, with few exceptions.

From my perspective, the CDCR health care division had made no demands of staff with respect to mission, vision, and goals. The statewide leadership was mired in managing day-to-day issues and emergencies. The truth is, the Health Care Division was continuously overrun by the legislature and governor's office who demanded answers, practically every day, to the barrage of prison law office inquires and allegations. The federal court had not yet assigned the Receiver when I was promoted to AW, but the threat of that foregone conclusion was ever present.

****

Locally, the CMOs ran the health care units like fiefdoms. If you didn't acquiesce to the demands of the CMO, you would be treated like an outcast. The stronger the CMO exerted his or her leadership, the more dictatorial the atmosphere. CIM had one of the stronger minded CMOs. He also was a shrewd politician, having made friends over the years with each new warden to protect his fiefdom. Custody managers didn't understand the health care arena and really didn't care about it. It wasn't a priority for them...and that, in a nutshell, was the main problem for CDCR statewide.

I had just been announced as the new AW for Health Care during the executive staff meeting and was warmly greeted by all the custody and non-custody managers. The CMO and Southern Regional Administrator for Health Care were also in attendance at the meeting. The regional administrator was acting on a limited basis until someone could be assigned. She was the CMO for the California Institution for Women, CIM's sister prison less than five miles away. Immediately following the meeting, I received a call from the CMO's secretary who advised me that the CMO wanted to meet with me. I graciously said yes. Before I left my office, I received a call from Health Care Division Headquarters. As "luck" would have it, the call would prove to be timely. I promptly went to the CMO's office to see what was cooking. Little did I know, I was the main course!

As the secretary led me into his office, I could smell the stale air of outdated wall paneling and old furniture. It seemed nothing had changed in the room for forty years and, judging by the looming exchange between us, the atmosphere was nearly perfect for the occasion. I sat across from the CMO, in a chair that seemed shorter than his and that of the acting regional administrator, who was seated to my left. The CMO never made eye contact, but only looked at a paper for what seemed like forever. I could hear the old clock behind him ticking louder by the minute. Finally, he started. He shook the crumpled paper in his hand and asked me, "Do you know what this is?"

"No, I don't," I responded.

"This is your duty statement for the job!" he bellowed.

"Oh, okay, I've seen it," I said sheepishly while nodding my head.

"Do you know what I think of it?" he said, his voice rising a bit.

I finally recognized what was coming and I wanted to maintain some self-control, for two reasons: First, I wanted to keep my new job. Second, I really, really wanted to keep my new job! I quickly glanced at the Regional who looked at me, then looked away. I responded, "No, I don't," almost at a whisper.

He yelled, "Nothing!" and angrily tossed it in my direction on the table. He continued, "I'm in charge here and I decide what we do and when we do it; no one else!"

I looked at him and could see this fiery rage and disgust flashing across this old man's face. I'd seen the look before, so I maintained my composure. Keeping eye contact, I quickly stated, "I know you're in charge. I work for you and the warden. My function is only to ensure that custody personnel are getting the inmates to where your staff needs them and also to provide advice on any health care delivery issues you deem appropriate."

It was his turn now to get his composure. Maybe he wanted me to go off or something, but I wasn't about to let it happen. The CMO ended the meeting saying, "Good, I just wanted to make sure you know how things work around here. You can leave now."

I was pissed, but didn't show it as I left the office. His office is located in the hospital on the Minimum Support Facility just behind the administration building. I was furious that he would make a "grandstanding" spectacle in front of the acting regional administrator at my expense, and for no other reason than to exert his power and, apparently, to put me in my place. I already knew the pecking order, but I realized now…I was about to challenge it.

****

One thing CDCR had taught me was self-discipline in the face of adversity. It happens nearly every day with disruptive inmates and pompous supervisors. Inmates were an easy fix because, ultimately, we—prison personnel—had the power. But with supervisors, a much different battleground existed. Staff that fought their bosses head-on were doomed to failure; not so much by their deeds but by the "Car."

The Car is CDCR's cultural euphemism for who has power (The Driver), and who was a passenger, lucky to be in the "Car." Those in the "Car" were the favored ones. If you didn't have some in-house mentor, or worse, you'd been given the "shine," then you weren't going to catch the ride for the next special assignment or promotion and move forward. I learned the hard way that those you "piss off" one day may become your boss, or worse, become the next director. (But that's a story for another day!) This was an informal pecking order that plays out in any organization, but is magnified in a prison setting.

It didn't matter in this case, I had been disrespected. The CMO had insulted me in the presence of another administrator. From a young man to this day, I was always quick to respond when someone offended me. As a youth, all my fights occurred because I had been disrespected or challenged in some adolescent way or another. I could tolerate most things, but when I was disrespected, I'd go off!

I recall an associate warden (AW) who was shouting at me and two other captains about not wanting to be surprised with bad news during a meeting. He and I already had a personality clash that was growing larger by the day. On this occasion, he was speaking in generalities about another captain's failed actions and not me personally. But when he said, "If it happens again, I'll kick your ass!" and looked directly at me as he said it, that was it! We were sitting not two feet apart at the table and I quickly responded, "You're not kicking my ass!"

At that moment, I waited for him to move, thinking; if he moves, I will argue at my disciplinary hearing that I hit him to protect myself. He didn't move, but stated, "You take everything personal."

I responded, "Only to threats." In these situations, I couldn't care less about any "car" or the consequences for my actions. Maybe it was foolish pride; I'm not sure.

I had no problem keeping my cool when convicts, prisoner family members, or subordinate staff flew off the handle. But if a peer or supervisor was unprofessional, I would not tolerate it. I expected more from them because I was one of them. So, there I was again, a newly hired AW "pissed off" about remarks made by the CMO, my superior, and me making a beeline to the warden's office, like a kid running to tell Mommy, but this time with a bit more savvy.

****

The warden was a seasoned correctional professional. She had worked her way up and had seen all there is in a prison. Prison politics, like with most wardens, was her forte. As I entered her office, she could sense my anger. I was her newest AW and in my mind, being frank and to the point was the best and only option. "Warden, I just got back from the CMO's office and you need to know what just happened." I proceeded to share the grim details.

As I outlined the drama, she just kept shaking her head in disbelief, stating, "I can't believe it...why would he do that...we don't need this right now."

Once I had presented the details of the meeting, I said, "Warden, I want to share something with you that I think might be in our best interest." She looked at me wondering what was next. "I got a call from Headquarters; they want me to work as the administrator for the southern region."

She nodded. "Yes, I got that call yesterday, too. I told them no, you just started here and we need you."

I smiled. "Warden, let me give them four months so they can have time to find someone else." She is shaking her head "No" as I continued. "Look, as the regional, I will still be available to you and can route resources to CIM. I don't want to remain in Health Care, my job is here and I want to remain with the custody side of the house. The call I got today was to tell me that they are going to go over your head to make it happen." She looked startled, but was listening intently as I continued, "If you approve, I will tell them I will only work a few months, but I can guarantee you that, within the first week, the CMO will likely retire."

She seemed intrigued, asking, "What makes you say that?"

I responded quickly, "I could see it in the CMO's face; he can't stomach the thought of working with me. Once he finds out that I'm now his boss, he won't know how to handle it; I just know he'll want to leave."

The warden studied my face for a minute and then said, "Okay, but only four months."

I was smiling now. "Yes Madame, four months."

She looked at me sternly. "I mean it Richard, do you understand?"

I responded, "I got it, four months and no more."

The following day, Friday, it was announced by the Division of Health Care Services that I would be assigned as the acting southern regional administrator. My responsibilities included oversight of the ten southern prison health care operations. All the southern region prison CMOs would report to me.

The next day, Saturday morning, CIM's CMO tendered his resignation. The following Monday, the CMO from CIW, who had witnessed the exchange between the CMO and myself, came by to apologize. I told her not to concern herself about it and just keep her focus on our health care mission. She appeared to be relieved. In my mind, she had only been a misled "team" player. I stayed four months in the regional post and returned to CIM as promised, declining a permanent position as the Southern Regional Administrator for Health Care Division.

The Federal Court Invasion

By 2005, CDCR could no longer ignore the enormous elephant in the room, the Prison Law Office (PLO). The PLO represents individual prisoners by engaging in class action and other litigation that affect prisoners. The PLO was instrumental in seeking federal court redress on three primary issues: Medical, Physical Disabilities, and Mental Health. The federal court presiding over three major law suits; Plata, Armstrong, and Coleman, sought remedies addressing issues that were characterized by the court as "deliberate indifference."[114]

In October of 2005, the federal court ordered that the prisons' medical care system be placed under the direction of a court appointed "receiver" An extraordinary decision to take control of an agency's business based on its failure to achieve adequate medical care for inmates. The PLO was successful in showing the court that CDCR had consistently failed to provide constitutionally adequate care to inmates:

> The court found that the system is "broken beyond repair," causing an "unconscionable degree of suffering and death." Among the shocking findings are that, on average, an inmate in one of California's prisons needlessly dies every six to seven days due to grossly deficient medical care. (Prison Law Office, 2013)

The federal court had determined that CDCR's failure to provide constitutionally adequate care resulted in poor or inhumane care and, in some cases, unwarranted deaths of prisoners. It was not surprising that a receiver was appointed to take charge. The court's action bi-furcated the leadership role in CDCR and at the local prisons; the receiver having complete control of health care operations and CDCR retaining control of security and operations of the prison. A clash of cultures (Medical and Custody) had always occurred in the prisons to varying degrees over the years, but this time the clash was decidedly different. This time one of those prison cultures was armed by the court!

Judge Thelton E. Henderson presiding judge from the Ninth Circuit Court placed Robert Sillen as the receiver with extraordinary powers to revamp the medical delivery system for California prisons. His appointment was a lightning rod for CDCR staff, particularly executive and administrative custody staff at all levels who viewed his brash and sometimes condescending style of leadership as offensive. Nearly fourteen months after his appointment, Sillen spoke to the Sacramento Press Club in July of 2007.

> So, we've been at it for fourteen or fifteen months, something like that. And we've accomplished a lot, but we have not scratched the surface. Okay, we increased the salaries. In this day and age of, you know, "You can't get nurses, you can't get pharmacists, you can't get this kind of personnel,"…we had to waive state law to do it, because the state wouldn't do it. The state somehow thinks it can get pharmacists, paying 49 percent of market, and then signing up with registries to pay four times what you have to pay if you paid them a

reasonable salary and wage. I mean, it's just nuts. It's just the most wasteful thing in the world. There's several billion dollars in the CDCR that shouldn't have to be spent, and some of it in medical care.

Many of the clinicians in the prison system, too many, not most, not a majority—and there's some good people in the prison system—but far too many are only there because they don't have a career or a livelihood. They can't make it outside the walls of the prison. But somehow the state of California thinks it's okay to have them providing "medical care" in the prison system. And that's a function of politics, political imagery, not willing to spend money...

It's going to cost a little to get out of it. And we're going to spend it. We're going to redesign the system. We increased salaries. I've hired over 300 registered [nurses] in the last three or four months. I've hired over 700 licensed vocational nurses. We've transferred out all the MTAs—the medical technical assistants out of the prisons who were this strange hybrid of peace officer and LVN. And I told them, you can only have one choice. You can be a cop, or you can be a technician. You can't be both—that's a conflict. We've transitioned them out, as of June, and then created the classification we're hiring for—LVNs.

We're ordering up vehicles for transportation. **Most people do not understand the incredible linkage between custody and medical care.** If there aren't correctional officers, there's no transportation for my patients. So, I buy wardens correctional officers. I don't buy them the bodies because CDCR can't get recruiting done. There's a backlog of 10,000 applicants for CO [correctional officers] positions. There are 3,500 vacancies of COs. **The prisons are unsafe; they're understaffed.** There's not adequate transportation.

So, I provide financial resources to at least pay for the overtime, the transportation of medical patients.

It has to be a team effort, ultimately. The whole idea of the receivership is to bring care, quality to…bring it up to constitutional levels and then to turn it back to the state.[115] (**My emphasis**)

His candid characterization of the problems and remedies with CDCR's medical delivery system was probably more refined in the presence of the media that day than when he visited the prisons and spoke more candidly with staff directly. But his message was clear. He was in charge and was not interested in excuses. He would take any path, regardless of the economic impact, as long as it would benefit his mission to vastly improve health care delivery in the prisons.

In the original PLO complaint in Plata, the key concerns regarding the delivery of medical services included, but was not limited to: insufficient qualified medical staff including physicians and nurses; inadequate training and supervision of all medical personnel; delays in access, follow-up, or specialty care and finally the administrative grievance system did not provide timely or adequate responses to complaints.[116]

However, by 2010, five years after the appointment of the receiver, most correctional employees complained that inmates were receiving "Cadillac Care." Meaning, inmate health care was more responsive and superior than that provided to most citizens in the community. It's not hard to see why that became the prevailing view among correctional personnel. One of the primary outcomes of court oversight was the hiring of more qualified and knowledgeable doctors. To achieve that, the court receiver had to "weed out" incompetent doctors by having all the doctors pass a competency exam. Secondly, the receiver enacted a pay schedule that was competitive with the open market to draw more seasoned and highly qualified clinicians. Thirdly, nursing staff were increased state-wide to compliment the rigorous health care mandates imposed by the federal courts. Fourth, a significant increase in correctional officers' positions occurred at each institution that was dedicated only to delivery of inmates to clinical appointments and security coverage of clinic and hospitals. Those officers were budgeted and supervised by health care custody supervisors and managers under the direction of the receiver.

What correctional staff observed was a pronounced promptness to inmate requests for medical service, follow-up care, and access to specialty clinicians for chronic and acute care treatment. Inmates could submit a medical request form and a nurse would review it within twenty-four hours and determine what level of care was needed. Inmates were informed by the PLO via Inmate Advisory Councils and/or posted bulletins about their right to prompt health care intervention. Inmate appeals were also streamlined to ensure that health care concerns were addressed promptly by the medical department within court-ordered timeframes.

All the above was audited and monitored by court or PLO representatives who made routine and unannounced visits regularly at all the state prisons. It was a remarkable time for CDCR, addressing unprecedented health care changes while being under the microscope of the court. Whether true or not, the general feeling among staff was that convicted felons were receiving better treatment than that afforded in the community and all at tax payers' expense. The perception of "Cadillac treatment" quickly became an open wound that festered in the minds of most staff obliged to meet the court mandates. What oozed out from that "perception wound," unfortunately, was blame, frustration, and envy.

Prison Culture Clash

Appearances can be deceiving. Regardless of the changes being made in health care administration, as Sillen so aptly stated three years earlier, "... we have not scratched the surface." Within the underbelly of the institutions, where the rubber met the road, problems were brewing larger and larger. The problems were a combination of resistance to change, loyalty to old dogma, logistical challenges, and infrastructure limitations. All these issues rested comfortably in the hornets' nest of what was the biggest obstacle facing CDCR—the correctional culture.

CDCR had never formally acknowledged conflicting cultures in a prison setting, nor had they trained managers or supervisors about managing socio-cultural distinctions in a prison setting. There was also very little impetus for developing the "soft skills" in communication, cooperation, teamwork, etc. It is understandable that, in a paramilitary organization where nearly half the employees are peace officers, a "command presence" and "take charge" attitude would prevail and influence the style of management of all employee classifications. The result was a competitive "silo" approach to communication and personal leadership agendas that infused almost all the various organizational systems (Medical, Custody, Records, Plant Operations, etc) to work separately in the prisons.

The "Who's in Charge" story at the beginning of this chapter alluded to the mindset that exemplified aspects of the prison culture that still somewhat languishes today. This is not to be construed as totally negative commentary. On the contrary, this dictatorial style of management worked effectively for many years and for good reason. Prior to 1985, prisons had a higher rate of violence with less security enhancements. Having strong-minded "Alpha" personalities in charge, was the norm simply because that's what worked in a prison setting.

Accordingly, a "command presence" was the *standard operating mindset* for nearly all the "silo" employee groups; including: Plant Operations, Investigations, Custody, Medical, Mental Health, Nursing, Education, Clerical, and the Administration. *Bloomberg Business Week* correspondent Evan Rosen refers to an organization that suffers from "silo syndrome" as being unable or unwilling to work with other parts of the organization thereby reinforcing its own culture and creating roadblocks to collaboration.[117] He writes:

> Command-and-control-oriented cultures breed silos. In such cultures, fear prevails. Managers focus on guarding turf rather than on engaging colleagues outside their group. Instead of reaching across the organization, people in command-and-control cultures primarily move information and decisions vertically.

There were obviously exceptions to this characterization, but most groups working in the larger prison security environment were influenced by the larger prison custody mindset. As a result, cooperation took a backseat to authoritative control measures.

All employee groups had the same response for the other groups. "I don't work for you," and/or "I'm not responsible for that work," were common responses. And they were correct. Unfortunately, this was not a good organizational management formula when fundamental change, ordered by the federal court, was needed in day-to-day prison business. Worse, when you consider change was on-going amid contentious and politically-charged stakeholder groups, very little cooperation could be expected.

Byzantine Health Care

Providing meaningful health care in a prison setting is a complex web of coordinated effort between nursing, custody, physician, pharmacy, and records. Take, for example, an inmate who has just arrived to state prison. Whether a parole violator or new commitment, the health care protocols are essentially the same. He first undergoes an *Intake Health Care Screening*, preferably in a private setting with computer access. Then, he is reviewed for mental health concerns. Any need for medication is forwarded to the pharmacy to prepare medications to be delivered that evening. A Medical Activity Report (MAR) is initiated by a nurse. A subsequent physician appointment is completed or scheduled for the next day. When "hiccups" (inmates needing special or immediate care) occur, then the Intake Health Care Screening process is interrupted to accommodate the immediate medical or mental health needs. All the above activities occur with constant custody staff coverage and/or escorts for the inmate throughout the intake process.

For those inmates determined to need additional health care intervention, the following day another round of nurses, doctors, or pill line is completed, more medications and/or specialty clinic (x-ray, dialysis, blood tests, etc.) are done at the prison clinic or scheduled for outside (the prison) hospital. The MAR entries must be made with each clinical encounter by a nurse. Unfortunately, the inmate may be moved from various units or facilities, possibly one, two, or three times within the span of a day or two. Consequently, the medical team must find the Unit Health Record (UHR), MAR, and the custody team must locate the inmate. The whole process can replicate itself each week for one inmate that has ongoing medical or mental health concerns.

The aforementioned medical delivery process is a regular occurrence especially for the Reception Centers. As a result, tracking an inmate's movement daily becomes a fulltime job for custody, medical, and clerical staff. Moreover, they must locate the UHR file, transport the file, and return the file for storage at the end of the day. Inmate movement at a prison is a constant event especially for RCs and level I and II prisons, since the inmates at those facilities are closer to release dates, or house PVs, with minimal time to serve. Additionally, cell fights, lower bunk requests, population pressures, enemies, all influence bed moves within a prison. Multiply this "record-keeping voyage" with thousands of inmates at one prison and you can see where mistakes can occur.

Complicating the delivery of care are the aging infrastructures that were neither equipped to house inmates in large numbers nor capable of capturing information electronically for both custody and medical staff to use. The CDCR had been relying on over 100 antiquated and independent electronic and paper database systems to provide daily information critical to managing the population in a safe and secure manner. These systems were primarily stand-alone systems that could not share information. In addition, some of the most widely used systems required data downloads from the other systems in order to maintain their usefulness. These systems are used to locate, identify, and track critical inmate/parolee case factors (crime, current release date status, disciplinary, medical, and custody history). The most widely used systems were not used by the Health Care Division who had their own information technology system in place.[118]

The CDCR recognized that the antiquated information systems needed a complete overhaul and began a search for the best solution for statewide application. As a result, the Strategic Offender Management System (SOMS) was born and began to roll out in November of 2009.[119] Under the auspices of the CDCR's Enterprise Information System Division and in contract with Hewlett Packard, Oracle, and other IT consultants, the SOMS is anticipated to be a far-reaching answer to a besieged bureaucracy. Once fully implemented, SOMS will allow a routine action such as a disciplinary hearing or medical appointment to be documented and shared with a click of a button.

What had normally taken many hours to do could conceivably be done in less than a minute! CDCR's J. Pandora, Chief Information Officer and Director of Enterprise Information Services reported that CDCR has more than 36,000 desktop PCs connected to its network. It also has an additional 19,000 non-networked educational devices and 3,500 network devices such as hubs, servers, and databases.[120] The initial startup for SOMS focused on intake, movement, and scheduling for inmates; once "on-line" all prisons will have access to the same secure data.

Although the SOMS remains a work-in-progress for CDCR, for all its bugs and learning curve challenges, it appears to be steadily gaining wider use and applications. Imagine San Quentin (SQ), the oldest prison and CIM, the third oldest male prison both having Reception Centers with the largest intake of all other prisons for the past twenty years. CIM and SQ averaged no less than 500 inmates arriving each week with the same number leaving. Envision a minimum of no less than one thousand bed changes weekly at CIM and SQ without benefit of modern information technology to make the job easier. Mistakes were bound to occur and they did frequently. Bed and housing errors were normally corrected within twenty-four hours. They had to be, because accounting for a convicted felon's whereabouts was always the first priority for public safety. But missed medical and/or mental health appointments or failure to deliver doctor-ordered medications were not. Those indiscretions were significant violations of the federal court mandates and, for all their best effort, CDCR correctional personnel could not help making mistakes. The workload was beyond the prison's ability to remain error-free.

Just What the *Receiver* Ordered

Receiver, Robert Sillen wisely improved the quality of doctors and nursing staff. He not only substantially increased the pay for clinical staff and demanded more qualified doctors, he also awarded them equal status to a warden, as "hiring authority." The CMOs were renamed, *Health Care Manager* (HCM)—one for each prison. But a critical cultural problem arose that neither he nor any administrative effort could resolve. The new HCMs and chief psychiatrists were now making twice the income that wardens were earning.[121]

Wardens remained equally accountable for the implementation and delivery of health care, yet only the wardens remained accountable for everything else in the prison; facility management, personnel, accounting, training, investigations, plant operations, security, education/vocational programs, visiting, food services, inmate appeals, inmate discipline, classification, employee relations, and volunteer programs. All the aforementioned functions touched health care delivery at the prison, but the health care managers were only accountable for the clinical delivery portion. As a result, a growing undercurrent of frustration and anger was felt that was only spoken among those closest to the warden's ear.

The health care operation at each facility was dependent upon the work functions of plant operations staff, clerical staff, appeals office, staff investigative services, and personnel services staff. Although, some additional health care positions were assigned for appeals and clerical function, the oversight and management of all those areas remained with the wardens. Custody supervisors generally viewed the doctors as competent regarding clinical intervention, but not very good at organizational management and leadership. This is precisely where the receiver's prescription was lacking. Sillen's initial remedy—gargantuan pay raises— was akin to pouring salt in the frail confidence wounds of correctional managers and wardens statewide. Even worse, the receiver's persona was like a sharp knife stabbing at the character of CDCR's executive staff and the field custody leadership, as he made remarks during visits to the prisons that were surely meant to reinforce who was in charge.

For example, his dissatisfaction with legislative inaction was appreciated by some, but harsh, nonetheless, to the ears of the prison leadership. "If we have to, we will back up a Brinks truck to the general fund coffers to get the money to make this happen…some agencies will lose funding for their pet projects, that's just the way it is…if that means you (custody) don't get new vehicles, so be it…"[122] Vehicles were a high priority for the reception center processing since those inmates were paroling, going out to court, and attending more frequent off-site hospital visits. The purchase of new vehicles in the field was reduced, more likely from pre-determined budget cuts, but staff believed the receiver influenced the decision. Perhaps his greatest failing was not anticipating the impact of discarding MTAs in the prisons.

MTAs were the "drivers" of all medication management in a prison setting. They were licensed vocational nurses with badges: Part nurse and part peace officer. They prepared the daily pill dosages, delivered medications to the pill lines, and went cell-by-cell to administer the medications. They routinely responded to medical emergencies and provided life-saving treatment within the scope of their license. They were the implementers of the doctor's orders. Sillen's approach to improving the nursing efforts was simple, as he made clear his intentions, stating, "Nurses cannot have two masters."[123] His rationale made sense. Nurses either work for him or the warden, but the manner in which he proceeded by terminating the MTA classification and replacing it with LVN and RN positions statewide, created havoc in the statewide prison medical departments.

Perhaps there was no easier way to make the change in classification, but it had significant blowback.

Statewide, a recurring trend was observed. Newly hired RNs and LVNs were afraid of the inmates and had not been clearly informed about the working conditions and security protocols of a prison. It wasn't their fault, they were "fish" and not accustomed to the manner in which prisons ran. They were also not well received by many other correctional employees (officers, clerical, plant operations, etc) who had working relationships with the MTAs. Many MTAs that were transitioning out to become officers, demoting to LVN status, or leaving to other employment, were not inclined to assist the "newbies" who were taking their jobs. This period of transition lasted a year with bargaining units representing both the MTAs and nursing staff at odds with Sacramento and the prisons.

It didn't matter to the receiver or the PLO that a cultural "melt down" was occurring at the prisons, and very little was being said or done to quell the distrust and poor morale at all levels. Even though the vast majority of custody and medical staff wanted to understand and accomplish the ever-changing mission mandates, the infrastructure limitations, logistical barriers, and ill-prepared new medical "drivers" (LVNs and RNs) continually got in the way of success. Communication between custody and medical had been poor before the change in nursing classifications; it was decidedly worse after.

The focus on medication management protocols was the least of the problem; it was the internal prison communication links that badly needed repair. CDCR executive staff in Sacramento had a good indication that morale was low at the prisons statewide and recognized that such rapid changes made by the receiver were part of the problem. They also recognized that the PLO and the court were driving the changes and they had no recourse except to enforce accountability for anyone that failed. This meant more salt in the morale wounds for all staff working in the prisons.

The Prison Patient Variable

Making matters worse, the inmates were not being "good" patients. It is arguable that citizens in the community also make lousy patients.

One study suggested that medication non-compliance is responsible for at least ten percent of all hospitalizations in the nation and costs the health care system up to $289 billion per year.[124] If that is the norm for the community, then what can be said about inmate patients? Inmates have a higher rate of chronic or acute care needs because of poor eating habits and habitual drug usage. So it can be assumed they have a greater need for health care intervention. In a controlled setting like a prison, it seems reasonable that it should be easy for "Johnny" to get proper care. Guess again!

The failure in medication management in a prison setting can neither wholly be blamed on staff incompetence nor "deliberate indifference." Some inmates may simply not want to take the medication. Some cannot make it to the pill line because custody personnel limit movement based on immediate security concerns or incidents. Some inmates are "gaming" the clinicians for psychotropic medications to sell or get high on. Others are requesting nurse or doctor visits as a ruse to make contact with other inmates or to advance some nefarious criminal activity like stealing syringes or hoarding pills to be sold to others. Still others seek attention as habitual patients with no real medical problem. This is certainly not representative of what occurs in the community, but it is absolutely reflective of the convict character and gang subculture that drives inmate behavior in prison.

CDCR was in a no-win situation regarding medication management regardless of the amount of money being poured into health care delivery, because some inmates were not cooperative and some staff couldn't keep up with the changes being driven by the receiver. This perspective is based on two recurring examples. The first was the requirement of having an officer available at all pill lines. One of the duties of a pill line officer included assisting the nurse in making sure the inmate had taken his Direct Observation Therapy (DOT) medication. After the inmate would presumably take his pills with a cup of water, upon the nurse's request, the officer would direct the inmate to open his mouth, lift his tongue, and he would confirm the inmate had, in fact, swallowed the medication. However, it was almost routine to find discarded medications strewn around the vicinity of the pill line each day.

This was not a reflection of the officer failing his/her duties at the post. On the contrary, some inmates not requiring DOT would simply discard medications and some under DOT may have "beat" the officer and nurse in concealing the pills to sell or hoard. Imagine 300 inmates in a continuous pill line with 20 percent DOT (sixty) inmates requiring observation. If only 5 percent of the DOT inmates succeed in concealing the medication (three inmates), and the same percentage of non-DOT inmates (twelve inmates) also discard or conceal medication, that amounts to a 95 percent success rate for administering medications.[125] But consider that the fifteen inmates who missed their medication cycle are now either unknown to the health care staff or worse, suffering unknown complications from failed medication delivery. This number doesn't include the additional inmates that simply refuse to go to the pill line. This scenario only reflects the surreptitiously failed medication deliveries that happen each day at each pill line at every prison in the state.

The other reason medication management was problematic rested squarely on the mission. The number of inmates requiring medication rose as the health care delivery system improved and the inmate population soared. Pill lines normally occurred before meals in the morning and afternoon. In addition, a special pill line (HS meds) occurred at 8:00 p.m. The management of these lines in conjunction with the nurses' line, doctors' line, and any specialty clinician appointments each day became the primary obligation for Health Care and Custody each day. Assuming all things to be equal, any prison's medical resources seemed capable of handling the workload.

But things are rarely equal in a prison setting. Frustrating custody and health care management included the everyday prison business requirements for meals, count times, educational/vocational programs, exercise yard time, and related activities. Inmates behave just like citizens do with regard to doctor visits and follow-ups. They tend to ignore them if something of greater interest comes their way. A family visit, sporting event on TV, program cell or job move, meeting with custody staff, phone call with family, etc, all took precedence among inmates over medical appointments.

When an inmate does not attend a medical ducat (summons) appointment, custody is required to locate him and bring him to the medical team to complete the treatment or document the refusal. If the inmate cannot be found in a timely fashion, an "emergency count" would occur that stops all programming which requires all inmates return to their bunks for count before resumption of activities. But if the inmate fails to report to the pill line for routine medications, the MAR is noted as a "no show." After repeated failures (three) to be present at pill line, the LVN would schedule the inmate for nurse or doctor line review. This would entail duplicating work for clerical and nursing staff to re-ducat an inmate who failed to show for pill, nurses, or doctor lines. This was a daily exercise that was slow to develop into a routine but nonetheless was fraught with errors and required massive resources of personnel and time to make happen.

Unfortunately, the extent of the federal court oversight didn't see the challenges of improving health care delivery from the same lens as prison staff did. When a twenty-year-old federal court-initiated health care bureaucracy is created and given power through the courts, it inevitably must sustain and maintain itself. It almost becomes a self-fulfilling prophecy to justify its existence. Clearly, CDCR had enormous issues relative to improving its health care delivery and quality of service. However, by 2010, it had significantly improved both those concerns.

Muddy Water Ripples

As it happens, audit teams from the Coleman, Plata, and Armstrong plaintiffs, court experts, and PLO all found issues during court mandated tours. These were issues that were not representative of any major systemic failure, but individual issues of non-compliance in documentation service or follow-up—issues related to appeal responses, infrastructure repair snafus, and worse, "potential" issues about *path of travel*, privacy, and uncooperative staff. The larger issues of general accessibility, medication management, and quality of care had largely been addressed. Instead, the auditors focused on inmate complaints to view specific instances of non-compliance.

The gradual change from systemic policy and procedural compliance to an *individualized* focus at each prison for determining court compliance was akin to throwing rocks in a dirty pond. With each issue, and there were many, the "ripple effect" created new and ever-changing court compliance directives. CDCR was in a no-win situation. For example, inmates would embellish mistakes or simply make up issues. Likewise, uninformed or disgruntled custody or medical staff would also make allegations or report discrepancies during tours regarding the health care delivery. It wasn't hard to find some errors on a daily basis. It was to be expected with the sheer volume of movement, work, and documentation required to both meet the health care mandates of the court while providing verification of the work done. What's more important is that CDCR finally had a system in place to capture mistakes or errors and rectify them. The PLO and court experts teams acknowledged this fact by 2010, but nonetheless reported non-compliance to the courts on a consistent basis—which begs the question, why?

The Plata, Armstrong, and Coleman litigation efforts to provide constitutionally adequate care to inmates, created or compounded institutional infrastructure and procedural issues. Building and clinical equipment needs that stood in the way of meeting the health care mandates were beyond the ability of the state to resolve. For example, in living units or areas that housed disabled inmate-patients, specialized toilets were required for mobility-impaired inmates. In fact, most of the old cell blocks were not wide enough for wheelchair access. Plumbing changes and wall-breaching construction was no simple matter in a prison and at a cost much higher than was normal for toilet replacement.

For example, space for a wheelchair to fit alongside the specialized toilet with sufficient grab bars sometimes required removal of an adjacent toilet. This may seem to be an easy fix, but it wasn't. Inmates didn't care that the "special toilet" was for a certain class of patient. And it was not that easy for a Black or White mobility-impaired inmate to "share" the same commode in a dormitory setting. Inmate ethnic groups had a history of claiming areas as their own and, many times, that included sinks, toilets, and showers.

The receiver, PLO, and the court didn't recognize prison culture (behavior) as an issue because inmates rarely acknowledged it. This is not a complaint of the PLO's drive to represent the best interests of inmates. On the contrary, it is a consequence of the litigious environment CDCR was struggling to address. The new paradigm for change in CDCR was now "court-driven and court-managed." But you can't litigate culture; in this case, prison culture. An environment, ironically, that was not contributing to effective patient care. What had been a concern about the health delivery system, soon proved to be an "overcrowding" issue since the sheer volume of patients was too much for CDCR's prison infrastructure and health care system to manage.

The "Crowding" Dilemma

A federal three-judge court was convened to consider placing limits on California's prison population. The orders were issued after U.S. District Court Judges, Lawrence Karlton, and Thelton Henderson and Ninth Circuit Court Appeals Justice, Stephen Reinhardt concluded that California prisons are unable to provide constitutionally adequate medical care (Plata) and mental health care (Coleman) due, in part, to severe overcrowding. The trial in front of the federal three-judge court began on November 18, 2008. On August 4, 2009, the three judges found that overcrowding was the primary cause of unconstitutional conditions in California's prisons such as the system's inability to provide competent and timely health care for prisoners. The judges also found compelling evidence that reducing the prison population is the only way to address the problems.

In May 2011, the U.S. Supreme Court ruled that overcrowding in California's prisons resulted in *cruel and unusual punishment* in violation of the Eighth Amendment to the U.S. Constitution. As a result, the Court's ruling required the state to reduce its prison population by approximately 32,000 prisoners within two years. This was a significant court determination that overcrowding was a cause for inadequate health care treatment. The focus was no longer entirely on access to care and quality of service; the focus was now directly placed on the number of prisoners housed in state prison. This was not an operational issue for the prisons; it was now a policy issue for the state—a policy issue that continues to be debated among the governor's office, legislature, and the courts.

Since the CDCR had failed to provide adequate delivery of health care in the prisons and had not achieved any discernible reduction in the prison population, CDCR was ordered to reduce the offender population to 155 percent of the state capacity by March of 2012. Governor Brown signed into law AB 109, Public Safety Realignment Act as the means to address the court directives. In November of 2011, a CDCR deposition to the court projected the prison population numbers by June 30, 2012 to be 136,614 (Fig. 5). Roughly, twelve thousand inmates above the court mandated target. As of March 20, 2013, the state in-custody population was at 123,147 (CDCR, 2013). To date, the CDCR has not yet met the federal court mandate of 110,000 inmates.

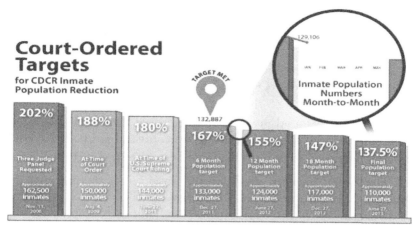

Figure 5 (CDCR, 2012).

In January of 2013, Governor Brown declared the "…prison crisis over and launched a legal and public relations crusade to end court oversight of inmate healthcare…"[126] In April of 2013, the three-Judge panel rejected the governor's bid to end restrictions on overcrowding stating, "At no point over the past several months have defendants (state of California) indicated any willingness to comply, or made any attempt to comply, with the orders of the court…in fact they have blatantly defied them."[127] The Governor and CDCR leadership were now pushing back and rightly so, given the effort being made statewide in all the prisons.

The *Los Angeles Times* reported that CDCR Spokesperson Deborah Hoffman criticized the federal judges' decision in a prepared statement:

> "…The truth of the matter is that California has invested more than a billion dollars to transform its prison health care system into one of the best in the country. Our prisons now provide timely and effective health care to inmates that far exceed what the constitution requires…"

To be clear, the federal court judges had ordered the state to reduce crowding to 137.5 percent by June of 2013, which amounts to about 9,600 offenders being released or moved outside the prisons (county supervision or out-of-state placement). According to a report released to the *Los Angeles Times* in April of 2013, "...the prison population for California stood at 119,542 inmates or 149.5 percent of the number they were designed to hold..." The governor and CDCR agency secretary and directors may be found in contempt of court if the prison population does not go down. As of this writing, the court had given the governor until January of 2014 to meet the inmate population reduction.

How this "crowding" predicament played out in the prisons was a much more alarming problem. The operational dilemma faced by correctional practitioners from all classifications; nursing, doctors, officers, counselors, psychologists, plant operations, clerical records, and managers was staggering. All those groups were trying to wrap their heads around delivery of services in a prison setting and all had failed as far as the courts were concerned.

The delivery system created by the court receiver and dictated from Sacramento was initially implemented as a broad policy directive affecting all employees, but was treated in a silo fashion with each group adhering to their own protocols and culture. The health care managers and wardens were not sharing the same mindset regarding their roles and expectations for others. Even the most enlightened wardens statewide—and there were many—had a hard time finding straightforward communication links among the differing cultures within Health Care (Nursing, Medical, and Mental Health) who were competing amongst themselves for the same court resources. But it wasn't solely a health care challenge.

Plant operations staff had historically responded to custody infrastructure needs before health care needs. After 2005, the priority changed, but the infrastructure needs remained the same. CDCR had shot itself in the foot years earlier by cutting back jobs in plant operations to save on budget costs statewide. As a result, what normally had been routine sink or toilet repairs in the cells became priority job orders for clinical needs. Correctional leadership would have to decide what was more important, health care delivery or operable cells. CDCR headquarters chose the health care delivery system as the priority. But in the field, prison administrators, especially those in the reception centers, continued to focus on operable cells. They had no choice since the county jails were overcrowded with inmates headed to prison. Not a good choice for CDCR prison management, given the court oversight, but the back-and-forth rollercoaster decision-making process spurred by which stakeholder demanded immediate action (receiver, PLO, court monitors, governor, legislature, county jails, etc) had already become the norm for CDCR and the prisons. Crisis bed management was an everyday occurrence.

The same conflicting and competing resource issues applied to the clerical arena, too. Records functions (medical and custody) didn't agree on time tables for sharing information relative to transfers and releases. Record functions were by-and-large manually completed, and both record operations were not using compatible information technology. Phone and the facsimile communication were the primary movers of information, both suffering inconsistent and error-prone delivery woes. All the failed efforts were painstakingly documented and shared by the PLO with the federal court to "prove" CDCR's failure to make a concerted effort to meet the court mandates. The sheer number of prisoners needing medical, dental, mental health, and disability treatment was beyond the space and resources needed to meet the court mandates. This was especially the case within the original twelve prisons, whose infrastructures didn't support the needed space or logistics. Those antiquated buildings lacked room to support additional telephone, computer, plumbing, or disability access, all of which were required functions for today's modern health care delivery systems.

No demonstrable improvements made, whether infrastructure or systems methodology, satisfied the court edict of *constitutionally adequate* medical care. In fact, the *Los Angeles Times* reported that the judges put the blame squarely on the governor for failing to address the crowding issue, saying "...he had provided no 'convincing evidence' that overcrowding is no longer a problem...his recent actions raise serious doubts as to the governor's good faith in this matter and in the prison litigation as a whole." Governor Brown had asked the Supreme Court to delay the order to release 9,600 offenders and give the state time to take its appeal to the higher court. On July 3, 2013, the Supreme Court refused to stay the June 20, 2013 order by the U.S. District Court Judges, Lawrence Karlton and Thelton Henderson and Ninth Circuit Court Appeals Justice Stephen Reinhardt to intervene. California would nonetheless be forced to release 9,600 more offenders back to the community.

The Tail Wagging the Dog

In 2009, the PLO had effectively argued to the California Ninth Circuit Court that overcrowding results in constitutionally inadequate care for inmates. The United States Supreme Court upheld the state court ruling in 2011 citing overcrowding as "cruel and unusual" punishment. Although, CDCR had made significant effort to reduce the statewide population by the end of 2013, the inmate population remained some 9,000 inmates above the court decree. Governor Brown's last minute request to the court for more time to work out a long range plan; instead, got a one month reprieve from the Ninth Circuit Court. The PLO maintained that, by doing nothing about the unprecedented inmate population would, "...prolong ongoing irreparable harm—including illness and death..."[128] The court agreed, citing the four years of population reduction "non-compliance."[129]

However, this was not the view held by most correctional health care practitioners in the prisons. A definitive improvement had occurred since 2005 that clearly brought better continuity of service and quality of care that had not been evident before. While it was true that further reducing the inmate population would benefit the onerous workload suffered at all of the prisons, especially in the reception centers, the question of what was "constitutionally" adequate care was, for all practical purposes, a question about "overcrowding." The issues of health care access or service were no longer relevant to the bigger issue of *too many inmates* for limited resources.

For correctional staff, the "Cadillac service" (meaning: *the best health care* taxpayers can buy) being provided to inmates was above and beyond what was perceived to be available to the community. The CDCR staff was not alone in that observation. The governor argued that "the state has spent almost two billion dollars since 2008 on [health care] upgrades...the prison population also has been reduced quite a bit more than the judges seem to recognize."[130] From CDCR's perspective, the legal arguments for CDCR failing to meet undefined "constitutionally adequate care" was no longer true. The alleged unwarranted death rate was remedied as well as the ability to request, track, and provide care. But the care was never consistent or sufficient to meet the audit tool goals of 90 percent.

What was true, at least in the opinions of most correctional employees, is that the PLO appeared to be a self-perpetuating legal bureaucracy that the court was unknowingly paying deference too. What perplexed

CDCR headquarters was the inability of the local prison administrative staff to resolve or comply with the PLO demands. At the same time, what frustrated prison administrative staff was the consistent and subtle expansion over the years of PLO oversight into areas that previously had not been at issue. The PLO focus of adequate health care delivery in a prison had expanded to a policy debate about "crowding." But the PLO didn't stop there.

The Madrid Ghosts

It was just a matter of time before the PLO would take CDCR's Use of Force Policy to task. The PLO had already addressed Use of Force in a previous landmark case; Madrid v. Gomez. In 1990, inmates at Pelican Bay State Prison had filed a class action law suit against CDCR alleging:

> that the defendants unconstitutionally condoned a pattern and practice of using excessive force against inmates, failed to provide inmates with adequate medical care, failed to provide inmates with adequate mental health care, imposed inhumane conditions in the Security Housing Unit, utilized cell-assignment procedures that exposed inmates to an unreasonable risk of assault from other inmates, failed to provide adequate procedural safeguards when segregating the prison gang affiliates in the Security Housing Unit, and failed to provide inmates with adequate access to the courts. (PLO, 2013)

The Madrid Court assigned a court master and CDCR was duty-bound to create a Use of Force Policy consistent with the Madrid decision and amenable to the prison environment. As a result, since 1995, CDCR had been using *less-than-lethal* force options (OC spray and/or physical holds) to gain compliance with inmates refusing or unable to follow directives based on their mental health concerns.

When an inmate was suffering a delusional episode and doctors required that he/she be medicated for his own safety, correctional staff were obligated to gain physical control of the inmate whether he be in a cell or office or exercise yard...it was doctor's orders. The same applied to an inmate that refused medications. If the doctor determined that "forced medication" was required to stabilize or save the life of the inmate-patient, correctional staff was obliged to forcibly restrain the inmate for the treatment.

The protocols were spelled out and had been under the scrutiny of the Coleman court monitors for many years. Correctional supervisors were trained and followed procedures mandating that required questions are asked before force options are used: At the time of the mental health breakdown, was the inmate in restraints or not? Was he in a cell? Was he alone? Was he an immediate threat to himself or others? Had sufficient clinical intervention to attempt resolution of the episode taken place? Did the clinician order medication be provided to the inmate? Did the inmate's actions (destroying state property, barricading door, or covering windows) constitute an immediate security breach?

All these questions and more had to be discussed, performed, and approved by correctional and clinical management before any action could take place. Psychiatric doctors and psychologists, alike, all shared their views on the best means to address disconsolate inmate-patients. This process had been the established *calculated* Use of Force protocol for all health care patient interventions. But the PLO sought more far-reaching remedies as the years passed. It has expanded litigation and the courts were now listening.

For example, U.S. District Court Judge Lawrence Karlton had been reviewing videos of mental health inmates being sprayed with pepper spray (*Los Angeles Times*, October 2, 2013). In April of 2014, Judge Karlton ruled that California's treatment of mentally ill inmates violates constitutional safeguards against cruel and unusual punishment through excessive use of pepper spray and isolation. The PLO had asked the court to restrict CDCR from using pepper spray on the mentally ill. This amounted to additional court oversight of the CDCR Use of Force Policy.

The policy already required the attendance of a custody manager (captain or above) and a medical clinician to be present to determined that a medical or mental health need requires staff to remove an inmate from a cell by force. The policy also required that, in all instances, the event be videotaped. The use of pepper spray is a non-lethal and safer measure to immobilize the inmate before staff enters the cell. This has proven to reduce injury to staff and inmates, alike, from not having to use physical force to subdue the inmate. You would think that was sufficient to ensure appropriate oversight. Apparently, it isn't enough. CDCR is currently revising the extraction policy on calculated use of force and will probably go back to using physical force protocols as was the practice many years ago. The same protocol that the Madrid court found wanting.

What strikes the psyche of persons unfamiliar with prison Use of Force situations is the appearance of pain and suffering caused by OC pepper spray. OC pepper spray causes an intense burning sensation in all the mucus membranes of the body (nose, mouth, and eyes). It creates a sensation of affixation as the body tries to secrete all fluids. It is a nasty, but effective deterrent. Inmates generally want the spraying to stop and respond instantly to staff directions to lie down or cuff up. In all cases of OC pepper spray usage, inmates are decontaminated with fresh air and water with their body fully recovering from the effects within about thirty minutes. Each case must be observed and documented by staff. What was presented to the court as the issue is the "cruelty" of the OC application to mental health patients who may or may not understand what is happening in that moment.

What is not fully recognized is the causes; uncooperative inmates with feces smeared in the cell, thrown at staff, or eaten by the inmate. Or worse, imminent danger to the inmate's safety when they are harming themselves by cutting or banging their head and bodies against the steel bed or cell wall. The options available to correctional staff include, baton rounds fired from a projectile firearm or physically entering the cell and taking control of the inmate. In both cases, some degree of injury is likely to both the inmate and staff. Ironically, in assessing what constitutes "cruelty" to mental health patients in crisis, is what is conveniently ignored; OC spray has proven to be more effective in gaining compliance without elevating the threat of injury.

Another example of the PLO in-roads on the operation of the prison has been the outbreak of valley fever at Pleasant Valley State Prison and Avenal State Prison. Valley fever is a fungal infection that causes flu-like symptoms and can be lethal. It was alleged by the PLO medical expert that "62 prisoners died throughout the state from 2006 through January 2013 after coming down with the disease...African Americans and Filipinos are particularly vulnerable to the lethal form of the disease...71

percent of the prisoners who died between 2006 and 2011 were African American" (SFGate.com, April 28, 2013).

The PLO wanted all inmates susceptible to valley fever to be moved. The PLO argument was akin to saying cold weather causes more colds. Although, valley fever susceptibly in the Central Valley of California may have some validity, in fact, it was stewed in a big pot of assumptions. First, the PLO data supporting the risk-of-death argument applied to the total state inmate population which amounted to only sixty-two inmates or less than.04 percent. Moreover, the.04 percentage at risk covered a seven year period. This is without considering what other secondary causes may have contributed to their deaths. The CDCR rightly challenged the arguments presented by the PLO to the court, but no formal resolution has been forthcoming.

If the state were forced by the court to comply with this demand, it would open the floodgates of other issues. One impact would be the forced segregation of ethnic groups by region. Imagine Avenal or Pleasant Valley housing White and Latino inmates and/or Folsom with all Blacks. There is always power in numbers so this potential outcome would be a dangerous precedent for the CDCR. Besides, any agreement with the PLO on this issue would open the door for staff to demand the same alleged health protection. Staff susceptible to valley fever could demand moving (at state expense) to another "safer" prison. The domino effect would continue to fall on other potential health care claims, as well.

The medical/mental health debate has also bled into the recent hunger strike by inmates. The PLO is challenging the state's right to forcibly feed hunger strikers when they are determined to be in a life-threatening status. It is ironic that the CDCR health care effort to save lives in prison, a principle cause of the Plata and Coleman lawsuits, has now turned down the rocky road of managing *custody protocols* for the sake of the perceived health concerns of offenders. The ripples in CDCR's muddy litigated ponds continue to expand.

CHAPTER 7
HUNGER STRIKE

You said you'd never compromise,
With the mystery tramp, but now you realize,
He's not selling any alibis, as you stare
into the vacuum of his eyes,
And ask him, hey mister, do you want to make a deal...

Bob Dylan
"Like a Rolling Stone"

"You Lost Control!"

I got the call about 9:00 a.m. on Saturday morning. The lieutenant advised that inmates in Dorm 302 were refusing to eat or program. They refused to go to work, school, yard, or chow. The first question I asked, "When did this start?"

He replied, "Yesterday morning, I think."

It was the lieutenant's first day back to work and he had just been made aware of the issue when he arrived. "What's their beef?" I asked.

He indicated that the inmates in the dorm were angry at the new officer. They claimed the officer had been changing their program by strictly enforcing the rules and was disrespecting everyone. The lieutenant revealed that all the races, Blacks, Hispanics, and Whites, were participating in the strike. Having all the races involved was significant, since ethnic groups don't usually jump to support one another unless there's something in it for themselves or there is a legitimate mutual concern. Regardless of the motive, they wanted to get staff's attention.

Four days earlier, we had staff personnel "Post Assignment Schedule" job rotations completed. Officers bid for posts (job assignments) throughout the institution. The job assignments were based on seniority and previously-negotiated non-seniority posts. During the mid-1980s, management at local prisons had begun to lose the ability to control who and where staff was assigned. The negotiations for the statewide Bargaining Unit 6 (correctional officers) contract were handled in Sacramento, where politics and money determined outcomes more readily than managerial or operational necessity. This gradual change in how and who got job assignments would have a profound impact on management of local facilities for years to come and continues unabated today.

One of the major outcomes was the loss of supervisory control of housing unit staff assignments. Most search and escort (S&E) posts had weekend days off (Friday/Saturday or Sunday/Monday). These posts were coveted by many officers and the union fought hard to get those prized posts included in the bid process. The union argued that only management's "kids" or "favored" staff was getting premium weekend post assignments. They argued that some of those posts provided experience that would aid them in promotional exams and that those posts also provided exposure for staff to administration. There was absolute merit to those arguments. But some supervisors and managers saw it differently.

A good S&E could pick up the slack for busy sergeants. Since the posts were administratively controlled, if an officer didn't meet muster, it was easy to simply job-change him/her for someone else. Alternatively, sergeants would reward their S&Es with insider knowledge of upcoming special assignments, recommend them for promotional or coveted posts, and transfer the S&Es with them when the sergeant was moved to a new assignment. The S&Es were generally "go getters" who knew the inmate population, were familiar with the unit "paperwork," and were the first to give supervisors the "heads up" when staff morale or inmate tension was brewing. When the contract provisions reduced administrative control of post assignments in 1986, the department began to see a gradual slippage in the work ethic and productivity of critical posts. "Critical posts" meaning; assignments that were important to supervisors and managers.

Sergeants were not able to pick and choose the best or loyal S&E to get their work done. They could not depend upon the new breed of officers who got the post to volunteer to do paperwork, errands, etc, that the previous loyal S&Es would do. On the contrary, the new breed of S&E saw their job in a more limited perspective. They were only obligated to follow the "post orders" or written job duty statements, such as: Monitor chow, canteen, unit work crews, and pill lines; respond to assistance calls; and provide "count-time" coverage. The other "stuff" was not required because the "post orders" (job description) didn't say so. What had been the norm of extra work and loyalty was now becoming the exception. This is not a negative reflection on officer dedication to the job. On the contrary, they continued to function satisfactorily with security and control matters, but, as time passed, fewer and fewer "additional duties" could be imposed. The new contracts had taken valuable position control leverage away from custody managers and supervisors.

Some of the new breed S&Es did excel as a matter of their own work ethic and professional demeanor. Also, some sergeants that had the leadership skills to demand it, prevailed in maintaining a solid crew regardless of the contract changes. Most sergeants, however, discovered a diminished work force pool of dedicated officers. It would take a mountain of paperwork to remove a recalcitrant, or worse, incompetent officer. This is not meant to disparage the majority of custody staff who did their jobs well. It is an observation regarding the impact a single officer in a "critical post" can have that could adversely affect security protocols, or worse, create undue risk of harm to staff or inmates.

S&Es are first responders in any disturbance or incident. They must be proficient report-writers and keen observers to ensure witness and evidence is properly secured. More importantly, the better ones can gauge the climate of a facility and take proactive steps to ward off trouble between inmate groups or inmates and staff. Their custody awareness and communication skills are not something that is outlined in a post order; on the contrary, it's a function of solid peace officer character.

****

I reported to Facility III at the California Rehabilitation Center about 10:00 a.m. I was not happy because the supervisory staff had failed to report a serious issue to me in a timely manner. An inmate strike is like a virus that can spread and escalate quickly. This one started maybe two days or so before I got the call. The staff could visibly see I was in no mood for pleasantries. The *sergeant and lieutenant briefed me again about details that were being said by numerous inmates in the dorm. We toured the "striking" Dorm 302 and some random dorms for perspective. Facility III housed 1,300 felon inmates, all level II inmates in a dorm setting. The dorms were dilapidated wood-framed buildings all connected by a large snaking breezeway. The dorms were built during the 1940s as a Navy hospital barracks, which later were given to the state to house Civil Addict Commitments and low level felons.*

The Dorm 302 officer had been accused of being totally obnoxious with inmates cursing "dick head" to any inmate that confronted him. Some of the complaints included the officer's penchant for ripping and throwing away extra sheets and blankets that he found in the bunk areas of the dorm. Inmates were aware that they weren't allowed "extra" items, but that wasn't their concern. They were angry at the rude and disrespectful manner the officer went about removing some personal and extra items on the bunks. The inmates' demand was simple: remove the officer from the dorm and they would stop the strike.

I asked the lieutenant, "When is the last time the dorm went to chow call?"

He looked at me and said, "Yesterday morning, as I understand it, but this is the second dorm that isn't programming."

I was stunned. "What did you say? The second dorm? What other dorm is refusing to eat?"

The lieutenant had been made aware, after calling me at home, that Dorm 307 was also refusing to program. The officer in that dorm had also "pissed off" the inmates. They had started the sit-down strike the day before Dorm 302. The Dorm 307 inmates also wanted the officer removed. I called the 3rd watch lieutenant who worked from 3-11 p.m., and directed him to report to work an hour earlier before his shift began. I asked the 2nd watch lieutenant if the Men's Advisory Council (MAC), inmate representatives for facility units and dorms, had been spoken with about the issues. He indicated in the affirmative. He had spoken to them individually, but they could not offer, or would not offer, any other resolutions. I directed him and the sergeant to round up the MAC Reps from Dorm 302 and 307 and deliver them all to the Facility III sergeant's office

****

MAC inmates represent the ethnic races consisting of Blacks, Whites, Latinos, and Asians. In some cases, a Mexican or Central American

National—"border brother," as they are referred to—is included to represent their interests. MACs are an unusual breed of inmate. Generally speaking, none have direct power or influence in the housing units. Rather, they are mouth pieces for the real inmate shot callers that run the units. MAC inmates report to their respective races on all matters that the unit lieutenant or sergeant wants the inmate population to be aware of in the unit. They are useful in squashing rumors, finding "lost" items, providing general information from administration. MAC reps are not peacemakers. But they do deliver messages of interest or concern from the inmate population to custody staff on matters like visiting, property, or canteen issues. Additionally, they are not above assisting nefarious activities at the behest of the prison gangs or shot callers, either. Generally speaking, I had no use for them, but in this particular incident I saw their value.

At approximately 11:30 a.m., the MAC reps for Dorm 302 and 307 were escorted into the sergeant's office in a straight line. The inmates recognized me immediately as the captain for the unit. I waited until all were present and standing facing me. Three S&Es were positioned around them. The lieutenant and sergeant stood behind me. As I began my "speech," I knew exactly who my lecture was intended for. My message was for the S&Es, not the inmates. The MAC reps didn't give-a-shit about anything I had to say, because they were only going to follow the lead of the shot callers in the dorms. I knew that, too, but I also knew the S&Es would get the word out to staff on what we were going to do as the custody team.

In a loud and stern voice, I said, "I want to make it very clear and make sure you get the message back to the units." The MAC reps looked disinterested; some looked away, some with their heads down, as I continued, "The officers will not be removed from the units in your dorm. In fact, I intend to put more officers in the dorm with my sergeant. I will make them the safest dorms in this prison!" I raised my voice for effect, "No inmate is going to tell me how to run these units. I expect everyone to program! Sergeant, take these inmates back to the dorms!"

"Yes sir, Captain," the sergeant responded affirmatively, as he motioned the inmates out the door. This dramatic "song and dance" to the MAC meant nothing to me. What did matter was for staff to know that we would not accept the inmate hunger strike demands to remove staff.

****

As I exited the sergeant's office, I reminded the lieutenant that I wanted a plan on what we would do to stop the strike. About ten minutes later, I called a seasoned S&E to my office. He was familiar with most of the inmate leaders in the units. I told him to bring me the shot callers from Dorm 302 and 307 one at a time so that I could speak with them. My fear was that once the word got out about the strike, other dorms would close ranks and support the other two units in the strike. Time was ticking away and I didn't want to lose control of the dorms.

When the 3rd watch lieutenant arrived, both lieutenants came to my office. They sat at a large table that protruded out from my desk. Each lieutenant sat on either side facing me. I started, "I am not happy about no one calling me on Thursday night to inform me that Dorm 307 had started a strike. Now this morning, on Saturday, we have another unit doing the same. Let me be clear," I said, as I looked directly at the 3rd watch lieutenant, "your officers lost control of those two units, then your sergeants lost control of the units, and now we are sitting here and I, for one, will not lose my facility because two officers can't work their way out of a cluster fuck!" I stared across the table and asked point blank, "Now, what's the plan?"

They were a bit startled by my statement about "losing control." I didn't exactly blame them, but the inference was clear. By including myself in the question, it softened the accusation, but didn't reduce their aggravation.

In any law enforcement organization, it is always a mixed bag of personalities, but what stands out is the "A" type persona. There are a lot of them because agencies search for, encourage, and develop individual acumen with emphasis on command capabilities. Law enforcement agencies need to have staff that engenders a "take charge" attitude to maintain control when all hell breaks loose. CDCR is no exception. There is no shortage of strong-willed personalities who are in control, non-emotional, with reasoned by-the-book demeanors. In a house full of felons who feed off the fear of others, a strong para-military ego, that maintains a command presence and is more than willing to engage, is a formidable adversary.

The plan described by the lieutenants was simple: Continue to provide extra coverage by assigning an additional officer to each dorm. Also, have the S&Es and sergeants make extra rounds in those dorms. Search the dorms and speak with the dorm MAC reps again to see if they changed their minds. This was CDC "101" (meaning basic correctional practice). Both lieutenants *revealed that the officers in question were "by-the-book" meaning everything was black-and-white with them. Both officers enforced procedures to the letter. There was no "grey" area when it came to inmates adhering to the rules. Each ran a structured dorm and, as a result, both were not well liked by inmates.*

I still wasn't happy, but I knew the plan described by the lieutenants was the best course to take given our situation. We would not allow the inmates to dictate the terms of engagement (removal of the officers). More importantly, I was not going to allow myself to wait for the inmates to decide when and under what circumstances the strike would end. However, at the moment, the concern was not to exacerbate the situation by creating more tension in the dorms and riling up a "hornets' nest."

****

Some calculated risk was needed to resolve the conflict and reduce the tension building in the dorms. For rank and file "boots-on-the-ground," when a crisis situation develops on the yard between inmates, a calculated risk could cost a staff or inmate's life. Most officers successfully negotiate "good behavior" and quell minor disputes by the force of their reputation. They are respected by the inmates because their word is good. In those cases where decisions are needed for program changes above their pay grade, they defer to their supervisors. It is the supervisor's duty to ascertain the issue and take a definitive action to resolve it. This is a daily occurrence in prisons statewide.

The same "risk-taking" label doesn't always apply to supervisors and managers. For management, any proactive engagement in addressing staff and inmate disputes could cost a reputation and possibly a career path, both of which are considerably less risky concerns than what officers face each day. Unfortunately, I've witnessed many a supervisor and manager who readily relinquished their decision-making authority to the "higher ups" to avoid having "ink spilled" all over them for taking some unwanted action. Seeing managers and supervisors that steered clear of making the hard decisions disgusted me to no end. In prison, there can be no claim of "risk-taking" when fear of disciplinary action is the only danger. But when the risk involved the possibility of serious injury to staff and inmates, that was a totally different matter!

Supervisors and managers are responsible to their teams first, especially in a crisis situation. Everything else was secondary. I've known plenty of men and women who were solid leaders at every level and every position. But I've seen the opposite, too! Unfortunately, leadership traits among supervisors, managers, and administrators are eroding more and more each year. Custody personnel are less inclined to make decisions as our litigious criminal justice environment seeks more and more victims in the dysfunctional prison environment.

I recognized that if I had contacted my superiors and advised them of the hunger strike occurring in my unit housing 1,300 inmates, I would soon be sitting in an office with other administrators and the warden. I did not want the warden and executive team deciding the resolution—namely, the removal of the officers or possible lockdown of the entire facility. Not that the warden would make that particular call, but I didn't want to chance it. In my mind, that option would be opening a Pandora's box for future episodes of inmate discontent. To oblige the inmate demands was tantamount to disempowering the officers. The truth was, the officers had already done that to themselves. What was needed was to find a way to get them back in charge.

****

It was approximately 2:00 p.m. when the facility S&E brought the first inmate shot caller to my office. He, like the others to follow, was a seasoned convict who had done time at other prisons. In fact, with each convict, I asked the same questions: "Where are you from? How much time left to serve? How do you feel about this situation?" One thing I learned early on in the department about inmates is, the closer they are to their release date, the more willing they were to talk about the program. They didn't want to chance getting more time added to their sentence or continued inconvenience in the prison. Even parole violators who were doing "straight time" and could not have "good time" taken away for disciplinary infractions, were more inclined to cooperate if something could be held over their heads that they wanted badly (i.e. visits, phone calls, dorm change, etc). The trick was figuring out what got their attention.

On the last question (how do you feel...), I never asked what they knew because the answer would be similar to the popular television program Hogan's Heroes character, Sergeant Schultz, who would say, "I know nothing!" But when I ask convicts what they think or feel about a situation, they were generally more responsive. In this situation, the answer from the inmate shot callers was the same, "Hey Captain, I'm just doing my number, I don't get involved in the small stuff."

I responded, "I know but you're a Veterano (older as in 'did more time' inmate) and get respect from others in the dorm. I'm sure you didn't start this business, but I also know that some will listen to you."

The White and Latino convicts both responded the same, "Captain, if you just remove that officer, I'm sure the dorm will stop this mess."

I gave all shot callers, separately, the same response, "Look, let me explain my predicament. Say, for example, if I were to book you for conspiracy to instigate a strike or disturbance, you'd have disciplinary rights that the hearing lieutenant would have to abide by, correct?"

They nodded in agreement, but weren't sure what I really meant.

I continued, "Well, that process could take thirty days; the same applies to that officer. He has rights, too. I can't start to look into his conduct when I have a dorm full of inmates that aren't programming. I cannot focus on his behavior until my units are back at work and going to chow regularly."

The inmate shot callers I spoke to were not sure if I meant to write them up. They studied my facial expressions and listened intently for clarity. I wanted them to be clear about my intentions, but a little confused about where they stood in the situation.

In a calm, almost whispered voice, I said, "Look, this is what I need; I want all the dorms to go to chow tonight and start back to work and school on Monday. If that happens, then I will address the officer's conduct. It could take thirty days or so, but I will get the officers' attention. That doesn't mean they will be moved, but something will change. You have my word. If I don't get that cooperation, then I will need to identify any inmates that I believe could have stopped this mess and ship them to Ad-Seg (CRC used CIM Palm Hall as its Administrative Segregation). If I don't get any cooperation, then I will move my team dorm-by-dorm in the whole facility removing anything and everything I suspect may be a security risk to inmates. There will be no contraband or extras (sheets, blankets, pillows, mattresses, personal property, etc). You have my word on that, too. It's not what I want to do, but I will if I can't get any cooperation."

The discussion and message was pretty much the same for the Black shot caller as with the other two. This was the first time I had met any of the shot caller inmates face-to-face, but the MAC reps had seen me touring the unit dorms many times. My reputation as a fair, but firm captain had already been established after a year in the unit. They knew I was telling them the truth.

I was trying to let these inmate shot callers know two things and not so subtly. First, I knew who they were and secondly, they now knew that I knew who they were. In their minds, I wasn't blowing smoke because I had the authority to do what I said I would do. In fact, I had done it many times before when a fight or skirmish broke out in a dorm between races.

Minor racial disturbances in a 100-man dorm can escalate quickly in a unit. CRC was no different. I had little patience for fights, but interracial fighting demanded more consequences. Both scenarios put custody staff in harm's way to quell the disturbance. But those with racial overtones were like waiving a match over gunpowder; you're inviting trouble you can't control. In those instances, I'd have the lieutenant and sergeant "clean house" of everything not nailed down in the dorm. The inmates would be confined to their bunks in skivvies and not allowed to use their personal TVs or radios. Boredom can be a great motivator. This adult "time out" which could last a while, was also a message that "if you play, you pay."

It was time for the 3:00 p.m. custody shift change. Both lieutenants remained in the unit, but I wanted to speak to both sergeants before the shift changed, I had the lieutenants sit in, as well.

"Sergeants, I want you both to understand how I see this mess with both dorms, 302 and 307. As far as I'm concerned, the officers lost control of the dorms. It was your job to get it back, but that didn't work. You lost control, too."

One of the sergeants interrupted me. "Captain, that's not fair, it didn't start on my shift."

I quickly responded, "Is that right? Are they going to chow on your shift? Are they working on your shift?"

"No sir," he responded.

"Does your obligation to this facility end with those two dorms?"

"No sir, it doesn't," the sergeant responded.

I continued. "Now the lieutenants and I are here, tell me when does it end? If we fail, does the associate warden come down or chief deputy or the warden to fix it?"

They both stared at me, but said nothing as I continued. "I have said it many times before; you run the facilities, not me and not the lieutenants. You both allowed the dorms to get out of hand. Now I expect you both to get it back. Those dorms will not be given to the inmates and those officers will have to do whatever is necessary to regain control, but on our terms."

Both said nothing, only nodded in agreement. They were angry, but they also knew what had to be done.

About 4:30 p.m., evening chow had started. The meal was a popular one: noodles and meat with bread rolls and string beans. There would be ice cream for dessert. I was encouraged. I toured the chow hall, which fed over 400 inmates from Facilities II and III at the same time. As the inmates poured in and out in a rhythmic fashion, keeping tables filled just long enough for the next unit to arrive, I got the word...Dorm 302 had just exited the dorm and was next in line to serve. Dorm 307 followed in short order. I acted like nothing had happened and went about touring the chow hall talking with the inmates who were eating dinner. I suspect the sergeants and lieutenants had also made the rounds and read the "riot act" to some influential convicts. Regardless, the matter had been resolved...but I had one more job to do.

****

It was 6:30 p.m., chow time had finished and the inmates were on their bunks for count. It was quiet and the right time to close the loop. I had spoken with the union representative for the facility. I explained the situation about the dorms and asked that he be in my office when I met with the officers. I gave him no further details about the pending discussion. Neither the sergeants nor lieutenants were present. As the officers came into the office, I could see the deer-in-the-headlights look on their faces. Normally, on 3rd watch, they don't have this type of interaction with the captain, but I was determined to finish my message to all personnel attached to the inmate hunger strike.

"Gentlemen, you don't need to speak and I will be brief. Your union rep may speak up, if at any time he believes I'm violating your rights. Do you understand?"

They nodded yes.

"Good, there's no nice way to say what happened these last few days in your dorms, but I'll put it bluntly: both of you lost control. I don't know what was said or done to piss off the dorms, and all the races, to the point where they refused to eat or work, but you both did it!"

One blurted out, "Sir, I was just enforcing the rules..."

I cut him off, saying, "I believe you AND I believe the officers in the other ten dorms are enforcing the rules, too! But they didn't lose control of their dorms, you did!" I looked squarely at both officers as I continued, "The state doesn't pay sergeants to baby sit or sneak around checking up on officers. The state expects facility staff to be professional and courteous, just like your training dictates that YOU be at all times. But both of you lost control because of something you did or said and only both of you can take control of the dorms back. Do you agree?"

They both nodded yes.

But I wasn't done getting my pound of flesh. I continued, "If an officer is calling an inmate a "dickhead" or telling him he "has nothing coming" and is tearing up his house (the inmate's locker and bed area), then he's not going to get much cooperation. But it doesn't end there. It also makes it harder on the next cop to do his job because Johnny (inmate) looks at all of us the same."

The room was deftly silent for a moment. Both officers looked at me not sure what to say or do.

"Report back to your dorms," I ordered, "but you'd better reflect on what you need to do to change the way you handle your business. Am I clear?"

Yes sir," said one officer as he rose to leave.

"Yes sir. I'm a good officer," said the other almost pleading.

I quickly interjected, "I have no doubt, but you lost control, now be a 'good officer' and get that dorm back!"

"Yes sir," he responded, without making eye contact as he left. The job steward rose from his chair, having never uttered a word during my rant, looked at me, and smiled nodding in the affirmative as he left the office.

Opening Pandora's Box

Hunger strikes, work stoppages, and refusals to program (facility or education/vocation class strikes, yard, or chow-hall sit-downs, etc) occur somewhat routinely in state prisons with a broad range of intensity and risk. Most are handled discreetly and immediately by staff working the unit or facility. Most are resolved without the dramatic flair described above. More often than not, the issue or complaints alleged by inmates are a matter of misinformation that a respected officer, counselor, sergeant, or lieutenant clarifies to the satisfaction of the inmate population. It has been part of the history of prison culture that inmates take correctional leadership at "its word." This is not to be confused with trust. A person's word in prison has more to do with respect. You don't tell an inmate what you think…you tell them what you mean to do and then do it.

These aren't negotiations in any sense of the word; it is plain speak about issues both sides know very well. Negotiations involve a bargaining give and take process between two or more parties (each with its own aims, needs, and viewpoints) seeking to arrive at a mutual agreement. There can be no give and take in prison. That would invite a paradigm shift for the overseer/prisoner model: control, structure, and obedience for the overseer and compliance, cooperation, and servitude by the prisoner.

The overseer/prisoner model works well in correctional facilities for one reason only, "power." Prison staff is routinely out-numbered. There are no less than 100 inmates to one officer, in most instances, but sometime less and often times more. Having the ability to control the environment without the need for violence is an everyday exercise for all staff. The facility structure and logistical floor plans provide one degree of control. The other is policies and procedures that require redundancy in security protocols (strip searches, cell searches, monitored phone calls, count procedures, and armed perimeter coverage and patrols, etc). These are all non-negotiable matters for maintaining security.

Negotiating with convicts was counter intuitive to the historical perspective of most custody personnel. For example, inmates may want extended (or a resumption of) phone, visits, canteen, and/or yard privileges. Inmates don't care about the "why" as much as they care about whether or not they will get them. Accordingly, in any individual or group work stoppage or hunger strike, CDCR didn't "negotiate" terms of engagement or even solutions, but would always outline the intended outcomes. The issue of "fairness" was the only consideration seasoned correctional personnel would consider, as long as inmates adhered to the directives of the staff (i.e., return to program, removal from the yard, squash racial conflict, exit the cell, or chow hall, etc). To do otherwise, would be perceived as opening "Pandora's box" for untold drama in a prison setting. The "drama" referred to the unknown issues or new expectations that would become fodder for more negotiation dealings in future conflicts that had rarely been done before in prison.

This conflict resolution mindset was a historical practice that long ago probably found its root from the department's longstanding hostage policy. The CDCR has a "No Hostage" policy, meaning it will not negotiate trade or barter for the release of hostages in exchange for possible escape assistance.[131] Instead, there are protocols in place that derive specific strategic or tactical advantages to resolve hostage situations. But the outcome is always the same—neutralize the threat. So it was, with this historical perspective, that all other conflict resolution would be treated in the same fashion; the surrender of inmates to authority.

A calculated and direct response was always the best remedy, especially when prison gangs were involved. During the initial segregation efforts to separate prison gang members from the general population during the 1980s, CDCR had no qualms about locking them away in the newly created Security Housing Units (SHUs). The Ninth Circuit Court in Toussaint v. Rushen had left its mark on the obligation to ensure inmates rights to due process in any restricted housing such as Ad-Seg or SHU.[132] Attention to due process and appropriate cell and yard placement was a priority, as was the intended outcome; the isolation of prison gang members and associates to reduce violence in the prisons. But seasoned inmates, like convicts, are always looking at avenues to "beat the system." And they are good at it.

Super Max Faux

There wasn't a management control unit, Administrative Segregation (Ad-Seg) or Security Housing Unit (SHU) protocol the prison gangs couldn't beat some of the time. These units were managed by humans, so there was always going to be human error. "Beating the system" refers to the prison gang's ability to introduce contraband and drugs into the cell units of the Ad-Seg and SHUs and to communicate information regarding nefarious activities without being detected. Any number of methods were used; mail, visiting, staff, and contact with other inmates during movement escorts or health care appointments. It was a cat and mouse game for staff and convict to outsmart each other. For the convict, time and circumstance was always in his favor. The department's answer was to create a "Super Max" a prison designed for those "super predators" needing higher control measures. Unfortunately, CDCR was not ready for the twenty-first century criminal mind, but the prison gangs were!

Pelican Bay State Prison (PBSP), a Level IV facility (known as a "Super Max" prison), houses the most notorious prison gang leaders from throughout the state. PBSP contains a Security Housing Unit (SHU) where the leaders from the EME, Aryan Brotherhood (AB), Nuestra Familia (NF), and Black Guerilla Family (BGF) are housed.[133] Not to be excluded are the convict "remnants" from the Texas Syndicate, Northern Structure, PINI, Border Brothers, Nazi Low-Riders, and a potpourri of high profile murderers and other prison predators.

This tightly controlled and limited-movement prison setting did little to deter the prison gangs from continuing nefarious activities within and outside the walls. Visitors, staff, and inmate workers all continued to be intended or unintended assistants for the prison gangs for communicating with street gang soldiers in the streets and other prisons. As well as, letters, packages, kites, and even sign language. Nothing had changed as far as how and why convicts sought to obtain, sell, or control contraband. Coded messages continued to be the primary key to prison gang communication within and outside the prison walls.[134]

In late 2006, PBSP administration decided to further restrict communication between the prison gangs and confederates to deter nefarious activities as much as possible. The recognized leadership of the four main prison gangs; AB, NF, EME, and BGF were moved to a smaller multi-occupancy corridor or POD, duly named the "short corridor." With fewer housing cells, there was even less inmate movement and no possible contact with other inmates in the SHU. For PBSP Investigative Services Unit (ISU) personnel, placing the prison gang shot callers in the short corridor was a very effective means to intercept messages and clamp down on communication. But it had an unintended outcome. It left the prison gang leadership with little choice but to communicate amongst each other.

The "Short Corridor Collective"

These prison gang shot callers were "alpha" personalities who recognized their tier companions as the enemy. But they soon realized they also had much in common. The "Short Corridor Collective," as they called themselves, was comprised of the following prison gang leaders: Todd Ashker, C-58191 (Aryan Brotherhood); Arturo "Tablas" Castellanos,

C-17275 (Mexican Mafia); Ronald "Sitawa Nantambu Jamaa" Dewberry (Black Guerilla Family); and Antonio "Chuco" Guillen (Nuestra Familia). They all shared the same kind of prison experiences and rise to power. Each had, at some time in their prison life, directed, conspired, or acted in a ruthless, sociopathic manner to reach the pinnacle of power they held in the gang. Likewise, each had been disciplinary-free for much of the past decade.

To be sure, each member of the Short Corridor Collective recognized each of the others as a leader with the same interests. All of them wanted out of the SHU. Each of them wanted to maintain their power on the mainline and the streets. Finally, all of them realized that there was power in numbers. What was initially a successful CDCR "control" tactic to intercept the communication links of the prison gangs, would ultimately introduce a more calculated and, arguably, more effective strategic response by the prison gangs, which the CDCR was not ready to address in any organized fashion. CDCR was about to engage the prison gangs in a public "fire fight" and didn't even know it was providing the ammunition!

The *Los Angeles (LA) Times* reported that in 2009, Denis O'Hearn, a sociology professor at Binghamton University in New York, had established correspondence with convict Todd Ashker, a validated Aryan Brotherhood member. Ashker had been corresponding with Professor O'Hearn's classroom students. As a gift, Professor O'Hearn provided Ashker with a copy of a book he had written. The book was about "the prison hunger strike of the Irish Republican Army member Bobby Sands, who died after sixty-six days of his fast. The book made the rounds of the Short Corridor."[135] *The Los Angeles Times* revealed that "after a group of Ohio inmates staged their own hunger strike in early 2011, Ashker said, 'The idea of a California protest was launched and spread via the grapevine.'"[136] The grapevine was a combination of the prison gang contacts throughout the state prisons and local communities where they had influence. More importantly, it included their new "kite" system outside the prison walls: social media and the Internet.

The dawn of society's advanced information technology cannot be ignored in this discussion. SHU inmates, by and large, are avid readers (it helps pass the time and keeps the mind busy on something else besides their immediate circumstance), but they have very little knowledge about the nuances of social media and the Internet. However, their family members, attorneys, and friends are familiar with today's social media craze. What can only be described as "luck" was an eerie combination of "double isolation" (PBSP SHU + the Short Corridor), a book about the prison hunger strike of the Irish Republican Army, and the soon-to-be seeds of "torture-awareness" sown on the Internet.

The Age of Ares

Housing prison gang leaders in the Short Corridor at PBSP created an opportunity for sworn gang enemies to be unified. By 2011, the members of the Short Corridor Collective were ready to engage in a bastardized "social protest" against a common foe, CDCR. Like the Greek God of War "Ares," the Short Corridor Collective would begin a calculated course of action that would create chaos in the prisons and hallways of CRCR headquarters in Sacramento.[137] CDCR was fighting an enemy they knew very well, but now the fight was going to venture outside the walls of the prison and into the battlefield of public opinion. Unbeknownst to CDCR, the only landmines being planted in this battlefield were of their own making!

The first hunger strike occurred in July of 2011. The Short Corridor Collective had five core demands[138]:

1. Eliminate group punishments

2. Abolish debriefing policy and modify active/inactive gang status criteria

3. Comply with recommendations of US Commission on Safety and Abuse in America's Prisons (2006)

4. Provide adequate food

5. Provide constructive programs and privileges for SHU prisoners

Approximately, 6,000 inmates were initially involved in the hunger strike that began on July 1, 2011.[139] Most of those included inmates housed in the Ad-Seg and SHU units throughout the state. By July 7, 2011 only 1,700 inmates were refusing to eat state supplied meals.[140] On July 22, 2011, after CDCR had concluded "some dialogue" with prison rights advocates representing the Short Corridor Collective, the hunger strike was ended.

The CDCR had agreed to consider reviewing the way inmates were assigned to the state's three security housing units. Scott Kernan, Under Secretary of Operations for CDCR was quoted after the hunger strike ended that the department "determined there was some validity to what the inmates' concerns were…the department is reviewing its procedures."[141] Everything appeared to be resolved, except for an apparent "fairness" concern that the department would evaluate, as long as the inmates cease the hunger strike. CDCR, having feasted for years on its own overseer/prisoner model, would soon find itself eating its own words.

On September 26, 2011, the hunger strike was renewed by the Short Corridor Collective. A total of 4,200 inmates at eight prisons were identified by CDCR as having refused state-issued meals. The Short Corridor Collective argued that their demands had not been fully addressed. Specifically, the unspecified length of time served in SHU based on supposed gang ties and requirements to "snitch" in order to debrief, were the primary issues of debate.

The CDCR was caught off guard with the size and public response to the July and September Hunger Strikes. Internally, headquarter staff and field staff debated the department's response to the Short Corridor Collective. An interesting statewide conference call with wardens and prison executive staff, conducted by Scott Kernan, Undersecretary of Corrections, proved to be a telling prophecy of things to come.[142]

Undersecretary Kernan shared the uneasiness of many executive branch personnel in negotiating with SHU convicts. (He never mentioned the Short Corridor Collective by name.) His candor in sharing the conflict said volumes about what most staff were thinking: You start negotiating with convicts about prison policy and you will open Pandora's box for negotiating all correctional procedures. It was too late. CDCR agreed to reform two SHU policies: Increase the requirements for substantiation needed to support evidence of gang activity for placement in the SHU, and create a four-year step-down program to leave SHU confinement without requiring snitching as a prerequisite.

Understanding the political pressure that headquarters was under during the hunger strike is important. The Short Corridor Collective had exposed glaring issues of dispute for public consumption—the uneven and seemingly unfair placement of inmates in a SHU for unspecified time periods and the length of stay in solitary confinement without recourse. The factual representation could not be overlooked. These "super predators" were inmates that had not been involved in any misconduct for years. There was no "proof" that they were involved in criminal activities within prison or outside the wall. The only evidence was the statements of other inmate informants. Informants were hardly a very good witness as character traits go. Moreover, to prove their own innocence, alleged prison gang members were required to snitch on other inmates. To a reasonable citizen, it would beg the question, "If the inmate is innocent, how can he snitch on someone or something he knows nothing about?" From a common sense and legal standpoint, the question deserved investigation. The head of CDCR, Secretary Matthew Cate, was a former lawyer who had worked in the attorney general's office. It was almost a foregone conclusion that SHU policies would be re-reviewed.

The "Muddling Thru" Stew

For CDCR, the prison management "battlefield" throughout the state was limited to day-to-day prison functions, the enormous county jail intake, and parole-related street gang activities. However, what happened in July of 2013, almost two years after the first Short Corridor Collective hunger strikes, would change how corrections manages major prison conflicts for years to come. On July 8, 2013, the Short Corridor Collective orchestrated another hunger strike statewide. This time an estimated 30,000 inmates refused meals. The resumption of the hunger strike was based on "Governor Brown's and CDCR Secretary Cate's failure to make the changes agreed upon during the July/October 2011 negotiation process…"[143] The extent and dramatization of this coordinated effort cannot be underestimated.

First, the Short Corridor Collective "posted" the notice to resume the hunger strike or "peaceful protest," as they described it, in February of 2013 on the Internet. This use of social media was a "first" for inmates in California staging protests behind walls and fully five months in advance of the event. Secondly, in June of 2013, the department agreed to concessions never considered before in SHU; unlimited amounts of candy, instant soup, and additional clothing within a six-cubic-foot limit already allowed. The basis for the concessions are unknown, but the timing of them suggests a "last ditch effort" to persuade the convicts to stop the strike. Lastly, legislative leaders, social activists, and even United Nations observers began publicly questioning CDCR's apparent draconian measures. The Short Corridor Collective appeared to be winning a decisive battle for public support.

This time, CDCR officials behaved like "the train-headed for the proverbial-wreck." Moving "full steam ahead" to stop the deluge an internal memo in which George J. Giurbino, Director of the Division of Adult Institutions for CDCR outlined the process for dealing with mass hunger strikes: Isolating inmates participating in the strike, disciplinary measures, and provisions to deny strike leaders access to contact with visitors, removal of food canteen items from the cells, etc.[144] This official mindset was no different than the mentality that guided most law enforcement officers on the street, or working the county jails and prisons; maintaining an authoritative stance and requiring absolute compliance with directives to prevent a wrongdoing. The overseer/prisoner model was still alive and kicking; if you play, you pay.

To be fair, the CDCR directorate was under tremendous pressure to find some palatable solutions to the hunger strike. CDCR headquarters was being pulled in different directions from powerful interests, each with their own agenda and none willing to compromise. The prison leadership and bargaining units represented an array of different members-officers, nurses, custody supervisors/managers, and health care—each impacted directly by the hunger strike. Likewise, the governor's office wanted no new prison issues on the front page and T.V. stations while it was in a volatile fight with the PLO and federal court decrees on overcrowding and health care management. Similarly, inmate family and friends saw an opportunity to impact the living conditions for prisoners long-held in administrative segregation or SHU units.

Charles Edward Lindblom, Sterling Professor Emeritus of Political Science and Economics at Yale University was one of the early developers and advocate for *Incrementalism*, what he termed the "Science of Muddling Through."[145] He argued that public policy did not arrive from a systematic and careful analysis of alternatives and best options. On the contrary, bureaucracies limit their analysis to small limited options that differ in relatively small degree from the policies already in place. This "small-steps" approach to public policy was, in his view, normal and realistic in government agencies. A result of the impossible task of sorting out all the various constituencies—government officials, legislators, citizen, organizational stakeholders—in order to determine which preferences are the most important. Essentially, as Professor Lindblom posits, CDCR was "muddling through" a policy decision regarding the hunger strike issues.

One unidentified intimately involved onlooker observed both PBSP management and CDCR Directorate during the hunger strike events. He indicated that every effort to expose the Short Corridor Collective's true agenda fell on deaf ears. CDCR trying vainly to maintain a firm stance on the hunger strike demands while placating the various competing interests amounted to what the onlooker described as "a death by a thousand cuts." CDCR had no choice but to address some of the hunger strike concerns or face court-imposed action. The policy changes, limited to a small portion of the SHU policy, nevertheless had a profound impact to the larger constitutional issues of confinement.

In most circumstances, CDCR's *old guard* custodial approach was appropriate. Security and safety, in all its various forms and functions, had always been the best solution for maintaining control. But the Short Corridor Collective hunger strike was different. First, Ad-Seg and SHU inmates were already "locked up," so there was no risk for them of losing what they didn't have. Second, the "blowback" to the Giurbino memo in the media characterized the CDCR as being retaliatory and reactionary.[146] Lastly, the hunger strike foray led by the Short Corridor Collective, would provide meaningful advantage for their cause as they had quickly learned the value of public opinion and found *food-for-thought* from CDCR's mistakes, too!

Déjà Vu-doo

The Short Corridor Collective was made up of a cast of very dangerous and cunning killers. They shared a history of orchestrating and controlling the drug trade inside the prisons. They also pursued similar wicked interests outside the prison walls. Most of the power they exercised was a direct result of the violence they perpetrated or directed against anyone not yielding to their demands. Yet, none had a history of violence for over ten years. On paper, they were "model inmates" as far as their behavior was concerned in the SHU. Herein, lay the dilemma for CDCR. Over thirty years of court battles, regarding conditions of confinement, had taken place legitimizing current policies and procedures. But now those policies were being challenged again, but in a different court—the court of public opinion.

Since the 1980s, a due process structure had been developed that provided certain rights to prison gang members housed in the SHUs. That included disclosure of confidential information used to determine their association with prison gangs, involvement of a classification committee chaired by the warden or his/her designee to review information leading to SHU housing, and participation of the convict in that committee review. This process was a direct result of two key federal court cases brought by inmates Toussaint vs Rushen (1983) and Madrid vs Gomez (1990).[147] The Madrid decision is important for another reason; it originated at Pelican Bay State Prison (PBSP) where the Short Corridor Collective lived and the statewide hunger strike had originated.

The Madrid decision exposed the worst side of the CDCR. In 1990, the Prison Law Office brought a class-action suit alleging that conditions in the SHU were unconstitutional. Allegations of staff brutality and poor medical/mental health care were proven to be true by the Ninth Circuit Court:

> Guards snapped one inmate's wrist, knocked out four front teeth of another inmate, and hammered a third on the head with the butt of a gun so hard that he lost consciousness...the judge detailed the sickening case of Vaugh Dortch, a mentally ill inmate who ranted that he was a killer bee and was left to wallow in his own feces for 10 days in 1992, until the stench became so overpowering that officers forcibly extracted him from his cell. They marched him in shackles to the infirmary and forced him into a bath filled with water so hot that his skin peeled off. A nurse overheard one of the officer's quip, "Looks like we're going to have a white boy before this is through." (*Sacramento Bee*, August 2013)

The judge "appointed a special master to oversee the prison which was not lifted until 2011, when he concluded the Department of Corrections complied with the reforms he had ordered."[148] It is hard to fathom that a federal court had approved "due process" and "living condition remedies" that were in place over twenty-one years, then suddenly were of no significance in the debates that followed in the media following the hunger strikes of 2011 and 2013. The CDCR public relations team was in *defense mode* against a mob of protagonists supporting the Short Corridor Collective. On hindsight, a proactive attack against the misguided perceptions of the public using the federal court reforms as evidence, may have been the smarter strategy. But in the "smoke and mirrors" world of perceptions, CDCR was blind.

The Madrid Court had addressed unconstitutional issues like staff brutality, limited programs, poor living conditions, and due process for placement in Ad-Seg and SHU. But the Short Corridor Collective had effectively sought "higher court of approval"—public opinion. It didn't matter that a federal court had already "blessed" the departmental policies and procedures regarding placement and housing protocols in SHU. It didn't matter that the Short Corridor Collective represented the most dangerous convicts in the prison system, predators that preyed on other predators. All that mattered was the perception of the new buzz words flying off the journalists' pens and the social media presses. *Inhumane treatment, cruel and unusual punishment, and torture;* emotionally charged words that fed our worst fears about prison conditions. CDCR was re-living the Madrid ghosts of prison past.

The "Word" Game

The hunger strikers were supported by prison advocates, lawyers, and committed family members and celebrities who began to earnestly use the media to frame their demands.[149] It wasn't CDCR's fault that it failed to project the impact of isolating prison gang leaders together in the short corridor at PBSP. It was a sound security tactic. What CDCR failed to recognize was the creativity of these Alpha dogs when cornered. The use of social media to dramatize the prisoner plight and solidify the Short Corridor Collective position became too overwhelming for CDCR to digest. In fact, the language used to describe their prison condition became like a beacon illuminating all that was seemingly wrong with the "Super Max" environment. Journalist Ian Lovett of the *New York Times* reported in July of 2011:

Most of the prisoners who remain on hunger strike are in security housing units like the one at Pelican Bay, where they are kept alone in windowless, soundproof, concrete cells. To communicate, they have to yell from one cell to the other, although prisoner-rights activists in contact with the prisoners did not know if this was how they had organized the strike. The **lack of human contact** often leads to depression and bouts of rage, psychologists say.

Prisoners and activists say that such **conditions are cruel and unusual punishment**. Most inmates end up in these **extreme isolation** blocks because of ties to gang activities. To get back into the general prison population, activists say, they are **pressured to divulge information** about other gang members in prison, a process known as "debriefing," which can jeopardize their safety.

"We do see this long isolation and debriefing process as **torture**," said Carol Strickman, a staff lawyer with Legal Services for Prisoners with Children, an advocacy group in San Francisco. "These are **inhumane conditions** designed to extract information from someone." (Author's emphasis.)

The use of emotionally charged words like; *torture, cruel and unusual punishment, and inhumane conditions* resonated with many people who decried the "barbarous" living conditions of California's prisoners. These words were the same used to describe the horrendous conditions imposed at Abu Ghraib and Guantanamo Bay (Gitmo), where suspected terrorist and "enemy combatants" were housed.[150] The SHU inmates were now being viewed on an equal platform with other prisoners around the world.

Freelance Journalist David Mizner reported in a 2013 article for *The Nation* magazine, "Starving for Justice" on the increased trend of hunger strikes worldwide:

Prisoners have made up the majority of hunger strikes in the modern era, and this year is no exception… they fasted to protest abuse, unjust imprisonment, and inhumane conditions. The fast is a logical form of protest in a place that breeds desperation and robs people of autonomy. To refuse to eat is one of the few ways prisoners can exercise control, and usually the only way they can pressure the state…The hunger-strike watchers I spoke with agreed that the tactic is being used more frequently. They cautioned, however, that **a lack of comparative data makes it difficult to distinguish fact from perception.** But perception influences fact: social media increases public awareness of hunger strikes, which in turn increases their prevalence.[151] (Author's emphasis.)

Mizner's comments suggest an upward trend and continuation of hunger strikes to crystallize *perceptions* of torturous and inhumane conditions within the SHU environment of California's prisons.

Perhaps a comparative look at the conditions and circumstances of prisoners held in Abu Ghraib and/or Gitmo could prove useful in deconstructing the "word game" used to describe conditions of confinement in California SHUs. Abu Ghraib and Gitmo currently house detainees from the post 9/11 attacks on the Pentagon and the Twin Towers in New York. The detainees have been described as "terrorists" or "enemy combatants" captured from throughout the Middle East and Europe. The issues of cruel and unusual punishment and inhumane treatment surrounds the use "torture" tactics; water boarding, degrading or sexually offensive posing of detainees (in particular the pictures of naked bodies in a pyramid or a female military officer holding a detainee with leash and collar) and other torture techniques meant to ridicule or shame the detainee to the point where he is willing to share critical information.[152] This view of the terms "torture," "inhumane treatment," and "cruel and unusual" certainly goes well beyond the descriptions regarding California's prisoners' conditions of confinement. To be sure, the inmate's treatment faired far better than the detainees in Abu Ghraib and Gitmo.

Scholar Walter Hart, theorizes that a "cycle of assumptions" is created when the author (Short Corridor Collective), the director (television, newspapers, social media) and audience (American public) shape how we view and comprehend the *language* of torture, cruel and unusual punishment, and inhumane treatment. Hart explains:

> The cycle of assumptions is not simply a one-way mediation of information from the media to the public, rather the media crafts its messages based on its assumptions about the existing beliefs of its target audience. Therefore, as the public relies on the media to evaluate the decisions and rhetoric…the public receives only the information that aligns with their existing beliefs… The role of identification in the process of rhetoric leads us to interrogate the role of the audience's perceptions in the development of messages…, as Wynton C. Hall emphasizes, "In a world where perception is reality, a rhetoric that ignores perception is… doomed to fail."

In short, the role of the Short Corridor Collective, media, and American public in developing its own "cycle of assumptions" about words like; torture, cruel and unusual punishment, and inhumane treatment, had become limited to perceptions void of any critical analysis, but heaped in factual snippets.

The public outrage (or at least discomfort) with actions taking place at Abu Ghraib and Gitmo by American military personnel may have had less to do with the torture and more to do with the fact that no charges had been brought against the vast majority of the detainees. Rights normally provided to United States citizens were denied these prisoners on the grounds that they were not American, but *suspected* terrorists. They were considered prisoners-of-war who may hold critical information related to the on-going "War on Terror." Accordingly, rights normally guaranteed American citizens like; presumption of innocence, to remain silent, representation, speedy trial, etc., were denied them. In fact, nearly half the detainees have been found to be innocent of any terrorist activities, but remain in custody.[153] The arguments claiming injustice and inhumane treatment of Abu Ghraib and Gitmo detainees has some factual support; however unpleasant a thought to some Americans.

But the same injustices can't be claimed for California's SHU inmates. The prison gang members housed in Pelican Bay have a very different profile from the "War on Terror" detainees. First, the SHU inmates were all convicted felons, most for murder, and all with a history of violent offenses in and outside of prison. Secondly, they were recognized leaders of the four main prison gangs; Mexican Mafia, Aryan Brotherhood, Black Guerilla Family, and Nuestra Familia. Third, they all were validated and documented prison gang members whose prison disciplinary history could arguably be labeled as "prison terrorism." It is a considerable reach of the imagination to see their confinement as even remotely resembling the experience endured by detainees at Abu Ghraib and Gitmo. Yet, the "cycle of assumptions" between the Short Corridor Collective, the media, and the public, effectively "massaged" the language of; inhumane treatment, torture, and cruel and unusual punishment to make those far-fetched perceptions a reality for the prison gangs.

"Corridor 4" Acuity

It would be unfair to totally blame CDCR officials for the public perception mess surrounding the Hunger Strike of 2013. In fact, no one could have predicted the extent to which social media played a part in orchestrating the dialogue. But to balance the scale of perceptions, a review of the Short Corridor Collective or "Corridor 4" needs to be addressed. The Aryan Brotherhood, Mexican Mafia, Black Guerilla Family, and Nuestra Familia all have a vested interest in seeing changes in SHU policy. It is doubtful they believe change will result in freedom from prison, but they would certainly want to be freed to the general population mainline. The critical question to be posed is not for prisoner advocates or CDCR officials to ask and answer. It is for other inmates not aligned with the Corridor 4 to ask. What would happen if these prison gang members were released from the SHU? To answer that question requires a look at what prison gang leaders do in prison.

Todd Ashker, the fifty-year-old AB leader and principle writer for the Corridor 4 was nineteen years old when he first arrived to prison. He had a history of assaultive behavior against staff and other inmates before he was convicted of the 1987 stabbing assault against another AB member. Over the years, he became a "prison lawyer" who was adept at filing lawsuits and winning in court. *Sacramento Bee*, journalist Dan Morain reported that when Ashker first arrived to Pelican Bay in September of 1990:

"he kicked open his cell door—a defect costing $8 million to fix—and tried to kill another inmate. A guard broke up the fight shooting Ashker in his wrist. Though he was the aggressor, Ashker filed a suit …and won. A federal jury in Oakland awarded him $225,000."[154]

Other prison gang leaders took notice and realized that, with his legal research skills, they could forge a formidable argument against what would soon be viewed as archaic and suppressive SHU policies. Ashker can hardly be viewed as a victim. And the same can be said for the other Collective members.

"Chuco" Guillen, a high-ranking leader in the Nuestra Familia (NF) was convicted of narcotic sales and assault with a deadly weapon in 1990. He was released from prison in 1999 and out less than a year before his arrest for murder, believed to be a NF sanctioned "hit."

Ronald Dewberry is serving a life sentence for a murder he committed in 1981. He has been living in SHU since 1987. He is believed to hold the rank of lieutenant in the BGF and was alleged to be an enforcer.

"Tablas" Castellano, Mexican Mafia (EME) member was convicted of murder in 1979 and sentenced to twenty-six years to life. His prison record included six documented stabbing assaults. Gang investigators consider him to be the "undisputed" leader of Florencia 13, one of Los Angeles County's oldest gangs. A recent federal indictment alleges that the EME used Florencia street gang members to traffic narcotics. The indictment also alleges that Florencia 13 is allied with La Familia Michoacán, a drug cartel based in Michoacán, Mexico. Tablas was also suspected of fashioning the weapon used by Gabriel "Sleepy" Huerta (also a member of the Short Corridor Collective Representative Body) to murder Niko Velasquez in the Tehachapi SHU.

The Corridor 4 and other prison gang members have proven to be cunning and treacherous in holding power and control over other prison gang members. Jeffery Beard, Secretary of CDCR in an Op-ed piece for the *Los Angeles Times* said:

> Some prisoners claim this strike is about living conditions in the Security Housing Unit, commonly called SHUs, which house some of the most dangerous inmates in California. Don't be fooled. Many of those participating

in the hunger strike are under extreme pressure to do so from violent prison gangs, which called the strike in an attempt to terrorize fellow prisoners, prison staff, and communities throughout California…the corrections department created SHUs to safely house gang members and their associates while minimizing their influence on other prisoners. Restricting the gangs' communication has limited their ability to engage in organized criminal activity and has saved lives both inside and outside prison walls…So what is this really about? Some of the men who participated in the last hunger strike and have since dropped out of the gangs…said it best…"We knew we could tap big time support through this tactic, but we weren't trying to improve the conditions in the SHU; we were trying to get out of the SHU to further our gang agenda on the mainline." [155]

The notion that four inmates and a small cadre of other SHU inmates could somehow influence 30,000 inmates statewide to heed their call for "justice" but not wield the power CDCR claims they have, has little merit. They do have power and they proved it. If the conditions of confinement in California prisons were similar to Abu Ghraib or Gitmo, it well might be possible to see many more inmates unite in protest, but that argument doesn't hold much weight, either.

Massaging the Madness

The truth of the matter is that California prisons have had a history of federal court incursion and oversight to remedy the very issues (due process and conditions of confinement) that continue to spark debate at Abu Ghraib and Gitmo. It is more probable that the Hunger Strike Protest was manufactured by the Corridor 4 to support the hidden agenda goals of the prison gangs. Author, Chris Blatchford describes EME dropout Rene "Boxer" Enriquez's view on prison gang "goals" from previous hunger strike protests when the EME used inmate Steve "Smiley Castillo a known jailhouse lawyer. Castillo filed lawsuits on behalf of SHU inmates and eventually won reforms regarding the SHU program, claiming it to be "…capricious and cruel…" his intent was to have prison gang members released back the main yard and out of isolated housing. Castillo had gained support from the state legislature, including Senator Gloria Romero who chaired the Senate Select Committee on Corrections.[156]

Author Blatchford reported that Castillo, a validated EME associate was eventually assaulted by the EME who suspected him to be an informant. He wasn't, according to dropout "Boxer" Enriquez. Castillo's lawsuit, contending that "...'hundreds of prisoners' were misidentified as gang affiliates with 'flimsy and trivial' information and held in the SHU unjustly for indeterminate amounts of time," was eventually dropped.[157] However it did spur some legislative interest. On September 15, 2003, Senator Gloria Romero convened a hearing of the Senate Select Committee on the CDCR's SHU policies and practices. Nothing of substance came from that hearing since the federal court was already engaged with the living condition issues in the SHUs.

Ironically, ten years later, the July/August 2013 Hunger Strikes have spurred the senate to conduct more hearings. This time there was substance to the "living conditions" complaints. On October 9, 2013, a Joint Legislative Hearing on "Segregation Policies in California Prisons: *Current conditions & Implications on Prison Management and Human Rights*" was conducted. Loni Hancock, Senate Public Safety Committee Chair and her counterpart, California Assembly member Tom Ammiano, Chair of the Assembly Public Safety Committee, both raised concerns regarding the hunger strike and conditions in California's supermax (SHU) prisons.[158] The Corridor 4 had pursued the same strategy that inmate Castillo had pursued ten years previously. Although, the hunger strike strategy appeared more indicative of the "Just Us" goals driving the Corridor 4 than "justice" regarding living conditions of the SHUs, the advent of public opinion had sparked a political regurgitation on prison reform and genuine public attention to the prison policies heaped in apparent draconian forms of punishment.

CDCR can no longer hope to close the lid on its self-imposed Pandora's box outcome—*negotiating the Hunger Strike*—because it's too late. The public outcry has crystallized over perceptions of inhumane treatment and torture in the SHUs. The dialogue is moving very quickly to legislative and/or federal court action. CDCR has already revamped the procedures related to documenting gang involvement and has provided a shorter timeline and less invasive (no snitching required) means to walk away from gang activity. But that is clearly not enough to satisfy the naysayers.

Taming of the SHU

During the joint legislative hearing of October 2013, the California Inspector General, Robert Barton testified that over 4,000 inmates reside in the SHUs statewide with over 500 having lived in the SHU environment beyond five years.[159] As many as 60 percent are serving "open-ended terms" or "indeterminate" SHU status based on their alleged gang associations. This is the crux of the SHU placement issue—why gang association and not specific behavior—for determining the reason for separation from other inmates? More importantly, how long must gang members remain in continued isolation?

There is some truth to the demands made by the Corridor 4. The "torture," characterized by them and their supporters as: long periods of non-contact with other inmates, limited movement outside the cell, and restricted program opportunities remain intact and unresolved. Research has determined that prisoners who are subjected to long periods of sense-deprivation: lack of touch, sound, and movement, are more prone to mental illness. The United Nations has long decreed that long periods of non-human contact and isolation are torture. In fact, testimony at the Joint Legislative Hearing indicated that, in 2011, the United Nations, "...Special Rapporteur on Torture and Terror called for a ban on solitary confinement lasting longer than fifteen days and an absolute ban on solitary confinement for youth and the mentally ill."[160]

Likewise, federal court decrees, and many mental health experts have already weighed in on the subject of SHU housing creating a "hot bed" for mental health breakdowns. During federal court Coleman hearing before U.S. District Judge Lawrence Karlton, lawyers representing inmates showed mentally ill prisoners were many times more likely to have force used against them by correctional officers. In fact, they showed that in some prisons they accounted for more than ninety percent of the incidents. Based partially on that testimony, the court determined that "solitary confinement can and does cause serious psychological harm" and the practice must be limited.[161]

Arizona Senator, John McCain and Shane Bauer, an investigative reporter, have weighed-in on the atrocity of isolation and non-human contact as inhumane and torture based on their real-life experiences.[162] And the evidence to support their contentions about the negative impact of prolonged isolation is hard to dismiss. Depression and mental decomposition are not uncommon. Worse, the high rate of suicide in segregation units cannot be easily ignored.[163] As a result, in April 2014, the federal court ordered new limits on solitary confinement, pepper spray and baton use applied on inmates with mental health conditions. This may signal an increase in mental health claims made by more SHU inmates, whether genuine or contrived.

During the Joint Legislative Hearing on Segregation Polices it was revealed that the federal government and many states are reevaluating the continued use and benefit of long-term solitary confinement. Many organizations and most state correctional agencies oppose prolonged segregation for inmates with mental illness. CDCR is stuck between the proverbial "rock and a hard place." Like Shakespeare's characters in the *Taming of the Shrew,* Petruchio (CDCR) must attempt to "tame" Katherine (prison SHUs) by asserting its authority; a not so simple proposition. Change can come slowly in large agencies like CDCR but in prisons, particularly closed environments like the SHUs, change is nearly non-existent.

However, a proactive approach on the principle issues—lack of human contact and long periods of isolation—would allow CDCR to control the terms of engagement. Unfortunately, this stance would pose a significant challenge for CDCR, as the stakeholders (court receiver, unions, inmate advocates, legislators, and media pundit) on all sides hold considerable influence. But failing to act could result in changes no one would benefit from, namely a court imposed release of prison gang members back to the mainline.

Occam's Razor

In the history of penology, the one maxim that seemed to always percolate after all the custodial, therapeutic, and rehabilitative undertakings failed or lost support was, keep it simple. David Leung, J.D., in his book, *Power Vocabulary*, describes the teachings of William of Occam as "…the best explanation should contain only the simplest forms…everything else shaved away to eliminate complications."[164] Similarly, Ad-Seg or SHU units need to work in a basic manner that meets the security needs, but also avoids the trappings of inhumane treatment. Accordingly, addressing seemingly contradictory goals is a matter of going back to what worked before the introduction of the Super Max prisons.

Let's acknowledge first, that prison gang members need to remain in segregated housing because they pose a demonstrable threat to the general population of inmates. They are predators who prey on weaker inmates. But they don't need to be isolated in single cells or yard walk-alone pods without human contact. Justification for prolonged isolation (as is practiced today in the California SHUs) will not meet federal court muster, so why fight the inevitable?

Indeed, the honeycomb design of the California SHU buildings created a formal barrier to communication. An above ground control booth officer monitors the housing sections as doors are opened electronically. There's minimal verbal communication and physical touching in a sterile environment. Likewise, recognizing spatial (the scale of space) environments in a prison setting and how they influence human behavior has been the subject of discussion:

> The impact of scale…is typically misunderstood or completely ignored in the design of detention facilities…narrow long corridors…disparate masses of space. The gravity is completely overwhelming, and our sense of the space is muddled or completely lost. In addressing scale, the most effective manageable solution is likely through programming and movement. Movement provides a haptic (sense of touch) understanding of space that cannot be accommodated through passive viewing and decreases the isolation that can arise in such a sterile environment. It establishes an auditory and visual landscape that reduces the scale of a space to that of a human dimension.[165]

Unfortunately, "safety and security" pundits will perceive giving prison gang members more "movement" (access to each other or programs) as a potential threat to the safety of the public, staff, and inmates. That is a very limited viewpoint, since every time a prisoner is released from a cell, he potentially poses a higher level of threat to others. "23/7" in a cell has been the *safety* remedy of choice for custody personnel. Today that option can no longer be the proscribed cure, however distasteful it may appear to be to officers working the SHUs. It is not a safety or security question any longer, but a constitutional rights question.

It is the mission of every correctional professional to ensure public safety by providing a secure and safe environment for staff, the public, and prisoners. But keeping correctional facilities "secure and safe" doesn't require unconstitutional living conditions. In other words, CDCR simply can't keep inmates locked up twenty-three hours a day and seven days a week anymore, and peace officers can't limit interaction among or with prisoners because it's perceived to be too dangerous. Of course inmates are dangerous that is why they are in prison. CDCR must seek some internal compromise relative to increasing movement, and reducing isolation in the SHUs. If not, these concerns will be resolved by the courts.

Back to the Future

We've already acknowledged how dangerous the Corridor 4 is and the cunning methods prison gangs use to orchestrate power in prisons and the communities. One fact is clear: They will continue in that effort regardless of where or how we house them. Accordingly, giving them more freedom of movement really won't make a difference in their behavior. Access to group yards with compatible inmates has already been the practice in most SHUs. Can the same access apply for cell housing, phone calls, and day rooms?

The court-of-public-opinion will no longer stand idly by allowing draconian SHU policies to dictate living conditions for prisoners. The 23/7 in a cell may well be a thing of the past. If CDCR doesn't take proactive measures to remedy the long periods of isolation and non-human contact, it is only a matter of time when change in SHU policies is going to happen in California either by legislative or court interdiction. So, why wait?

There is a flip side to providing some measurable increase in movement and programs in the SHUs. The prison gangs would not be thrown together in some helter skelter mob. They would remain separated, but allowed to interact amongst their own cadre. This is already the practice on most Ad-Seg and SHU yards. The addition of phone calls, enhanced programs, group yard, etc could all be done incrementally. This would avoid court or legislative action and would deflate the growing support for abolishing the SHUs. The Corridor 4's social media leverage would likely dissipate, too. Perhaps more importantly, increasing programs, contact, and movement in the SHUs would also reduce mental health issues.

There is another advantage; more movement and programs has always provided meaningful avenues for intelligence-gathering. The more inmates are interacting with staff and amongst themselves, the more nefarious activities are revealed to staff. Yes, they pose an on-going threat to staff, but that has always been the case. The idea that 23/7 cell-time is the best option will not suffice in today's courts. That draconian ship has sailed. CDCR has already had experience with secure SHU and Ad-Seg units that allowed movement and had less isolation. That was the case at the CIM Palm Hall Ad-Seg Unit, Tehachapi's SHU Units, and the Corcoran SHU Units, too. As one seasoned "old guard" correctional officer remarked about inmates, "They might not all be talking, but they all be telling..." It is the nature of human interaction. Not quite what the legislative hearings were driving at, but true, nonetheless.

CHAPTER 8

Well those drifters' days are past me now,
I've got so much more to think about,
Deadlines and commitments,
What to leave in, what to leave out…

Bob Seger
"Against the Wind"

"Stand Down!"

*M*y last year with the department, 2011, was probably the most dismal year of my professional life in the criminal justice arena. CDCR had already suffered its worst budget years following the 2008 economic disaster. For the three years that followed, it meant significant job cuts in custody, plant operations, and clerical positions. It also meant serious departmental oversight on spending for all unbudgeted items. Just my "luck" that CIM led the state in custody overtime. We were under a microscope.

Fortunately, we could justify the overtime since the majority of it was directly related to medical transportation and guarding costs; two areas never adequately financed over the years. It didn't matter, because headquarters continued to demand a reduction in overtime regardless of the reason. The turnips (prison staff) in the field had to squeeze out the last ounce of blood in their workload and budgets or face the dire consequences.

In fact, CIM was visited by the deputy director of Adult Institutions in July of 2011. He was there to get a "pound of flesh" according to the best laid gossip. In prison, the rumor mill is always a driving force regardless if there is any truth to it. In this case, rumors sprang out that the warden and I would be removed. I recall a seasoned lieutenant approaching me saying that an unnamed union representative had heard that the warden and I would be "walked off" referring to our removal from office. I laughed, responding, "Good, I need a vacation!"

As Career Executive Appointments (CEA), we worked at the pleasure of the governor and CDCR directorate. We retained civil service rights to our last jobs as associate wardens, but could be moved anywhere in the state. In the field, especially among supervisory and management staff, "CEA" meant, if you get in-a-wreck with headquarters, your "Career Ends Abruptly." Since I was the Chief Deputy Warden (CDW) for Operations, all budget and personnel matters fell under me. So, if rumors were true, I was prepared for whatever was coming my way when the deputy director visited.

When the deputy director arrived, he sat across from me at the large rectangular table in the warden's office. He read the "riot act" to the warden, me, the program CDW, and the regional administrator (the warden's boss), who was in attendance, too. The deputy director had his game face on and focused mainly on budgetary issues. He demanded to know why CIM had not curbed its overtime. I didn't know him and wasn't sure if he was serious or only wanting to get our attention. I listened intently and scanned the faces of the others. They all looked like scared sheep ready for the slaughter. I was becoming irritated, but not at the deputy director.

I was irritated because I knew I would probably be standing alone in my convictions. This was not a testament to any profound courage or leadership skill on my part. On the contrary, I was "short to the house" as they say in prison jargon. With only six months to retirement, there wasn't much the state apparatus could do to me. I could take a career ending "hit" with little impact except possibly a bruised ego. So, I didn't feel intimidated or nervous. In fact, when the deputy director was finished talking, I took over. I only had one serious objective, and that was reducing his target zone to one person, me.

I began, "Mr. 'S' everything you've talked about falls under my duties and responsibilities. The warden has put his trust in me to resolve those things you spoke about. The CDW for programs had no part in any decisions I made relative to the budget and custody operations. If you need to hold someone accountable, it starts and ends with me."

He interrupted. "Do I need to hold you responsible?"

I answered quickly, "That's the warden's, regional's, and your call to make, not mine. But let me be clear that the management team of captains and AWs here at CIM are committed and have earnestly been working to meet our budget challenges. They are future leaders for the department and shouldn't be included in any negative characterization of what you believe has been occurring at CIM."

I continued, "I want to share with you that, during this past budget cycle, we reduced overtime by over a quarter of a million dollars and reduced sick leave usage by over 30,000 hours. Unfortunately, what has continued to impact us is our off-grounds guarding costs. As you know, we don't control when and if the medical team determines an inmate requires off-ground treatment…" I continued my diatribe for about ten minutes outlining in detail, actions we'd taken to reduce costs in medical guarding—some of which were knowingly in direct violation of departmental policy and bargaining unit contract provisions.

When I finally stopped, the room was quiet. The deputy director looked at me and paused before saying, "That's what I needed to hear…I came here to find out if anyone cared or knew what was going on and what has been done. I appreciate the effort, but this is what I need. I want you to balance the department's checkbook not CIM's…use the budgeted positions only for what they were intended."

I responded, "I can do that, but you realize our overtime will skyrocket if we do."

He nodded in agreement. "Yes, I realize that, but we need to provide Department of Finance (DOF) a clear picture of how we look using the positions they have authorized us."

I got the message; he wanted me to "stand down" on our local effort to rein in overtime.

Headquarters also got the results I said would occur. The next few months saw a definitive jump in overtime costs. But I actually appreciated the exchange between the deputy director and myself. It made clear the focus headquarters was pursing and it made sense given the political dark cloud hanging over CDCR's budget woes at the time. If he was not happy with the field, CIM in particular, it was certain that the DOF was not happy with the CDCR Directorate. From my view, it amounted to the agency shouting, "public taxpayers be damned!" This budget tactic was clearly about enabling funding source improvements for the department. I understood it, complied with the strategy, and made sure staff followed the orders. The strategy didn't work as the CDCR continued to suffer deeper cuts in budgeted position authority. December, my retirement month, could not come fast enough.

****

The workplace didn't get any better during this period. CDCR was standardizing staffing packages statewide in anticipation of the Assembly Bill (AB) 109 Public Safety Realignment rollout. This meant layoffs and cutbacks in positions. Some of the cutbacks in positions were understandable. But the statewide process of demotions and transfers created confusion locally and could not be mitigated by wardens. Headquarters was directing the process and the field had to "stand down" on any involvement.

For example, Employee A could not transfer to Prison Z, which had a vacancy and was closer to home, because it was outside the county. But Employee B could voluntarily demote to that position even if he/she had no experience. Hence, we had teachers demoting to locksmith posts and staff service analysts demoted to personnel technicians. The learning curves for these positions could take a year or more, yet the employee was expected to work immediately. If staff was already frustrated with three years of increasing workload and furlough pay cuts, they were damn near going crazy with the demotion/transfer process. Anyone with less than ten years on the job was vulnerable to involuntarily transfer or being laid off!

Statewide, staff received letters advising them about layoff and involuntary transfers, but months would pass without any new instructions or results. Everything was controlled by Headquarters Personnel Administration. This left the field Personnel Office staff unable to respond to inquiries by prison employees. What do the employees tell their families? What do they do with their homes, school, and any extended family obligations? Morale was at an all-time low throughout the state. Yet, prison management had to "stand down" on any participation in the staffing realignment process.

Not to worry, the implementation of AB 109 would distract staff from their personal problems! CDCR had gotten one thing right about AB 109. The projected inmate population drop was fairly accurate. As would later prove to be true, the projected final population numbers were well below the *court-ordered population cap by nearly 10,000 inmates. CDCR projections couldn't pull out a magical number from all the data to meet the court edict, but would be darn sure to meet its own projections.*

This wasn't intentional. On the contrary, Population Services Unit was adept at projecting the statewide prison body count. The numbers provided in 2011 would be proven to be fairly accurate for a two-year projection—an impressive task given the monumental changes in offender movement and location on the immediate horizon. Ironically, that meant the implementation of AB 109 would also require approved overtime—overtime for staff, who were on the departmental chopping block for demotions, involuntary transfers, and/or layoffs. Once again, the field prison turnips were being squeezed for more blood.

****

I had a professional and personal stake in the implementation of AB 109, Public Safety Realignment Act that was due to start in October of 2011. First, I was very proud of CIM's executive staff because many would promote to AW, CDW, and warden within one to three years. They had seen and done it all during their careers and I had been fortunate to have them carry me during my tenure at CIM. Realignment could be the crown jewel for their careers if implemented correctly. It could also be their Achilles heel. Secondly, I was completing my last year in the Public Administration Master's program at the University of La Verne and had focused my thesis research on AB 109. I knew this was the biggest conversion in California's criminal justice arena that could either present a national blueprint for effective change in crime and recidivism models or potentially pose a costly and serious public safety threat to communities.

The CIM executive staff realized that a significant number of CIM's inmate population would be impacted by the Realignment. The Parole Violator "frequent flyers" would be the primary benefactors of Realignment as many met the three "Non" criteria; non-violent, non-serious, and non-sex offenders. Yes, the same PVs responsible for one of the largest prison riots in the state's history were now going to be turned over to county probation departments. Over three-quarters of the nearly 5,800 felons at CIM were parole violators. Over one-third easily met the criteria.

I witnessed firsthand the difficulties in initiating a far-reaching policy that had significant impact to both the institutional mission at the California Institution for Men (CIM) and the local counties' efforts to wrap their hands around the increase in offenders coming to their communities. From the time the counties first got wind of Realignment to the day of implementation, it was a public outcry and political whirlwind of denial, anger, refusals, and veiled threats of court action. Not to mention, the logistical barriers and mountainous communication doubletalk between fifty-eight counties, CDCR Headquarters, and field staff.

****

In April/May of 2011, I met with the Riverside Community College President, the Chief Probation Officer from Riverside County, and Robert Presley, former State Senator and head of the Presley Group, for lunch. Mr. Presley was also the former agency secretary, for the Youth and Adult Corrections Agency before its dismantling and renaming as CDCR. Presley was a resident of Riverside County and served over twenty years in the state assembly and senate. The Presley Group was introducing a community rehabilitation program to the county and I had been asked to lend some advice with respect to program needs as they apply to offenders. My background with the Riverside County Probation Department served me well as I soon befriended the chief probation officer.

As it happened, I extended an invitation to the chief probation officer to visit CIM. He had shared many concerns during our lunch meeting regarding AB 109 offender release packet inquiries, conditions of release issues, and managerial staff contact information. I gladly offered CIM's assistance. I soon realized the same concerns were evident throughout the southland and extended the invitation to the entire southern region Probation Departments.

In July of 2011, CIM hosted executive personnel from Riverside, San Bernardino, and Orange Counties Probation Departments to address common concerns. Attendance at the meeting included representatives from local Division of Adult Parole Operations, CIM's Chief Medical Officer and Chief of Mental Health, Classification and Parole Representatives, and Facility Associate Wardens and Captains.

It was clear that the details of a collaborative organizational structure to meet the counties' needs were in its infancy. This is not a criticism, rather an observation of the normal stage development for any new program or policy implementation. I was impressed with the frank and open dialogue from the counties and institutional staff, as it should be when wrestling a nebulous offender group that all state prisons were tasked to identify quickly and the counties were very soon to inherit. All of this was evolving before our eyes as

CDCR strove to meet the AB 109 implementation date of October 2011 as the counties gamely tried to prepare, project, and address its impact.

The information void appeared to be fairly simple matters; for example, how to notify the inmates on changes in their Conditions of Probation or reporting instructions. The probation personnel only needed a facsimile or phone contact number and staff person responsible at each prison. Even though, the statewide contact information had already been provided by CDCR headquarters to the fifty-eight counties, for whatever reason, it was not relayed down the chain-of-command to the personnel staff that needed it at the probation departments. Likewise, key inmate case factor information and related reports on offenders were not consistently delivered, or worse, lacked the breadth of detail needed for the probation teams. All these issues were to be expected, given the newness of forms and processes for both sides. Even CDCR's Counseling and Records staff, tasked with implementation of the Realignment casework, was experiencing the same "newness" tensions.

The meeting was very illuminating for both sides, and all the agencies wanted to meet again with lower level staff in attendance to understand and meet key communication links. Not that we were all singing "Kum-ba-ya" but it was a welcome relief to know there were some simple answers and fixes to the first stage of implementation; identifying "Johnny," clarifying contact information, and massaging the implementation protocols.

Headquarters saw things differently. Teri McDonald, Undersecretary for CDCR, addressed the Reception Centers during a telephonic conference call a week after I had hosted the CIM-Probation Departments meeting. She advised that all communication with the counties relative to implementation of AB 109 will be conducted only through Classification Services. Her concern, albeit a good one, was to avoid miscommunication about the law and policy and to insure a standardized implementation. Rightly so, AB 109 was brand new and moving too fast for CDCR and the counties to clearly understand. She acknowledged the problems voiced statewide, but made it clear that all the prisons are to "stand down" on any assistance or communication with the county probation departments. I suspect that Headquarters had heard about CIM hosting the regions probation department leaders and was not happy it had occurred. I had no choice but to direct prison staff to refer all county probation questions to Headquarters.

Terri McDonald would leave CDCR and accept a post with the Los Angeles Sheriff's Department in March of 2013. As the new assistant sheriff *for custody operations, she now has complete oversight and management of the largest jail operation in the nation. Ironically, her new post as head jailer would put her in the crosshairs of AB 109's newly created Post Release Community Service Offenders (PRCS) and other former parolee offenders that were now subject to county oversight. As had been forecast, the jail population saw an immediate increase due to the addition of PRCS offenders. With "no-room-at-the-inn," I have no doubt Assistant Sheriff McDonald has had little time to stand down, too!*

The AB 109 Public Safety Realignment Challenge

On April 4, 2011, Governor Edmund G. Brown Jr. signed Assembly Bill 109, California Public Safety Realignment Act, into law (hereafter referred to as Realignment). Realignment began in earnest October of 2011 statewide. Realignment has been called "....a dramatic new path...a momentous decision...a seismic shift...an experiment of unparalleled national significance..." in criminal justice reform.[166] Yet, most Californians don't realize its sizable impact to the local criminal justice arena. Moreover, based on California's gargantuan offender population, Realignment may prove to be the national model if it succeeds. Success will be measured from two key components; a reduction in local crime and, for those offenders returning to the community, a reduction in the recidivism rate. But this policy didn't arrive with those auspicious components being touted across the state. Indeed, it became the policy choice for the state of California to address overcrowding and reduce the cost of incarceration.[167]

Instead of pouring money into construction for more prison beds or release offenders before they had completed their sentence, the state shifted responsibility for *non-serious, non-sex, and non-violent* (3-non) offenders to the local counties. Supervising, tracking, and imprisoning the 3-non offenders were no longer a CDCR Parole Division function. Instead, the fifty-eight counties became responsible. Realignment was, for all practical purposes, the state's best response to cumbersome federal court directives to reduce the prison overcrowding dilemma. California simply had no choice.

But a funny thing happened on the fast-track to Realignment. County agencies throughout the state initially blamed CDCR for the overcrowding that brought Realignment to their door—as if CDCR, a state agency, had solely been responsible for who got charged and convicted in a court of law. Those commitment decisions had always rested with the fifty-eight counties. Yet, the public dialogue viewed it differently, and for good reason, since nearly 60 percent of the returning offenders to prison were Parole Violators (PVs) who fell under the auspices of CDCR. But the counties had a significant hand in the overcrowding mess, too.

All PVs serving a "new" sentencing term and first-term felon commitments to state prison originally had been prosecuted and convicted in the county. Moreover, new commitments to state prison included 40 percent of the counties' probation revocation cases, strongly suggesting that county rehabilitation efforts had failed at least 40 percent of the time. The truth of the matter was that the fifty-eight counties shared equal blame for prison overcrowding. The public discourse conveniently ignored that fact.

Instead, critics charged CDCR with "dumping" felons back into the communities. This initial public opinion "blow back" regarding Realignment was to be expected. It has always been the community NIMBY (not in my backyard) outcry. But wiser heads prevailed as the topic soon changed to money. The county district attorney, sheriff, probation and police departments all wanted to know how much funding would be provided to address the *post release community service* (PRCS) offenders returning to the counties. The governor and legislature were listening and with good reason. The three-judge federal panel in the Plata court case had ordered the state to reduce its prison population to 137.5 percent of design capacity in 2009. By mid-year 2011, the United States Supreme Court had affirmed the order. If Realignment was going to succeed, it made sense for the state to provide the necessary funding to make it work. As a result, during the first two years of Realignment, counties have received in excess of two billion dollars affecting the sentencing of over 100,000 offenders since 2013.[168]

So what were the *dramatic and seismic* changes brought about by Realignment? Realignment shifted responsibility for an estimated 30,000 "low level" offenders released from state prison and county jails back to local county jurisdictions.[169] The intent was to keep low-level offenders in the community, offering alternative sanctions while reserving state prison beds to those offenders who posed significant risk to the community—a seminal, if not dramatic change in crime policy. At its onset, Realignment was effective in reducing the state's total prison population. Nearly six month after its implementation, approximately 17,000 offenders were released to California's fifty-eight counties. Since 2012, there has been a 41 percent reduction in new prison admissions and a drop of 28,300 in the prison population and a nearly 50 percent drop in parole numbers-without a doubt, a definite *seismic* change in CDCR's offender population.[170]

Unfortunately, these offenders have not gone away. On the contrary, they have only changed jurisdictions. California's *probation population* has seen a jump in the number of offenders on probation.[171] In fact, the total number of offenders under *correctional control* (Prison, Probation and Parole) has grown. Before Realignment, offenders under correctional control in 2010 numbered 677,586, after realignment those numbers increased to 694,158 by 2012. The prisons and parole offenders comprise only 29 percent of the total number of offenders in the state; whereas, the counties comprise 71 percent of the total state offender population. It can be arguably stated that Realignment has, in fact, had a *dramatic* affect in the criminal justice arena. It has shifted the state's offender *location* base from state prisons to the fifty-eight county jails.

Scholars Joan Petersilia and Jessica Greenlick Snyder describe Realignment as the "biggest penal experiment in modern history."[172] They portray the national debate and actions in rethinking the policies over mass incarceration as the largest effort in the nation owing to its overall correctional (prisons, parole, jail, and probation) populations.[173] In fact, other scholars have noted that Michigan, South Carolina, and Virginia had already implemented some form of Realignment similar to AB 109 beginning in 2000, but California was by far the largest.[174] Petersilia and Snyder neatly illustrate Realignment's potential for best or worst outcomes:

> "…At its best, as programs develop, information sharing will allow cross-county sharing of effective practices. At its best, realignment will return criminal justice to local control, reduce recidivism, and reserve prison for California's most dangerous offenders…At its worst; the state will have dumped tens of thousands of crimi- nals back to cash-strapped counties with imaginary

treatment plans that are never delivered upon. At its worst, the state will have simply transferred its crowding problem to local jails, sheriffs will be required to resort to early releases to alleviate crowding, and crime rates will rise.

(Past the Hype: *10 Questions on Realignment.* Page 267)

During the initial Realignment rollout, many issues foretold of long-term problems that foreshadowed Petersilia's and Snyder's "at worst" image. First, no funding was earmarked for evaluation. During the first year of implementation, 367 million dollars were provided to the counties with no provision for collecting data and research. Many critics rightly asked the proverbial question, "How do we know, what we don't know?" about the impact of Realignment's fiscal spending.

Secondly, the PRCS offenders were being released to the county jurisdiction with only the jail system as the "backup" reservoir for housing offenders. Scholars David Ball and Robert Weisberg reported that Realignment had "…amended about 500 criminal statutes by eliminating…the possibility of a state prison sentence upon conviction. Virtually all drug and property offenses are now served in jail."[175]

Jails have typically been taxed for bed space, staffing, and other resources. In fact, seventeen counties' jails were already under a federal court imposed population cap before Realignment. Some of the biggest counties (Los Angeles, Orange, San Diego, Sacramento, and Imperial) had average daily offender populations that were above the number of beds available.[176] The knowledge that Realignment could result in a flood of offenders being released early from jail based solely on overcrowding was a real public safety threat.

Worse, all fifty-eight counties operated different probation systems, each mirroring the cultural and political nuances of their particular county. Each court, district attorney, county jail, and probation team exercised their own policy interpretation of the law, sentencing habits, alternative sanction usage, and treatment program availability. Likewise, most probation departments had experienced limited funding support over the years leading to imperfect or underfunded probation treatment, and rehabilitative services. Realignment would require a larger "probation footprint" in alternative options to incarceration that were not readily available to meet the initial PRCS incursion into the counties.

Between a Rock and a Shell Game

One of the mandates that Realignment is meant to accomplish is a reduction in recidivism.[177] Barring that outcome, can we then expect to see an increase in crime? This isn't a theoretical construct; it is quite nearly a prediction based on historical fact. The fifty-eight counties have taken over the management of returning PRCS offenders and they're also taking responsibility for the majority of offenders who previously would have been serving parole or time in a prison. Before Realignment, California's offenders were returning to prison at a rate reaching well above 65 percent; the highest recidivism rate in the nation. If California's counties decide not to fundamentally change the way they attack crime and recidivism, it will only be a matter of time before the county jails suffer the consequences of overcrowding on a scale that would mirror, if not surpass, the state's prison experience.

Another significant change Realignment produced was the concept of *Mandatory Supervision.* Realignment provided two sentencing options. The first was the traditional jail term; wherein, the offender would serve all his time in jail. The second option allowed sentencing judges to impose a prison sentence and then "split" the time to serve between jail and probation. One of its features was the fact that the time spent on probation counted for the total sentencing term.[178] Unlike before Realignment, now the offender doesn't have a choice. The conditions imposed by the court are mandatory, hence, the term Mandatory Sentence. Also, there is no probation period to follow once the total split term sentence is completed, which means the "former" offender can go his/her merry way without any probation or court oversight.

Mandatory supervision with court-imposed terms and conditions included participation in rehabilitative programs. This created a mixed bag of potential blessings (community programs and treatment) in rehabilitation but also potential crime reduction reverses if another crime was committed.[179] Retired Judge, J. Richard Couzens reported a study completed by the chief probation officers of California which revealed approximately "…23 percent of the sentences to county jail are split sentences. In eighteen counties, judges used the split sentence more than half of the time, but in Los Angeles, it is used in only about 5 percent of the cases."[180] This suggests that the use of split sentences remain an anomaly rather than the norm for the counties. One legitimate reason for so few split sentences may be that probation departments in some larger counties are not prepared for a potential court onslaught of split sentences.

Judge Couzens also identified two other Realignment changes that directly impacted the supervision of offenders in the community. First, PRCS inmates released from state prison were no longer supervised by the CDCR Parole Division. That function became a county probation responsibility. Secondly, beginning in July of 2013, Judge Couzens reported that most:

> "serious and violent crimes would also be supervised by county probation officers...court sanctions of up to 180 days...a modification of the terms of supervision and treatment...only in very limited circumstances may the offender be returned to state prison."
> (Rodríguez, page 218)

Initially, the results of the Realignment sentencing changes led to a 31 percent reduction in the *average daily population* of state prisons.[181] But it also led to the increase in the number of offenders under county (jail, probation) correctional control.

From 2010 to 2012, statewide county jails saw an increase of 8.3 percent while probation departments saw a substantial increase of 29.7 percent.[182] What do these numbers mean in terms of the recidivism challenge? It means that Realignment has made statewide probation departments responsible for 60 percent of California's offenders. That means over 100,000 more offenders under the auspices of probation departments since 2010.[183] If probation departments are going to successfully meet the recidivism challenge (less crime and lower returns to confinement), the answer is certainly going to be found where the funding dollars are spent.

The Community Corrections Partnership

It's been said that trying to get a different result by doing the same thing over and over again and getting the same result, only validates you're stupidity. But the name-calling only applies if your intent really is a different result. In the case of Realignment, the jury is still out since many of the stakeholders remain committed to being "tough on crime" as the most effective public safety approach. However, much has also been written about the public safety intent of Realignment. The California Penal Code identifies its rehabilitative goal and the legislature certainly alluded to the benefit of local intervention as key to Realignments success. However, the counties had a much more pragmatic approach to the changes Realignment brought. They collectively sought funding commitments from the state that would ensure the cost of "rehabilitation" would not overwhelm local agency (Sheriff, Probation, Police, and Court) efforts. Accordingly, the best measure of judging the intent of the counties is by following the funding trail for Realignment.

It is understandable that the initial implementation of Realignment statewide would resemble previous budget patterns. The counties didn't surprise anyone except for when they fought for a larger share of the 4.4 billion dollar prize the first two years. Likewise, a sizable portion of the funding continued to support the jail and probation functions since the initial PRCS offender outpouring would presumably hit those agencies first. In fact, the first year's (2011-2012) spending pattern reflects that thirty-five of the fifty-eight counties had plans to expand jail capacity using Realignment funding.[184] This pattern should have been expected, given that the political wheels and local budget cycles had already been geared for that effort prior to the implementation of Realignment. However, the next three years will bear witness to whether or not the counties pursue alternative options to rehabilitation beyond more jail beds. Unfortunately, recent Realignment allocations don't look substantially different from the past, which suggests the counties Community Correctional Partnerships (CCP) are continuing to do the same things, but hoping for different results.[185]

The CCP is the principle avenue by which the counties will assess, implement, and evaluate the implementation of public safety for offenders under Realignment. When Realignment first rolled out, the fifty-eight statewide counties CCPs were required to develop implementation and budget plans for county approval. The executive committee of the statewide CCPs in each county is comprised of the chief probation officer, chief of police, sheriff, district attorney, public defender, presiding judge of the superior court, and a representative from local social service agencies. These are the very important people who are tasked with creating and implementing the Realignment policies, procedures, and practices for each county.

Throughout the fifty-eight counties, the board of supervisors was required to designate a county agency to be responsible for the post-release supervision of offenders. That decision came with much debate and controversy (*Los Angeles Times*, 2012). However, it is interesting to note that, in all fifty-eight counties, the boards appointed the chief probation officers as lead agency and chair of the CCP. This was a wise decision owing to the probation department's role in supervision and rehabilitation, but only a ceremonial gesture in practice, given that each agency participating in the CCP has independent budget authority. Simply stated, the local CCPs have no jurisdictional authority for how, when, and why each participating agency acts on offenders.

"Ramping Up" the BS-CC.

There is reason to believe that the current CCP approach in all counties may turn the corner on Realignment. On July 1, 2012, the Board of State and Community Corrections (BSCC) was established to serve as an independent body providing leadership and technical assistance to the adult and juvenile criminal justice systems. A central part of its mission was to oversee the prison and public safety realignment goals. The BSCC's history dates to 1944 when the *Board of Corrections* (BOC) was established by Governor Earl Warren to establish a system-wide reorganization that improved prison conditions and centralized management. In 2004, the *Corrections Standards Authority* (CSA) replaced the BOC within the California Department of Corrections and Rehabilitation.

Today, the BSCC is "vested with the CSA's rights, powers, authorities and duties," and sets standards for the training of county corrections and probation officers. Its mission includes, but is not limited to, maintaining data on Realignment and is a clearinghouse for information regarding evidence-based strategies and programs, compliance of standards and directs funding for construction of local adult and juvenile detention facilities and ensures that the local jail projects meet Legislative mandates to provide program space for offenders.[186] The BSCC comprises a large public safety mandate to be sure.

Even though Realignment began throughout the state in October of 2011, the BSCC remains in embryonic form since the Chair, Linda Penner and its executive director only came on board in October on 2013. Two years into its existence, the BSCC has been described as "... still 'ramping up' which was expected to be a long process involving much cultural change."[187] Ironically, an expectation not afforded to the county CCPs, courts, jails or prisons when Realignment first rolled out for them.

To be fair, the BSCC mission can provide uniformity and accountability as it applies to program effectiveness and data collection, but only with consistent support from key stakeholders in the legislature and governor's office. Presently, its members include the chair appointed by the governor and approved by the legislature, the Secretary of the CDCR, the DAPO Director, County Sheriff in charge of a local detention facility, a local Police Chief, a community provider, an advocate of rehabilitative treatment and programs and lastly, a member of the public appointed by the governor. This is a very powerful group whose influence will be sorely tested on the question of crime reduction and recidivism.

The Fuzzy Facts

The American Civil Liberties Union (ACLU) reviewed the county Realignment allocations in 2012. Their review revealed that the "Big twenty-five counties" of California's fifty-eight counties receive the bulk (92.2 percent) of the Realignment dollars. Interestingly, Southern California cities were well represented among the "Big twenty-five." In fact, Los Angeles, Orange, Riverside, San Bernardino, and San Diego represented almost 59 percent of the "Big twenty-five" Realignment Program Allocations. These same counties also represent nearly 65 percent of all felons committed to state prisons. If Realignment is going to succeed, it is clear that these southern region counties will be critical in determining what outcome will be attained for the long term.

Therein lies the challenge for all fifty-eight counties. The debate (if there is one) between more programs versus more jail beds is a complicated topic for most of the Realignment stakeholders. There is no simple answer because what works best or what is needed most in Monterey County is significantly different from what works or is needed in Riverside County. The context from which the various counties' political machines, community culture, multi-agency status, and socio-economic history must interact with the nuances of offender type, number, and circumstance all come into the Realignment equation.

This is all *fuzzy math* which may lead to dire consequences if the decisions made today don't add up to lower crime rates and lower recidivism tomorrow. That is why today California has fifty-eight different approaches for addressing the recidivism challenge. Each has its own issues and resource challenges. This is not an auspicious beginning for the counties Community Corrections Partnerships (CCP) or the BSCC. The BSCC and local county CCP participating agencies, whose colossal task of leading Realignment have no statewide vision, standardized data collection methodology, or statewide rehabilitation benchmarks to guide its path.

CHAPTER 9

**City Rage Feeds Man's Desire,
Confused Minds Have Souls for Hire,
American Dreams of Dignity,
Out Looking for a Real Reality**

Daniel Valdez
"Real Reality"

"Wandering Dogs"

*I*first met Steve Slaton at the Riverside Juvenile Hall in the summer of *1982-83. We were both group counselors assigned to manage the ward housing units. I don't remember the first time we jammed together, but it happened; and what a strange combination it was. At the time, he was into bluegrass music and I was into oldies and soul music, but we both loved classic rock. We merged somewhere in the middle and found something that we've enjoyed ever since. Like our careers, we didn't stay with one sound for too long. He became a very good lead guitarist and bass player for rhythm and blues bands on weekend gigs, while I suffered the indignity of never mastering rhythm guitar, but finding solace in "closet" songwriting.*

Some years later, it took another LEO, Rick De La Rosa, an accomplished drummer/percussionist in the Inland Empire region of southern California, to convince me to "come out of the closet" and play my songs publicly. Together, the three of us formed a group called the "Wandering Dogs" playing original blues and classic rock music. Eventually, we expanded, adding a bass, saxaphone player and drummer, Tommy, Ybarra (another LEO who had also worked at the juvenile hall). We had fun, but the experiment didn't last too long. Thankfully, we had kept our day jobs!

Steve treated his profession much like his music—always finding a better and more challenging assignment during his celebrated career. I recall one evening when we worked together in the Security Unit at the juvenile hall. It was the Administrative Segregation Unit for wards that were considered "high risk," meaning they were violence prone or escape risks due to their commitment offenses. Also, wards that were awaiting transfer to prison or Youth Authority would be housed in the Security Unit. As "luck" would have it, we had a high notoriety case pending transfer to Youth Authority.

The high notoriety case was a sixteen-year-old Crip, I'll refer to as "Nathan." He had committed a murder robbery in the Moreno Valley area of Riverside County. The circumstances of the offense revealed his sad pathological personality. After robbing the victim, Nathan had made the victim lie prone. The victim complied. Instead of leaving, Nathan calmly walked up to the victim and shot him at point blank range in the back of the head. The case had received a lot of media attention, but my only concern was his behavior in the housing unit. He had spent nearly a year in the county jail before he was committed as a juvenile and remanded back to the juvenile hall by the Riverside County Superior Court. Nathan had spent most of his time in isolation at the county jail because of his age. Nathan, now seventeen years old, was in the security ward of the juvenile hall, awaiting placement in Youth Authority for first degree murder.

Nathan had been in the unit about a month and I began to notice a troubling behavior pattern. He would always try to bend the rules. He made a habit of being the last to return his meal tray or enter his cell at the end of the day. Staff would find items in his cell that were not allowed. Staff were vigilant and he never challenged them. Instead, he was casually polite, but always indifferent with staff. Yet with visitors and teachers, he appeared engaging and interested. His behavior was not random, it was calculated.

One evening I allowed Nathan to join a group of kids for Bible study with a volunteer visitor. Before I released the group, I cautioned them about not removing anything from the classroom. Nathan had already been reprimanded earlier in the day about taking a book from the classroom. The classroom had glass windows which allowed staff to easily monitor the group. About an hour or so later, as Bible study ended, all the kids were released from the classroom back to the living unit. I made a quick tour of the classroom and realized the leather-bound Bible was missing. I walked out of the room directly to Nathan.

"Do you have the Bible?" I asked.

"Yeah," he replied, looking right at me.

I responded, "Hand it over and go to your cell!"

He complied, reaching into his shirt and removing the book. He handed it to me and we both started walking down the long corridor to the last cell. I stayed within arm's reach, not really sure what would happen next. Unbeknownst to me, Steve had seen us and was quietly trailing the escort.

I opened the cell and directed him to remove his shoes and pants, which he did without saying a word. As we entered the cell, he turned and faced me. I had the Bible in one hand and the Folger-Adam key (large steel key especially made for prison cell doors) in the other. I didn't move. Instead, I tapped the tip of the key against his chest as I stated, "When I tell you not to remove anything from the classroom, I damn well mean it!"

I sensed that he wanted to take a swing at me. I wanted him to, as well. Nathan only gave me a cold stare for a moment then replied, "You know what? You are an evil man."

I responded, "Yeah whatever, remember that. Get on your bunk." He complied, without saying anything more.

As I exited the cell, I realized Steve had been standing at the side of the door quietly listening, but out of sight from us. I secured the cell and, as we walked away, Steve whispered to me, "He's here for murder and he's calling YOU an evil man?" We both just shook our heads in disbelief.

I lost track of Steve for some time after we both left Riverside County Probation. I went to work in the prisons and he to the parole division. A few years later, I happened to read in the departmental newsletter that he'd received a commendation medal for a major drug bust in Victorville. I remember looking him up to tease him, but he got the last laugh. It turns out the rural dirt roads out in that area all look the same. When Steve, his parole agent partner, and several deputies approached a house, a guy ran out the back. A deputy detained him and, although it turned out they were at the wrong location, the runner turned out to be on parole. One thing led to another and they came away with a cache of weapons, several stolen vehicles, and a good amount of illegal narcotics. Even though they had gone to the wrong place, their timing couldn't have been better! In the world of crime-fighting it is always good to have a little "luck" on your side.

Steve completed twenty-five years with CDCR and retired in 2008, as a Special Services Unit Agent—a very well respected unit in police/detective circles. He had become a gang expert during the ensuing years and is now a consultant with various law enforcement agencies today. Steve had a unique perspective on Realignment since he had worked as a Parole Agent I (PA-I) in the field for nearly ten years before he was moved to the Parolee At Large team. He was promoted to Special Services Unit Agent the last ten years of his career. In fact, he returned to PA duties as an annuitant in 2010, two years after he retired. It was this involvement that provided him a clear comparison to his previous training and work experience. I interviewed him on April 16, 2014.

Q: How would you characterize the caseload changes from when you started and then retired twenty-five years later?

A: First, they got so big…they (Headquarters) did audits and you had to meet the "stats." What happened then is you started getting really shoddy casework…many agents did these "drive-by" casework contacts. Before, when you were assigned a case, it was yours; from release through the whole course of supervision. When the caseloads grew, they [Department of Adult Parole Operations-DAPO] demanded more "stats" and the quality of work diminished greatly. Before then, you'd sit with Mom and Dad, explain parole, and sit with the family to "put a face on the parole process." Parolees got to know me as a professional; you establish a rapport. This is not to say that the parolee didn't sometimes return to prison. Recidivism is recidivism…there's the one-third rule. One-third of them are going to do well no matter what you do, another one-third are going to screw up no matter what you do…I think it's higher than that, but a third of them might benefit from what interventions you provide them. I'm not sure the break down is exactly thirds, but the concept is valid. If you capture a moment in time, I think you'd find the number… but it's a fluid number…I've been doing this so long, but I've seen it.

…I recall this long time offender with a rap sheet a mile long…he got released and was found passed out drunk on the street the same day. I was new to the job and was gonna throw him back (to prison on a violation) but my seasoned partner said, "No take him to the residential program in Victorville." We did and I don't know what happened, but he got well. He went to a school and got an air conditioning/heating certificate and never looked back. Those types of successes are all too rare, but they do happen. The trick is to identify the ones who are truly open to interventions. I had misread this guy, thinking he was way beyond help and too dangerous to leave out.

...When I started as a PA-I, the caseloads were manageable to the point where you weren't just "checking boxes," you actually went into the home, could talk to family and the parolee. Over the ensuing years, as caseloads became larger the emphasis, sometimes misplaced, became on just meeting the "specs." If you had a high control parolee, you had to have one face-to-face in the office, one face-to-face in his home, and one collateral contact (employer, neighbor, family member, etc) each month, and you really had to hustle and manage your time well.

This whole emphasis on "stats" probably began during the mid-nineties. It just got ridiculous...No quality in work, agents would make home contact appointments and do a drive-by, not really going inside the home. That's not a home call, there is a process involved and that process includes making good casework decisions based on intelligent and practiced observations. To be fair, it wasn't always the agent's fault. There were no measures for the quality of the contacts, only that the contacts happened.

There was no continuity of supervision. Caseloads were on a point system so if, for example, the supervisor says Richard you have 180 points and Fred has 101 points, so give him ten of your cases...and if Richard hadn't been doing the case work, Fred has to catch up in a hurry. Or worse, Richard received them from me and now he has to turn them over to someone else. The cases are now twice removed. There was no continuity of caseloads anymore. Before, the parolee knew me and I knew him, but that was not the case anymore. Now you have Probation. They couldn't handle their caseloads before AB 109, with the large numbers of cases coming in to the counties it's the same impact for them, too.

...In 1996 the Parolee-At-Large (PAL) Team was created. I went to PAL and it was the best thing that ever happened to me. I'd always been a problem-solver and you're dealing with other law enforcement, so I was *solving crimes. I liked that...I also had a theory: That at any given time 80 percent of the caseload was committing a crime.*

Q: *How did you come to that 80 percent conclusion?*

A: *I came to that conclusion based on the criminality of drug use. Look at it this way, if you or I had been locked up away from our loved ones and, as a condition of getting out, we are required to do certain things and not do some other things, including not using drugs, we would do whatever it took to remain free. But many of those sent to prison either can't, or choose not to comply with conditional release requirements. Even though we told them not to and put it in writing, and had them sign conditional release documents, they would still use drugs and sometimes remain otherwise criminally active. This is a criminally active population—a certain percentage is criminally active at any given time. Now if you de-criminalize drug use that would take care of a bunch of it...*

...You know I went back as a retired annuitant in 2010 to the Parole Unit in Victorville, the same unit where I started out as a PA-I. That's when I noticed the difference; the number of Hispanic gang members and the number of parolees—it just exploded. I also noticed that parole was more ineffective because it had been burdened with the "stat driven concept." They took away the offender risk and needs assessment from PAs and made it an institution-based function. I thought, "What are you doing?" They (prison) would sometimes make them a high control case when he (parolee) was really just a run-of-the-mill case. You know, high control cases were traditionally serious offenders, but these case assessments coming out of the prison just seemed screwy.

Sometimes serious offenders came out with lower risk assessment scores, and agents were reluctant to suggest an override because it meant more work. Parole supervisors didn't want to bump a high control case down and get into a mess. They were thinking, "What if I bump him down and the case blows up?" Instead, they wait sixty or ninety days and then reclassify. In the meantime, PAs had to push the "stats."

There was also a new computer-aided decision matrix that was being used. By and large, the computer decisions were okay...some were not.

When they took the human element out of it, and "dumbed down" the offender evaluation process, it really hurt the parole division a lot. I had a feeling about this computer-based behavior matrix...you put the data in and it spits out the result. In a sense, it was good because it made it easy for people to put information in and be presented with reasonable conclusions. But taking human judgment out of the immediate process always bugged me.

Q: *What caused that?*

Q: *First, it was bad hires, they (PAs) were supposed to have college degrees, but didn't. The caseloads grew so fast that it seemed they were just getting warm bodies to fill positions. Remember, the number of positions were driven by the number of cases and that number was skyrocketing...so we sometimes got people who were not self-starters, they were institutionalized—used too simply following orders. Some carried the old prison guard work ethic of, "Do your eight and hit the gate" to the Parole Division. Not all of them, of course. I worked with some very good agents who came to the division from correctional officer and correctional sergeants positions. But all in all, when pay compaction issues allowed officers and sergeants to obtain a lateral transfer to Parole, the mission suffered.*

*...See, when I started, me and my senior partner, we were "booting" doors every week. We were very proactive in enforcing parole conditions and one of them was "not break any laws." Remember this was in the 80s and our area of responsibility was vast, the entire high desert area of San Bernardino County. That's everything from the Cajon Pass to the Arizona Border, and from the LA County line to Joshua Tree, and there were only two of us. That meant we relied heavily on local law enforcement for backup and many of those officers also relied on us if we were available. We worked very well together. We were "hooking and booking" a lot...then I come off the Victorville Mountain thinking all PAs were working like us. I'm looking around thinking, Oh, my god...I mean I was just astounded to learn that people were working out ways **not** to get their jobs done. I wasn't raised that way.*

...I couldn't believe it! Where was the pride of a job well done? To get a perspective of the growth and contraction in the Parole Division consider this, when I started in 1987 there were two agents and one supervisor

covering the whole area. By the time I left Victorville in 1997, we had a full unit of about seven agents and two supervisors. When I returned in 2010, before Realignment, there were four completely staffed units and about ten agents in each unit, four supervisors, and six to eight support staff. Now, after Realignment, they are down to two units.

Q: *Did you see a change in the characteristic makeup of gang members during your career?*

A: *No, I didn't. What happened was, when I started as a parole agent in the 1980s, gangs were not as big of a problem in Victorville as they are today. When I went to the PAL Team, a fugitive's gang status was only useful if it helped us find him. As a special services agent dealing with the prison gangs I didn't start at the bottom, I started at the top, dealing with the Mexican Mafia, the Brand (Aryan Brotherhood), NLR (Nazi Low Riders). When you're talking about gangs, particularly the EME… you can't think Black Angels, Puente 13, you know, street gangs. You got to imagine, the T.V. program, The Sopranos. You got to think like Tony Soprano, and the Italian Mafia. That's what I dialed right into. That's when I started really working with gangs because that's the level of sophistication they are working at. I fell right into it…. The EME has become more sophisticated, more deadly, and more treacherous. Their covert communications have become better from the prisons; the coded messaging, very sophisticated. They have created better lines of control from the prisons to the streets and they are known to have ties to Mexican drug cartels and other organized crime syndicates.*

The Mexican Mafia is the most sophisticated of all the prison gangs in California. When they started out, their whole concern was profiting from criminal behavior in the prison community. So if someone got a load of dope in, they were gonna "break off" (share) something for the Mafia, or suffer at least a beat-down if they didn't. What they did was— and Pete "Sana" Ojeda, I believe did it—they took the strategy of "I'm gonna tax anything or anyone who comes on my prison yard" and they took it to the street. In the 90s the EME had these meetings supposedly to help stop the drive-by shootings by brokering a "peace treaty" among rival street gangs in Southern California. What the EME actually told them (street gang members) was if you're gonna shoot someone, then walk up and shoot them. Don't be a coward and shoot from a car.

It was about that time that Ojeda took the inmate taxing [strategy] to the streets. I think when he saw the number of local gang members who showed up at those meetings, a light went off in his head. If he could command the same respect-out-of-fear in the community that he held inside a prison, why not manipulate that into a money-making enterprise? That is when they really strengthened their communication from prisons to the streets. In the 90s the Mexican Mafia consolidated their control of the street gangs.

Q: *Using the Soprano analogy, so what are they doing with the money?*

A: *Anything from fighting court cases, to becoming more active in taxing legitimate businesses to funding other illegal activity such as drug manufacturing and drug trafficking on a very large scale. In extorting local businesses they might say, "You know what? We can keep the taggers from putting graffiti on the wall," and then get a monthly fee for not tagging up the place. In some jurisdictions, they go after the food trucks. It's like "If you're going to park in this neighborhood and sell stuff, then you must pay us—we control this area." But they get greedy, starting at fifty bucks a week and then increasing the amount. In one case, it went to $300 and the victim finally got tired of it and reported it to the police. They use local gang members to do it, and the other prison gangs try to emulate them.*

Q: *What's your opinion about the impact of Realignment to the counties?*

A: *They are experiencing many of the same problems the state system had, and maybe a few new ones. Jail population growth, inmate health care issues, mental health care issues, staff training, and safety issues, and a rapidly rotating revolving door that allows more contraband in and makes it easier for gang members to communicate with fellow gangsters in the community. They also have the community supervision aspect to deal with and many of the smaller jurisdictions were really caught off guard by the level of sophistication some dedicated criminals possess.*

Q: *Are we doing anything substantially different to reduce crime with AB 109 Public Safety Realignment?*

A: No... Well I think you mentioned the numbers, we're not dealing with it meaningfully. You can do a "drive-by" home call, send them on a referral, and then move on down the road. Besides, most violent crime is committed by young adults sixteen to twenty-five years of age. You can't discount the demographics. There is research that suggests the reduction in the number of violent crimes and a reduction in the number of sixteen to twenty-five year olds is more than coincidental. You can have a parole agent or a probation officer doing the same things, which is to say they are doing nothing different. They say Probation is "community-based." But what does that really mean? Parole agents also live and work in the same communities with the same programs. What has changed?

...One-third (of offenders) are going to do well, a third are going to screw up, and a third might respond to intervention. I might be wrong on the number, but the pattern exists. The concept of rehabilitation in a free society is interesting, too. We have freedom of choice. You can choose to break the law. Society can't take that choice away, but if you do choose to break the law and are caught, there are sanctions. Then you have Correction Departments who are held responsible for these "free choice inmates." And we tell them, "You have to quit doing this." We make programs for them to reinforce our desire that they change. I remember telling this parolee, "You have to quit doing this," (meaning stop using dope and breaking laws) and he said, "Man, I've been doing this since I was twelve years old. What's your problem?" To them, it's like having a beer, or taking the kids to the park. Getting locked up was just part of doing business as usual. It certainly was no deterrent.

I'm not opposed to rehabilitation; I've sent many guys to programs. For the sake of argument let's say all offenders are the same and they victimize the same in the community. If you take them out of the community, the public is safer. That's where the argument and complaints about the "revolving door of corrections" kind of falls short in terms of public safety policies. If you aggressively investigate criminals every chance you get and return them to prison, it disrupts their flow and organization; they can't get their (nefarious) business activities going. It's expensive, but, for the most part, a criminal in prison is less dangerous to the free community than one who is not.

Q: *If you were heading the Community Correctional Partnership, what things would you do to make AB 109 effective?*

A: *First, align the laws with the sentences...make the crime fit the punishment. If someone steals a car and gets two years, but only does six months, what message does that send? I would also decriminalize all simple drug use, and lessen the penalties for possession of small amounts. I think we're on the right path with the marijuana decriminalization laws. From a public health point of view, other things can be done...*

Steve, Rick, Tommy, and I still play music, but the "Wandering Dogs" band is no more. I had chosen the band's name because it had a double meaning. The name Wandering Dog is translated from the ancient Native American Nahua word "Chichimeca." The term Chichimeca referred to nomadic tribes that wandered the valleys and mountains of Mexico. They were considered to be savages, but accomplished at war and hunting. It is said that these Wandering Dogs would offer protection to warring tribes from their enemies and trade their warrior skills for food, shelter, and clothing. The Chichimeca were the ancestors of the future Aztec Warriors in Teotihuacán society. From my perspective, they were the first centurions of ancient Mexico.

I had the romantic notion that LEOs like Tommy, Rick, and Steve were modern day centurions wandering thru one assignment after another, whether it be in the street, jail, prison, or special assignment duties. In fact, today, in retirement, Steve continues to be a valuable gang consultant for various law enforcement agencies on the West Coast. Tommy owns and manages therapeutic homes for juveniles. Rick, also retired, is a Mayor in a southern California community. As for me, I'm also retired, but remain active as a board director for a small credit union in Southern California serving correctional employees and their families and I teach criminal justice courses part-time. It's pretty clear wandering dogs just can't sit still.

The Lords of the "Fly"

The primary problem and/or solution to making Realignment work ironically resides with the "fly"—the fly being the offender sitting in the Realignment ointment. Offenders tend to follow old habits that inevitably lead to law enforcement contact. But offenders cannot dictate the "new rules" for Realignment engagement because probation, county jail, and other local law enforcement personnel decide how to react to crime and engage criminals. As much as Realignment signifies a call for proactive programs and therapeutic treatment, our collective (community, media, and criminal justice stakeholder) response to crime remains fixed.

The *Wandering Dog* interview pointedly reveals the distinction between rank and file behaviors that don't mesh with the stated mission of CDCR. Former Special Services Agent (SSU) Slaton's candid perspective that "...a criminal in prison is less dangerous to the free community than one who is not..." has been the guiding mindset of most LEOs and with good reason. They have seen the tragedy of crime and the merits of justice for victims through lens of arrest and incarceration. The mission of DAPO and the CDCR has always spoken about public safety but it has also spoken about the reintegration of offenders back into society. Unfortunately, where the rubber meets the road, only one side of the criminal justice coin was tossed.

Like Pavlov's dogs, we have become conditioned to the benefits of the crime prevention model that targets, arrests, and detains criminals. We readily "salivate" a disgust and have been quick to use "heavy-handed" responses to crime and repeat offenders who ignore or dismiss parole/probation conditions. Slaton recalled when he was a parole agent, "We were very proactive in enforcing parole conditions and one of them was, not break any laws." Not much has changed in that regard among LEOs. Unfortunately, all the flies look the same and all the crimes feel the same so, it is hard to discern any other option than the one we've grown accustomed too. We dismiss the fact that flies just like offenders, don't routinely follow the same path-of-travel and behavior.

The Public Policy Institute reported that in year 2011-2012, property crime increased in California as a direct result of Realignment. Likewise, auto theft had increased by 24,000 in California, a 14.8 percent jump. However, violent crime remained relatively unaffected.[188] These crime numbers strongly imply two points. First, most of the Realignment "crime wave" is property related and therefore more than likely tied to drug and alcohol abuse. Secondly, if we agree that drug use plays a significant role in offender behavior or misbehavior, then our past *conditioned* response to *lock-them-up* will not be enough to deter future drug-related behavior. We've already proven this theory by our forty year experiment called the "War on Crime." This is the challenge the counties are struggling with today, how to change the culture of the law enforcement

"Lords" (the CCP; including, jail, police, probation, and court person-nel) to collectively embrace a decidedly different path that can reduce crime and recidivism.

Part of the state's solution to reducing recidivism was the passage of Senate Bill (SB) 678, The California Community Corrections Performance Incentives Act, in 2009. SB 678 provided a sentencing means where the counties would share a portion of the savings to the state if offenders were successfully maintained on probation instead of going to prison. SB 678 provided funding to increase the use of evidence-based sentencing practices. SB 678 funding was an incentive for the counties to try alternatives to incarceration. As a result, the counties had received $87.4 million from the state in year 2011-2012 and received approxi-mately 136.3 million in year 2012-2013.[189]

Roger K. Warren, President Emeritus, National Center for State Courts reported that prior to implementation of SB 678 in 2009, 50 percent of California probationers were not actively supervised. Moreover, the probation failure rate was 10 percent above the national average. Roughly 20,000 probationers revoked to prison annually cost tax payers over $1 billion dollars per year. Following implementation of SB 678, California saw a 23 percent reduction in the probation revocation rate in 2010 and a 32 percent reduction in 2011. Also, violent crime rates continued to decline in year 2010 and 2011.[190] These numbers suggest that alternatives to incarceration can work if given continued budget support that is tied to performance. More importantly, SB 678 provides all the counties a monetary incentive to reduce probation fail rates. This is a good start, but much more is needed in the way of program alterna-tives to jail.

Judging from recent attempts to change our attitude about drug-related crimes, Realignment still faces an uphill battle in redefining what constitutes a crime. For example, California Senator Mark Leno introduced Senate Bill 1506, in 2012, which sought to reduce simple possession of heroin, cocaine, and methamphetamine from a felony to a misdemeanor offense. Senator Leno maintained that, "there is no evidence to suggest that long prison sentences deter or limit people from abusing drugs…people trying to overcome addiction because they are unlikely to receive drug treatment in prison…"[191] This was a great complimentary crime bill to Realignment which would have saved the counties in excess of $159 million annually. Sadly, the bill failed to muster the needed votes to pass. The "Lords" of crime prevention didn't actively support the bill, thereby giving it little chance to pass.

One year later, 2013, the Attorney General of the United States, Eric Holder actively sought to reduce the penalties for drug-related offenses that originated with the Anti-Drug Abuse Act of 1986. The 1986, bill was introduced by Congress after the very public overdose death of Len Bias, a member of the Boston Celtics. The bill imposed minimum sentences for drug-related offenses. Public support of the bill stemmed from its focus on "kingpins" and other major drug dealers. It passed with little opposition.

But the law was triggered by possession of small amounts wherein, a first-time offender could receive a five year sentence for selling as little as five grams of crack cocaine. Instead of major dealers going to prison, the nation saw an explosion in the federal prison population. 25,000 in year 1980, became 80,000 by 1990. By the year 2000, there were over 150,000 offenders housed in federal prison. By year 2012, the number was 219,000, a jump of nearly 700 percent in thirty years.[192] While there has been plenty of public support to overturn what many believe to be a draconian law, there is no consensus in Congress to reduce the harsh penalties created by the 1986 Act. Like the book, *Lord of the Flies* portrays; conflicting human impulses always seem to get in the way of rational actions, rules, and humanity.[193]

The conflict in human impulses, as it applies to crime, has been the underlying theme of this book. It examines our collective mindset about crime, fear of criminals, and adherence to locking them up resulting in the mass incarceration of offenders. Ironically, having the largest prison population in the world may not be the primary issue or concern facing society today. To be fair, taking a criminal off the streets absolutely mitigates against the threat of more crime from that offender and acts as an immediate deterrent by disrupting their pattern of destructive behavior. But that is only one part of the trifecta crime solution gamble.

The more important question is, what's being done with them *during and after* incarceration? It is a sad commentary on our nation that notions of humanity or moral obligation aren't enough to bring the discussion of offenders to the forefront. Instead, the cost to taxpayers has sparked national debate on incarceration the past few years. More frightening, perhaps, is the impact Realignment may have on how the "flies" engage each other that could pose a greater threat to public safety.

"Guerilla" Warfare

All the research previously cited regarding Realignment speaks to specific prescriptions to make it more effective. It makes sense that independent evaluation that quantifies the strengths and weaknesses of evidence-based practices can help agencies determine more reliable or effective Realignment strategies. Likewise, better communication and coordination among stakeholders in the Community Corrections Partnership (CCP) can go a long way in providing consistent intervention at all levels of the criminal justice process, such as, programs, policing, probation, and ultimately the court. But in all the literature, the onus for meeting the goals of reducing crime and recidivism rates rest primarily on two factors: *Alternative options to incarceration and individual offender desire for rehabilitation.* Both are necessary and can achieve measurable success, but they ignore the bigger criminal justice threat on the Realignment landscape. That being the "Guerilla" in the room; organized crime in the form of the Mexican Mafia.[194]

The prison gang mentality has infiltrated all levels of the prison and jail systems in California. As SSU Agent Slaton pointed out, their web of influence, particularly the Mexican Mafia, reaches out in most urban communities where loyal street gang members live. The idea that the EME or any other prison gang could start a race riot in a prison or jail setting is of no surprise to any correctional professional. It has happened time and again since the advent of organized California prison gangs in the late 1950s and 60s. The August 8, 2009, riot at the Chino Prison exemplifies that fact.

But to most citizens, media, and politicians, that kind of obscene power is almost considered acceptable in a hostile prison environment. What else can be expected from angry, uneducated, sociopathic personalities with little redeeming social values? On the other hand, the idea that the EME could orchestrate a statewide prison hunger strike using social media to manipulate a change in CDCR's departmental policy seems farfetched. It shouldn't be, because that is exactly what occurred in 2013. More importantly, the likelihood of the EME orchestrating another major hunger strike, work stoppage, or large scale disturbance statewide remains hauntingly real.

Because Realignment changed the correctional landscape from the state to local counties, the "playing field" has changed, too. Herein lies the criminal justice threat that is looming larger and larger in California's county jails—the unbridled influence of organized crime that can now reach more easily into our communities. For example, one unintended outcome of Realignment has been the increase in time spent in county jails for all offenders. Some are awaiting trial, others are serving their time, and some are cycling in and out. This is similar to what prison Reception Centers were experiencing statewide with Parole Violators except for one key difference. The length of stay at the county jails can be much longer than the one year maximum stay that Parole Violators could be held in state prisons.

The jails and county facilities housing offenders are being taxed for resources and program availability. Limited program access may not be remedied in the immediate future. As a result, the idle time in jails is only increasing as more bodies arrive with nothing to do. This is the idle time "petri dish" that spawns a deadly poison of new recruits for the Mexican Mafia.

Imagine a tough but naïve street gang member who, after repeated arrests and/or probation violations, arrives to do his time in the county jail. More than likely he will be asked to do "a favor." This is normal for the "pecking order" social dynamic that occurs among offenders in correctional facilities. The "favor" could range from merely watching for staff, sending a message to the streets, moving contraband or kites, holding dope or weapons, assaulting another inmate, or completing a sanctioned "hit." Offenders have little choice but to agree or they become the next target. This isn't mere speculation because it is happening today, just like it happened yesterday and in years past and will happen tomorrow.

Prison gang recruitment had previously been the mainstay of the general population prisons and Reception Centers where idle time was rampant and "doing time" meant adjusting to prison life. It still occurs there, but now has been moved *closer to home* locally at the county jails where gang recruitment can be manipulated more easily. Just like the unintended strategic plan of placing the prison gang leadership in an isolated corridor at Pelican Bay, which ultimately led to their unexpected cooperation. Likewise, Realignment has indirectly isolated "career offenders" for longer periods of time in the county jails. This change in the correctional landscape makes it easier for strengthening the EME foothold in the communities.

The Reception Centers held offenders from all the counties, making communication and alliances more difficult to traverse. To be sure, prison gang recruitment happened, but at a much slower pace, because inmates were more often separated and didn't personally know or have an allegiance to the gang players. But today we are housing offenders primarily from one county locally, making recognition and communication easier among them. The EME can now more easily engage Surenos who are doing more time languishing in jail with nothing to do, with no available options to crime, but having greater neighborhood ties to each other. Fashioning alliances and trust doesn't take as long when you know the players. Notwithstanding, if they are from an opposing street gang, these offenders more than likely know each other from previous school, juvenile hall, and community experiences. Besides, in jail and prisons street gang associations take a backseat to prison gang business. Cooperation is easier when you have a guiding hand. In this case, the guiding "black hand" belongs to organized crime in the form of the Mexican Mafia.

The New Prison Prism

The prisons too, have not escaped the impact of Realignment from a custody management perspective. The offender demographics in prison were once more egalitarian in terms of the array of counties, crimes, age, race, and time to serve. That is not the case today. What Realignment has changed for the counties remain nebulous as all fifty-eight counties struggle to determine what fits and works for each. But for the state prisons, a very clear picture is being produced that has escaped the attention of the media, politicians, and the public. It is an image that is both real and may have frightening consequences, if not addressed effectively.

An intended outcome of Realignment, was to house only the most dangerous criminals in state prisons. That goal has been achieved. As of June 30, 2013, over **70 percent** of the total prison population in California state prisons are serving time for serious or violent offenses including, but not limited to murder, manslaughter, robbery, assault with a deadly weapon, rape, lewd act with child, oral copulation, sodomy, and kidnapping. But somehow along the way, unintended demographic trends have come to pass.

Nearly **44 percent** of adults incarcerated in state prisons are between the ages of eighteen and thirty-four.[195] This is a critical age period because research has shown that most crime is committed by people between the ages of eighteen and twenty-five. But for offenders doing "hard time," the age increases, since there is no deterrent effect for continuing criminality. In prison, "continuing criminality" is the accepted norm. Likewise, Blacks and Latinos represent over **70 percent** of the inmate population with Latinos representing over 40 percent of the statewide population.[196] This unique socio-cultural aspect to prison life makes ethnic group ties stronger. As a result, California prisons today are housing more violence-prone offenders, who are younger and have a common ethnic heritage.

The only thing that hasn't changed is where the offenders who land in prison are coming from. The counties representing the most incarcerated felons remain in the southern region: Los Angeles (34.5 percent), Riverside (7.2 percent), San Bernardino (6.6 percent), San Diego (6.9 percent), Orange (5.3 percent), and Imperial (.2 percent). Combined, these counties represent over **60 percent** of all felon commitments residing in California prisons. Taken by itself, this statistic is uneventful, especially since that trend has existed for over twenty years. But when considered with the current demographic of younger aged offenders and a prison population decidedly more dangerous and ethnically tied by culture and region (namely *Surenos*) is bound to find common ground on which to unite.

The Asphalt Jungles

In California, the influence of the Mexican Mafia is not limited to the state prisons or community barrios where they tax local drug dealers or extort local businesses. They have ventured into other states and crossed the Mexican border as well. Investigative Journalist, Anabel Hernandez, in her landmark book, *NarcoLand*, describes in detail the corruption and usurpation of socio-political power structures in Mexico by the Mexican Drug Lords.[197] Hernandez revealed one aspect of the Mexican drug cartels control efforts was the use of the Mexican Mafia to aide their endeavors in the United States and Mexico. Hernandez, cites a 2005 Federal Bureau of Investigation, Criminal Investigative Division and San Antonio Texas Field Intelligence Group reports, linking the EME (used as hit men) with the notorious Los Zetas group.

The threat Los Zetas and other para-military criminal organizations hold for Mexican society looks eerily similar to the threat the EME poses here in the states. Hernandez describes the attraction of membership in the cartels as "...*the droves of Mexican youth without a future are fertile ground for them and other criminal organizations—mere boys and girls, robbed of all chance for a meaningful life.*"[198] Clearly, security on both sides of the border has not been a deterrent to criminal activity.

Hernandez revealed that today the bulk of cocaine, heroin, methamphetamine, and marijuana sales and distribution in the United States are controlled by Mexican cartels. They have moved ahead of Columbian, Chinese, and Russian mafias to control the illegal drug market into the United States maintaining Mexican drug trafficking organizations (DTOs) in every single region of the United States. Mexican DTOs have increased their cooperation with street and prison gangs in the states, representing approximately 20,000 street gangs in more than 2,500 cities.[199]

Hernandez passionately describes Mexico's fragile system of governance and the corrupt democratic processes that underpin any strategic consolidation of the drug cartels. She argues that Mexican and United States leaders would prefer to fight one cartel as opposed to 100. However, Hernandez persuasively contends that any such "Narcocracy" would collapse the Mexican government institutions creating a "Mafiocracy." Fortunately, the United States system of government is not so crudely corrupt (despite all our political defects), but our communities may well be vulnerable given the enormity of the financial incentives. Hernandez points out that the cost of a kilo of cocaine in Columbia was $2,500 in 2010. The larger drug kingpins would share a piece of the action with smaller dealers who could move a quarter-ton each week, generating an incredible profit worth the risk for persons lacking education and viable work skills. As Hernandez poignantly states the obvious, "Two hundred and fifty kilos of cocaine fit easily into a couple of suitcases, and drug traffickers on that scale are two a penny in our country."[200]

It is no secret to law enforcement that the EME has taken a larger role in drug trafficking, especially in Southern California. The EME ties to Mexico's DTOs remain fluid, but real. It's a simple case of economics and power. There is easy money to be made by those with the guile and grit to control nefarious activities. The EME has both which, in our prisons, jails, and urban locales, makes them look like kings of the asphalt jungles to a younger generation of gullible and disenfranchised youth that want to be gangsters. Street gang members who may soon be as Journalist Hernandez labels, "two a penny in our country."

California prisons and jail cauldrons are now housing a higher percentage of violent offenders than ever before. These inmates are younger and serving longer sentences. They are also primarily offenders of color: Black and Latino, mostly from Southern California. This is the stock ingredients of the street gang brew that will produce a poisonous concoction in prison and most certainly in the communities. Ironically, this offender demographic trend is a direct consequence of our best efforts to manage criminals and cope with an evolving Realignment policy quagmire. This is the larger public safety threat that has gone unnoticed in our crime discourse. This is the reason this book has argued for a different way to view crime today. Because if we don't, crime, or more accurately criminals, will be more difficult to address tomorrow.

All babies together,
Everyone a seed,
Half of us are satisfied,
Half of us in need...

The Isley Brothers
"Harvest For The World"

"Crime Pill Prescription"

The sky isn't falling just yet, nor is the writer crying "wolf." But, it is clear based on the aforementioned crime trends, what the outcome will be if we fail to talk and act differently about crime. Chances are we will see criminality increase at an alarming cost and consequence as offender population's increase and public safety is diminished. Compounding that ugly scenario will be the crystallization of organized crime in Southern California, the likes of which, we have not seen before.

The United States socio-political environment cannot be compared to the communities and governments in Latin America that have ignored, allowed, and in some cases encouraged and benefited from the growth of political corruption via drug cartel manipulations. But our inner cities could be ripe for exploitations if we don't make a concerted effort to reduce the inequities that invite criminal organizations in the form of DTOs like the EME. Accordingly, the following six concepts are offered as a macro remedy for what I think are the key instigators of crime in California:

1. **BSCC and CCP Expansion:** First, it's time to create a czar at the statewide level. The position already exists, but doesn't have the real *bully pulpit* power that chiefs of police and district attorneys wield locally. The czar would chair the Board of the State and Community Corrections (BSCC) (formerly the Corrections Standards Authority and Board of Corrections). Envision someone with the persona of William Bratton or Magic Johnson as the head of the BSCC! They would tender more political leverage in the legislature and, more importantly, the public forum—Bratton, because of his law enforcement lineage, and Johnson, because of his sports persona and entrepreneurial savvy.

Neither of them would be managing the BSCC, they would be *leading* the fifty-eight counties to the next level in crime prevention! The current BSCC Chair is responsible for reporting to the legislature and governor's office on all performance incentive funding outcomes that are specifically tied to SB 678 funding and/or any other funding tied to CCP programs. The chair is also tasked with coordinating research and evaluation of the CCP efforts as it applies to reducing criminality and reducing recidivism. But the chair of the BSCC should also have the authority to withhold funding for training and programs when agreed upon benchmarks have not been reached. Having a centralized leadership arena, with stronger budget authority over the counties, would expedite the BSCC effort to create a standardized approach to evaluating and implementing best practices for all fifty-eight counties in the state. Very few people know who the chair person is for the BSCC. Imagine if someone with the bravado of Magic Johnson or William Bratton were chair; everyone would know and all the CCPs would be listening or suffer the political consequences. If there are no effective penalties at the statewide level to encourage CCPs to remain on a restorative criminal justice path, then the CCPs have no reason to change. Additionally, *community treatment provider* representation should be provided a voting seat on the CCPs. Almost all treatment providers are informal members without voting privileges on the CCPs. Making them part of the CCP will enhance a systemic *bridge-building* link for rehabilitative programs. Inclusion invites change.

2. *Evidence of Programs* **Based in the Community**: Evidence Based Programs (EBPs) are not the issue. Not enough programs *is* the issue! The fact remains that there are not enough of them and those (EBPs) that have proven to be successful, still remain far removed from the budget looking-glass. Split sentencing (Mandatory Sentencing) under Realignment has been used sparingly by the courts. The statewide average of split sentences is only 26 percent of all cases. More EBPs in the community would provide a sustainable option for courts to exercise split-sentencing while simultaneously reducing overcrowding in the jails. And as we have learned, overcrowding is the linchpin of greater issues like: racial conflicts, federal court decree violations

and health care concerns. Why not flood the libraries, parks and recreation, middle schools and high schools with programs? We can pull the ineffective programs out like weeds in the garden and enhance programs that are sprouting positive outcomes. This may appear to look like a waste of money thrown randomly in the wind. But benchmarks and evaluation standards aside, if we have something to offer after school and on weekends that young people will participate in, we will immediately be ahead of the crime rate curve. To paraphrase Father Gregory Boyle's perspective on rehabilitation programs; it's not *outcomes* that are important, it's the *in-coming* seekers of treatment and jobs that should be our objective. California voters recently passed *Proposition 47* that will reclassify current felony drug possession offenses to misdemeanors. Estimates are that over the coming days, months and year up to 10,000 more offenders in jails and prisons will be released. The need for programs couldn't be more urgent.

3. **Summer Youth Job (SYJ) Programs**: Why the distinction between EBPs and SYJs? Simple, even though both improve self-discipline, educate, and provide skills in a variety of areas, only jobs give youth and young adults something tangible—money. And money matters, when expressing self-esteem. Not to mention, jobs provide real life practice at taking direction, team work, and routinized schedules…the "arts" of stable employment! The SYJs can and should be directed toward all youth, not just "at risk" or "low-income" candidates. Positive self-imaging begins with *not* being categorized by strangers as poor or delinquent. Instead, a broad brush solicitation of jobs, under a federal and/or state initiative, can be inclusive not exclusive. For youth, it would be then treated as an opportunity, instead of a handout. For employers, it provides a low cost "employee-trainee" incentive to hire.

4. **Strategic Law Enforcement targeting of Drug Trafficking Organizations (DTOs)**: There is already an on-going effort among and within most law enforcement agencies to fight prison and street gang drug trafficking. However, within the fifty-eight CCPs, each law enforcement agency acts on its own in addressing what is probably the greatest threat to public safety

today—organized crime. Presently, active and effective coordination relies on individual leadership and networking acumen among the various law enforcement agencies. Unfortunately, each is subject to the internal politics of that agency's budget process and local political priorities. The CCPs may readily acknowledge that bureaucratic pitfalls exist, but this should be an area that the BSCC can easily take the lead in without much political blowback. Every agency and county wants to beat down drug trafficking in their communities. The BSCC can provide an enhanced strategic plan for all counties to tackle together by formulating a persuasive funding argument for the legislature to confront DTOs at the statewide level.

5. **Viable Expansion of Educational/Vocational Programs in Jails and Prisons**: During the early 1990s, a conference call to all wardens from the director's office was made following a cluster of escapes that had occurred statewide. The director quipped, "Our mission is real simple, we get 'um and we keep 'um. If you can't do that, then you don't need to be here..." Since that time, the CDCR has been successfully keeping inmates inside the prison walls. But that approach didn't mean much once the offender left the prison after serving his/her term. They came right back in again and again and again. It isn't enough to just lock them up because most will return to the community. Providing programs that improve reading, writing, pre and post-release activities, and vocational skill certification has already been proven to reduce recidivism. We are not spending the monies to increase jail and prison programs for three main reasons: First, the stakeholders are not in agreement about its usefulness. Secondly, many citizens don't believe convicts deserve it. (Do the crime and do the time and nothing more). Lastly, many citizens believe that the monies would be better spent on our youth. These are all legitimate arguments for not spending money on prison and jail programs. But only if we want to continue in a vicious circle of offender "frequent flyer" recycling. This is the Realignment *slippery slope*: We cannot resolve our collective NIMBY (not in my back yard) feelings about releasing criminals back to society when we are adamant about the reasons we don't spend money and time on prison or jail programs.

6. **Viable Realignment Leadership and Management Training for Supervisors and Managers, at all Levels, in Law Enforcement and Correctional Facilities via the BSCC**: It seems obvious that a Realignment strategy should include training. After all, the agencies expend a significant amount of time and energy training staff in all manners of mandatory courses. Equal Employment, Affirmative Action, Use of Force, Americans with Disabilities Act, state and federal certifications in firearms and arrest protocols, are all standard features of most departments. What is lacking is the leadership and ethics training as it applies to the public safety mission. Staff among all CCP agencies generally know what their daily duties entail and can readily articulate those functions when asked. But a large percentage of all criminal justice employees cannot discern *what their role is* in the agency's or CCP's mission as it relates to Realignment. Some agencies provide management training as a vehicle to groom the next cadre of department leaders. But employees, who are not interested in moving up the ranks are left without understanding the "big picture." Realignment has opened the door for a broader view of the criminal justice arena that has not been articulated among the participating agencies in the CCP. This is perhaps, the greatest on-going failure—the lack of any visionary plan laid out for all fifty-eight counties to embrace as a collective mission viewpoint. Put it another way, what are the *six degrees of separation* between the community, criminal, victim, law enforcement, court, probation, jail, and prisons? Sounds simple enough, and most readers can easily connect the dots. Yet each entity by and large works independent from the other in terms of seeking to address recidivism and reduction of crime efforts. The BSCC should actively take the lead in collective training cycles on the Realignment mission, values, and benchmark goals for all the counties to help cement the connection dots.

EPILOGUE

Jaded, got a broken past,
Trying to get narrow, got to be fast,
Cause I'm losing, time in the sun,
Trying not to end, what I haven't begun

JANO
"Yesterday's Gone"

My intent in writing this book was to create a "new" dialogue about crime. The "new" part was how and where crime intersects with law enforcement, prisons, parole, probation, and gangs. My goal was to get LEOs and community correctional practitioners and citizens to ask, "What are we doing *differently* to reduce crime and recidivism rates?" The question may not be new, but the LEOs being asked to respond may be. Since boots-on-the-ground are the first contact offenders have in the criminal justice arena, they should be the first asking the question. They aren't asking and frankly most LEOs don't care to ask at all since most are satisfied with arresting and incarcerating criminals.

Fortunately, not all LEOs think the same. In fact, some earnestly go against the grain in the criminal justice arena—not an easy thing to do in law enforcement circles. Some of the important players don't get much of the spotlight or any of the credit when rehabilitation works. This includes community and church volunteers who work with local treatment programs, probation, and court personnel. Among all these dedicated citizens and contrarian LEOs, two persons stand out that need to be mentioned because of their impact on California, CDCR, and more importantly, on me. They both have had a profound influence on my perspective about crime. Leonard Greenstone and Robert Presley.

Leonard Greenstone volunteered fifty years of service to changing broken lives. During the latter part of my career I had the opportunity to meet Leonard Greenstone, the Vice-chair of Prison Industry Authority for the CDCR. He was a self-made entrepreneur, builder, and real estate investor/developer. If you asked him, he'd say "I'm just a plumber." He was, by trade, a master plumber. Leonard was a gregarious man with a booming voice and strong willed personality. But he had a heart of gold. He was a boxer and one of the original Navy Salvage Divers during World War II. He also helped establish the Los Angeles County Sheriff's Department's Underwater Search and Rescue Team while serving for nearly twenty years with the Sheriff's Reserves.

Leonard shared his story about how he came to develop an interest in prisoner rehabilitation. He made a visit to San Quentin in 1960 to see a relative who was working there. During the visit, an inmate captured an officer and held him hostage, but the man was eventually freed by other prisoners. Leonard was struck by the humanity of the rescuers' actions. He reasoned that even hardened criminals may have something inside that can allow them to do the right thing when the right circumstances exist. Leonard, a man of action, soon donated tools and equipment for a fledgling program to teach plumbing and other trades to San Quentin inmates.

Through his efforts and unrelenting determination CDCR embarked on rehabilitation programs unlike no other since CIM's beginning as a prison "without walls." His early efforts would eventually grow into the *California Prison Industry Authority (CALPIA)*. The CALPIA was a semi-autonomous agency, originally patterned as a self-budgeting industry. Greenstone was appointed by successive governors to serve on the board of the agency. The crown jewel among all the CALPIA programs was the CIM Diving Program. It remained close to Leonard's heart since his love of marine diving and salvaging remained strong throughout his life.

Leonard started the CIM Diving Program in 1970. Using his own resources and funding, Leonard created a viable program that provides teaching in diving physics, navigation, report-writing, air systems, welding, seamanship, blueprint-reading, diesel engines, and marine construction. He and his hand-picked marine instructors even had the inmate divers build the tanks, pool, and platform structures from which they would train. The instructors all had previous experience in the marine industry and gladly used their industry network to keep abreast of current needs and standards.

Nowhere else in prison vocational programs was a promise made like the one given to the CIM diving students: *You pass our rigorous program and you are guaranteed a job when you leave.* The program trains inmates for jobs in underwater construction, dam repair, and offshore oil drilling. The CIM diving students became known nationally as the Chino Divers, recognized as the best trained divers coming into the marine industry. Over the years, one of the ironic truths said about the program was "… you have to commit a crime in order to attend the best underwater diving program in the world." This wasn't hyperbole. Most community marine programs involved forty hours or so of training with limited certification and underwater application. At the MTTC, the Chino divers were immersed in hundreds of hours of training and underwater application that included on-the-job repairs. Employers could readily see the work ethic, knowledge, and confidence the Chino Divers brought to the job. They were the best of the rest. That industry view remains the same today.

Although the graduates of this program consistently maintained a recidivism rate of less than 7 percent, the program was closed in 2003, due to budget constraints. However, Leonard was not deterred in his belief that the program needed to be revived. When I became Associate Warden over the facility that housed the defunct program, it was an easy decision to help him revive it. On December 1, 2006, CALPIA re-established the commercial diving center at CIM as the *Leonard Greenstone Marine Technology Training Center* (MTTC). It continues today as one of the few successful vocational programs left at CIM.

I once asked Leonard why he believed vocational programs were vital to any philosophy about rehabilitation. He said, "Richard, through all my years of working with inmates I've realized one important thing, you give a man a viable job and half of his problems are over." This statement came from a man who dropped out of high school to serve his country honorably in war time and continued to serve his fellow man thereafter the rest of his adult life. Leonard passed away October of 2012, content that his effort in rehabilitation behind prison walls continues today. But

Leonard wasn't alone in his effort to establish the CALPIA. He had influential friends helping him. One of those was Senator Robert Presley.

****

Robert "Bob" Presley is one of California's iconic law enforcement leaders. Bob, like Leonard Greenstone, volunteered to serve during World War II, receiving a Bronze Star for his efforts. Bob moved to Riverside, California and served twenty-four years as a member of the Sheriff's Department before entering into politics. Bob, promoted thru the ranks, becoming a detective in the Homicide Division, Lieutenant, Captain, and eventually Undersheriff. He never forgot the trauma felt by victims and their families from the death of loved ones. Bob's experience in law enforcement would greatly influence his legislative policies.

Bob Presley was a California State Senator from 1974 to 1994. He represented California's 34th and 36th Senate Districts which included cities within Riverside and San Bernardino Counties. Bob's unimpeachable character and amiable approach to politics endeared him to many politicians and community stake holders. He was one of a few politicians who could walk both sides of the political aisle getting support for Senate Bills from Democrats, Independents, and Republicans alike—a feat almost unheard of in today's combative and impotent state legislatures. Bob's political tenure was made notable by his work on domestic violence, law enforcement reform, transportation, clean air initiatives, and other important areas as well.

California had been suffering one of the highest crime rates in the nation from 1970 through the mid-1990s. During the same period, California had the unenviable distinction of also leading the nation in violent crime.[201] In response to the unparalleled crime wave, Bob proposed and passed two bills in 1982 to build new prisons in southern and northern California. This was a period of unprecedented prison construction in the nation, particularly California. But he didn't stop there.

Bob worked diligently to improve faults he observed in the treatment of crime victims. He proposed bills that would establish domestic shelters, provide restitution for victims, and improve communication with them throughout the court process. He also recognized the benefits of programming in prisons and was a key legislative supporter of Leonard Greenstone's efforts in establishing CALPIA. Bob's leadership in the legislature and innovative spirit in the criminal justice arena (two titles he would humbly deny) led to his sponsorship of a package of ten bills in 1991, to reform the Corrections policies in California.

Bob proposed a package of bills that were the most far-reaching correctional policy changes that had been seen since 1951, when the California State Detentions Bureau was renamed the California Department of Corrections. Among them, the bills sought to standardize the statewide operation of the department by redistributing the power of wardens back to the Director. He sought to give educational and health care decision-making back into the hands of professional physicians and educators. He proposed that wardens and chief deputy wardens be required to have a Master's degree or Bachelor degree. He also proposed prisoner testing for AIDS to protect officers. All of these proposals did not pass, but some were ultimately imposed by the federal court and others eventually became policy directives. He had anticipated the need before others could see the problem.

He even proposed several bills to reduce the state's overcrowded jails and prisons. One in particular, Senate Bill (SB) 187, the Community Offender Re-entry Act, sought to allow judges and parole and probation officers more options than simply incarceration for punishment of non-violent criminals. Another, offered in 1984, SB 365, increased the number of Superior Court Judges in several counties to decrease the case backlogs. After retirement from public office, Bob has continued to support and sponsor local rehabilitation programs in California. The *Presley Group* has created one community vocational program for parolee and probationers in Northern California and is actively seeking another like program in Southern California as well.

Bob steadfastly remains committed to scholarly research that focuses on the criminal justice arena. In 1998, the California legislature established funding as part of a $12 million dollar federal effort targeted at steering youth from gang involvement. *The Presley Center for Crime and Justice Studies* at the University of California, Riverside was borne out of Bob's determination to find strategies that can reduce crime and recidivism rates among repeat offenders. The center continues to conduct research today.

****

I have known Leonard and Bob, first as mentors and then, as time passed, family friends. California and in particular, CDCR, should be grateful to have crossed their paths. They individually made a profound impact of how crime has been tackled in California. Budget constraints, notwithstanding, California's criminal justice arena would have fared much worse if not for their valued public service. I recall sharing many a dinner and drink listening to these two men debate the pros and cons of our crime prognostications. No one knew the politics of crime fighting better then these two warriors of World War II. They were both LEOs, but they didn't blindly follow common law enforcement perspectives nor did they cradle criminals. They just saw things for what they are. It simply cost too much to lock all offenders up and not do something constructive with them before and after they come back to our communities.

Accordingly, I don't have any trepidations sharing my views about crime in this book. Any errors or oversights are my fault. At times, I spoke directly to issues and other times, like the Hunger Strike events and Realignment implementation, I focused on the macro issues to reveal the criminal justice trends and impact. But always, my intent was to challenge the assumptions about future criminal justice outcomes. I am thankful for the many field leaders; wardens, managers, supervisors, and rank and file peace officers that guided my path. The stories and views I shared were real. And all of the people I wrote about believed they were doing the right thing and for the right reasons when they were in the middle of a mess. They all did their jobs differently, but all striving for the same outcome, to make a difference and to go home safely.

Unless, you have spent considerable time working in the criminal justice arena, you cannot truly understand the contradictions, conditions, and crisis in which LEOs, correctional practitioners, and offenders find themselves in daily. However, understanding the impact of the AB 109 Public Safety Realignment Act and the very real demographic changes occurring right now in California's prisons and jails is a start. My "crime-pill prescriptions" may seem idealistic and wholly unachievable in today's budget conscious and politically impotent climate. But I had the unique opportunity to see the harvest of two men who ignored the criticisms and challenged the prevailing wisdom. They weren't alone and neither are others that think the same way in law enforcement today.

****

The Greek philosopher, Aristotle is credited as saying, "Poverty is the parent of revolution and crime." I agree because the basic nature of mankind first and foremost is about survival. Our poorer communities—barrios and ghettos—have people facing limited options. Most are hardworking, full of hope and grit for themselves and their family. But there is a growing generation of youth that can't see a future because they are living in the moment. They have lost the ability to dream and only suffer the despair and frustration of getting through the day. Their lives have no normal routine or schedule. It is a sad irony that in a crowded city they know too well, they are lost and lonely.

Some of these young people have a poor sense of right and wrong and are prone to criminality as the easier solution for their selfish needs. They become the loyal street gang members whose only sense of pride comes from an attachment to the image of gangsters; strong, fearless and popular. They become the predators that prey on others, like themselves, who are struggling to make it through each day. But we can minimize this poisonous gang mentality by limiting the feeder-dish of despair when we educate, sustain, and provide opportunities for this millennial generation of lost youth. This is the public safety challenge.

Crime is a wicked problem. It will always be in our neighborhoods, like a cold that comes and goes but is never too far away. We can manage it, but the more sinister disease that has proven to be more symptomatic on society is drug trafficking organizations, like the Mexican Mafia. We need to attack the plague we call *organized crime* and its insidious impact on struggling youth in urban cities. Realignment can be the starting point. Our effort to reduce crime and recidivism rates begins when we ignore and overcome fear-mongering dialogue and create opportunities that breed dreams for our youth. President Woodrow T. Wilson once said, "We grow by our dreams." For the youth in our cities, dreams are the embodiment of what they want and ultimately where they hope to be some day. Perhaps, the best way to fight crime is by helping keep dreams alive in our communities.

GLOSSARY OF TERMS

AB-109/Realignment	Assembly Bill 109 is the Public Safety Realignment Act. Signed into law on April 4, 2011 by Governor Edmund G. Brown. Initiated statewide October, 2011.
AW	Associate Warden is the 3rd highest ranking administrative position in a prison and reports to the Chief Deputy Warden and Warden.
Barrio/Ghetto	Latino/Black slang: Used in reference to poor or impoverished minority neighborhoods.
BSCC	Bureau of State and Community Corrections: Established to serve as an independent body providing leadership and technical assistance to the adult and juvenile criminal justice systems. A central part of its mission is to oversee the prison and public safety realignment goals.

Carnal	Used by inmates in reference to a validated Mexican Mafia member.
Canteen	Where inmates can purchase sundry items such as Ramen Soups, candy bars, soda, etc. if they had money on their prison account.
Convict/Inmate	Convict: Is an offender with a long prison record who considers incarceration home. Inmate: Any offender in state prison.
CCI	California Correctional Institution located in Tehachapi, California.
CCP	Community Correctional Partnership- the county consortium of agencies headed by the Chief Probation Officer. The CCP is the principle avenue by which the counties will assess, implement, and evaluate the implementation of public safety for offenders under AB-109. Committee includes— Chief of Police, Sheriff, Superior Court Judge, Health Director or Mental Health Director and possibly community treatment vendor.
CRC	California Rehabilitation Center located in Norco, California
CDCR/CDC	California Department of Corrections and Rehabilitation

CDW	Chief Deputy Warden is the 2nd highest ranking person in a prison and reports to the Warden. Both are career executive appointments who work at the pleasure of the Director and Governor's office
C-File	Central File - is the entire history of inmate from the time he first enters the prison system and subsequent incarcerations.
CIM	California Institution for Men, a State Prison located in Chino, California.
CMO	Chief Medical Officer. Also, known as the Health Care Manager.
CRT	Crisis Response Team, a tactical team highly trained in hostage rescue, riot interdiction and high profile escort coverage.
Culinary	Dining Hall for inmates.
DAPO	Division of Adult Parole Operations
DTO	Drug Trafficking Organization
EOC	Emergency Operations Center is the heartbeat of any emergency/riot. Information is reported back to the Incident Commander as it happens minute by minute.
Fish	A new inmate or staff person in the prison system. A "newbie."

LEO	Law Enforcement Officer: Refers to all local, federal and state law enforcement agency peace officers.
LVN	Licensed Vocational Nurse
MSF	Minimum Support Facility: Provides low-level housing for inmates that work in clerical, plant operations, program and culinary assignments to augment prison functions.
MTA	Medical Technical Assistant. Generally, a LVN or RN.
Placa	Spanish slang for the police.
PLO	California *Prison Law Office* monitors the prisons and represents the inmates in court litigation.
PRCS	Post Release Community Service: Refers to the offenders released as a direct result of AB 109. Non-sex offenders, non-serious and non-violent offenders.
R & R	Receiving and Release. A secure location at prisons that is responsible for all intake and release of inmates.
RC	Reception Center is the processing unit for all inmate intake.
RCC	Reception Center Central, located at CIM

RCE	Reception Center East, located at CIM
RCW	Reception Center West, located at CIM
RVR	Rules Violation Report is a written document that outlines a violation of prison rules and regulations.
SAB	Security Administration Building/ Watch Office.
Shank	An inmate manufactured weapon.
Shot Caller	A "top dog/boss" inmate who is the recognized leader among the inmate races and unit living areas.
SHU	Segregated Housing Unit.
SOMS	Strategic Offender Management System allows access to an inmate's C-File including disciplinary hearing, medical appointments, visiting info, etc.
SSU	Special Services Unit- A unit within the Division of Adult Parole Operations.
Veterano	Refers to old time street gangster or convict.
Warden	The Warden is the highest ranking position in a prison and reports to Headquarters.
Watch Commander	A Correctional Lieutenant in charge of the facility or watch shift.

Song List Bibliography

- Jimenez, J. A. (Circa 1945). El Rey [Recorded by Jose Alfredo Jimenez]. Universal Music Publishing Group, HALL OF FAME MUSIC.

- Page, J. and Plant, R. (1969). What Is and What Should Never Be. [Recorded by Led Zepplin]. On *Led Zepplin II* (Album). North America and United Kingdom: Atlantic Records.

- Cooper, A. Bruce, M., Buxton, G., Dunaway, D., and Smith, N. (1970). I'm Eighteen [Recorded by Alice Cooper]. On *Love it to Death* [Album]. Los Angeles, California: Warner Bros. Records.

- Henley, D., Kortchmar, D. (1982). Dirty Laundry [Recorded by Don Henley]. On *I Can't Stand Still* [Album]. Los Angeles, California: Asylum Records.

- Kirke, S. and Rodgers, P. (1973). Bad Company [Recorded by Bad Company]. On *Bad Company* [Album]. Swan Song, Island.

- Howard, S., Brown, H. (1971). Slipping into Darkness [Recorded by War]. On *All Day Music* [Album]. Los Angeles, California: United Artists.

- Fogerty, J. (1969). Bad Moon Rising [Recorded by Credence Clearwater Revival]. On *Green River* [Album]. San Francisco, California: Fantasy Records

- Dylan, B. (1973). Knocking on Heaven's Door [Recorded by Bob Dylan]. On *Pat Garrett and Billy the Kid* [Album]. Columbia Records.

- Felder, D., Frey, G., Henley, D. (1976). Hotel California [Recorded by the Eagles]. On *Hotel California* [Album]. Asylum Records.

- Carter, B., Ellsworth, R., Layton, C., Shannon, T., Wynans, T. (1989). Crossfire [Recorded by Stevie Ray Vaughn and Double Trouble]. On *In Step* [Album]. Los Angeles, California: Epic Records.

- Hayward, J. [1967]. Nights in White Satin [Recorded by The Moody Blues]. On *Days of Future Passed* [Album]. United Kingdom: Deram Records.

- Traditional; Arranged by Price, A. [1964]. The House of the Rising Sun [Recorded by The Animals]. On *The Animals* [Album]. London, England: Columbia Graphophone.

- Slick, G. [1966]. White Rabbit [Recorded by Jefferson Airplane]. On *Surrealistic Pillow* [Album]. RCA Victor.

- Dylan, B. [1965]. Like a Rolling Stone [Recorded by Bob Dylan]. On *Highway 61 Revisited* [Album]. New York, New York: Columbia Records.

- Seger, B. [1980]. Against the Wind [Recorded by Bob Seger and the Silver Bullet Band]. *On Against the Wind* [Album]. Capital Records.

- Valdez, D. [1973]. Real Reality [Recorded by Daniel Valdez]. On *Mestizo* [Album]. Unknown Label.

- Isley E., Isley M., Jasper C., Isley R., Isley O. and Isley R. [1976] Harvest for the World [Recorded by the Isley Brothers]. On *Harvest for the World* [Album]. Los Angeles, California: T-Neck Records.

- Alvarado, A. [2009]. Yesterday's Gone [Unreleased Recording by Jano].

BIBLIOGRAPHY

Blatchford, C. (2008). *The Black Hand; The Bloody Rise and Redemption of "Boxer" Enriquez. A Mexican Mafia Mob Killer.* New York, NY. HarperCollins.

Boyle, G. (2010). *Tattoos On The Heart; The Power of Boundless Compassion.* New York, NY. Free Press.

Chaskin, R. J. (2010). *Youth Gangs and Community Intervention; Research, Practice, and Evidence.* Chichester, West Sussex, NY. Columbia University Press.

Dunn, W. (2007). *The Gangs of Los Angeles.* iUniverse.com

Gladwell, M. (2000). *The Tipping Point: How Little Things Can Make a Big Difference.* New York, NY. Little, Brown and Company.

Hagan, J. (2010). *Who Are The Criminals? The Politics of Crime Policy from the Age of Roosevelt to the Age of Reagan.* Princeton, New Jersey. Princeton University Press.

Hernandez, A. (2010). *Narcoland; The Mexican Drug Lords and Their Godfathers.* London, England. Verso.

Hayden, T. (2004). *Street Wars; Gangs and the Future of Violence.* New York, NY. The New Press.

Leap, J. (2012). *Jumped In; What Gangs Taught Me about Violence, Drugs, Love, and Redemption.* Boston, Massachusetts. Beacon Press.

Levitt, S. & Dubner, S. (2005). *Freakonomics: A Rogue Economist Explores The Hidden Side of Everything.* New York, NY. HarperCollins.

Mirande, A. (1987). *Gringo Justice.* Notre Dame, Indiana. University of Notre Dame Press.

Rodriquez, L.J. (1993). *Always Running, La Vida Loca: Gang Days in L.A.* New York, NY. Simon & Schuster.

Wilson, J. Q. (2013). *Thinking About Crime.* (2nd Ed.) New York, NY. Basic Books.

Mendoza, R. A (2005). *Mexican Mafia: From Altar Boy to Hitman.* WGA Registered.

Endnotes

Chapter 1

1   The California Penal Code Section 1.02 states, in part, "The general purposes of this code are to establish a system of prohibitions, penalties, and correctional measures to deal with conduct…the provisions of this code are intended, and shall be construed, to achieve the following objectives: (1) to insure the public safety through: (A) the deterrent influence of the penalties hereinafter provided; (B) the rehabilitation of those convicted of violations of this code; and (C) such punishment as may be necessary to prevent likely recurrence of criminal behavior…"

2   To be clear, the California Department of Corrections and Rehabilitation has an emergency code response protocol that can be elevated according to the immediate circumstances. Normally, officers don't announce a "10-33 in progress at such and such location." Instead, they use a numeric system to describe the response requirements. In the case of the August 8, 2009 riot, the 10-33 code was immediately on its highest level.

3   Other notably large riots: **Folsom** prison on Thanksgiving Day, November 24, 1927; a small group of inmates with the intent to escape incited a riot among approximately 1200 inmates who had just finished watching a movie at the school facility. Two officers died (one stabbed to death the other suffered a heart attack), three inmates killed and thirteen wounded. It took two days before the riot was ended. See www.militarymuseum. org and http://www.odmp.org for details. Another larger riot occurred on January 17, 1967: 1,800 black inmates and 1,000 white inmates clashed on the main yard at **San Quentin** resulting from the murder of an alleged

Nazi-prison gang member the day before. Prison officers broke up the brawl by firing shots into the mass. Five inmates were wounded by the shots and another inmate suffered severe head trauma from being assaulted by other inmates. Two other inmates suffered non-fatal heart attacks. See, http://www.crimemagazine.com/blood-blood-out-violent-empire-aryan-brotherhood. Also, the **California Rehabilitation Center** (CRC) had a history of sizable riots during the 1970's and early 80's. CRC housed primarily Civil Addict Commitments and some felons but the ratio's reversed with more Felons doing time at CRC by the 1980's. CRC riots involving large number of inmates (ranging from 200 to 1,000) at times would erupt inside the 100 man dorms and/or on the main yard requiring staff to use lethal weapons (shotguns, mini 14) inside the secure perimeter to regain control. These previous disturbances were not as well documented as the modern day CDC 837, Incident Packages that provide more extensive response details.

4   See: D'Elia, Carole (2010) *The Politics of Public Safety Reform in California*. Federal Sentencing Reporter, Vol. 22, No.3. Pages 144-147; Little Hoover Commission, Solving California's Corrections Crisis: *Time is Running Out* (2007); and Little Hoover Commission, Back to the Community: *Safe and Sound Parole Policies* (Nov. 2003). Also see, The Pew Center; *One in One Hundred*, (2008).

5   Simon, Jonathan. (2000) *Megan's Law Crime and Democracy in Late Modern America*; Law and Social Inquiry. 25 (4) 1111-50.

6   Bert Useem, Raymond V. Liedka, and Anne Morrison Piehl; Popular support for the prison build-up *Punishment & Society January 2003 5: 5-32*.

7   Campbell, Michael. (2012) Criminology & Public Policy, Vol. 11, Issue 2: *Perpetual "Crisis" and the Dysfunctional Politics of Corrections in California*. Pages 411-413.

8   Population Trend from 2000 to 2011, CDCR, 2013. http:/www.cdcr. ca.gov/Reports_Research/Offender_Information_Services_Branch/ Projections/F00Pub.pdf.

9   Spector, Donald. Everything Revolves Around Overcrowding: *The State of California's Prisons;* Federal Sentencing Reporter, Vol. 22, No.3 February, 2010.

10 Useem, et al. (2003). Hagan, John. (2010) Who Are the Criminals?: The Politics of Crime Policy from the Age of Roosevelt to the Age of Regan Princeton University Press.

11 Bert Useem, Raymond V. Liedka, and Anne Morrison Piehl; Popular support for the prison build-up *Punishment & Society January 2003, 5.*

12 Green Judith, Pranis, Kevin; Gang Wars: *The Failure of Enforcement Tactics and the Need for Effective Public Safety Strategies.* A Justice Policy Institute Report. July 2007.

13 Pew Center on the States; One in One Hundred: *Behind Bars in America.* 2008 (Page 5).

14 Hayden, T. (2004). *Street Wars; Gangs and the Future of Violence.* New York, NY. The New Press. (Page 338)

15 Wicked problems have been described by scholars as historical social issues that have no lasting solution like; poverty, war, hunger, revolutions, and crime.

16 The 1993 kidnap and murder of 12-year-old Polly Klaas by a California parolee and the barrage of criticism that followed this crime is symbolic of very real emotional impact of a horrible event. On October 1, 1993, Klaas invited two friends for a slumber party. Late in the evening, a parolee (Richard Allen Davis) entered her bedroom, carrying a knife. He tied up the two friends, pulled pillowcases over their heads and told Klaas' friends to count to 1,000. He then kidnapped, raped and murdered Klass. In the wake of the murder, politicians in California and other U.S. states supported the "Three Strikes Law" which California signed into law on March 8, 1994.

17 Aaron Rappaport, Kara Dansky, State of Emergency: *California's Correctional Crisis.* Federal Sentencing Reporter. Vol. 22, No. 3. February, 2010.

18 Under Indeterminate Sentencing, the Board of Prison Terms (later renamed Board of Prison Hearings) would make the decision as to an inmate's readiness to reinter society. Under the DSL, the court would have already provided a set term. So, if an inmate received a 5 year sentence for 1st Degree Burglary with enhancements, a prison Records Office calculation of "time to serve" would be necessary to subtract "good time" credits from the court. The Inmate would know they had up to 5 years to serve but could serve less depending on the calculation for good time credits. However, this date was fluid since the inmate could receive additional time if he violated prison rules and regulations (CDC 115 Rule Violation Report). In any event, the inmate could not be extended beyond his total prison sentence from the court.

19 The Urban Dictionary describes *"the belly of the beast"* as being locked up in prison or jail. See, http/www.urbandictionary.com.

20 Joan Petersilia, *A Retrospective View of Corrections Reform in the Schwarzenegger Administration*, FED. SENT. REP. 148-153 (2010).

21 *Street Wars*, Page 148.

22 **California Proposition 36:** The Substance Abuse and Crime Prevention Act of 2000, was an initiative statute that permanently changed state law to allow qualifying defendants convicted of non-violent drug possession offenses to receive a probationary sentence in lieu of incarceration. The proposition was passed with 60.86% votes in favor and 39.14% against on November 7, 2000 and went into effect on July 1, 2001 with $120 million for treatment services allocated annually for five years. *"Bridging" Education Program*: The *2003–04 Budget Act* included funding to begin implementation of an independent study program that continues today to bridge the gap between when an inmate arrives in prison and when he or she is placed in an education program or work assignment. Inmates work independently and are to meet with instructors weekly to assess their progress. Approximately 16,000 inmates were in bridging programs throughout the state prison system in 2008. Additionally, the California parole system changed in 2009, in large part due to the passage of **Senate Bill 18 (S.B. 18)**. S.B. 18 created a class of low- and moderate-risk parolees who will serve administrative or banked parole. This created a $100 million savings which presumably allowed agents to focus their attention on higher-risk parolees. S.B. 18 also established and expanded drug and mental health reentry opportunities for parolees rather than being returned to prison for violations. S.B. 18 also required application of the Parole Violation Decision Making Instrument (PVDMI) in all cases under active parole supervision. The PVDMI was intended to create a more consistent and fair revocation decision-making system by giving the Board options other than prison for dealing with parole violations.

See http://www.lao.ca.gov/2008/crim/inmate_education/inmate_education_021208.aspx

Also, http://www.vera.org/files/FSR-Editors-observations-February-2010.pdf.

23 Statewide numbers for *average daily jail po*pulation has increased by approximately 10,000 offenders since the implementation of AB 109. However, the increase has more to do with the time spent in jail which has increased as a result of AB 109 provisions.

[24] Scholar John Hagan posits that President "Roosevelt famously challenged narrow ideas of "gangsters" with broadened images of "banksters." During the depression era of the 1930's bankers faced prosecution when their banks failed. Much has changed in America since then regarding our view on white collar crime. See Hagan, John. Who Are the Criminals? *The Politics of Crime Policy From the Age of Roosevelt to the Age of Reagan.* Princeton University Press, 2010. (Page 212)

[25] Ibid, Page 3.

[26] Ibid, Page 41.

[27] See, W. Dunn, (2007) The Gangs of Los Angeles. iUniverse.com, Page 2.

[28] Kelling, George L. and Wilson, James Q. (1982) Broken Windows: *The Police and Neighborhood Safety.* March 1982, Atlantic Journal. (Page 1 & 2) Retrieved on January 23, 2014 from www.theatlantic.com.

[29] George Kelling was a consultant for the New York Transit Authority during the 1980's. The new subway director David Gunn and William Bratton no doubt received first-hand schooling on the Broken Window's Theory. See, Gladwell, M. (2000). *The Tipping Point: How Little Things Can Make a Big Difference.* Boston: Little, Brown and Company. Pages 142-144.

[30] Ibid, Page 145.

[31] Scholar John Hagan speaks about "collective action frames" that politicians and "Broken Window" advocates created by seeking "…to build consensus around new definitions and meanings…" thereby changing the definition of crimes and misdemeanors in the social context (Page 139). Professor Bernard E. Harcourt critical of the broken window theory describes it as "small forms of disorder…you let them go…then they lead in some way to serious crime…that was the idea…that disorder was somehow communicating to criminals, disorderly people, that they could…get away with crime" (NPR Interview, October 17, 2002, Los Angeles). Essentially, broken windows theory was framing people as either law abiding or lawless. Regardless of the nature of the offense; taggers, jay walking, squeegee men, thieves, gang members, rapists or murders were all together in the broken windows continuum.

[32] Tom Haden points out that the "searching and frisking" of "…several thousand of the hundreds of thousands…undesirables" most of which were not reported. He argued that "…at the height of the gang wars, LAPD and many other departments were training their officers to circumvent

Miranda..." and pursuing interrogations of suspects. Failure to advise on the right to remain silent and right to an attorney were eventually rebuked in 2003 by the California Supreme Court which ruled against "the widespread official encouragement "of such police practices..." Street Wars, Pages 124-125.

33 Street Wars, Page 147.

34 There is no data to support this contention. Except the trend in specialized law enforcement units appears to exponentially increase as Compstat data managerial systems were introduced nationwide. The crime data simply pointed to a need (gangs, graffiti, car thefts, burglaries, fraud, etc) to "separate out" policing efforts which quickly turned to task force and eventually new departmental units to address those specific crime concerns. Over time those units became separate line items in police budgets.

35 Wilson, J. Q. (1994). Prisons in a free society. *Public Interest, (117), Page, 39.*

36 Street Wars, Page 128.

37 Ibid, Page 148.

38 Ibid, Page 148.

39 Fulda, Joseph S. (March, 2010) The 'Broken Windows' Theory and the New York Experience Reconsidered. *Economic Affairs, Volume 30, Issue 1.*

40 Moskos, P. (2012, March16), James Q. Wilson's Practical Humanity. *Chronicles of Higher Education.* Page B2.

41 Most seasoned officers who worked the line maintain open communication with convicts. This isn't to establish any rapport; on the contrary, it allows an informal avenue for inmates to address personal and/or group grievances with officers they respect. Most officers are able to address minor concerns without the need for supervisors to intervene. Sgt's and Lt's know which staff have control of their units by how it is managed and the number of incidents, appeals or complaints coming from those areas too. The notion that "your word is your bond" is literally the most important mediation tool officers have in prison. More importantly, open lines of dialogue results in officers knowing more about what is going on among the inmate population.

42 There is no accurate data reflecting the number of parole agents who began their careers working in prison. But interviews with retired regional and district parole administrators suggests that the "career path" trend began

in the mid-1990's and continued until 2011 when budget constraints and implementation of AB 109 significantly reduced prison and parole populations. Likewise, as the bargaining unit (California Correctional Peace Officers Association) gained more parity in pay, officers with sufficient time in service were able to laterally transfer to the Parole Division as Parole Agents (At one time, parole agent and Lieutenant pay were equal). The need to meet previous qualification requirement of college (minimum Associate of Arts Degree) and case load experience could be traded for years working in corrections. It is estimated that well over 60% of today's parole agent in the field began their career in prison as a correctional officer.

[43] Presently, DAPO oversees the following: Electronic Monitoring Unit (responsible for Global Positioning System, Electronic In-House Detention and related Gang Monitoring); Sexual Assault Felony Enforcement Team; California Parole Apprehension Team (Parolee-at-Large recovery); and Special Services Unit (Gang interdiction teams). At one time Community Reentry Services like, Day Reporting Centers and Cal Trans Parolee Work Crews were under DAPO management but a separate unit called *Community and Reentry Services Unit* was created under the Office of Offender Services to address rehabilitative efforts.

[44] Retrieved on February 16, 2014 from paige.stjohn@latimes.com.

[45] Dwight Thompson, a Field Representative for Los Angeles County Probation Officers commenting on 80 offenders the department "lost" in 2013, "If a person's not being properly monitored or supervised, then what's going to stop them from taking it [GPS] off and leaving? If they take it off, what is the point of putting it on?" Retrieved on February 16, 2014 from paige.stjohn@latimes.com.

[46] Retrieved on February 16, 2014 from www.cdcr.ca.gov.

[47] Paparozzi, M. (2003). Much Ado About Nothing: "Broken Windows" Versus "What Works". *Corrections Today*, 65(1), 30-33.

[48] Ibid, Page 31.

[49] Street Wars, Page 146.

Chapter 2

[50] The California Correctional Institution in Tehachapi was built in 1932. It was initially built to house women prisoners.

51   Scudders, Kenyon J. (1952) Prisoners are People. Double-day and Company, Inc., Garden City, New York. Page 282

52   Scudder, Kenyon J. (1954) The Open Institution. The ANNALS of the American Academy of Political and Social Science. 293: 79-87, doi:10.1177/000271625429300111

53   Ibid, Page 81.

54   From 2001 to the present, a number of class action law suits were pursued by inmates relative to access to adequate health care, disability rights, and mental health treatment. The Federal Court presiding over three major law suits; **Plata, Armstrong and Coleman** argued that health care treatment was severely impacted due to overcrowding (Prison Law Office, 2012). Since the CDCR had failed to provide adequate delivery of health care in the prisons and had not achieved any discernible reduction in the prison population, CDCR was ordered to reduce the offender population to 155% of the state capacity by March of 2012. On April 4, 2011, Governor Edmund G. Brown Jr. signed Assembly Bill (AB) 109, Public Safety Realignment, into law.

AB109 is the most far reaching public safety policy enactment since the implementation of *Determinate Sentencing* in 1977 and the subsequent *Three Strikes Law* enacted in 1994. However, AB109 has had a more global effect for California because it effectively shifted responsibility for approximately 30,000 "low level" offender's prison back to local county jurisdictions. The inmates who fell under AB109 would complete their existing prison sentence but would report to county Probation Departments instead of State Parole. The AB109, Public Safety Realignment Act served as a means to help reduce the statewide prison population by releasing non-violent, non-sex and non-serious offenders into the counties for supervision, community programs and local incarceration. However, the prison population cap of 136,000 inmates order by the Federal Court remains unattenable to this date (Capital Alert@sacbee.com. Retrieved January 8, 2013).

55   Initial intake processing included: New Commitments (N/C); Parole Violators, Returned to Custody (PV/RTC); Parole Violators, Pending Revocation (PendRev); Parole Violators, with a New Term (PV/WNT); as well as Minimum Support Facility (MSF), Camp, and Community Correctional Facility (CCF) Higher Custody "rollups" (inmates who cannot remain due to infractions/disciplinary detention/health, etc).

Each month 52% of the inmates at RCW would "turn over" as a result of Detention Processing Unit (DPU), Parole, Continuing on Parole (COP), or In Custody Drug Treatment Program (ICDTP) releases (Figure 3).

	3/09	4/09	5/09	6/09	7/09	8/09	Total:	Average:	Percentage:
DPU's:	315	309	344	255	227	169	1619	270	18%
Paroles:	234	251	199	204	201	394	1483	247	17%
COP/ICOTP:	250	245	349	319	224	112	1499	250	17%
Total Per Month (Base on the RCW capacity of 1482):									52%

Source: CDCR; After Action Report, January 25, 2010.

[56] Aaron Rappaport, Kara Dansky, State of Emergency: *California's Correctional Crisis*. Federal Sentencing Reporter. Vol. 22, No. 3. February, 2010. Also see: Ryken Grattet, Joan Petersilia, Jeffrey Lin, & Marlene Beckman; Parole Violations and Revocations in California: *Analysis and Suggestions for Action*, 73, FED. PROBATION 1, 2 (2009).

[57] The Pew Center on the States; One in One Hundred: Behind Bars in America (2008). Retrieved from http://www.pewstates.org/.

[58] California Department of Corrections and Rehabilitation. Retrieved January 17, 2013 from http://www.cdcr.ca.gov/Reports_Research/ Offender_Information_Services_Branch/Monthly/.

[59] Public Policy Institute of California: Who's in Prison? *The Changing Demographics of Incarceration*. Retrieved on January 17, 2013 from http:// www.ppic.org/main/home.asp.

[60] Below is the breakdown, by placement score, of the inmates housed on the RCW facility on 8/8/09, the day of the riot. Parole Violators, as indicated below, will have points assessed, based on their prior level of custody. No Classification Score indicates the number of New Commitments. The average processing time for inmates at RCW at the time of the riot was 61 days

RCW BREAKDOWN		
Levels	Number of Inmates	%
Level I	763	59%
Level II	427	33%
Level III	91	7%
Level IV	0	0%
No Score	17	1%
TOTAL:	1298	100%

CDCR Placement Criteria

Levels	Points
Level I	0-18
Level II	19-27
Level III	28-51
Level IV	52+

CDCR, After Action Report, October 27, 2009

61   Informal measures of control included; phone sign up, extra sack lunches, contact with counselors or records staff on release dates or sentencing issues, allowances for extra blankets, pillows or sheets, passes to library, church services, and/or special evening programs.

62   The following number of prison gang associates and members of street gangs were identified and validated as a result of the operation: EME-13; NLR-1; BGF-1; Street Gang members- 78.

Chapter 3

63   RC-Central Incident Report dated May 21, 2009. Incident log #CIM-RCC-09-05-0204.

64   CDCR; After Action Report. October 27, 2009.

65   Mesa is a Spanish term for "table". In a prison setting it refers to a leadership table or council. This leadership table normally comprises three to five Southern Hispanics (Surenos). They are charged with making decisions and conducting illegal activities, most of which is on behalf of the Mexican Mafia (EME) prison gang. They may or may not be EME members but are considered associates of the EME.

66   California prison inmates have an informal but definitive practice among the various street gangs. In each facility, housing unit and even a tier, there are recognized leaders or "shot callers" that the other gang members pay homage too. The prison gangs are at the top of the leadership chain of command and select who will speak or act on their behalf. The Crips and

Bloods are unique since they normally act on their own without direction from the Black Guerilla Family-the only recognized Black prison gang in California. "Pilli" is an Aztec/Mayan Nahuatl language term meaning "Noble or Prince". It is used as a sign of respect by Mexican Mafia associates or Surenos for a member of the EME. The EME uses the Azteca language and symbols to disguise their messages and/or to identify themselves to others

67 "Lock down" refers to the process of modifying the daily routine programs in prison. Generally, it requires facilities to place all inmates back in the living units either in cells or on their bunks for an unspecified time period. Given the circumstances in the instant matter, additional security enhancements were employed; including but not limited too, interviews, searches, additional patrols, and monitoring unit behavior more closely.

68 It should be noted that the day rooms at RCE housed approximately 38 inmates in a secure gated area. The same day rooms at RCC housed similar numbers. The day rooms ordinarily were meant for T.V. and table game functions but due to overcrowding statewide, the space was used to house RC process cases.

69 All RCW dorms have two Correctional Officers normally assigned to supervise 198 inmates. In addition, the facility has Search and Escort Officers (3) to assist with coverage and related escort functions. An additional Search Team (4) was assigned that shift to assist in the event of any disturbance.

70 CDCR has prescribed protocols for emergency response situations. "Skirmish" lines and "cover/contact" teams are part of the tactical response formations used by staff. All correctional officers and supervisors have assigned less lethal force equipment on their person during working hours. In addition, all correctional staff are trained in use-of-force options, including but not limited to, Baton, Mk-9, Mini-14, 37 & 40mm Projectile Launcher. Tactical application is taught at Range and On-Site in a *Reality Based Training* environment.

71 CDCR has set response teams that are formed from existing staff at all facilities who respond in stages as directed from the Watch Lieutenant.

72 Prior to the author's' assumption of the Incident Commander post the following staff assumed specific duties associated with the National Incident Management System emergency response protocols: Operations-T. Diaz, Lieutenant; Logistics-M. Hill, Captain; Planning & Intelligence-D. King, Captain; Public Information Officer-M. Hargrove; Finance-H. Provencher, Chief Deputy

Warden, Safety Officer-R. Juarez; Law Enforcement Liaison-S. Cleland, Sergeant; and Crisis Response Team-R. Guerrero, Correctional Counselor I.

73 The location of the CPD and Critical Care Triage Areas were located outside the entry gate of the Prison complex. This would prove problematic for movement of critically injured inmates from inside the secure perimeter of the RCW facility to outside the confines of the prison since identification of all the inmates could not be verified until sometime later.

74 Both the California Rehabilitation Center and the California Institution for Women are within a 15 mile radius of CIM. Both prisons provided officer support. The Crisis Response Team is a highly trained tactical response team for hostage recovery, riot and extraction response capabilities, and high profile/high risk transportations.

75 CIM utilized the National Incident Management System (NIMS) and Incident Command System (ICS) components to carry out responsibilities in responding to the riot. The NIMS was developed and administered by the Secretary of Homeland Security under the direction of the President of the United States on February 28, 2003. NIMS provides a consistent nationwide template to enable Federal, State, and local governments to work together to prepare, prevent, respond and recover from the effects of incidents regardless of size, complexity, location or cause.

76 The Chief Deputy Warden arrived at 2150 hours and assumed the role of Incident Commander having determined the Watch Commander was needed to manage the remaining facilities which had on-going parole releases and related medical care, count and staff concerns. The Warden and Associate Director were excused from the EOC to the Warden's Office where they initiated direct contact with the headquarters personnel in Sacramento. During this time, the Office of Correctional Safety (OCS) sent out emergency notifications and soon thereafter activated the Department Operations Center (DOC) at approximately 0330 hours.

The primary role of the DOC was securing additional staff, identifying and coordinating relocation of inmates involved in the riot. The DOC coordinated lodging and feeding of staff responders. The DOC dispatched a representative of the California Emergency Management Agency (Cal EMA) and contacted the California State Warning Center (CSWC) who received daily briefings throughout the Response and Recovery Phase of the incident.

77   This is an important custodial duty to "count" and verify the inmate population. It is done at various times throughout a 24 hour period to ensure no escapes and all inmates are accounted for each day.

78   RCW had an Electrified Fence surrounding the facility. By placing armed officers in the normally vacant Towers provided enhanced security coverage and ultimately allowed for the Western Zone to be turned off when the CVIFD later entered the facility.

79   The officer later reported that the culinary workers (all races) who all lived in Angeles Hall didn't want to participate but were fearful of retribution from other inmates if it was later determined they had not participated. The Hispanic inmates in particular, bruised and cut themselves to have proof of their supposed participation.

80   All 1298 inmates being removed from RCW would be without any hygiene materials (tooth brush, paste, soap and deodorant). These items were included in "fish kits" commonly given to newly arriving (fish) inmates. Stark was a Youth Authority facility that was in the process of being decommissioned. It had cell block configured housing units, three of which remained vacant at the time of the riot.

81   Inmate Transfer Details

8-09-09	1298 I/M's
Institution	Transferred
Hospital	55
CTF	0
CAL	78
CRC	92
Stark	0
SCC	30
Transferred	255

8-10-09	1043 I/M's left
Institution	Transferred
CTF	154
CAL	0
CRC	0

Stark	482
Transferred	636

8-11-09	407 I/M's left
Institution	Transferred
CTF	122
CAL	0
CRC	0
Stark	253
Misc Trans	32
Transferred	407

[82] Inmate Injuries: Per the completed Medical Report of Injury or Unusual Occurrence (CDCR 7219) reports, 249 inmates received injuries requiring medical treatment.

Hispanic/Mexican	62
White	39
Black	139
Other	9

Of those, 54 inmates were transported by ambulance to outside hospitals for further medical treatment; no inmate deaths were noted. There were 86 abrasions, 32 active bleeding wounds, 4 broken bones, 37 bruises, 1 burn, 3 dislocations, 144 cases of multiple lacerations, 7 OC spray exposures, 38 puncture wounds, and other lesser injuries.

Staff Injuries: Nine staff reported non-life threatening injuries during the riot. A subsequent review of the associated, Crime/Incident Staff Reports (CDCR 837-C) indicated eight staff had sustained injuries:

- One employee sustained an injury to his right shoulder/arm and a possible spider bite on his right hand.
- One employee suffered a pulled groin muscle.
- One employee was exposed to blood.
- One employee injured his lower back and was exposed to blood.
- One employee suffered a bruised left thigh and was exposed to blood.

- Four employees exhibited symptoms of Post Traumatic Stress Disorder (PTSD).

[83]   Disciplinary Actions:

Due to the large number of inmates identified as being involved in this riot, CIM assembled a task force to specifically address the disciplinary issues (refer to **Attachment D**). A total of 215 Serious Rule Violation Reports (RVR), CDCR 115, have been written. They are summarized as follows:

Specific Act:	Number:
Division "A-1" Offenses:	**48**
Arson	1
Attempted Murder	12
Battery with a Deadly Weapon	7
Battery with Serious Injury	26
Conspiracy to Commit Attempted Murder*	2
Division "D" Offenses:	**167**
Inciting a Riot	13
Participation in a Riot	154

Of the 215 inmates receiving RVR's, 199 inmates were placed into the Administration Segregation Unit (ASU). 20 inmates paroled and one is currently out to court on an unrelated matter.

[84]   The DOC required that all the inmates from RCW be identified via "Live Scan" and photographs. Live Scan technology was limited to one unit at RCC and used for reception center processing. Two other Live Scan units were borrowed but took much time to set up and configure. Suffice to say that the process was long and arduous and created animosity with EOC personnel and the DOC.

Chapter 4

[85]   Glouderman, Nikki (2009). Mother Jones. Rage in The Cage: *Nine prison riots to remember;* Retrieved on January 24, 2013 from http//www.motherjones.com.

86   Inland Empire Daily Bulletin....

87   Huffington Post.com

88   Inmate Incidents include: Assault/Battery; Possession of Weapons; Suicide; Possession of Controlled Substances, paraphernalia; Destruction of Property; Theft; Resisting Staff; Cell Extractions, etc. For this discussion, the ratios are limited to Assault/Battery violence. See, http://www. cdcr.ca.gov/Reports_Research/Offender_Information_Services_Branch/ Annual/Beh1Archive.html.

89   The term "ugly beds" referred to the use of non-traditional sleeping arrangements throughout the state. Day rooms, chow halls, and gyms, and at times, hallways were used to "bed down" inmates who could not be placed in a regular cell or dormitory bed. Statewide the use of ugly beds was the norm until 2007 when the statewide population began to drop to more acceptable levels.

90   Graeve, Christine; DeLisi, Matt; Hochstetler, Andy (2007). Prison Rioters: *Exploring Infraction Characteristics, Risk Factors, Social Correlates, and Criminal Causes.* Psychological Reports, 100. 407-419.

91   The 1993 kidnap and murder of 12-year-old Polly Klaas by a California parolee and the barrage of criticism that followed this crime is symbolic of the very real stigmatism that ordinarily follows parolees, sex offenders and other violent offenders. In the wake of her murder, politicians in California and other U.S. states supported the "Three Strikes Law" which California signed into law on March 8, 1994.

Chapter 5

92   See, Ramon A. Mendoza, *From Altar Boy to Hitman* (2005) www.convictand-cops.com and Chris Blatchford, *The Black Hand* (2008), HarperCollins, New York, NY.

93   "Mondo" is a different aka not to be confused with the EME dropout "Mando." "Surenos" is prison slang (although LEO's are using it today in the communities they work) term that refers to Hispanic street gang inmates that claim or who reside in southern California. Their counterpart in Northern California are called Norteños. There is one other distinction among Hispanic inmates. Those inmates who originated in Mexico and have ties to street gangs and/or drug cartels in their home country have been

called "Border Brothers." A caste system of sorts forms in prison; where the more one group is represented, the more influence they have on illicit activities occurring. However, they are quick to forget their country allegiances and become one "group" when a race riot is imminent.

94 There is information that the "shot caller" in question was, in fact, in trouble with the Mexican Mafia leadership at Pelican Bay State Prison (PBSP). PBSP houses validated prison gang members in the Security Housing Units. During this time period, inmates were questioning "Mondo's" leadership but chose to follow his "green light" on assaulting Black inmates. It was later determined that he had been "green lighted" by the EME. The author has not included the name and prison number of the inmate in question for security and confidentiality reasons.

95 California Department of Corrections and Rehabilitation; Offender Information Services Branch. 2009. Retrieved from http://www.cdcr.ca.gov.

96 During the calendar year 2012, felons from southern California account for roughly 66.4% of the statewide prison population. Hispanic represented approximately 44.3% of the total inmate population. Blacks and White inmates represented 25.4%. While 5% were other nationalities. Retrieved on June 20, 2013 from http://www.cdcr.ca.gov/Reports_Research/Offender_ Information_Services_Branch/Annual/ACHAR1/ACHAR1d2012.pdf

97 "13" is reference to the 13th letter of the alphabet "M". "EME" is the phonetic Spanish term for the letter M. Surenos began using the number 13 to signify allegiance to the Mexican Mafia.

98 CDCR had implemented a formal process to determine (validate) whether an inmate is a Mexican Mafia member, Associate or Street Gang member. Normally, three separate source validations are necessary. For example, self-admission, letters or other material that reflects EME communication or verifiable associations (cell mate approval, yard assignments, and/ or known credible informant information). This past year a new policy has emerged called the *Security Threat Group Prevention, Identification System and Step-Down Program* for gang interdiction and management.

99 Palm Hall Unit located in RCC at CIM was a well recognized housing unit among convicts throughout the state. It was an Administrative Segregation Unit that held the most violent and notorious inmates, including validated prison gang members pending court proceedings. It had a storied history for inmates and staff and was a source of pride to all working and/or doing time. If a validated prison gang member was not housed in "Palmas" then

he was considered either a protective custody case in another adjacent segregation unit or not perceived to be as critical a member warranting such placement.

100   Literally meaning a "goat sucker." Chupacabras were the celebrated mythical animals that inhabit parts of the Americas. The name comes from the alleged habit of attacking and drinking the blood of its victims (livestock). This appears to be mostly local legend in parts of the southwest, Mexico and other Latin American countries. Like the Jackalope; part jackrabbit and antelope. My use of the label is really just a humorous attempt to underscore *Leo's* innate prison ability to hunt down information and turn a suspected gang member (sucking the "intel" out of them). *Leo* made a career at finding critical intelligence or contraband on gangs-he was scarier than the bogie man in prison because he was for real!

101   Howell, James, C. and Moore, John P.: *History of Street Gangs in the United States;* National Gang Center Bulletin, No. 4 May, 2010. Office of Juvenile Justice and Delinquency Prevention, Bureau of Justice Assistance, U.S. Department of Justice.

102   Ibid, Page 4.

103   See Moore, J.W. (1978). Homeboys: *Gangs, Drugs and Prison in the Barrios of Los Angeles*. PhiladelphiA: Temple University Press. Also, Virgil, J.D. (1990). Cholos and Gangs: *Cultural change and street youth in Los Angeles*. In C.R. Huff (ed.), Gangs in America (page 116-128). Newbury Park, CA. Sage.

104   See Vigil, J.D. (1998) From Indians to Chicanos: The Dynamics of Mexican-American Culture. 2nd edition. Prospect Heights, IL: Waveland Press. (Page 42).

105   This "crime wave" put pressure on local law enforcement to round up Mexican teenagers based on race and the vaguest suspicions most of which centered on their Zoot Suit appearance. The *Sleepy Lagoon Case* became the backdrop for the Mayor and police targeting of Zoot Suiters during the Zoot Suit Riots that occurred in May of 1943. (See, Meier, Matt S. and Ribera, Feliciano (1993) Rev.: Mexican Americans/American Mexican: *From Conquistadors to Chicanos*. Union Square, New York. Hill and Wang. Also, Howell, James, C. and Moore, John P.: *History of Street Gangs in the United States;* National Gang Center Bulletin, No. 4 May, 2010. (Page 11)

106 Mirande, A. (1987). Gringo Justice, Notre Dame, Ind. University of Notre Dame Press. Page 185.

107 After the convictions in the Sleepy Lagoon Case, minor incidents between zoot-suiters and Anglo military personnel took place in Los Angeles and in Oakland. Typically the cause stemmed from quarrels over girlfriends. However, tensions mounted as media depictions of marauding Mexican gangs attacking servicemen ignited organized assaults by servicemen. Military personnel roamed the city streets, seeking out and attacking zoot-suiters, ripping off their clothes and cutting their hair. These attacks quickly became attacks on any Mexican-American youth. From early June to July of 1993, military personnel were unrestrained in their assaults on young Latino men in Los Angeles. Meier and Ribera describe the period, "*To make matters worse, police responded by following the cabs, full of service personnel, at a distance and then arresting the victims…What had begun as a series of street brawls quickly turned into a full-fledged race riot incited by the press and condoned or ignored by major law enforcement agencies… Time magazine later called the Los Angeles violence "the ugliest brand of mob action since the coolie race riots of the 1870's*" (Meier and Ribera, Mexican Americans-American Mexicans, Page 164).

108 See, Official Website of the Los Angeles Police Department. Retrieved on July 4, 2013 from http://www.lapdonline.org/get_informed/content_basic_view/1396.

109 C. Schoville (2008). Surenos 2008 One Rule, One Law, One Order: *A Special Report from the Rocky Mountain Information Network.* Funded by the Bureau of Justice Assistance. Retrieved on July 30, 2013 from http://info.publicintelligence.net/surenosreport.pdf.

110 The Central File was the main harbinger of an inmates history. It included: Legal Documents; medical history; prison classification documents and chronos; custody level score sheets; Court documents; Parole documents; criminal and in-prison disciplinary history. These voluminous files are only recently being converted to digital form.

111 The author spent 5 years as a "rank and file" employee with CDCR: As an officer in various assignments in a Level II facility at the California Rehabilitation Center, Norco and as a Correctional Counselor assigned to the facility 4B SHU and the Max Level IV Facility at the California Correctional Institution in Tehachapi. On many occasions, inmates would express their indifference about "politicking" but acknowledged that if

something happened they'd have no choice but to participate. Their best effort to "lay low" was futile if a riot or racial incident in a cell block, dorm or yard were to "kick off". This was recognized by staff as a matter of "prison business" among the inmate population.

112   Also, the prison gangs would ignore some things since they used many of the clerks, porters and crews to assist them in the introduction of contraband. It is noted that on the days prior to and following the August 8, 2009 riot the SNY dorms at RC-East and RC-Central did not participate. Likewise, Angeles Hall at RC-West which housed the clerks and culinary workers did not participate.

113   Credit earning status can be a complicated discussion. Simply put, inmates are generally receiving 1/3 credit off their calculated release dates. However, once they begin a program (work, school or vocational assignment) they begin to earn "day for day" credit. That essentially makes their release date shorter. Some inmates cannot earn day for day credit due to court determinations that prohibit the earning status. For example, some commitment offenses require the inmate to complete 80% of their total term by law.

Chapter 6

114   For a more definitive discussion on the primary court cases; Plata, Armstrong and Coleman see: http://www.prisonlaw.com/cases.php#health_care. To be sure, there were other significant cases: Dental Care (Perez v. Tilton, 2006), Developmental Disabilities (Clark v. California, 1996), and Licensed Health Care Facilities within Prisons (Budd v. Cambra). But Plata was the "*Mother of all law suits*" as was described by a high ranking Director during a conference call to the Wardens in 2002. It overshadowed the others because its focus was the delivery of health care systems at each institution thereby addressing or including related concerns in the other complaints.

115   Frank. D. Russo (2007). *California Prison Medical Court Receiver Robert Sillen Bares All Before Sacramento Press Club*. Article posted July 11, 2007 in the California Progress Report. Retrieved on July 19, 2013 from http://www.californiaprogressreport.com.

116   Other key issues included: Inadequately trained Medical Technical Assistants;; prisoner medical records incomplete, disorganized, and not transferred with them to other prisons; inadequate medical screening of incoming prisoners;; untimely responses to emergencies, officers interfering

with delivery of care; lack of quality control, peer review and death reviews; and lack of established protocols for chronic illnesses. See Amended Complaint Plata v. Davis No. C-01-1351 for more detailed information. Retrieved on July 19, 2013 from http://www.prisonlaw.com.

[117] See Evan Rosen (2010). *Smashing Silos.* Article posted February 5, 2010 in the BloombergBusinessweek, Companies and Industries. Retrieved on October 14, 2014 from http://www.businessweek.com/managing/content/feb2010/ca2010025_358633.htm.

[118] CDCR routinely used the following systems: The **Distributed Data Processing System (DDPS)**, an integrated information-sharing system for institutions that includes inmate housing, classification, assignments, and trust accounting; **The Offender Based Information System (OBIS)**, developed for the CDCR, captures information regarding commitment, offenses, cases, movement between prisons, and descriptive data; **Revocation Scheduling and Tracking System (RSTS)**, is used to facilitate the tracking of parolees, to schedule hearings and to report revocation actions; the **Correctional Offender Management Profiling for Alternative Sanctions (COMPAS)**, a tool used to assess the risk and needs of adult offenders in an automated system, with the intent to reduce recidivism; **Law Enforcement Automated Data System (LEADS)**, the tracking system used for supervisory purposes by CDCR parole agents and other law enforcement entities to access demographics, photos and information on parolees; and the **California Identification and Information System (CI&I)**, that includes individual identifiers and describes an individual's arrests and subsequent court dispositions.

[119] SOMS Project Update (PowerPoint presentation). Warden's Meeting June 23, 2009.

[120] Quote from B. Heaton, *California Prison Realignment Spurs IT Projects.* Government Technology article August 24, 2012.

[121] Some doctors made substantially more depending on their medical and forensic background. For example, salaries in the range of 300,000+ was not unusual for Chief Psychiatrists.

[122] Quote from R. Sillen during a visit to CIM during the summer of 2006.

[123] Ibid.

[124] C. Pearson (2013). Medication Adherence: *Are Women Worse Than Men at Taking Their Meds?* Online article dated May 24, 2013. Retrieved on July 19, 2013 from http://www.huffingtonpost.com.

[125] Check the math but the equation is: *15 inmates (3 DOT + 12 non-DOT) is what percentage of 300 inmates? The answer is five percent.* Retrieved on Oct. 14, 2014 from http://www.mathgoodies.com/lessons/percent/proportions.html.

[126] April 11, 2013. Los Angeles Times Article by Chris Megerian.

[127] L.A. Times, et al.

[128] P.S. John, *Judges Refuse to Stay Prison Order*, Los Angeles Times, July 4, 2013.

[129] Ibid.

[130] G. Skelton, *A Strong Hand on Prisons.* Article in the Los Angeles Times, July 1, 2013.

Chapter 7

[131] The author was a member of the CRC & CCI Negotiation Management Team (NMT) from 1986 to 1994. NMT worked in concert with the Special Emergency Response Team in tactical situations to resolve inmate unrest, work stoppages and hostage situations. The training protocols included the basic tenet "No Hostage" policy which required resolution without bartering policy or procedural changes, release or escape. But trading a hostage for food or family phone call could always be a no-brainer tactic!

[132] The Toussaint preliminary injunction reaffirmed due process rights held under Ruiz v. Estelle, Supra 679 F.2d (1980) and specifically addressed living conditions including, but not limited to, regularly scheduled shower, exercise, visits, law library and mail privileges. See Toussaint v. Rushen 553 F.Supp 1365 (1983) The "...Findings of Fact and Conclusions of Law, as well as the Preliminary Injunction to which they relate, are predicated upon the decision in *Wright v. Rushen* (9th Cir.1981) 642 F.2d 1129..." And includes, "...Plaintiffs' motion for a preliminary injunction involves the second phase of *Wright v. Enomoto* (N.D.Cal.1976) 462 F.Supp. 397, a class action..." The aforementioned precedential cases dealt specifically with due process and living conditions of inmates in administrative segregation or any restrictive housing environment. Retrieved on December 7, 2013 from http://www.leagle.com.

[133] Pelican Bay State Prison (PBSP) was opened in 1989. As of September, 2013, PBSP houses 2,715 inmates: 983, Level IV, General Population; 1,179 Security Housing Unit; 127 bed Psychiatric Services Unit; 244 Administrative Segregation Unit and a 400 bed Level I, Minimum Support Facility. http://www.cdcr.ca.gov/Facilities_Locator/PBSP.html.

[134] Inmate written notes or "kites" can be written on anything and passed on via letters, "fish-lines" (string slung between cells, or thru pipes), legal mail or other inmates. Generally, the prison gangs use a code system to confuse staff and to ensure the reader knows from where and whom is communicating information.

[135] July 29 2013, Los Angeles Times article by Paige St, John.

[136] Ibid

[137] In Greek mythology, "Ares is the son of Zeus and Hera. He was disliked by both parents. He is the god of war. He is considered murderous and blood-stained but, also a coward…His bird is the vulture. His animal is the dog." Retrieved November 29, 2013 from http://edweb.sdsu.edu/people/bdodge/scaffold/gg/olympian.html.

[138] Prison Hunger Strike Solidarity, 5 Core Demands. Retrieved on December 31, 2014 from www.prisonhungerstrikesolidarity.wordpress.com

[139] *Hunger Strike by Inmates is Latest Challenge to California's Prison System*; July 7, 2011, New York Times article by Ian Lovett. Retrieved on November 29, 2013 from http://www.nytimes.com/2011/07/08/us/08hunger.html?ref=us.

[140] Inmates housed in Ad-Seg and SHU's are also allowed limited access to Canteen supplies with money from their personal trust accounts. Although, they refused state supplied breakfast, lunch and dinner meals, many had already retained a supply of food purchased from the canteen: Tuna, crackers, peanut butter and assorted nut packages, etc. Most inmates gave "lip service" to the *short corridor collective* call for a Hunger Strike but cooperated to avoid reprisal. Most relied on their personal canteen to get them through the ordeal.

[141] *Prisoners Renew a Protest in California*; New York Times article by Erica Goode. Retrieved on November 29, 2013 from http://www.nytimes.com.

[142] Scott Kernan was a seasoned prison professional. He was respected by most correctional leaders in the field (prisons) because he was one of them who had "been there and done that"! The mid-September 2011 conference call

was unusual for two reasons. First, Kernan was not directing policy or delivering instructions to the field. He was sharing the controversy that executive members in headquarters were debating on over the hunger strike. Second, the decision to change some SHU policies had already been made and he was attempting to prepare the field in understanding the complexities. You could sense the conflict in his voice. I queried a number of prison managers from different prisons after the call and each was disappointed that CDCR had elected to negotiate terms to end the hunger strike. Regardless of the fact that headquarters never admitted that any "negotiated" terms were agreed upon.

143 Short Corridor Collective Notice: *Peaceful Protest to Resume July 8, 2013, If Demands Are Not Met*. Retrieved on September 20, 2013 from http://prisonerhungerstrikesolidarity.wordpress.com/.

144 Inmates claimed that prison officials at a central California facility stated, "If they wanted the world to think they were going hungry, then it would be made so they were hungry." Canteen items; like peanut butter, crackers, chips and candy were personal items bought by inmates with their trust account monies and not considered state property were allegedly confiscated. *Striking Inmates Tell of Threats*; July 11, 2013 Los Angeles Time article by Paige St. John.

145 See The Texas Politics Project: The Science of "Muddling Through." Theory and Reality in Public Policy Formation. Retrieved on September 24, 2014 from http://texaspolitics.utexas.edu/archive. Also, Lindblom, Charles E. 1959. The Science of "Muddling Through." Public Administration Review 19:79–88

146 *California Prison Hunger Strike Resumes as Sides Dig In*; October 7, 2011, New York Times article by Ian Lovett. Retrieved on November 29, 2013 from http://www.nytimes.com.

147 See Toussaint v. Rushen 553 F. Supp 1365 (1983) and Toussaint v. McCarthy 597 F. Supp. 1388 (N.D. Cal. 1984) Aff'd. 801 F. 2nd 1080 (9th Cir. 1986) regarding the preliminary injunction addressing: Administrative Segregation (Ad-Seg) and Security Housing Unit (SHU) placement, living conditions, access to programs and due process right. The Toussaint case was brought forward by inmates from Folsom, San Quentin and Soledad. The case was appealed five times regarding clarification of issues arising from the first case. Retrieved on November 18, 2013 from http://www.leagle.com/decision/19831918553FSupp1365_11703.

The second seminal case regarding Ad-Seg/SHU placement and conditions of confinement was Madrid v. Gomez 889 F. Supp. 1146 (N.D. Cal 1995). On January 10, 1995, the Ninth Circuit Court granted injunctive relief to the inmate plaintiffs, holding that: 1) there was unnecessary and wanton infliction of pain and use of excessive force at the prison; 2) prison officials did not provide inmates with constitutionally adequate medical and mental health care; 3) conditions of confinement in the Security Housing Unit, which included extreme isolation and environmental deprivation, did not inflict cruel and unusual punishment on all inmates, but conditions in the Security Housing Unit did impose cruel and unusual punishment on mentally ill prisoners; 4) some procedures used to validate inmates as gang members and thus transfer them to the Security Housing Unit violated due process. Retrieved on November 18, 2013 from http://www.clearinghouse.net/detail.php?id=588.

[148] August 11, 2013, The Sacramento Bee article by Dan Morain. Retrieved August 14, 2013 from http://www.sacbee..com.

[149] California Prison Focus, a prisoner advocacy group has been supporting prisoner rights and bringing their cause to the public for at least 12 plus years. See http://www.prisons.org/index.htm.

A paid advertisement in the Los Angeles Times dated August 28, 2013 titled: Join Us in Stopping Torture in U.S. Prisons! Listed notable supporters include a long list of social activists: Jay Leno, Susan Sarandon, Gloria Steinem, Jesse Jackson, Cornel West, Noam Chomsky, Viggo Mortensen, Luis Valdez, Fr. Gregory Boyle, James Lafferty, Daniel Elsberg, and Blasé Bonpane to name a few. See www.stopmassincarceration.net

[150] See, Page St. John. *State Prison Hunger Strike Ends*, September 6, 2013. Los Angeles Times. Also, Katherine Driessen's Report in Amnesty International dated March 21, 2009. Retrieved on December 6, 2013 from www.amnesty.org.au. Also, Amy Goodman, *Prisoner Protest at Guantanamo Bay Strains Obama's Human Rights Record,* article dated March 14, 2013 in the Guardian. And Luke Harding, *Pleading Prisoners and Families Outside Protest at the Horrors of Abu Ghraib Jai;* The Guarding

[151] David Mizner, Starving for Justice: *From California to Israel, Hunger Strikes Are Erupting All Over the World.* The Nation, December 23/30, 2013

[152] Hart, Walter Edward (2012) Framing Abu Ghraib: The Interaction of Presidential Rhetoric, the Media, and the Public in the Cultural Industry's Cycle of Assumptions. Inter-University Seminar on Armed Forces Society,

November 3, 2012. Hart argues that "Abu Ghraib turned into a scandal about the administration's authorization of interrogation techniques on June 8, 2004 when the Washington Post revealed memos authored by the Office of Legal Counsel's (OLC) Alberto Gonzalez and Jay Bybee. The "torture memos," as they became known, showed that the Bush administration authorized and implemented policies that legalized torture and denied the authority of the Geneva Conventions. The American public was then aware of the Abu Ghraib scandal as well as the torture policies put forth by the Bush administration." Page 7-8

[153] Therese Postel, reported in the *Atlantic* that "at least 42 inmates are participating in a hunger strike to protest their continued detention. But those 42 are only part of the ongoing story. There are still 166 prisoners being held at Guantanamo Bay. 86 of these individuals have been cleared for release. 46 others are being held 'without enough evidence' to prosecute, but are still 'too dangerous to transfer.' Only 6 people being held at Guantanamo Bay are facing formal charges." See, *How Guantanamo Bay's Existence Helps Al-Qaeda Recruit More Terrorists*. April 12, 2013. Retrieved on December 7, 2013 from http://www.theatlantic.com.

[154] *The Real Story Behind Hunger Strike.* August 11, 2013, The Sacramento Bee. Article by Dan Morain. Retrieved August 14, 2013 from http://www.sacbee..com.

[155] Jeffery Beard, *Hungry for Control*; Article in the Los Angeles Times, August 6, 2013.

[156] Blatchford, Chris, *The Black Hand* (2008); HarperCollins, New York, NY. Page 270.

[157] Ibid, Page 275.

[158] *California's solitary-confinement policies scrutinized at hearing.* Jeremy B. White, Sacramento Bee. October 9, 2013. Retrieved on January 1, 2014 from http://blogs.sacbee.com/.

[159] Ibid

[160] During testimony at the October 2013 Joint Legislative Hearing, Margaret Winter, Associate Director of the ACLU National Prison Project advised the panel regarding a number of agencies, associations and states who have revamped their solitary confinement policies. In some cases like Mississippi the state chose to close them down. Retrieved on January 2, 2014 from http://sfbayview.com.

[161] See, Page, St.John. *Limits Ordered on Pepper Spray Use.* April 11, 2014. Los Angeles Times. See also, federal court case: Coleman v. Brown, Case 2:90-cv-00520-LKK-DAD. Document 5131. Filed 4-10-2014.

[162] John McCain was a Vietnam War fighter pilot that was shot down and held for five years as a POW in Vietnam. Living in deplorable conditions and sustaining lifetime injuries from the plane crash McCain is a staunch advocate against torture and solitary confinement. Shane Bauer was arrested while hiking near the Iranian border of Iraq and spent four months of his 26 month incarceration in solitary confinement. Bauer was accused of being a spy which was proven to be untrue.

[163] Helen Vera, National Prison Fellow with the American Civil Liberties Union (ACLU) reported that the suicide rate is "dramatically heightened" among inmates housed in segregated housing (SHU and/or Ad-Seg). She indicated that in 2011 "...more than one-third of all suicides in the first half of 2012 were housed in segregation and 58 percent of the 19 people who have taken their life to date in 2013 occurred in segregation units." See, ACLU website, *Confronting California's Abuse of Solitary.* November 19, 2013. Retrieved on January 1, 2014 from www.aclu.org.

[164] Leung, David. (2011), *Power Vocabulary.* Lingua Franca Publishing, Limited. Hong Kong. Page 223

[165] Justice Design Exchange: *The Dilemma of Scale.* Retrieved July 20, 2013 from http://justicedx.com.

Chapter 8

[166] Much has been written since AB 109 first came on the state and national stage. The quotable descriptions are from: Rappaport, Aaron J. *Realigning California Corrections;* Federal Sentencing Reporter, Vol. 25, No. 4, Realigning California Corrections (April 2013); Vera Institute of Justice. pp. 207-216. Also, Quon, Lisa T., Abarbanel, S., Mukamal (December, 2013). Reallocation of Responsibility, *Changes to the Correctional Control System in California Post-Realignment.* Stanford Criminal Justice Center, Stanford Law School (Page 1); Rodriquez, Lisa. *Criminal Justice Realignment: A Prosecutor's Perspective. Federal Sentencing Reporter*, Vol. 25, No. 4, Realigning California Corrections (April 2013), pp. 220-225. And, Hopper, Allen, Dooley-Sammuli, Evans, Keli (March 2012). *Public Safety*

Realignment: California at the Crossroads. American Civil Liberties Union, California (ACLU).

167 See, Rappaport, Aaron J., and Dansky, Kara (2010). State of Emergency: *California's Correctional Crisis.* Federal Sentencing Reporter, Vol. 22, No.3 (Page 133). Also, see Hopper, et al. (Page 1)

168 See also, Ball, W. D., Weisberg, Robert (January, 2014). The New Normal? *Prosecutorial Charging in California after Public Safety Realignment.* Stanford Criminal Justice Center, Stanford Law School. (Page 7)

169 The Plata Court required California to reduce its prison population by 33,000 by March of 2013. See, Public Safety Realignment, *California at a Crossroads,* ACLU Report 2012 (Page 7). Retrieved on October 10, 2013 from www.aclune.org/realignment. More recently, the court gave the Governor a 2 year stay on the prison population cap as long as the inmate population continues to be reduced and effective programs are put in place to reduce recidivism.

170 Rodríguez, Lisa, (April, 2013).*Criminal Justice Realignment: A Prosecutor's Perspective. Federal Sentencing Reporter,* Vol. 25, No. 4, Realigning California Corrections. (Page 220)

171 Quon, Lisa T., Abarbanel, S., Mukamal (December, 2013). Reallocation of Responsibility, *Changes to the Correctional Control System in California Post-Realignment.* Stanford Criminal Justice Center, Stanford Law School. (Page 1)

172 Petersilia, J., Snyder, J.G. (April, 2013). Looking Past the Hype: *10 Questions Everyone Should Ask About California's Prison Realignment.* 5 California Journal of Politics and Policy 266-306. Stanford Criminal Justice Center, Stanford Law School.

173 New York, Washington, Illinois, and Texas had already begun reductions in prison and parole populations by a combination of alternatives; including but not limited too, changes in sentencing, alternative parole monitoring, community programs targeting newly released offenders, to name a few.

174 Ball, et al. (Page 7)

175 Ball, et al. (Page 19)

176 Hopper, Allen, Dooley-Sammuli, Evans, Keli (March 2012). *Public Safety Realignment: California at the Crossroads.* American Civil Liberties Union, California (ACLU). (Page 5)

177 The California Penal Code, section 17.5 states, in part, "…Legislature reaffirms its commitment to reducing recidivism among criminal offenders…Criminal justice policies that rely on building and operating more prisons to address community safety concerns are not sustainable… Community-based corrections programs require a partnership between local public safety entities and the county to provide and expand the use of community-based punishment for low-level offender Populations…" The penal code also defines community-based punishment as "…correctional sanctions and programming encompassing a range of custodial and noncustodial responses to criminal or noncompliant offender activity." On paper, at least, the onus is on finding and using alternative options instead of incarceration as the focus of the *justice re-investment.*

178 Prior to Realignment, the sentence in some cases could have been suspended and reinstated if the offender misbehaved. This provided an incentive for the offender to behave which unfortunately wasn't always the case.

179 Rodríguez, et al. (Page 218); and Couzens, J. Richard. (April, 2013). *Realignment and Evidence-Based Practice: A New Era in Sentencing California Felonies. Federal Sentencing Reporter*, Vol. 25, No. 4, Realigning California Corrections. (Page 221)

180 Couzens, et al. (Page 219)

181 Ibid (Page 218)

182 Quon, et al. (Page 2)

183 Ibid, Page 4.

184 Hopper, et al. (Page 6)

185 The state provides monies to the Community Corrections Performance Incentives Fund (CCPIF) for purposes of implementing the community corrective practices and programs. Additionally, the CCPIF is made available to the Chief Probation Officers statewide (Penal Code § 1230(a) & (b). The Community Corrections Partnership (CCP) is primarily responsible for the following: Prepare and vote approval for the implementation of the local public safety realignment plan to the Board of Supervisors; Provide advice in the development and implementation of the programs receiving CCPIF funding; Insure CCPIF funding is to be used to provide services for adult felony offenders subject to probation, and spent on evidence-based community corrections practices and programs; and lastly, present the local realignment plan to the Board of Supervisors for approval.

186   See: http://www.bscc.ca.gov/s_historyofthebscc.php.

187   The Association for Criminal Justice Research (CA). 78th Semi-Annual Meeting, October 24-25, 2013.

Chapter 9

188   Lofstrom, Magnus, and Steven Raphael. (2013) Public Safety Realignment and Crime Rates in California. Public Policy Institute of California. Retrieved on April 23, 2014, from www.ppic.org/main/publication. asp?i=1075.

189   Couzens, J. Richard. (April, 2013). *Realignment and Evidence-Based Practice: A New Era in Sentencing California Felonies. Federal Sentencing Reporter*, Vol. 25, No. 4, Realigning California Corrections. (Page 217)

190   2012, National Forum on Criminal Justice & Public Safety. Power Point presentation by Robert J. Warren.

191   Hopper, et al (Page 14)

192   Bouie, Jamelle. August 8, 2012 article. The Daily Beast: Eric Holders Decision To Back Away From Mandatory Drug Sentences Is A Positive Step. Retrieved from http://www.thedailybeast.com on May 12, 2014.

193   *Lord of the Flies* is a 1954 novel by the English author Sir William Golding. It is a fictional story about a group of British boys stuck on an uninhabited island who try to govern themselves with disastrous results. It shares the conflict of human nature (power, jealousy, fear, courage, etc) and the notion of individual welfare versus the common good.

194   I liberally use the term "Guerilla" as opposed to "Gorilla" to distinguish between the unspoken forces that may weigh heavily on the counties if not addressed by local law enforcement agencies. If we treat the Mexican Mafia as an "insurgent" force equipped like guerillas in the type of warfare seen during the Vietnam War or national wars fought in Central America, Europe and Africa "…fought by irregulars in fast-moving, small-scale actions against orthodox military and police forces and, on occasion, against rival insurgent forces, either independently or in conjunction with a larger political-military strategy…" we can see their potential threat more clearly. See, http://www.britannica.com/EBchecked/topic/248353/guerrilla-warfare.

195 California Department of Corrections and Rehabilitation; Offender Information Services Branch. Retrieved on June 3, 2014 from http://www.cdcr.ca.gov.

196 June 30, 2013 data compiled by CDCR reflects the statewide inmate population breakdown as follows: Blacks 29.4%; Hispanics 41.3%; Whites 23.0%; and Other 6.3%.

197 Hernandez, Anabel, *NarcoLand*, Verso, New York and London. 2010.

198 Ibid, Page 204

199 Ibid, Page 296

200 Ibid, Page 298-299

201 Based on 2012 data recorded by the Uniform Crime Report. California ranking by state from 1970 to the year 1995 for crime had a mean average of #4 among all 50 states. California also remained in the top 5 states for violent offenses from 1980 to 1994. Retrieved on October 30, 2014 from http://www.disastercenter.com/crime/cacrime.htm.

Made in the USA
Coppell, TX
22 April 2021